HARRY BRELSFORD'S SMB SERIES

MICROSOFT SMALL BUSINESS SPECIALIST PRIMER & 70-282 EXAM PREPARATION GUIDE!

Beatrice Mulzer
MCSE, MCT, USA SBS Hands-On Lab Instructor

Harry Brelsford
MBA, MCT, MCSE
CEO, SMB Nation, Inc.
Publisher, SMB Nation Press

SMB Nation Press

SMB Nation Press

P.O. Box 10179

Bainbridge Island, WA 98110-0179

206-842-1127

10 9 8 7 6 5 4 3

Printed in the United States of America

ISBN: 0-974858-03-X

Cover Design: Alyssa Johnson

Editors: Vicky McCown and Melinda Spencer

Interior Layout: Stephanie Martindale

Proofreader: Kevin Knudsen

Contents

About The Authors .... **xvii**

Dedication .... **xix**

Acknowledgements .... **xix**

Foreword .... **xxi**

Preface ....**xxiii**
What This Book Is About.. **xxiii**
How This Book Is Organized ....**xxiv**
    Section One: Small Business Specialist Community xxv
    Section Two: Exam 70-282 xxv
    Section Three: Additional Exam\Assessment........................... xxv
Who Should Read This Book... **xxvi**
Who Shouldn't Read This Book .... **xxvii**
    Who Wrote What? xxvii
March Forward! .... **xxviii**
PostScript .... **xxviii**

Section I - Small Business Specialist Community

Chapter 1
    Introduction **1-1**
Certification Exam 70-282 .... **1-1**
Certification Exam 74-134 .... **1-3**
Small Business Sales and Marketing Skills Assessment............... **1-5**

iv

MICROSOFT SMALL BUSINESS SPECIALIST PRIMER &
70-282 EXAM PREPARATION GUIDE!

Tips for Getting Certified 1-7

Experience 1-7

Enthusiasm 1-9

Education 1-10

    Microsoft Official Curriculum 1-10

    Self-Study/Online Study 1-11

    Workshops 1-12

    Annual SMB Nation Conference 1-12

Economics 1-13

Envy 1-14

Summary 1-14

Chapter 2

Small Business Specialist Community 2-1

The Case for Partnering with Microsoft 2-2

Definition 2-2

Partner Pyramid 2-3

Partner Points 2-4

Small Business Specialist Strategy 2-5

    Five-Step Initial Strategy 2-5

    Growth Strategy 2-6

Get Involved—Partner Community Building 2-7

Gives and Gets 2-7

Gives 2-7

    Program Sign-up 2-8

    Honor System Experience 2-8

    Purchase the Action Pack 2-8

    Successfully Pass One Certification Exam 2-18

    Successfully Pass the Online Small Business Sales
        and Marketing Skills Assessment 2-19

    Optional Training Labs 2-21

    Direct and Indirect Costs 2-23

Gone 2-26

Gets 2-26

    Amazing Customer Referrals! 2-26

    Affirmation and Affiliation 2-27

    Affinity Group 2-28

Access and Attention 2-29
Exclusive Premium Content! 2-32
Appealing Logo Usage 2-33
Exclusive Academic Education 2-34
Action Pack Content 2-34
Accrue Partner Points and Aspire for More! 2-34
Additional Gets 2-35
Historical Context **2-35**
Attempt #1: Sweet Success 2-36
Attempt #2: Small Business Partner Engagement Program 2-36
Attempt #3: Small Business Specialist Community 2-38
Elevator Ride Version **2-39**
Community Resources **2-40**
Summary **2-41**

Section II - Exam 70-282

Chapter 3
Analyzing the Existing Environment 3-1

Perform a Needs Assessment **3-1**
Identify and Analyze Business Problems 3-2
Critical Considerations 3-4
Identifying and Selecting Appropriate Hardware
and Software for the Environment 3-6
Hardware Functionality and Effectiveness 3-7
Software Efficiency 3-12
Practice Questions **3-12**
Answer Key **3-18**
Summary **3-21**

Chapter 4
Designing a Business Technology Solution
for a Small- or Medium-Sized Business 4-1

Design a Messaging and Collaboration Specification **4-1**
This Old House 4-1
SBS 2003 to the Rescue 4-3
Fax 4-3

vi

MICROSOFT SMALL BUSINESS SPECIALIST PRIMER &
70-282 EXAM PREPARATION GUIDE!

Real-Time Communications 4-4
Exchange Server 2003 4-4
Windows SharePoint Services 4-4
Shared Resources 4-5
**Design a Connectivity Specification for Networking
and Remote Connections** **4-6**
Broadband 4-6
Local Router with Static IP 4-7
Remote Web Workplace 4-7
Design the Application Specification **4-8**
Application Compatibility 4-8
SQL Server 2000 4-8
Backup 4-9
Utilities 4-9
Third-Party Applications 4-9
Design a Management and Operations Specification 4-10
E-mail, Networking, and Internet Connectivity 4-10
Active Directory 4-11
Server Administration and Management 4-11
Easy Setup of Client Computers 4-12
Monitoring and Reporting 4-13
Design a Disaster Prevention and Recovery Specification 4-14
Integrated Backup 4-14
Landing on Your Feet 4-15
Design a Hardware Specification 4-15
Database Server 4-16
File Server 4-16
E-mail Server 4-16
Fault Tolerance Considerations 4-17
Practice Questions **4-18**
Answer Key **4-25**
Summary **4-27**

Chapter 5
Installing Windows Small Business Server 2003 5-1
Deployment Planning **5-1**
System Requirements 5-2

Network Interface Cards 5-5
Disk Partitions 5-6
First-Time System Installation **5-7**
Setup Modes 5-8
Text-Mode Setup 5-8
GUI Mode Setup... 5-8
Small Business Server Component Installation
(Standard Edition).. 5-9
Small Business Server Component Installation
(Premium Edition) 5-10
Installing SQL Server 2000 with SP3a 5-11
Upgrading SharePoint 5-11
Installing ISA Server 2000 5-12
Completing Post-Installation Tasks (To Do List) 5-13
Upgrade and Migrations **5-15**
In-Place Upgrade from SBS 2000 to SBS 2003 5-15
Preparing the Server 5-16
Preparing the Client for an In-Place Upgrade 5-17
Performing the Upgrade 5-18
Migrating from SBS 2000, SBS 4.5,
or NT 4.0 to SBS 2003 5-19
Preparing for the Migration 5-19
Configure the Destination Server 5-22
Prepare Clients for Account Migration...................... 5-22
Performing the Migration 5-24
Practice Questions **5-27**
Answer Key **5-32**
Summary **5-35**

Chapter 6
Securing Windows Small Business Server 2003 ...... **6-1**
Configure User Accounts and Permissions **6-3**
User Rights and Permissions 6-3
User Rights 6-3
User Permissions 6-3
Security Groups 6-4
SBS User Templates 6-4

viii

MICROSOFT SMALL BUSINESS SPECIALIST PRIMER &
70-282 EXAM PREPARATION GUIDE!

Default User Templates 6-5
Custom User Templates 6-7
Securing File, Folder, and Printer Objects 6-8
Share Permissions 6-8
NTFS Permissions 6-10
Permissions and Volumes 6-12
Configuring NTFS Permissions to Files and Folders 6-13
Configuring NTFS Permissions for Printers 6-13
Security Guidelines 6-14
Configure Software Update Service **6-15**
Working with SUS 6-16
Approving Updates 6-16
History 6-16
Configure ISA Server 2000 and Firewalls **6-17**
Configure Access Using NAT **6-18**
How NAT Works 6-18
Configuring NAT 6-19
ISA Firewall Clients 6-19
SecureNAT 6-20
Web Proxy 6-20
Firewall 6-20
ISA Server 2000 Firewall Access Rules 6-22
Protocol Rules 6-22
Site and Content Rules 6-22
Practice Questions **6-23**
Answer Key **6-30**
Summary **6-33**

Chapter 7
Configuring Windows Small
Business Server 2003 .... **7-1**
Create and Configure User Groups and Group Policies **7-1**
Creating and Configuring Domain Groups 7-3
Group Scopes 7-3
Group Strategies 7-4
Using the Group Policy Management Console 7-6

**Configure Windows SBS 2003 for Networking
and Remote Connectivity** 7-6
  Using the To Do List 7-6
  Connecting to the Internet 7-6
    Networking 7-7
    Firewall 7-8
    Secure Web Site 7-9
    E-mail 7-10
    There Is More 7-11
  Configuring Remote Access 7-11
  Configure Faxing 7-12
  Adding Users and Computers 7-12
    User Templates 7-13
  Activate the Server and Add Licenses 7-14
    Internet Activation 7-14
    CAL Types 7-14
    Add License Wizard 7-15
    Transfer License Wizard 7-15
    License Backup/Restore 7-15
Configure DHCP and IP Addressing 7-16
  Configuring an Existing DHCP Service or Firewall Device 7-17
    Default Gateway 7-17
    Domain Name Server 7-17
    DNS Domain Name 7-18
    Windows Internet Naming Service (WINS) 7-18
    WINS node type 7-18
Configure the Domain Naming Service 7-18
Configure Terminal Services 7-19
**Manage Networks Using Simple
Network Management Protocol** 7-20
Configure Messaging and Collaboration 7-22
  Outlook Web Access 7-23
    Outlook Web Access Basic 7-23
    Outlook Web Access Premium 7-24
    Configure Outlook Web Access 7-24
  Configure Windows SharePoint Services 7-25
    Understanding WSS 7-25

x

MICROSOFT SMALL BUSINESS SPECIALIST PRIMER &
70-282 EXAM PREPARATION GUIDE!

Configuring WSS 7-27
Configure Real-Time Communications **7-29**
Recommend and Implement an E-mail Solution **7-29**
Configure the POP3 Connector 7-30
Migrating Mailboxes from POP3 to Exchange 7-31
Outlook Web Access 7-31
Cell Phones and Mobile Devices 7-32
Outlook 2003 7-33
IMAP4 7-33
Implement a Web Site Hosting Configuration **7-34**
Granting Non-Admin Access Permissions 7-34
Configure Firewall Settings to Publish the Web Site 7-35
Configure the File Transfer Protocol **7-36**
Installing the FTP Service 7-36
Configure FTP Permissions 7-36
Configure Resource Sharing **7-37**
Configure Print Servers 7-38
Configure File and Folder Objects Sharing 7-39
Configure Disk Quotas 7-40
Create and Configure Public Folders **7-40**
Creating a Public Folder 7-41
Configuring Public Folders 7-41
Practice Questions **7-42**
Answer Key **7-48**
Summary **7-51**

Chapter 8
Supporting and Maintaining Windows Small Business
Server 2003 8-1
Managing Windows Small Business
Server 2003 8-1
Using the Server Management Console 8-1
Standard Management Options 8-2
Advanced Management Options 8-7
Using the Group Policy Management Console 8-9
Applying and Configuring Group Policy
Using the Group Policy Management Console 8-9

Editing Group Policies 8-11
Configuring Folder Redirection 8-12
Resultant Set of Policies (RSoP) 8-13
Manage and Troubleshoot Small Business Client Computers .. 8-14
Adding and Removing Clients 8-14
Assigning Applications to Clients 8-19
Setting Up a Client Computer 8-23
Configuring Remote Client Computers 8-25
Configure Offline Mail Synchronization 8-26
Configure SUS Using Group Policy 8-29
Resolve Client Computer Connectivity Issues 8-30
Network Troubleshooting Utilities 8-31
Back Up and Restore SBS 2003 8-32
Creating a Backup Job Using the Backup
Configuration Wizard 8-33
Volume Shadow Service (During Backup) 8-36
Volume Shadow Service (Periodic Snapshots) 8-36
Backup Location and Media Considerations 8-37
Restoring from a Backup Job 8-38
Monitor and Troubleshoot SBS 2003 8-39
Configuring Monitoring and Alerts 8-40
Performance, Usage, and Server Status Reports 8-41
Changing Alert Notifications 8-44
Small Business Server Troubleshooter Utilities 8-45
Troubleshoot Outlook Web Access 8-46
Outlook Web Access Basic/Premium 8-47
OWA Client-Side Troubleshooting Remedies 8-48
Troubleshoot Company Network Connections to an ISP 8-49
Event Viewer 8-50
Configure and Troubleshoot Terminal Services 8-51
Understanding Terminal Services 8-52
Installing Terminal Services 8-53
Configuring Terminal Services 8-53
Terminal Services Manager Utility 8-54
Practice Questions **8-55**
Answer Key **8-61**
Summary **8-64**

xii

MICROSOFT SMALL BUSINESS SPECIALIST PRIMER &
70-282 EXAM PREPARATION GUIDE!

Chapter 9

Expanding the Windows Small
Business Server 2003 Network 9-1

Add Member Servers to the
SBS 2003 Domain 9-2
Adding a Server Procedure 9-3
Promoting Additional Windows 2003 Servers
    to Domain Controller Status 9-5
Configuring Member Servers 9-6
Create an Application Migration Strategy 9-7
Migration Considerations 9-7
Backing Up Data Folders 9-9
Installing Applications on the New Server 9-9
Moving Data Folders 9-10
Migration Open Minds 9-10
Practice Questions 9-11
Answer Key 9-16
Summary 9-20

Chapter 10

Installing and Configuring
Windows Server 2003 10-1

Install Windows Server 2003 10-2
    Windows Server 2003 System Requirements 10-2
    Preparing for the Installation 10-3
    Performing the Installation 10-4
Configure Your Server Wizard Components 10-5
    Troubleshooting Setup Issues 10-7
Upgrade from SBS 2003 to Windows Server 2003 10-8
Upgrade Guidelines from Windows 2000 Server
    to Windows Server 2003 10-10
    Ensuring Compatibility 10-11
    Preparing for the Upgrade 10-12
    Upgrading a Member Server or Domain Controller 10-13
    Upgrading Workgroup Servers 10-14
Configure Windows Server 2003 10-14

Configure File and Print Servers 10-15
Promoting a Domain Controller 10-19
Creating and Configuring User, Group,
    and Computer Accounts 10-20
Configure Networking Hardware 10-25
Secure Windows Server 2003 10-26
Configure and Secure Internet Access 10-26
Configure a VPN Connection 10-27
Manage Windows Server 2003 10-29
Managing User Environments with GPOs 10-30
Delegating Administration 10-32
Protecting Against Data Loss 10-35
Automated System Recovery 10-37
Monitoring Server Performance 10-38
Remote Administration of Windows Server 2003 10-42
Troubleshoot Windows Server 2003 10-43
Troubleshooting Utilities 10-43
DETECT 10-46
Practice Questions **10-48**
Answer Key **10-52**
Summary **10-56**

Section III - Additional Exam/Assessment

Chapter 11

**Exam 74-134—Preinstalling Microsoft Products
Using the OEM Preinstallation Kit** **11-1**

Steps to Passing the 74-134 Exam **11-2**
Purchase Microsoft Action Pack 11-2
Review the Exam Objectives 11-2
Visit the Microsoft OEM Site 11-4
Get To Know BOB! 11-5
Be the Webcast Warrior 11-6
Complete Applicable Coursework 11-8
Read OPK documentation 11-12
Complete Online Assessments 11-13

xiv

MICROSOFT SMALL BUSINESS SPECIALIST PRIMER &
70-282 EXAM PREPARATION GUIDE!

Schedule and Take Test 11-14
74-134 Certification Secrets **11-15**
Summary **11-17**

Chapter 12
Small Business Sales and
Marketing Skills Assessment 12-1
Why Are We Here? **12-2**
The World We Live In **12-2**
Finder, Minder, Grinder 12-3
Mapping to Finder, Minder, Grinder 12-4
Worldwide versus Domestic Perspectives 12-5
SWOT Analysis Exercise 12-5
Think Small – Microsoft's New Partner Paradigm 12-7
Forced Marriage **12-7**
Back To School **12-8**
Online Study Resources 12-8
Educational Value Adds 12-12
Segmentation 12-12
Licensing 12-16
E-Mail Order Diploma 12-17
A Day in The Life **12-17**
Coffee at 7a.m. 12-17
Starting the exam 12-18
Completion 12-21
Next Steps **12-21**
Summary **12-22**

Appendices

Appendix A **A-1**
SBS 2003 RESOURCES **A-1**
Small Business Specialist Community Sites A-1
Certification Sites A-1
SBS-MVP Sites and Blogs A-2
Microsoft Windows SBS Sites A-2
Microsoft Partners-Related Sites A-2

Additional Microsoft or Microsoft-Related Sites A-3
Third-Party SBS-Related Sites A-4
Newslists, User Groups, Trade
        Associations, Organizations A-4
Seminars, Workshops, Conferences A-6
Business Resources A-6
Media A-7
SMB Hardware & Software Companies A-8
Miscellaneous A-8

Appendix B B-1
More SNMP Stuff B-1
Manage Networks by Using Simple
        Network Management Protocol (SNMP) B-1
        SNMP Services B-1
        Configure Agent Properties B-2
        Configure Traps B-3
        Configure Security B-4

Appendix C C-1
Third-Party 70-282 Viewpoints C-1
Andy Goodman, SBS-MVP C-1
Exam Review C-2
The Main Areas Tested Break Down as Follows C-2
        Analyzing the Existing Environment C-2
        Designing a Business Technology Solution
                for a Small- or Medium-sized Business C-3
        Installing and Configuring Windows Small
                Business Server 2003 .... C-3
        Supporting and Maintaining Windows Small
                Business Server 2003 .... C-3
        Expanding the Windows Small Business
                Server 2003 Network C-4
        Installing and Configuring Windows Server 2003 .... C-4
        10 Things To Practice C-4
        Okay, here's my take... .... C-4
        Final Report C-5

xvi

MICROSOFT SMALL BUSINESS SPECIALIST PRIMER &
70-282 EXAM PREPARATION GUIDE!

Vladimir Mazek, Orlando SBS User Group Leader C-6
Welcome to Vlad's World! C-7
    The Bad C-7
    The Good C-7
    The Details C-8
    Consulting C-8
    Licensing C-8
    Servers C-9
    Networking C-9
    Taking the Test C-9
    Getting Psyched C-10

Index **I-1**

About The Authors

This book was thoughtfully written by two long-time Small Business Server users (affectionately known as SBSers) with significant international experience:

Beatrice Mulzer, Cocoa, Florida USA

Beatrice Mulzer, born and raised in Germany, is an SMB technology consultant with a hands-on approach. She built her business on Microsoft SBS and changing the perception of the "Computer Guy." She has taught the Microsoft Certified Systems Engineer (MCSE) Microsoft Official Curriculum at local college campuses and developed and delivered Microsoft Hands-on-Labs nationwide.

Beatrice is a contributing editor at *Reseller Advocate Magazine* and co-author of the *Advanced Windows Small Business Server 2003 Best Practices* book. She also writes for *Certification Magazine*, is an MCSE and Microsoft Certified Trainer (MCT), and is a member of the Better Business Development Board at the Cocoa Beach Area Chamber of Commerce. Since she moved to Florida, she hasn't been to the beach.

xviii

MICROSOFT SMALL BUSINESS SPECIALIST PRIMER &
70-282 EXAM PREPARATION GUIDE!

Harry Brelsford, Bainbridge Island, Washington, USA

As the author or co-author of 13 books, Harry Brelsford has dedicated much of his professional career to technology issues. He started working with SBS in early 1997, several months before its commercial release, and has consulted with SBS customers for over eight years. He delivers over 60 workshops annually in 25 countries. His annual SMB Nation Conference hosts over 500 small and medium business (SMB) consultants each September in the Seattle/Redmond area. His free monthly *SMB Technology Watch* newsletter is enjoyed by nearly 10,000 readers worldwide. And SMB Nation Press is all about delivering books like this one to your hot little hands with some sassy Texas spunk thrown in.

Dedication

To all eager small-business technology consultants around the globe seeking professional fulfillment and prosperity!

Acknowledgements

No writer is an island, although many writers live on islands. It takes a team to produce a book including the following kind souls who made good things happen to get this book to market!

Nancy Williams – tireless operations manager at SMB Nation who continues to impress her peers daily with new feats of accomplishment.

Stephanie Martindale – Proved to the team daily that hard working honest people still get up at the crack of dawn, work two jobs, and deliver service with a smile. Great page layout work, Stephanie!

Vicki McCown – affectionately known as VIX, she assumed the managing editor role for this book while keeping her keen copy editor hat firmly affixed.

Liz Halverson – a long-time former Microsoft employee who escaped Redmond, Liz is the incoming Communications Director at SMB Nation who blessed the works contained herein. She oversees SMB Nation Press, our web site and the *SMB Technology Watch* newsletter.

Mike Iem – SMB Nation 2005 conference director who contributed good old-fashioned Midwestern business sense!

SBS MVPs – for fact checking and feedback.

Microsoft Small Business Specialist Primer & 70-282 Exam Preparation Guide!

xx

Arlin Sorsenson and his team – Arlin, an SBS Channel Advisory Council member who advises Microsoft on the SBS product, is a class act and a solid contributor of some exam questions!

Amy Luby – small business owner who has dedicated her life to supporting and implementing infrastructure solutions built on Small Business Server. Amy is a former presenter at Harry's SMB Nation Conference, and is currently working on the Microsoft Retail Management System chapters for Harry's upcoming book, *Extending SBS*.

Kevin Knudsen – a super proof reader and Chicago SBSer!

The Appendix C Dudes – These two gentlemen contributed the Appendix C content: **Andy Goodman** and **Vlad Mazek**.

Melinda Spencer, who pitched in on some last-minute editing!

Foreword

Are You Ready for the New SMB Revolution?

Humanity's advancement can be charted along a timeline of exploration and innovation. From the advent of fire to the age of the microchip, mankind has steadfastly charted new paths, set new directions, headed for new horizons.

It's in this spirit that we celebrate the beginning of another great journey. It may not seem to be the simple genius of sliced bread or the noble sacrifice of a mission to Mars, but Microsoft's entrance into the small/medium business (SMB) partner space is certainly worthy of notice.

Some would say it's about time the software giant more aggressively played in the important, growing market beyond the Fortune 1000. Others would counter Microsoft has already reached all markets, if only through trickle-down theories. Either way, a more formal strategy is emerging, and the book you're holding here is a good guide for those ready to blaze an expanded trail.

Kudos and congratulations to Harry Brelsford, SMB/SBS guru and Microsoft expert, and Beatrice Mulzer, emerging SBS guru, for writing this helpful volume. *Microsoft Small Business Specialist Primer & 70-282 Exam Preparation Guide* sets out to help IT professionals prepare and certify themselves for careers as Small Business Specialists. In an industry beset by outsourcing, automation, and general malaise, IT professionals could do much worse for themselves by coming to the same conclusion Microsoft obviously has: Working with xxii

MICROSOFT SMALL BUSINESS SPECIALIST PRIMER &
70-282 EXAM PREPARATION GUIDE!

businesses of *all* sizes drives continued commerce and offers new avenues for growth and development.

That's a message we at *Certification Magazine* can certainly get behind. Since our first issue in the days before the burst of the IT bubble, we've been preaching the message of continued growth, ongoing learning and creative solutions to problems of all types, from technology trials to careers stuck in neutral. Even with recession worries seemingly less pressing, the new opportunity for expansion Microsoft is offering couldn't be timelier. We can certainly hope *Microsoft Small Business Specialist Primer & 70-282 Exam Preparation Guide* and the Small Business Specialist certification it supports are just the first salvo in a barrage of books, certifications and opportunities for Microsoft to interact with its channel and channel members to take advantage of the certified skills of a loyal army of IT experts.

At *Certification Magazine*, we support the three-sided partnership that can breathe new life into the careers of individuals and into businesses small, medium and super-sized. In Harry and Beatrice's thorough work, you'll find a roadmap to a new specialty, a guidebook to new challenges and directions to sustainable success.

It's a new era for the certified IT professional. Are you ready to take the one giant step into small-medium businesses?

Tim Sosbe
Editorial Director
Certification Magazine
www.certmag.com

Preface

Welcome aboard and congratulations on your first steps toward becoming a Microsoft Small Business Specialist! This is an exciting new partner opportunity that was introduced worldwide by Microsoft in July 2005. Read on!

What This Book Is About

First and foremost, this book is really about how to become a Microsoft Small Business Specialist. Microsoft has set some VERY AGGRESSIVE worldwide recruitment goals for this new program and we're delighted to provide this "How To…" resource to help you become a successful Microsoft Small Business Specialist. We're happy knowing you're using our guide to better your station in life and improve your standard of living. Last time we checked, you only go around once in life, and we want to help you make the most of it.

This book fulfils its goal of supporting the new Small Business Specialist Community by emphasizing preparation for the Microsoft 70-282 certification exam: Designing, Deploying, and Managing a Network Solution for a Small- and Medium-Sized Business, which is one of the ways you can fulfill the Small Business Specialist certification exam prerequisites. We detected a distinct lack of study materials for the 70-282 exam.

The alternative 74-134 certification exam: Preinstalling Microsoft Products using the Preinstallation Kit can be used to satisfy the certification exam requirement, xxiv

MICROSOFT SMALL BUSINESS SPECIALIST PRIMER &
70-282 EXAM PREPARATION GUIDE!

so we allocate Chapter 11 in this book to that exam. Microsoft also has a business development/sales assessment that is required to become part of the Small Business Specialist Community. Participants must successfully complete this assessment, and we provide guidance on how to do so in this book!

Something you've come to expect from SMB Nation books—balanced discussions of significant business issues and deep dives into technology areas—continue in this book. Our half-and-half approach is especially germane in the context of the Small Business Specialist Community. Why? Because the Small Business Specialist Community is really about business and technology. The materials speak to both camps and Microsoft is demonstrating a new appreciation that the small business technology consultant is really a business person and a tech-head!

This book wears a lot of hats: business, technical, preparation for different certification exams (with emphasis on the 70-282 exam), and preparatory discussion for a business-related assessment. Step back and reread that last sentence and think for a moment—doesn't that sound a lot like the multifaceted and joyfully fragmented day of a thriving small business consultant? Sure does, and this book captures that flavor from cover to cover.

And finally—this book is global. Beatrice started her life in Germany and is now an American citizen, so she brings a Euro-American perspective to the small business technology community. An American by birth, Harry is an experienced world traveler and he delivers SBS workshops in over 25 countries globally each year. Harry's international niche is developing countries, so you'll see appropriate discussion on opportunities that the "rest of us" can relate to!

How This Book Is Organized

This book is organized into three sections.

- **Section I** introduces you to the Small Business Specialist Community.

- **Section II** helps you prepare for passing the 70-282 certification exam.

- **Section III** considers the 74-134 certification exam and offers valuable insights on successfully completing the Small Business Sales and Marketing Skills Assessment.

Section I: Small Business Specialist Community

The discussion in this section is necessarily "business speak" to properly introduce the book and the Small Business Specialist Community. It sets the tone for this book and gets you jazzed about being a small business technology consultant. You'll see that your greatest wishes surrounding Microsoft and the small business community have been answered in spades. But you'll find the discussion balanced from a critical third-party perspective with "SMB Nation speak" and not "Microsoft speak." That's what you're paying for in this section.

Section II: Exam 70-282

This is the "red meat" of this book and clearly the topic area we're emphasizing. This cut-to-the-chase series of chapters map directly to the 70-282 exam topics. The content is presented at a sufficient level of depth to prepare the newbie, intermediate, and even advanced professional to PASS the 70-282 exam. We stay very focused on passing the exam, so when a discussion topic begins to stray beyond that scope, we point you to our other books where you can dive into deeper discussions. For example, for richer SBS setup and deployment information, who could forget the *Windows Small Business Server 2003 Best Practices* book, where over 100 pages are devoted to describing every nuance of SBS 2003 setup (to the point of being annoying!)? Want to know much more about SBS 2003 migrations beyond what you'll read in this book to pass the exam (and understand Microsoft's migration paradigm)? We refer you to Jeff Middleton's excellent Chapter 15 in the *Advanced Windows Small Business Server 2003 Best Practices* book. You get the point. Read this section, stay focused, and pass the 70-282 exam.

Section III: Additional Exam and Assessment

The third and final section presents a certification exam alternative (74-134), which is applicable if you are a system builder seeking to use the Original Equipment Manufacturer (OEM) Preinstallation Kit. The book concludes with a chapter we can all rally around, which is guidance for successfully completing the Small Business Sales and Marketing Skills Assessment. You will receive xxvi

MICROSOFT SMALL BUSINESS SPECIALIST PRIMER &
70-282 EXAM PREPARATION GUIDE!

some rich business discussion in that chapter. Those with a strong technical background but a weaker business skill set will truly appreciate this chapter.

Who Should Read This Book

Readers of this book fall into a few identifiable categories:

- **Newbies.** You're the apple of our eyes and much of the reason we wrote this book. Eat it up! We are salivating over the fact that there are thousands of newbies out there trying to improve their lives using Microsoft small business solutions and looking into becoming Small Business Specialists!

- **Experienced consultants.** The underlying paradigm woven in, around, and out of these pages is that more capable SBSers—those serving small business as trusted advisors and consultants—are aggressively seeking a leg up on their professional peer group and hoping to better serve their customers. Passing the 70-282 exam and becoming a Small Business Specialist are positive steps in this direction!

- **Other channel members.** In addition to consultants, there are system builders, independent software vendors (ISVs), and distributors who also constitute part of the channel. A surprisingly strong readership group, these channel partners are seeking to learn more about the SMB space and deliver much-needed services and solutions to starving small business customers. Engaging in educational endeavors like passing the 70-282 exam and the Small Business Sales and Marketing Skills Assessment is all good.

- **Curious cats.** We can't fault someone for simply having a deep interest in SBS 2003 and other Microsoft SMB product stack components! These readers want a book that expands their horizons. Good enough, mate! Enjoy the read and find ways to make the certification exam(s) and the Small Business Specialist Community work for you!

- **Gurus.** There are currently 34 SBS gurus in the world, known as SBS Most Valuable Professionals (SBS-MVPs). Of course, these guys and gals are welcome to read this book. In fact, a few helped in the review process (thank you!). But to be honest, no author or publisher can profitably write and print a book for only 34 readers, so if you're a guru, kindly understand that this book is written for the common man and woman and we're takin' it to the small business streets around the world!

Who Shouldn't Read This Book

- **Negative people.** SMB Nation Press books are positive. A lesson learned by many and emphasized in all our publications is you get a lot more in life with sugar, not hot chilies!

- **Enterprise technology professionals.** The technology field is huge, and there are many specialists who improve businesses and entire civilizations each and every day with technology! In this book we're committed to staying focused on the small business technology sector; a committed enterprise technology professional might not get much value from it. There are many excellent MCSE books on the market oriented more toward our enterprise brethren!

- **End user customers.** As many readers know, SMB Nation Press books typically speak to the consultants, resellers, and channel partners who serve the loyal end-user customer. That's our publishing paradigm and we're sticking to it! That is, we want end-user customers to **hire and engage** our core readership group who used this book to become fat and happy Microsoft Small Business Specialists!

Who Wrote What?

This book had two authors but occasionally we use the first person writing style to better tell our story. So just for the record, here is who wrote what!

Chapters	Author	Chapters	Author
1	Harry	9	Beatrice
2	Harry	10	Beatrice
3	Beatrice	11	Harry
4	Beatrice	12	Harry
5	Beatrice	Appendix A	Harry
6	Beatrice	Appendix B	Beatrice
7	Beatrice	Appendix C	Guest authors
8	Beatrice		Andy and Vlad

xxviii

MICROSOFT SMALL BUSINESS SPECIALIST PRIMER &
70-282 EXAM PREPARATION GUIDE!

March Forward!

Microsoft heard y'all loud and clear that it didn't "get it" when it comes to the small business technology space. Be careful what you ask for! With the introduction of the Small Business Specialist Community, it's time to get an umbrella over your head when you walk outside, as small business technology content, technology solutions, and CUSTOMERS will be falling from the sky. It's a nice problem to have!

We sincerely hope you enjoy this book. Feedback is always welcome!

Beatrice Mulzer (bmulzer@intellisysusa.com)

MCSE, MCT, USA SBS Hands-On Lab Instructor

Cocoa, Florida USA

Harry Brelsford (harryb@smbnation.com)

CEO, SMB Nation, Inc.

Publisher, SMB Nation Press

Bainbridge Island, Washington USA

July 2005

PostScript

Register this book using the back-of-book registration form to receive MORE sample test questions and a BONUS chapter!

Section I
Small Business Specialist Community

Chapter 1
Introduction

Chapter 2
Small Business Specialist Community

CHAPTER 1
Introduction

Microsoft has turned its attention to the small business space in a meaningful way, something you no doubt ascertained by picking up this book and thumbing through a few of its pages. This chapter introduces some key elements of the book, including certification exams and the Small Business Specialist partnership program. But from this paragraph forward, this book first and foremost remains loyal to its core mission: helping you pass the 70-282 certification exam: Designing, Deploying, and Managing a Network Solution for a Small- and Medium-Sized Business. However, this book goes beyond being a simple "cram" for the 70-282 certification exam because it provides the broader context of the new Small Business Specialist partnership program. The relationship is that the 70-282 exam can be used to complete your certification exam requirement to join the Small Business Specialist partnership program.

Let's get started!

Certification Exam 70-282

First things first. What is the 70-282 exam: Designing, Deploying, and Managing a Network Solution for a Small- and Medium-Sized Business certification? It is Microsoft's attempt to establish a certification program baseline whereby technology professionals can prove their skills related to small businesses and the deployment of Windows Small Business Server 2003 (SBS 2003) and the traditional Windows Server 2003 products. It's the newly created bar people must jump over if they want acknowledgement from Microsoft in this area. The 70-282 certification exam is broken into several major categories, as shown in Table 1-1. This exam flow is essentially the major outline for this book (although we've added additional value by discussing the new Small Business Specialist partnership program and other examinations).

Table 1-1

70-282 Certification Exam Categories and Flow

Category	Comment
Analyzing the Existing Environment	This is a traditional business systems analysis designed to build appreciation for using business tools in the deployment engagement.
Designing a Business Technology Solution for a Small- or Medium-Sized Business	The intent here is to honor the architectural planning role in the small and medium business technology deployment scenario.
Installing and Configuring Windows Small Business Server 2003	This is the testing category for the down and dirty details for installing SBS 2003.
Supporting and Maintaining Windows Small Business Server 2003	This is an appropriate exam area for the downstream support function after the SBS 2003 deployment concludes.
Expanding the Windows Small Business Server 2003 Network	This section addresses a key Product Support Services (PSS) issue of adding more servers to the SBS network.
Installing and Configuring Windows Server 2003	This section was added so that the 70-282 certification exam wasn't strictly SBS-focused and allowed for two other forms of competency testing: medium-sized organizations running Windows Server 2003 and those small businesses that might opt for Windows Server 2003 over SBS!

To be honest, the 70-282 certification exam has had a slow start over the past couple of years. Microsoft's traditional certification path is very enterprise-oriented, so the 70-282 exam has been something of an outcast in the context of the "get certified" message. Combine that with the lack of "butts in chairs" at training centers learning about SBS in the early part of this century, and you have historically low levels of excitement for the 70-282 certification exam. But hope is on the way!

Microsoft has given new life to the 70-282 certification exam by:

- Turning the bow of the Microsoft ship to focus on the small business segment.

- Creating a new partnership opportunity, the Small Business Specialist, which treats the 70-282 certification exam as one of two options for fulfilling the certification exam prerequisite (more certification exams are expected to qualify at a later date).

- Promoting the value of Microsoft Certified Professional (MCP)-level certification in numerous public no- or low-cost outreach efforts like hands-on labs and USA TS2 seminars, where you can interact with a Microsoft technology professional.

- Periodically offering reduced-cost testing vouchers and other inducements to complete this examination.

- Encouraging attendance at the Microsoft Official Curriculum course 2395a: Designing, Deploying, and Managing a Network Solution for a Small- and Medium-Sized Business, which is associated with the 70-282 certification exam.

You will learn much more about the 70-282 certification exam in Chapters 3 through 10 of this book. To review the Preparation Guide for Exam 70-282, go to the Microsoft Learning site: http://www.microsoft.com/learning/exams/70-282.asp.

Certification Exam 74-134

Chapter 11 of this book is devoted to the 74-134 certification exam: Preinstalling Microsoft Products using the Preinstallation Kit. Why? Because it is the alternative certification exam you can take to fulfill your examination requirement to become a Small Business Specialist. That is, you could take exam 74-134 instead of 70-282 as your required certification exam. But few people will take this exam because it really is focused on two types of individuals:

original equipment manufacturers (OEMs), like HP, and system builders heavily into the white box clone market. Historically, these haven't been the "doers" serving customers as consultants in the SBS and small business communities. But, as a courtesy, this examination is discussed here in Chapter 11.

A little bit of firsthand history on Microsoft's interest in exposing its partner channel to the OEM Preinstallation Kit (OPK): At the turn of the century, I was a USA hands-on lab instructor for a vendor who delivered the hands-on labs for numerous Microsoft products. (I toured upwards of 50 U.S. cities per year and very much enjoyed meeting many readers along the journey!) For about a two-year period, it seemed like any hands-on lab delivery included a section on the OPK. SBS hands-on labs weren't immune, and I often found myself lecturing on and demonstrating the SBS OPK during the final hour of the day. (Scheduling our OPK discussion late in the day allowed folks to leave early if the topic wasn't of interest.) Why was the OPK included in these training forums? It's not that Microsoft was necessarily trying to make deeper inroads with partners such as HP, Dell, IBM, and others. Rather, Microsoft was trying to get the local small-town computer builder to embrace the OPK approach to implementing its operating systems. While the motive is pure, I can state that my audience was underwhelmed by the OPK message. That's why we'll honor the 74-134 exam in this book, but not emphasize it.

The 74-134 certification exam contains the following components, as shown in Table 1-2.

Notes:

Table 1-2
74-134 Certification Exam Categories and Flow

Category	Comment
Use OPK tools to preinstall operating system	This is the OPK hands-on lab and content being put to the test.
Create and apply preinstallation images	This is a technical deep-dive section on imaging, using remote installation services and other approaches.
Preinstall applications, drivers, and updates	Covers the deployment of Microsoft and third-party applications, etc.
Comply with the licensing requirements	Obligatory licensing content that centers on the preinstallation environment. Microsoft is seeking to test your licensing knowledge here.
Troubleshoot the preinstallation environment	Delves into common maladies and associated troubleshooting approaches and resolution.
Preinstall SBS	condition for an SBS 2003 deployment, creating the domain controller, and configuring the installation of Exchange and other applications.

You can learn more about the 74-134 exam in Chapter 11 of this book and at the Microsoft Learning site: http://www.microsoft.com/learning/exams/74-134.asp.

> IMPORTANT: Passing either the 70-282 or 74-134 exam will qualify you to become an MCP. Either exam satisfies the Small Business Specialist certification requirement.

Small Business Sales and Marketing Skills Assessment

This book also addresses the online Small Business Sales and Marketing Skills Assessment, a required component of the Small Business Specialist program. Microsoft recognizes that its Small Business Specialists are indeed wearing multiple hats as technicians, business people, sales people, managers, and so on. This requirement—passing a business-focused quiz to demonstrate your basic sales and marketing comprehension—is a welcome addition. Why? Because I and other long-time small business technology consultants will attest to the importance of business acumen in the world of technology consulting and service delivery. The inclusion of a business-related assessment as a requirement in the Small Business Specialist partnership program speaks to the following small business consulting trends:

- **Backroom and Boardroom**. Microsoft is a technology company, and many of its past assessments and exams were technology and product focused. The inclusion of the Small Business Sales and Marketing Skills Assessment signals that the business boardroom is just as important as the technical backroom for the small business consultant.

- **Cultural Revolution**. Blue collar meets white collar. Let's face it; many customers still view the "computer guy" or "computer gal" as a tech-head and a business lightweight. Consider the Small Business Sales and Marketing Skills Assessment as one step toward turning the blue collar mentality a bit more white collar!

- **Analytical Advancement**. MBAs and MCPs getting along. As you ascend the small business consulting food chain, you'll need to have part of your brain thinking BUSINESS. So consider this Small Business Sales and Marketing Skills Assessment your "mini-MBA." Upon passing this assessment and joining the Microsoft Small Business Specialist partnership program, you're a card-carrying business person. Welcome to the club!

- **Communication Skills**. Sales people like to talk. It's as simple as that. With your legitimate exposure to the world of sales and marketing, you're going to also find your communication skills improving. Watch out, as you might go from gruff technical guru to optimistic super-salesperson without even realizing it!

- **Higher Pay**! Last and certainly not least, there is the economic advancement issue. Knowing all the "bits" surrounding the Microsoft small business product stack is dandy. But bringing home more BUCKS is even better! Hopefully the technical and business mix of the new

Small Business Specialist partnership program will let you have more "Bits" and "Bucks." The Small Business Sales and Marketing Skills Assessment exam is one path to greater financial success because many of us know that after a certain point along your career path, your sales skills will contribute more to your net worth than your technical thinking. You read it here first.

The Small Business Sales and Marketing Skills Assessment is discussed further in Chapter 12 of this book.

Tips for Getting Certified

I write this section from a place of passion because I feel many other Microsoft Certified System Engineer (MCSE)-type certification books speak to the "secrets" for getting certified rapidly, in your sleep, with little or no effort. I want to emphasize some practical paradigms for you to pass the 70-282 exam (in particular) and become a Microsoft Small Business Specialist.

Experience

Old hands in small business technology consulting will appreciate that I've listed "experience" first and foremost. While we're an inclusive community and we welcome new small business technology consultants into our profession, don't underestimate the role experience plays in your dealings. It can also be a great asset in passing the 70-282 exam (and becoming a SUCCESSFUL Microsoft Small Business Specialist). Granted, saying experience is important to a newbie creates the chicken-and egg construct. That is, while everyone acknowledges experience is essential, how do you get experience when you're new and can't get work until you have applicable experience? It's a problem all professionals face at some point; the time-honored path of doing good work, paying your dues, and just plain showing up are key success factors in becoming a well-respected, experienced professional. More practically speaking, experience will help you pass the 70-282 exam as much as any late-night study session will! So consider the following approaches for gaining experience:

- **Install SBS 2003 for yourself and use it**. Even for a home-based business like Amway or managing the madness of raising a family, use

SBS 2003 each and every day. BE your own best customer and think through the installation. It is a little-known fact that many Microsoft employees in Redmond run SBS 2003 at home so they can use and learn SBS 2003 in the "real world." Repeat this behavior and you are well on your way to success.

- **Volunteer**. Nothing like working for free to get experience. Talk to schools (deploy SBS at a small, private school), political campaigns, and even unprofitable small businesses and see if you can become a small business savior with SBS 2003!

- **Life experience**. Don't understate the life experience you've gained from going around the block a few times. Heck, even a stay-at-home parent has bona fide business experience: raising kids, scheduling activities, budgeting the family funds, balancing the checkbook, provisioning the pantry, and keeping the facilities sanitary all qualify as work experience in this book. Likewise, unrelated jobs you've had along the highways and byways of life have all contributed to your awareness and allow you to critically analyze situations. It's this core set of skills based on life experience that'll prove helpful when taking a certification exam or serving a small business customer. Trust me.

- **Get a mentor**. Attend your local technology user group, identify a successful professional in your chosen field, and HANG OUT WITH THAT PERSON! It's really the shortest path to business success and will allow you to gain experience rapidly. By being selective in the business friendships you make, you'll find yourself "invited" into business transactions, consulting opportunities, and the like. Hey—if you want to win the Tour de France bike race, start training with Lance Armstrong, a seven-time winner of that race. Hanging out with mentors typically creates interesting opportunities, such as customer engagements, which translate into obtaining valuable experience very quickly.

- **Maturity**. The simple passing of time, no matter what your station in life, results in experience. Heck, at a minimum, you've got finely tuned survival skills that'll allow you to hunt down customers as a certified small business technology consultant!

Enthusiasm

Honest enthusiasm and a positive attitude may not show up on your résumé, but they are real forces nonetheless, and they play a powerful role in helping you achieve what you want in life! Use your SBS-related PASSION to PASS that 70-282 exam, fulfill other requirements, and become a super Small Business Specialist. So how do you switch from being negative and reorient yourself in a more proactive and positive way? Here are three thoughts to build enthusiasm:

- **Simple steps**. When people with an addiction seek to fundamentally change their situation and improve their life, they often use one of the step-by-step recovery programs. Similarly, for today, discover something you LIKE about SBS 2003 and want to tell the world. Treat your local technology user group meetings as your recovery movement meeting. Attend and participate.

- **Smell the roses of financial success**. I don't know about you, but my attitude improves dramatically when I'm making a lot of money. Funny how everyone started to really like SBS once they started making money with the product. So, if you're new to small business consulting, have the maturity and wisdom to know that your enthusiasm will build exponentially as your wealth increases. There is no stronger direct correlation in business.

- **Be young again**. Remember how exciting people, places, and events where when you were a child? Some of us who are now older, seasoned small business consultants remember how excited we were when we met SBS for the first time. Personally, seeing the excitement of life in my two young boys has been a source of strength to keep me positive and excited about small business technology. So perhaps drawing from the fountain of youth will allow you to tap into the positive energy you'll need to prepare for and pass the 70-282 exam and succeed in your quest to become a Microsoft Small Business Specialist!

$$\boxed{\textbf{N}\text{otes:}}$$

Education

Hopefully, you're interested in knowing more about things in both your professional and personal life. Not only does such an attitude serve you well socially and make you more interesting, it also allows you to better serve your small business customers as a technology consultant. As a consultant, almost by definition, you need to know more than your customer. That's why the consultant gets paid by the customer. It's really a simple business model.

A commitment to being a lifelong learner and continually nurturing a desire to know *more* is a bona fide success factor in preparing to pass the 70-282 exam and ultimately becoming a Microsoft Small Business Specialist. Thus, being a lifelong learner and a seeker of knowledge keeps you relevant as a small business consultant. When you made the decision to serve small businesses as a technology consultant (and soon to be Microsoft Small Business Specialist), you hopefully accounted for the fact that you'd need to stay current or suffer the consequences of being put out to pasture at a tender age. Staying current is an important cornerstone to being a successful small business technology consultant, and continuous learning will always be important!

So, just how do you become educated with respect to the 70-282 exam and other aspects of the Microsoft Small Business Specialist partnership program? You've got to become educated the old-fashioned way—with a lot of elbow grease and other forms of hard work! Consider the following educational opportunities to increase your small business technology-related know-how.

Microsoft Official Curriculum

Microsoft historically releases a Microsoft Official Curriculum (MOC) course that is casually related to a certification exam. These courses are delivered at certified training centers that are Microsoft partners and are taught by Microsoft Certified Trainers (MCTs). The strength of the relationship between the course and exam varies, but historically the correlation, while positive, hasn't been high.

In the case of the 70-282 exam, the path is clear. You would take MOC Course 2395a: "Designing, Deploying, and Managing a Network Solution for a Small- and Medium-Sized Business," available from the Microsoft Learning site: http://www.microsoft.com/learning/exams/70-282.asp. For the 74-134 exam, there isn't as strong a MOC study path. As shown in Figure 1-1, the Microsoft Learning page lists multiple courses (not all MOC approaches) that are tied to the 74-134 exam (http://www.microsoft.com/learning/exams/74-134.asp).

Figure 1-1

To prepare for the 74-134 exam using Microsoft-based educational resources, you need to select parts of several different learning curriculum offerings, as shown here.

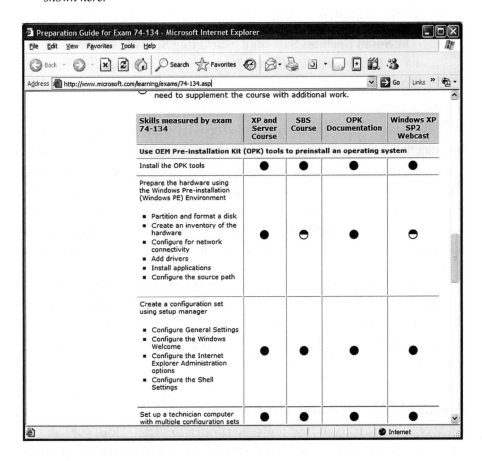

Self-Study/Online Study

We're delighted to report that this third-party book is one of your best resources for passing the 70-282 certification exam and completing the other steps needed to become a Microsoft Small Business Specialist! Microsoft also has many online and self-study resources available to make you successful on this journey:

- **70-282 exam**: A self-study version of the MOC course 2395a is being developed for your consumption and should be released in late summer or early fall 2005.

- **74-134 exam**: The Microsoft Learning page (http://www.microsoft.com/learning/exams/74-134.asp) offers several gold nuggets, including suggestions that you study the SBS 2003, Windows XP, and Office 2003 OPK document set.

- **The Small Business Sales and Marketing Skills Assessment**: Chapter 12 lists a boatload of free self-study/online training resources.

Workshops

At SMB Nation, we are proud of our global one-day workshops targeted toward boosting the technical and business performance of small business consultants. These workshops are one-day professional development or continuing education programs where attendees can step back from the madness of building a thriving small business consulting practice and think strategically. I liken it to a retreat where peer-to-peer interaction is just as important as receiving the technical and business content being served up. Visit http://www.smbnation.com for more details.

IMPORTANT: Rumor has it that starting in late 2005 or early 2006, Microsoft will offer, on a global basis, invitation-only training for Small Business Specialists. Chalk that up as another reason to get certified on the 70-282 exam and complete the other requirements to become a Small Business Specialist!

Annual SMB Nation Conference

Another sign of success and true professionalism is to attend at least one industry conference per year. The annual SMB Nation Conference, held each September in Redmond, Washington, is submitted for your consideration and approval. This event brings together over 500 small business technology consultants from around the world to talk the talk about walking the walk!

IMPORTANT: See Appendix A for additional resources that will assist you in preparing for the 70-282 certification examination and becoming a successful Microsoft Small Business Specialist. You'll find references to blogs, newsgroups, and much more.

Economics

Mind if I act like your beloved parents for a moment? Have you created a budget for getting certified and becoming a Small Business Specialist? While Microsoft has taken great strides to minimize the hard costs and direct financial outlay associated with passing the 70-282 exam and becoming a Small Business Specialist, there are hidden costs I want you to consider:

- **Courses/Courseware**. Either attending courses (expensive) or obtaining courseware (less expensive) is a bona fide cost you incur. Account for it.

- **Study time**. There is a "true opportunity" cost associated with studying for the 70-282 exam and completing the other requirements for hurdling the bar to become a Small Business Specialist.

- **Retakes**. Certification exam retakes have a real cost. As a general rule, you must pay $125 USD each time you want to take the 70-282 exam. Ouch!

- **Return on investment (ROI)**. Imagine this scenario wherein you've worked very hard and reached your goal of passing the 70-282 exam and becoming a Small Business Specialist (congratulations are in order). But, what if you've burned out along the way? What happens if you get to the finish line only to decide you want to hang up your running shoes!?!? You've just incurred massive sunk costs and definitively encountered negative ROI. They say economics is the dismal science, and this has certainly emerged as the most dismal paragraph of the book, but I want you to be "scared straight" as you move along so you are focused on making this entire process work for you in a most positive way! Make your ROI the highest possible, because you're incurring costs in the journey whether you know it or not.

- **This book**. You've made a huge step by purchasing a book that focuses on the 70-282 exam and the mechanics of becoming a Microsoft Small

Business Specialist. I'd like to think the cover price of the book will pay for itself many times over. Nonetheless, you've "bought the book," as they say in business. It's a real cost.

Envy

My final tip for you in passing the 70-282 certification exam and becoming a Microsoft Small Business Specialist is this: GET JEALOUS! When you attend your SBS user group meeting, scan the horizon and observe your brethren who appear more well-heeled (in the self-made sense, not the inherited wealth variety). Sit next to this person, buddy up, and get JEALOUS! When he or she drives away in a Volvo or Lexus and you're in a low-end car, let that burning feeling of envy MOTIVATE you to do better tomorrow, pass the 70-282 exam, become a Microsoft Small Business Specialist, and go out and KICK BUTT!

Summary

The purpose of this chapter is to get you excited about this book and motivate you to not only get certified on the 70-282 exam, but to run out and become a Microsoft Small Business Specialist! Microsoft is increasingly going to tie its interaction opportunities with small business technology consultants to those who are bona fide Small Business Specialists. It just makes sense. Wouldn't Ford or General Motors, the USA automobile companies, restrict sales opportunities to its network of car dealers? Yes!

This chapter painted the overall picture of the book with its focus on the 70- 282 exam and my unbridled excitement about Microsoft's new Small Business Specialist Community program. Hopefully, I've done my job and you'll now move along to Chapter 2 to learn much more about the Small Business Specialist Community!

CHAPTER 2
Small Business Specialist Community

Finally! A Microsoft partnership opportunity for the little fella. As you will learn in this chapter, Microsoft's new focus on small businesses has coalesced into the new Small Business Specialist Community after much evolution. This is a partnership program with three winners:

- **You** benefit from positive affinity and affiliation with the Microsoft Partner Program at a meaningful level.

- **Customers** enjoy the assurance that a small business technology consultant has met certain qualifications to hold the Small Business Specialist title.

- **Microsoft** gains a legion of certified partners dedicated to the small business space. Microsoft also learns more about the small business space.

In this chapter, the word "consultant" is used to generically include true technology consultants, value-added resellers, value-added providers, technology resellers, and even system builders!

IMPORTANT: For those readers who like to skip the wedding and go straight to the reception (naughty-naughty), you can drop to the end of the chapter and read the Elevator Ride Version to get a quick overview of the Small Business Specialist Community. Then look at he links in the Community Resources section that follows.

The Case for Partnering with Microsoft

One of the big reasons we're here in this book is to partner with Microsoft. Some readers who go back a few light years in the small and medium business (SMB) technology community will remember in the late 1980s and early 1990s when Novell's certification and partner program ruled the land (circa NetWare 2.x and 3.x). People loved the Novell partnering opportunity and Microsoft was a partner program no-show. That all changed in the early- to mid-1990s when Dwayne Walker (who worked for Microsoft between 1989 and 1996) fathered the modern Microsoft Partner Program with executive endorsement from Steve Ballmer. Walker later went on to run a dot-com called Network Commerce and ultimately sued Microsoft for patent infringement (2002-2003), but that's a whole different story. Fast forward to modern times and here's how Microsoft's Partner Program is defined and where the program is at, as shown in Figure 2-1.

Definition

Microsoft defines its Partner Program as follows:

> *The worldwide Microsoft Partner Program is for technology companies that use Microsoft software for building and distributing software or hardware solutions or as the building blocks for value-added services.*

What's interesting about the definition is how it sets expectations and boundaries. Clearly, the Microsoft Partner Program is focused on the consulting and reseller community and its stakeholders are expected to consider attending its annual Worldwide Partner Conference (WPC), last held in July 2005 in Minneapolis, MN. (For more information about this event, go to https://partner.microsoft.com/global/events, then click Worldwide Partner Conference in the Events section of this page.) However, the developers that support the Microsoft ecosystem possibly haven't even heard of the Microsoft Partner Program and attend very different

Microsoft soirées, such as the Professional Developers Conference (PDC) or TechEd. In short, Microsoft interacts with different stakeholder groups in different ways. One partner told me that the owner and sales people attend the WPC and the technical staff attend TechEd. There's boundary definition for you!

> IMPORTANT: In designing the Annual SMB Nation Conference, we attempted to cater to both crowds in the small business technology consulting space by having both business and technical tracks. That way, multiple people from the same Small Business Specialist Community firm could attend the same conference. For information on this event, held each September in the Seattle area, visit http://www.smbnation.com.

Partner Pyramid

Figure 2-1 presents a graphic view of the Microsoft Partner Program (nothing like a simple graphic drawn on a napkin to convey a concept!).

Figure 2-1

Microsoft's Partner Program can be viewed as a pyramid.

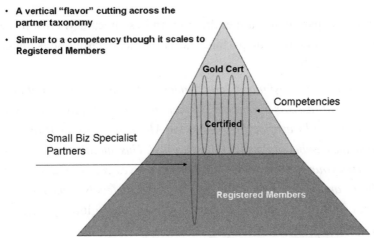

How does Small Business Specialist fit into the MS Channel Taxonomy?

- A vertical "flavor" cutting across the partner taxonomy
- Similar to a competency though it scales to Registered Members

Gold Cert

Competencies

Certified

Small Biz Specialist Partners

Registered Members

Starting at the bottom of the Microsoft Partner pyramid, you might be interested to know that the organizational and financial commitment increases as you climb upwards. For example, a Registered Partner simply registers at a Microsoft Partner site. I spell out the requirements to become a Small Business Specialist in great detail in the next section. A Certified Partner needs to have two Microsoft Certified Professionals on staff and pay a fee to join. A Gold Certified Partner pays the same fee but has to achieve additional milestones, such as more Partner Points and competency requirements. Here is sampling of current Certified/Partner fees:

- Australia: 3,465 AUD

- India: 80,454 INR

- New Zealand: 3,115 NZD

- United Kingdom: 1,050 GBP

- United Status of America. 1,450 USD

There are other requirements to become a Certified Partner and Gold Certified Partner that I won't explore here (the above discussion is a sampling to provide context). Visit https://partner.microsoft.com/global/30000104 for complete Microsoft Partner Program details.

Partner Points

Partner Points are part of the Partner Program and a scorecard Microsoft uses to reward its most committed top performers. The official definition is touted on the Partner Point web site:

Partner Points are designed to create a level playing field for solutions partners of all sizes. As a solutions partner you can qualify as a Certified Partner or Gold Certified Partner in the Microsoft Partner Program based on the number of Partner Points earned. This qualification method recognizes your success in the marketplace, gives you a great deal of flexibility, and helps open up the highest program levels to partners of all sizes and types. (https://partner.microsoft.com/global/program/partnerpoints)

As you will read later, when you become a Small Business Specialist, you are awarded 25 Partner Points!

Small Business Specialist Strategy

This section describes the initial and growth strategies surrounding the Small Business Specialist Community.

Five-Step Initial Strategy

How can you make a difference today as you read this early chapter in this book and ride the FAST PATH to becoming a Small Business Specialist Community member? When the clock strikes midnight tonight, is there any single task you could have completed to inch closer to the finish line? YES! Follow these initial strategy steps.

- **Step One**. Sign up as a Registered Partner at: https://partner .microsoft.com/global/program/levels/registeredmember. This gets you in the door and establishes a business relationship with Microsoft. Go do it RIGHT NOW; I'll wait for you to return.

- **Step Two**. Welcome back! The next step you can immediately undertake is to PURCHASE THE ACTION PACK! Read about the Action Pack before consummating your transaction, but understand that this is a requirement of the Small Business Specialist Community program. After reading this chapter, go to https://partner.microsoft.com/global/ 40009735 and purchase the Action Pack!

- **Step Three**. Sign up for a qualifying certification exam. See the IMPORTANT note that follows! We endorse the 70-282 exam as our favorite (and the focus of this book). You can sign up to take your certification exam by starting at this Microsoft Learning site: http:// www.microsoft.com/learning/mcpexams/register/default.asp.

IMPORTANT: Please set your certification examination date at least 14 days from today (30 days may be even better). This gives you time to read this book and completely prepare for your certification exam. The key point is to set a testing date so you have a DEADLINE and are motivated to complete your examination preparations!

- **Step Four**. Completely read this book. Hopefully, both authors have created such a compelling read that going cover to cover won't be difficult. So read the next paragraph, the next page, and the next chapter. Before you know it, you'll be done and ready to complete the process of becoming a Small Business Specialist!

- **Step Five**. Fulfill the other requirements. This chapter and the remainder of the book spell out the "gives" that you must extend to Microsoft to become a Small Business Specialist. It's really easy and soon you'll be a member of the club!

Growth Strategy

Both authors are acutely aware that some readers will simply use the Small Business Specialist Community as a stepping stone on the way up the partner ladder. Some readers don't intend to remain Small Business Specialists for long. For those, this is merely their starting point to building a relationship with Microsoft, acquiring some customers who are "referencable and referable," and becoming a Certified Partner or Gold Certified Partner going after upper/mid-market or enterprise-level work.

For what's its worth, here's our one-word reply: COOL! You are welcome to stay in the Small Business Specialist Community as long as you like and we'll miss you when you're gone.

IMPORTANT: It's a well-known and appreciated growth strategy to start small and become big. That's how the game is played and it's how the likes of Microsoft and HP and other great companies launched! Who knows? It's entirely possible that someone reading this chapter will ascend to stardom and be the next billionaire!

Along the same line, some people use opportunities like the Small Business Specialist program as a "station in life." Realistically, the opportunities available in the small business space allow you to make a good six-figure living. However, the small business opportunity probably isn't a seven-figure opportunity (to make you a millionaire just from installing SBS at customer sites). But you can use your small business consulting income to leverage into other opportunities, such as commercial real estate, where you then go on to make millions. That's the power of leverage.

Get Involved—Partner Community Building

There is another interesting way to interact with the Microsoft Partner ecosystem beyond just the official way. I cite a very successful SBS consultant in Houston, Texas—Tim Loney and his company SOLUTIONS Information Systems (www.solutionsis.com)—as a perfect example of this. Ever the businessman with a deep technical skill set, Tim understands the value of business relationships and the need to meet and greet regularly. It's what impressed me most about him: his Texas business moxie! Tim has been very active in a third-party trade association, the International Association of Microsoft Certified Partners (IAMCP, www.iamcp.org), to improve his business and the small business partner community. If imitation is the sincerest form of flattery, then you might want to mimic Tim's success and become a player in the Microsoft Partner community. Another prominent SBS partner, Michael Cocanower, from IT Synergy in Phoenix, AZ, has used this same IAMCP strategy with great success.

Gives and Gets

Every relationship is about giving and getting. This holds true in both business and personal settings, and the Small Business Specialist Community is no different. Frankly speaking, it should be that way, as relationships that last long term require both parties to have skin in the game and remain motivated.

Gives

Before you can "get" the Small Business Specialist benefits, you have to first "give" to get into the partnership program. Here are the gives.

Program Sign-up

It's been said that your odds of winning the lottery improve DRAMATICALLY if you purchase a ticket! That truism is indisputable. Likewise, your odds of improving your life as a small business technology consultant improve DRAMATICALLY if you complete the Small Business Specialist sign-up form! Consider this your first step. Visit https://partner.microsoft.com/global/smallbiz specoverview to start that sign-up process.

> IMPORTANT: More Small Business Specialist Community web site URLs are given at the end of this chapter.

Honor System Experience

The Small Business Specialist Community program is recommended for experienced small business technology consultants with at least six months of experience installing, configuring, and supporting SBS 2003, Office 2003, and Windows XP in small business environments. Clearly there is little Microsoft can do to enforce this requirement, but it is noble that Microsoft is trying to improve the quality of its program membership.

Purchase the Action Pack

The Action Pack is hardly a "give" because what you get clearly outweighs the $299 USD annual investment. Historically, Action Pack was a quarterly subscription service for Microsoft Registered Partners (the very lowest partnership level, also known as site-registered partners). If you were a Registered Partner, you could acquire Action Pack.

Action Pack currently contains front office and back office business applications that are particularly well-suited for use in small- and medium-sized businesses, as shown in Table 2-1. Action Pack, updated quarterly, is how SMB-class consultants and partners acquire their learning bits. With Action Pack, Registered Members of the Microsoft Partner Program have fully licensed, popular SMB-focused Microsoft applications that you can use in your own consultant practice to LEARN the products. Its generous licensing program allows you to climb the learning curve before delivering services to your customers.

IMPORTANT: Action Pack doesn't have strong "goodness of fit" for enterprise-class consultants and partners because its focus is on components that are better suited for the SMB space. And to be honest, Microsoft Certified Partners and Gold Certified Partners who are better equipped to serve the enterprise space would acquire their learning bits from the monthly mailer (a box of application software and partner-related materials), which is a separate deliverable for partners at these levels with the Microsoft Partner Program (MSPP).

Table 2-1

Action Pack Content (April 2005)

Component	Usage Licenses	Comments
Microsoft Business Contact Manager for Office Outlook 2003	10	This is "baby Customer Relationship Management" (CRM) that provides a holistic leads-tracking capability on a standalone basis.
Microsoft Business Solutions CRM	5	This is the "big dawg" CRM Professional. Tremendously valuable because it is the professional edition.
Microsoft Exchange Server 2003 Standard	1	The standard edition of Microsoft's widely accepted messaging server-side solution. It has a 16 GB information store limit and is limited to a single database.
Microsoft Internet Security and Acceleration (ISA) Server 2004	1	Microsoft's current update for its Internet security, firewall, and caching application.
Microsoft Live Communications Server	1 server, 10 clients	Microsoft's instant messaging and real-time communications application.
Microsoft MapPoint 2004 Standard Edition	10	A cool geography-related application in the North America edition only. See my worldwide discussion later in this chapter.

Visit www.microsoft.com/technet for the latest updates for any Microsoft product.

Table 2-1 (continued)

Component	Usage Licenses	Comments
Microsoft Mobile Information Server 2002 Enterprise Edition	1	This supports mobility extensions on your network infrastructure. North America edition only.
Microsoft Operations Manager 2005 Workgroup Edition	10	This is a managed services suite known as "MOM." Look for Microsoft to try to push this solution into the SMB space. Interesting!
Microsoft Office FrontPage 2003	10	Provides the ability to create and publish capable web sites.
Microsoft Office InfoPath	10	Very cool and gaining traction, this forms-based program is great for SMB organizations seeking to improve workflow.
Microsoft Office Professional Edition 2003	10	One of the true values in Action Pack is the 10 licenses for Office 2003 Pro. Use it!
Microsoft Office Project Professional 2003	10	An excellent desktop-based project management application that can be used by any business.
Microsoft Office Project Server 2003	1	Even the Project Server 2003 development team admits this product is for larger companies. Very powerful, but overshoots the small business market.
Microsoft Office Publisher 2003	10	A capable desktop publishing solution with some excellent newsletter templates.
Microsoft Office SharePoint Portal Server 2003	1 server, 10 clients	Provides server-based collaboration capabilities beyond Windows SharePoint Services (WSS).

Table 2-1 (continued)

Component	Usage Licenses	Comments
Microsoft Office Visio Professional 2003	10	An excellent drawing program to create business charts, graphics, and diagrams. Heaps of shapes included!
Microsoft Office OneNote 2003	10	Wow! A hidden jewel in Action Pack that is a "must use" if you have a Tablet PC. Allows you to instantly organize your thoughts.
Microsoft SQL Server 2000 Standard	1	A very powerful relational database that creates significant opportunities for Small Business Specialist Community members!
Microsoft SQL Server 2000 Service Pack 3a	1	Apply this to the above SQL Server 2000 product. This is an example of how Action Pack includes service packs, patches, and fixes in its quarterly mailers.
Microsoft SQL Server Reporting Services Standard Edition	1	This cool tool for MBAs allows the SMB organization to engage in business analytics with its SQL-based data.
System Builder Original Equipment Manufacturer (OEM)–OneNote 2003 W32 with Service Pack 1	1	The popular OneNote program is a system builder stock-keeping unit (SKU). This reflects how Action Pack is trying to cross over into the system builder crowd. (Also see the last components of Action Pack that have a system builder focus.)

Notes:

Table 2-1 (continued)

Component	Usage Licenses	Comments
Microsoft Virtual PC 2004	10	This is a really valuable addition to Action Pack. You can create "virtual environments" on a PC (e.g., laptop). For example, a Small Business Specialist Community member could create a "mini-SBS 2003" network on a laptop to demonstrate (and sell) SBS to customers. You could have a SBS 2003 server machine, internal Windows XP Pro workstations, and an external client computer – all SIMULATED – to demonstrate Remote Web Workplace!
Microsoft Windows Server 2003 Standard Edition	1	This is the "core" network operating system SKU from Microsoft. You can use this Action Pack item to create a second domain controller on your SBS 2003 network as part of a Swing Migration.
Microsoft Windows Server 2003 Web Edition	1	This is the channel-only reduced functional network operating system from Microsoft. It can't be a domain controller, but it's a darned good web hosting server.
Microsoft WSS Standard Edition	1	Action Pack is one avenue to easily acquire the WSS collaboration platform.

Notes:

Table 2-1 (continued)

Component	Usage Licenses	Comments
Microsoft Windows Small Business Server 2003 Premium Edition	1 server, 10 clients	This is a full-featured version of SBS 2003 you can use to run your SMB consulting practice and then provide SBS-related services to your customers. Ships with 10 Client Access Licenses (CALs) and you can add more licenses – up to 75 CALs. One of the GREATEST VALUES in Action Pack.
Microsoft Windows XP Professional Edition	10	A bushel of XP Pro licenses for your use. This is Microsoft's most current desktop operating system.
Microsoft Windows XP SP2	10	A necessary service pack to apply to the above product.
System Builder OEM Software: OEM Windows XP SP2 Professional, OEM Office 2003 Professional, OEM Small Business Server 2003 Standard Edition	Varies	A system-builder bonanza! Note that SBS 2003 Standard Edition is in the OEM version (not the Premium Edition). The rationale behind that is system builders and OEMs can easily roll out SBS 2003 Standard Edition, but not Premium Edition deployments, which are typically handcrafted.
Microsoft Partner Guides	N/A	Office System, Security Solutions, Small Business Resource Kit, System Builder
Additional Materials	N/A	Sales Tool Kit Partner Guide, Office Systems Developer Kit CD, Technical DVD Demo Toolkit

IMPORTANT: Revisit the system builder information in the above table. Not only will Action Pack provide you with the system builder bits to work your way through Chapter 11 of this book, but these bits will be the basis for you to pass the 74-134 certification exam. This is where you'll acquire the OEM Preinstallation Kits (OPKs).

The above list of Action Pack components exceeds $25,000 USD in value, if valued when compared to perpetual licensing! And the Action Pack subscription isn't just about software. It also includes professionally designed marketing collateral and self-paced training curricula (e.g., CD-based courses) that you can engage with. One of the Action Pack managers is shown in Figure 2-2.

> IMPORTANT: Action Pack is updated quarterly so application content offerings can be refreshed with updated versions, new releases, new partner guides, and even service packs and other fixes. To receive quarterly update kits, Partners must be Registered Members in the MSPP (which occurs when you purchase Action Pack) and have an active Action Pack subscription.

Figure 2-2
Sharon Erdman, Senior Marketing Manager for Action Pack for the USA region at Microsoft, visits with author Harry Brelsford to discuss this quarterly bounty of bits-based booty!

Financial Commitment

The Action Pack is a worldwide program that currently has an annual subscription fee of $299 USD annually for the Standard SKU (I discuss the Plus SKU in the note below). Prices vary by country and according to monetary currency fluctuations, but one thing is clear worldwide: YOU MUST RENEW your Action Pack subscription to continue using the learning bits in your business! Action Pack subscription prices are subject to change, so please check the Microsoft partner site for the most current pricing!

> IMPORTANT: Another Action Pack option in the USA is called Action Pack Plus for $399 USD for the first year. This includes all the content of the standard Action Pack, plus the ability to use the Microsoft List Builder tool to send out e-mail newsletters to your customers. For the first five years of my SBS-focused newsletter, *SMB Technology Watch*, I used List Builder as my delivery transport, and I can attest that it is an effective mechanism as long your newsletter doesn't exceed 250 KB in size or have more than 10,000 subscribers. My survey data supports this finding: the vast majority of Action Pack subscribers (80 percent) are enrolled in the standard program.

So why would you renew your Action Pack subscription in the second and later years if the learning bits are running just fine? Will the software police raid your domicile? (Action Pack Licensing Terms and Conditions violations are always subject to enforcement.) Will the bits burn up on the 366th day of use after your one-year licensing period expires? (No!) So why would you renew your subscription to Action Pack? I can think of two reasons:

- **Moral compass**. I believe that people are basically good and act in a positive, altruistic manner. (That is a time-tested political science theorem from some Greek philosopher whose name escapes me.) I believe you'll renew your Action Pack subscription simply because it's the right thing to do.

- **Staying Current**. In the body politic, there is a competing viewpoint that people act only in their best interest, and I'll accommodate that line of thinking, too. As actor Michael Douglas uttered while walking on a beach in the popular late-1980s movie *Wall Street*, "Greed is good." Greed will motivate you to renew your Action Pack subscription. Far be it from you to be seen using legacy Microsoft SMB product stack applications in your own consultant practice. Most embarrassing! More important, letting your Action Pack subscription lapse sets in motion the economic obsolescence of your knowledge-based technical professional skill set. You are no longer the most current SBSer and your days as a leader of the pack are numbered if you let yourself become an SMB technology dinosaur. Off with your head!

Your drive to stay current necessitates your Action Pack renewal!

You'll receive communication from Microsoft approximately 30 days before your subscription is set to expire. If for some reason you become disenchanted with Action Pack after one year or any subsequent annual renewal period, and/or you become otherwise disenfranchised from Microsoft and your Action Pack subscription lapses, then you must remove the learning bits provided by Action Pack from your technology infrastructure! Case closed.

Licensing

Another "heavy" comment that must be conveyed concerns the use of your Action Pack learning bits. The fact of the matter is that your Action Pack learning bits may not be utilized for your customers; they are for your private and specific use to enjoy these Microsoft front office and back office applications. And while I'm using simple Texas talk to convey a serious message, if somehow I am not getting through to you, kindly read the licensing agreement that accompanies your Action Pack subscription. I'll meet you back right here in a few minutes!

Worldwide Program

Another sage observation I want to share with you concerns Action Pack content and its positioning as a worldwide product offering from Microsoft. In some ways, Microsoft could potentially offer you more for less with Action Pack if it were only a USA product SKU. What, how, and why, you ask? Let me explain. In working closely with the USA and worldwide Action Pack teams at Microsoft in Redmond (two different and distinct groups), I've often suggested the inclusion of certain interesting business applications, such as Small Business Financials, in the quarterly distributions. I was then made privy to some international relations insights that explain why some products don't fit the Action Pack worldwide model. For example, the accounting applications offered via the Microsoft Business Solutions (MBS) organization—while very desirable for

SMB consultants seeking to elevate their SMB consulting practices above and beyond mere infrastructure—must be tailored for each country. That is, the Generally Accepted Accounting Principles (GAAP) used in the USA don't transfer easily or readily to foreign lands. Other countries have different accounting treatments, and Microsoft's MBS products in the accounting realm can't simply be dropped in a box and shipped out as part of a quarterly mailer. I completely understand this and can appreciate how such global dynamics affect the contents of Action Pack! And now you know the rest of the story on how, in part, applications are selected for inclusion in Action Pack.

Affinity and Adoption

I close this section with a discussion about Action Pack adoption rates and affinity-based acceptance based on geographic locations. When delivering my worldwide SMB Nation Summit one-day workshops in over 40 cities and 25 countries annually, I surveyed attendees about Action Pack and also gave away Action Pack as a door prize. Needless to say, this workshop format provided impressive data about Action Pack.

- **High positive affinity**. Worldwide Action Pack subscribers who attended my workshop LOVE ACTION PACK. It's all about value. For example, in the USA, Microsoft delivers the SMB application space library as the Action Pack subscription, valued in excess of $25,000 USD, for just under $300 USD annually (you must renew annually to continue to use that software library). What's not to love about that! Try this analogy on for size. In the U.S. Congress, an elected member who easily wins reelection is said to have a safe seat. The same could be said about Action Pack in the SMB consulting community—it has a safe seat.

- **USA traction, global need for action**. Over 80 percent of USA SMB Nation Summit attendees happily subscribe to Action Pack. However, in the worldwide community, I found that, at best, only 20 percent of attendees subscribe to Action Pack. This is ironic because Microsoft's SMB product stack, including Windows Small Business Server 2003, does so well worldwide and lags in the domestic USA market. Life sometimes delivers cruel punishment and unusual fates, and clearly this inverse performance relationship between Action Pack and the Microsoft SMB product stack is one of the paranormal phenomena I can't explain.

IMPORTANT: Bottom line? An Action Pack subscription is a prerequisite for membership in the Small Business Specialist Community. Learn more about the Microsoft Action Pack at https://partner.microsoft.com/global/40009735.

Successfully Pass One Certification Exam

Time to get serious after that lengthy Action Pack discussion! To become a Small Business Specialist, you must successfully pass a Microsoft Certified Professional (MCP) exam.

Currently, you can select from two MCP certification exams:

- **70-282: Designing, Deploying, and Managing a Network Solution for a Small- and Medium-Sized Business**. Discussed in detail in Chapters 3 through 10, this is clearly the major certification exam we focus on in this book. Both authors feel strongly that this will be the watershed examination event in the Small Business Specialist Community program with its focus on SMB consultants and value added reseller (VAR) partners. Ergo—we give you eight chapters to prepare for that specific examination. And what about the examination itself? It's very SBS 2003-centric, but it acknowledges the proper role of a Windows Server 2003 standard edition in an SMB organization.

- **74-134: Preinstalling Microsoft Products using the OEM Preinstallation Kit** (covered in Chapter 11). Including this niche examination is Microsoft's way of signaling its intention to be system-builder inclusive in the Small Business Specialist program. Microsoft would love to engage more with the system builder community in the SMB space; including the 74-134 exam in the Small Business Specialist Community certification testing requirements is part of that outreach.

- **Future exams**. The Microsoft program team behind the Small Business Specialist Community program is madly working to add more MCP exam options to satisfy the certification exam requirement. Look for this as a major area of growth in the Small Business Specialist Community program: more exams to select from!

IMPORTANT: Exam 70-282 qualifies the successful candidate to be a Microsoft Certified Professional and hold that title. Exam 74-134 does NOT qualify the successful candidate to be an MCP. Both authors recommend the 70-282 exam.

Applause extended to the Small Business Specialist Community team at Microsoft for demanding a certification exam requirement. Not only has it given new life to the above exams, but I really like how incumbent Small Business Specialists have to demonstrate basic technical competency. That is, not just anyone can become a member of this club—you have to earn this privilege!

IMPORTANT: Need motivation to complete and return the book registration form at the back of this book? By being a registered book owner, you'll receive notification of updated chapters that refer to new eligible MCP exams in the Small Business Specialist Community program!

Microsoft currently has the following exam retake policy:

Microsoft has revised its policy for retaking exams to increase security.

If you do not pass an exam the first time, you may retake it at any time.

If you do not achieve a passing score a second time, you must wait at least 14 days to retake the exam a third time. A 14-day waiting period will be imposed for all subsequent exam retakes. If you have passed an exam, you cannot take it again. Beta exams may be taken only once.

Successfully Pass the Online Small Business Sales and Marketing Skills Assessment

This is clearly one of my favorite components of the Small Business Specialist Community program and reflects the world we live in as small business technology consultants and VARs. The prototypical small business technology consultant is a sole proprietor businessperson serving other small businesses. As such, you must wear many hats including technician, business owner, and sales person.

So Microsoft has correctly determined that a successful Small Business Specialist must be sales and marketing savvy. Three cheers! Speaking only for myself, I can say that I've made more money with the sales and marketing skill set (namely, business development) than I have carrying the tools as a technician. But don't misinterpret that last comment, as it takes the "full package" to be a well-rounded and well-respected Small Business Specialist. The main point is this: embrace, don't fight, sales and marketing.

Time to get geographic and look at the online sales and marketing assessment from a popular sociology vantage point of global "haves" and "have nots." Sociologists in the research and academic communities are deeply concerned about a widening socioeconomic gap between developed and emerging countries. Study after study suggests that the rich get richer and the poor get poorer. That is, the "haves" get more and the "have nots" get less. I can offer casual support for the sociologists' empirical work from my own travels to over 25 countries to promote SBS and the SMB consulting opportunity.

Enter the Small Business Sales and Marketing Skills Assessment as one small step in trying to save the world. Hear me out on this theory. Whereas wealthy American small business technology consultants have grown up around a developed business community and probably have benefited from "table talk," where they overhear successful sales and marketing techniques and approaches, my friends in India, the Dominican Republic, and other emerging markets didn't enjoy the same competitive advantage growing up. Truth be told, I can think of some American small business technology consultants who might get lucky and be able to pass the Small Business Sales and Marketing Skills Assessment without studying (an approach I don't endorse, but I do acknowledge). But my friends in developing countries can truly benefit from studying for and passing the Small Business Sales and Marketing Skills Assessment. These "have nots" can take pride in passing this online assessment and quickly elevate and assimilate into the "haves" community. In sum, I see the preparation required for and the successful completion of the Small Business Sales and Marketing Skills Assessment being of the greatest benefit to the eager and earnest small business technology consultant in developing countries!

Chapter 12 is devoted to the Small Business Sales and Marketing Skills Assessment. After our technical deep dive into the 70-282 certification exam for several chapters and a look at the 74-134 certification exam, I elected to end the book by bringing you back to business reality and prepare you to pass this REQUIRED online assessment!

IMPORTANT: To further build credibility regarding my "pocket MBA" preaching, I direct you to a legacy article I wrote many years ago about the value of testing business drivers in the Microsoft Certified Systems Engineer (MCSE) certification program, submitted as evidence for your review at: http://mcpmag.com/features/article.asp?EditorialsID=17.

Optional Training Labs

To become a Small Business Specialist Community member, you should engage in appropriate educational opportunities. I like this requirement because it supports a "life learner" approach to the Small Business Specialist Community program and encourages ongoing professional development. You are strongly encouraged to complete 10.5 hours of online training as listed in Table 2-2. Two highly recommended courses, "Selling the Microsoft Solution to Small Business" and "Small Business Solutions Accelerators," are described in further detail on the following pages.

Table 2-2

Strongly recommended but optional training and readiness curriculum.

Sales and Marketing (3 hours)	Technical (7.5 hours)
Selling the Microsoft Solution to Small Business (1 hour)*	Designing, Deploying, and Managing a Network Solution of the Small- and Medium-Size Business (1.5 hours)
Volume Licensing Essentials (1 hour)	Windows XP and Office Small Business Edition (1 hour)
Competitive Selling With Respect to Open Source (1 hour)	Supporting Microsoft Windows Small Business Server 2003 Parts 1-4 (4 hours). See Chapter 12, Table 12-2 for a list of URLs.
	Small Business Solutions Accelerators (1 hour)

* Highly recommended by both authors and Microsoft's Small Business Specialist Community team!

Selling the Microsoft Solution to Small Business
Lesson 1: Selling to the Small Business Market

- Define the small business market.

- Describe the small business decision maker.

- Outline the keys for selling to the small business market.

Lesson 2: Identify and Reach Your Target Market

- Describe Microsoft Small Business segments

- Outline the process for creating a marketing plan

Lesson 3: Determining Customer Needs and Creating a Winning Message

- Describe the needs of small business segments.

- Identify which products to sell to which segment.

- Create a value proposition.

Lesson 4: Case Study Practice

- Define value and cost for customers' solutions.

- Describe how to keep customers

IMPORTANT: Guess what's missing from this course, which is a crying shame? A learning module on overcoming objections! That's what a superior salesperson does best. You try to get a customer to articulate one or two key objections and then you find creative ways to overcome them. I discuss overcoming objections at length in Chapter 6 of *SMB Consulting Best Practices* (ISBN: 0-974858-06-4, SMB Nation Press).

Small Business Solution Accelerators
Small Business Solution Accelerators

- Introduce the Solution Accelerator Model.

- Provide prescriptive guidance on how to get the most value from the accelerators for your business.

- Help make your solution implementations more predictable and repeatable.

Solutions Training

- Delivers prescriptive training on solutions for small business based on a SBS network.

- Helps make your solution implementations more predictable and repeatable.

Both authors can speak *ad nauseam* about the Small Business Solution Accelerators, found at: https://partner.microsoft.com/global/productssolutions/ smbsolutions. Harry wrote the *Peer-to-Peer Networking With Windows XP* solution accelerator and assisted with the technical and editorial review of the *Small IT Solution* document (and he maintains a close relationship with the Microsoft segment team to this day!). Beatrice holds a seat on the Small Business Solutions Accelerator advisory board. But self-promoting accolades aside, the real context is this: These excellent solutions accelerators are the basis of the current "SBS FRANCHISE" curriculum theme on the SMB Nation Summit global workshop tour in 2005. (Learn more about the SBS FRANCHISE at http://www.smbnation.com.) It is a good investment of your time to investigate these solution accelerators!

Direct and Indirect Costs

In the mid-1990s, I wrote a popular *MCP Magazine* article (http://www.mcp mag.com) on the true costs of obtaining the MCSE title. This article, which was widely distributed to budding MCSE candidates, provided an MBA overview of both the hard and soft costs associated with the tremendous commitment necessary to obtain the MCSE title. The MCSE title resulted in a positive return on investment (ROI), and readers felt reassured about committing the resources necessary to get their MCSEs. I encapsulate that same thinking in this section as the direct and indirect costs associated with becoming a member of the Small Business Specialist Community.

> IMPORTANT: There is no entry fee, cover charge, or other required membership fee to join the Small Business Specialist Community. Contrast that with a membership fee for Microsoft Certified Partners

and Microsoft Certified Gold Partners. This is good news for us! But please read the next section for two financial outlays you will be required to make.

Direct Costs

Here are the direct costs associated with becoming a member of the Small Business Specialist Community:

- **Action Pack subscription**: $299 USD

- **Certification examination fees**: $125 (see Figure 2-3). Microsoft periodically has certification exam promotions to encourage people to take exams. One current promotion involves discounted fees for initial testing and retakes. Read about it at: http://www.mcpmag.com/news/ article.asp?EditorialsID=804 and monitor *Certification Magazine* (http://www.certmag.com) and *MCP Magazine* (http://www.mcpmag.com) for current promotions.

Figure 2-3

A popular test provider's site shows the fees associated with test taking. If you must take the test multiple times to achieve a passing score, your certification examination fee component will necessarily increase.

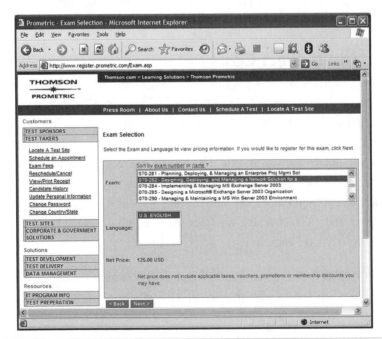

Indirect Costs

It's easy to overlook the hours spent on any endeavor that don't show up on an accounting report. These are the "lost hours" we should somehow recognize if we're true to ourselves about the time and effort expended to reach an achievement. Gaining membership in the Small Business Specialist Community is no different. You'll put in some off-the-clock hours en route to earning this designation performing the following types of activities:

- **Installing the Action Pack applications**. I know that when my Action Pack arrived, I was mesmerized by all the cool stuff inside. I spent many hours installing the software and perusing the Partner Guides. No doubt you'll engage in this same obsessive-compulsive behavior and need to recognize those hours spent along the way, albeit wisely, playing with the bits.

- **Preparing for the Certification examination**. Whether you take the 70-282 or the 74-134 exam, I honestly believe you need to schedule 20+ hours preparation time.

- **Completing the online Small Business Sales and Marketing Skills Assessment**. While this online assessment doesn't impose a test-taking fee, you are committing time to prepare for and complete this excellent assessment.

- **Reading this book**. Both authors are delighted you've elected to purchase, read, and review this book on your road to becoming a Small Business Specialist Community member. Allocate a few hours here.

- **Opportunity costs**. This financial concept concerns the cost of lost opportunities. Hey—if you spent all this time getting your membership into the Small Business Specialist Community, that took time away from becoming a realtor or other type of professional in another sector. Did you forgo another lucrative opportunity with the time commitment you made to this Microsoft Partner path? Perhaps, but both authors would hold up the Small Business Specialist Community as having high ROI and being something you'll enjoy. The opportunity-cost concept doesn't measure pleasure, so take this reasoning with a pinch of salt, as readers in the UK would say!

Gone

One thing you no longer have to "give" is a customer essay-writing exercise. One early rendition of the Small Business Specialist Community program had incumbents writing a few customer success story essays per year and submitting them to Microsoft. This was a non-cost way for Microsoft to receive another "give" from the incumbents and collect a significant amount of small business sector research at little or no cost. This requirement was later dropped. Too bad. Both authors feel writing skills contribute mightily to being successful in business! Plus, Microsoft was planning to use these customer reference submissions for future case studies and public relations for the Small Business Specialist.

Gets

Enough deferred gratification. Time for the good stuff: the GETS! This section outlines what you get as a Small Business Specialist Community member. Without further delay, check this out!

Amazing Customer Referrals!

At some level, we're all motivated economically, and the Small Business Specialist Community program recognizes that! When you become a Small Business Specialist, you are listed in the Small Business Partner Finder at http://www.microsoft.com/smallbusiness/partner/vendorsearch.mspx and as shown in Figure 2-4.

Notes:

Figure 2-4

Small Business Specialist Community partners will be listed above Registered Partners, showing a higher partnership status and level of expertise and commitment. All good!

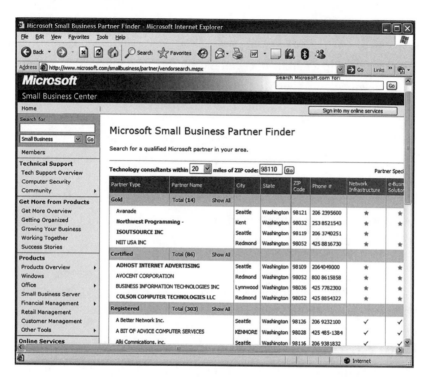

Receiving referrals from this Microsoft search site will likely emerge as one of the primary reasons many people jump on board the Small Business Specialist Community opportunity!

Affirmation and Affiliation

Membership has its privileges, and being a Small Business Specialist Community member is no exception. First, you have Microsoft's affirmation that you've achieved a significant accomplishment. It's an honor, not a right, to be a Small Business Specialist Community member. It wasn't handed to you on a silver platter—you earned it. Take a bow!

Second, the affiliation with Microsoft is invaluable. Whereas the "red meat" media often likes to focus on negative news about the big "M," this is a case where the media's version of the truth is inconsistent with the real world. On a global basis, I can attest that people in the SMB space overwhelmingly like Microsoft. It's not lost on folks that Microsoft started out as a home business with two eager entrepreneurs trying to create opportunity and improve their lots in life. Microsoft went on to be the richest corporation in the history of the world, with worth exceeding other great institutions like organized crime and the Roman Catholic Church! It's been the authors' experience that, rather than being green with envy about Microsoft, people really respect the software giant. Sounds like someone you'd want to partner with!

> IMPORTANT: Thankfully, the Small Business Specialist Community program is available worldwide. Why? Because the affirmation and affiliation message will really play much better overseas on the streets of Mumbai, India, than in the streets of Peoria, Illinois. Wealthy American small business technology consultants stand to gain less than their brethren in developing countries.

Some might view the affirmation discussion in terms of validation. Small business technology consultants who provide services to small businesses need the validation of the Small Business Specialist Community.

Affinity Group

Trade associations, fraternities, and social clubs all know one thing: People like to work together because human beings need social interaction. This "birds of a feather" benefit is clearly present in the Small Business Specialist Community, and it's not lost on Microsoft that it is providing real value to program incumbents by simply organizing such a community and providing opportunities for social interaction.

Submitted for further evidence is some of the interaction that occurs with the SBS Most Valuable Professionals (MVP). SBS-MVPs are technical gurus who volunteer support for a product such as SBS. One year, around the holidays, as the SBS-MVPs exchanged obligatory niceties, it occurred to me that being an SBS-MVP involves more than supporting a product. For these technical gurus from around the world, many of whom work alone, this was about participating in an affinity group. That was the value-add. I fondly remember one SBS-MVP subsequently posting a message saying, "…you are my family" in a highly complimentary manner.

So, for many readers, the Small Business Specialist Community is their new affinity group that allows these globe-wandering small business technology marauders to come in from the cold. Welcome to your new home!

> IMPORTANT: One way to shorten your path to becoming a Small Business Specialist is to utilize a great free technical resource: SBS-MVPs! Meet and greet the SBS-MVPs at http://www.microsoft.com/windowsserver2003/sbs/community/default.mspx or attend the annual SMB Nation Conference each fall in the Seattle area (http://www.smbnation.com), which many SBS-MVPs attend (and they have been known to hold court at a popular night club/pool hall!). Use 'em to meet your needs!

Access and Attention

During my Fall 2004 worldwide SMB Nation Summit workshop tour, I was allowed to show a sneak preview of the Small Business Specialist Community program to attendees to solicit feedback and conduct a follow-up survey. One of the overwhelming themes, something I discuss later in the chapter, related to small business technology partners feeling left out, ignored, and bereft of meaningful or productive relationships with live people at Microsoft.

This will change under the Small Business Specialist Community program. Microsoft is staffing positions that will serve the Small Business Specialist hand-and-foot!

Folks like small business segment expert Eric Ligman, formerly from the Microsoft Chicago office, have been called home to the mother ship (Microsoft Redmond) to replicate their in-the-field small business successes on a global scale. See Eric's epic small business community web site success story and his Redmond "calling" at http://blogs.msdn.com/mssmallbiz/archive/2005/04/11/407350.aspx. This blog entry inadvertently parts the curtains to give you insight into how Redmond is supporting and enabling the Small Business Specialist Community at corporate, regional, and local levels. The infamous web site that made Eric a small business star is shown below in Figure 2-5.

Figure 2-5

Bookmark http://www.mssmallbiz.com/default.aspx as your default Internet Explorer startup page. One of the authors has done exactly that—guess which one!

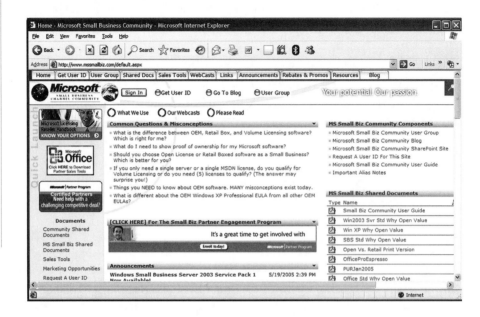

I'd like to make special mention of three USA small business partners who have used local Microsoft relationships to their business development advantage.

- **Fredrick Johnson**, Ross-Tek, Cleveland, Ohio (http://www.ross tek.com). A big part of Fred's successful business model is relationships. I swear Fred keeps a tickler file telling him when to call important people in the Microsoft small business community. Fred's friends (including local and regional Microsoft employees) can gladly anticipate receiving a check-in call about every four weeks. Very effective!

- **Alan and Lilly Shrater**, Solutions Unlimited, Denver, Colorado http://www.isolutionsunlimited.com/default.htm. "Playing the game" would sum up Alan and Lilly's success at cultivating local Microsoft relationships. These two just hang in there and go through official channels in communicating with Microsoft's Denver office. Their tenacity and toughness have allowed them to get past the Microsoft gatekeepers and benefit their business.

- **Pat Cooley**, RelianceNet, Annapolis, Maryland (http://www.reliance net.com). Pat claims that maintaining strong local Microsoft relationships has been the cornerstone to his success. Read about Pat's story in the April 2005 issue of the *SMB Technology Watch* newsletter at http://www.smbnation.com.

Similar positive relationship developments are occurring at the Microsoft worldwide subsidiary level. For those who are new to the Microsoft Partner Program, it is important to understand that Microsoft is organized into two entities: USA and Worldwide. When you work for Microsoft, you are affiliated with one or the other. Some programs are only USA, while other programs, like the Small Business Specialist Community, are both USA and worldwide. I want to highlight two global partners who have effectively converted their Microsoft international subsidiary-level relationships in the partner realm into cold, hard cash!

- **Matthew Dickerson**, AXXIS Technology, Dubbo NSW, Australia (http://www.axxis.com/index.htm). A sign of success is when people talk kindly about you behind your back. Such is the case with Matthew, whose name is mentioned with great reverence by the small business teams at Microsoft's North Ryde, Sydney, Australia office. Matthew is well respected for his sales and marketing expertise, and he exceeds Microsoft's expectations about what a small business partner should be. My wife and I had the distinct pleasure of going on a *Back to the Future* ride at Universal Studios at the 2002 WPC in Los Angeles with Matthew and his wife. You just never know where you'll bump into a superstar!

- **Nigel Mulholland**, Belfast, Northern Ireland (http://www.nitec.com). I had the pleasure of hearing about Nigel when my SMB Nation Summit workshop visited Dublin, Ireland, in the fall of 2004. Nigel was held up as the most successful partner in the region with his 300+ SBS customers out of 900+ total customers. What I liked about Nigel's approach was he not only maintained friendly diplomatic relations with the local Microsoft subsidiary, but he's also a big HP partner. He sees the power of small business partnership extending beyond just the Microsoft relationship (a common trait of many successful worldwide partners). Nigel was featured in the November 2004 issue of the *SMB Technology Watch* newsletter (read it at http://www.smbnation.com).

IMPORTANT: To learn more about how Microsoft operates and who's who, check out *Directions on Microsoft* at http://www.directionson microsoft.com. The Microsoft organizational chart is marvelous!

Also—*Advanced SMB Consulting Best Practices* (September 2005, SMB Nation Press) features several of the partners profiled above and many more VIPs! Learn detailed secrets of success, in their own words, in this book.

Here's Harry's list of the top five of most supportive small business Microsoft subsidiaries as of June 2005 (if I've omitted a subsidiary, it's because I don't have firsthand experience with it to render an opinion):

1. Australia/New Zealand

2. United Kingdom

3. Ireland

4. India

5. Germany

If you are a reader in these regions, congratulations! You have been born from the right womb! Go forth and meet your Microsoft makers at the next subsidiary-sponsored small business channel-facing event!

Exclusive Premium Content!

Access to the PRIVATE Small Business Specialist premium content is another benefit. There's only one thing better then belonging to a community-based affinity group, and that's being a member of an EXCLUSIVE community-based affinity group! Microsoft addresses this need for exclusivity for Small Business Specialist Community members via a private forum and premium content.

Appealing Logo Usage

I can't comment on the exhibitionist tendencies of Small Business Specialist Community members, but folks in general like to publicly proclaim their accomplishments with logo usage. This can take several forms, such as logo wear clothing and logo usage rights. Both are discussed here.

Logo Wear and Trinkets!

An enduring memory from a MCSE-era book from the late 1990s was a photo in which incumbents proudly wore logo clothing. There will be a provision for logo wear and trinkets for the Small Business Specialist Community. What is not yet known is how the logo wear will be acquired: free or fee. That is, will Microsoft give you an attractive shirt to wear to show customers your Small Business Specialist Community status, or will you have to buy it?

> IMPORTANT: Be sure to subscribe to the free *SMB Technology Watch* newsletter at http://www.smbnation.com so you can stay current with Small Business Specialist Community updates.

Logo Usage Rights

Microsoft has a well-established operational tradition of allowing its partners to use program and product logos subject to certain rules and regulations. (As you would expect, Microsoft wants to ensure appropriate use.) Small Business Specialist Community members are granted logo usage rights. When qualified, the logo will be available for download from the Partner Program website by clicking the Sales and Marketing link and using the Partner Logo Builder.

> IMPORTANT: Time for a global moment. I foresee the greatest up-tick in logo usage in the worldwide community, not the USA. In my travels, I've found that global communities tend to display a higher need to communicate achievement, success, and credibility by dress and logo use. This is especially acute in the Latino cultures. I think a small part of this cultural difference between the USA and the global communities relates to education. In the USA, many small business technology professionals are university-level degreed. In emerging markets, fewer people have access to university-level education and must display their accomplishments differently, such as manner of dress and achievement-based logos. I shared with the

Small Business Specialist Community team at Microsoft that the logo will play out very positively overseas!

Exclusive Academic Education

Small business technology consultants in the Microsoft community have long been jealous of Microsoft Certified Partners and Gold Certified Partners who received invitation-only technical and business training. The perception was that this gave those elitists a leg up on the competition (true!). That has changed with the Small Business Specialist Community program, where incumbents now get to attend by-invitation, partner-only training. The playing field with the big guys has effectively been leveled!

Action Pack Content

The Action Pack is a "blended beast" that was best presented earlier in this chapter rather than later. Clearly, you "gave at the office" to purchase the Action Pack subscription. But as you've concluded by now, you get SO MUCH STUFF from Action Pack (as listed in Table 2-1) that clearly the "gets" outweigh the "gives."

Accrue Partner Points and Aspire for More!

The Microsoft Partner Program correctly rewards achievers. That's just good free market behavior, where competition results in rewards for the winners! Small Business Specialist Community members receive 25 Microsoft Partner Points (this model was described earlier in the chapter).

I want to emphasize one item about the Partner Points system and aspiration. Around the world, fair-minded folks will use the Small Business Specialist Community program to improve their professional standing and their personal net worth. In short, the Small Business Specialist Community has opened a door for thousands to pull themselves up and do better economically than their parents did! This is a classic free market aspiration model that is honored globally. The Partner Points program provides a structure to move up the Microsoft Partner ladder. Perhaps you want to start out as a Small Business Specialist but you're really only biding time until you have enough customers to build up your references and go after mid-market and enterprise-level work. Hey—you're welcome to stay at the small business segment level as long as you like and free to leave for happier hunting grounds when the time is right. The Partner Points model supports such aspirations and you'll start out with 25 such points once you become a Small Business Specialist. Good on ya!

Additional Gets

A few other cool gets in the Small Business Specialist Community program are:

- **Marketing offers**. Small Business Specialists receive exclusive marketing offers and opportunities.

- **CRM templates**. Rumor has it that the Small Business Specialist Community program will offer "canned" or preconfigured Microsoft CRM templates for organizing, managing, and selling your small business technology services! Such templates are real time-savers.

- **Additions**. The only thing constant with the Small Business Specialist program is change, and you can reasonably expect that more gets will be added to the benefits of membership. As late as 30 days before the launch of this program, Microsoft was adding more goodies. Right on!

Historical Context

The old adage that Microsoft gets it right on the third try is very true when it comes to how Microsoft has entered the small business space. Let's face it—it wasn't until SBS 2000, the third major release of this application, that Microsoft got it right! In this section, I'll provide some historical context about how Microsoft has finally gotten it right with the introduction of the Small Business Specialist Community.

> IMPORTANT: The good news is that Microsoft hangs in there until it gets it right! Heck, with over $53 billion in corporate treasury cash (*Seattle PI*, April 2005, http://seattlepi.nwsource.com/business/169588_msftnotebook19.html), it's got some deep pockets to develop and refine programs and products until traction is achieved. Seems like a compelling reason right there to partner with Microsoft—it's in it for the long haul!

Attempt #1: Sweet Success

Upon the launch of SBS 2003 in October 2003, the Microsoft Partner Program launched a "Sweet Success" small business partner campaign where participants submitted SBS 2003 customer success essays in a context format. Monthly winners received a shopping spree at Best Buy (a retail store that later went on to buy the small business consulting firm Geek Squad), an Action Pack subscription, and cookie deliveries (the kind of cookies you eat, not those that infest your web browser!). The grand prize winners received cash, travel, and hardware. This was documented in my November 2003 *SMB Technology Watch* newsletter at http://www.smbnation.com/newsletter/Issue3-2.htm. This essay-writing campaign, where Microsoft gained heaps of valuable small business customer data, was the genesis for the inclusion of the three-customer essay submission requirement in the first draft of the Small Business Specialist Community (circa November 2004). As you read above, this essay-writing requirement was unfortunately dropped in later Small Business Specialist Community drafts.

Attempt #2: Small Business Partner Engagement Program

To pump up the small business technology community and refine its final versions of the Small Business Specialist program, Microsoft launched the Small Business Partner Engagement Program (PEP) in the USA for a sixth-month period starting January 2005 and terminating just before the launch of the Small Business Specialist Community in July 2005. In Figure 2-6, you can see the gives and gets of the channel-facing community-building outreach effort by Microsoft to boost the number of Registered Partners.

Notes:

Figure 2-6

Small Business PEP Gives and Gets

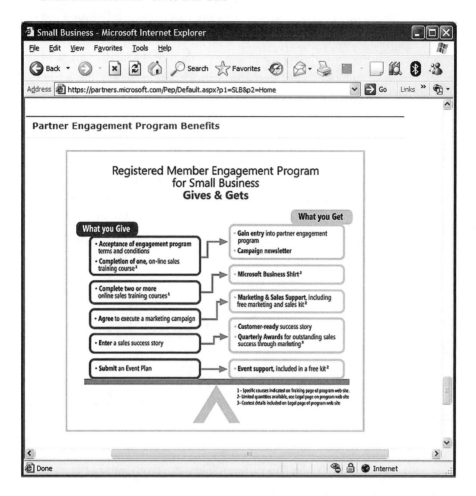

If you look closely at Figure 2-6, you can clearly see that Microsoft was testing the waters and softening the small business technology community defenses as it rolled out some gives and gets that are very similar to those incorporated into the Small Business Specialist Community. The Small Business PEP is discussed in detail in the January through April 2005 editions of the *SMB Technology Watch* newsletter at http://www.smbnation.com.

IMPORTANT: Time to share a mild partner program resentment. Microsoft has no provision to grandfather or "fast track" existing Small Business PEP participants into the Small Business Specialist Community program. That is unfortunate, because there is precedent in the technology industry for doing exactly that. How do I know? I was there! My Novell Certified NetWare Engineer (CNE) title (circa late 1980s/early 1990s) provided me an exemption into IBM's Certified LanServer Engineer (CLSE) program. Instead of having to complete six IBM CLSE-related exams, I was only required to take one "step-up" exam that I easily passed. No such step-up or fast track exists for expedited entry into the Small Business Specialist Community. But I'd be delighted to take a wager on the following: If for some reason Microsoft misses its aggressive Small Business Specialist Community recruitment goals (trust me—it is a very large worldwide number that I won't repeat here), you will probably see some grandfathering clauses introduced.

Attempt #3: Small Business Specialist Community

Believe it not, the Small Business Specialist Community has long been in the making. Microsoft conducted extensive research with its small business partners and found that small business partners:

- Want to provide more consultancy and business solutions.
- Want being a "partner" to differentiate them from non-partners.
- Want more from simply being a partner:
  - Services, and
  - Personal Contacts/Services.
- Have issues with Microsoft:
  - It is impersonal,
  - It is a very big corporation, and
  - They feel they are too small to be noticed.
- Want great dialogue with Microsoft

These findings, combined with other factors like the recent history outlined above, resulted in the first draft of the Small Business Specialist Community that was beta tested in the UK in the fall of 2004 and early 2005. Additional feedback from that beta period was used to refine the program you see in place today!

Elevator Ride Version

Okay—enough talk. Time to give you a condensed page you can walk around with and quickly tell the Small Business Specialist Community story! Check out Table 2-3.

Table 2-3
Small Business Specialist Community defined by Gives and Gets

Gives
Program registration *Acceptance of terms and conditions*
Purchase Action Pack *Microsoft front office and back office software library, Partner guides and more for $299 USD (Standard edition)*
Pass one Microsoft Certified Professional certification exam: • *70-282: Designing, Deploying, and Managing a Network Solution for a Small- and Medium-Sized Business* (see Chapters 3 through 10)* • *74-134: Preinstalling Microsoft Products using the OEM Pre-installation Kit (see Chapter 11)* • *Future qualifying certification exams to be added at a later date*
Complete mandatory online Small Business Sales and Marketing Skills Assessment (see Chapter 12)
Complete OPTIONAL but HIGHLY RECOMMENDED online educational offerings (10.5 hours) **Sales and Marketing (3 hours)** • *Selling the Microsoft Solution to Small Business (1 hour)* • *Volume Licensing Essentials (1 hour)* • *Competitive Selling with Respect to Open Source (1 hour)* **Technical (7.5 hours)** • *Designing, Deploying, and Managing a Network Solution of the Small- and Medium-Sized Business (1.5 hours)* • *Windows XP and Office Small Business Edition (1 hour)* • *Supporting Microsoft Windows Small Business Server 2003 Parts 1 to 4 (4 hours)* • *Small Business Solutions Accelerators (1 hour)*

Table 2-3 (continued)

Gets
Membership in the Small Business Specialist Community *Sense of accomplishment and achievement!*
Customer referrals via Small Business Partner Finder *One of the greatest benefits!*
Affiliation with other Small Business Specialists Community members *"Birds of a feather" group*
Microsoft corporate, subsidiary, regional, and local relationships *Value-added benefit if you procure and maintain meaningful Microsoft friendships!*
Small Business Specialist Community logo usage rights *Branding and advertising benefit!*
Invitation-only training events *Gain the latest Microsoft segment and product stack knowledge not available to nonmembers.*
Action Pack content *Generous supply of Microsoft application bits to use and learn the products, plus Partner guides. Contains heaps of small biz content!*
Partner Points (25 points) *Participate and grow in the Partner Points framework.*
Private Premium Content *Engage in relationship building online in a safe and secure environment.*
Additional Cool Stuff! • *Future marketing promotions* • *CRM consulting templates* • *More cool stuff to be added in the future!*

* Recommended by the authors

Community Resources

All right—time to move along and make good things happen. Your next steps are to visit the following program site links and use that toll-free telephone number (USA and Canada) for further assistance.

- **Overview**:

  https://partner.microsoft.com/global/40021563?PS=3#Over

- **Benefits and requirements**:
  https://partner.microsoft.com/global/smallbizspecbenefits

- **Training and exams**:
  https://partner.microsoft.com/global/40016933?PS=3

- **Readiness site:**
  https://partner.microsoft.com/global/40021525?PS=3

Toll-free telephone number: 1-888-613-3790

Summary

This chapter provided a deep dive into the Small Business Specialist Community program. You started with an insightful overview of the entire Microsoft Partner Program. We then dove right into the GOOD STUFF of gives and gets! That was followed by a historical view of how the Small Business Specialist Community came into existence, followed by the short "elevator-ride version" of how to quickly understand and communicate about this program. It was a lot of reading, and throughout this chapter heaps of context was woven in to provide maximum value. That's what a good book should do best!

Hopefully you're now super-psyched and jazzed about the Small Business Specialist Community and ready to turn the page and start preparing for the 70- 282 certification exam. See you there!

Authors Beatrice Mulzer and Harry Brelsford launch the new book at the Microsoft Worldwide Partner Conference in Minneapolis with Allison Watson, vice president of worldwide partner sales and marketing at Microsoft

Section II
Exam 70-282

Chapter 3
Analyzing the Existing Environment

Chapter 4
Designing a Business Technology Solution
for a Small- or Medium-Sized Business

Chapter 5
Installing Windows Small Business
Server 2003

Chapter 6
Securing Windows Small Business
Server 2003

Chapter 7
Configuring Windows Small Business
Server 2003

Chapter 8
Supporting and Maintaining Windows
Small Business Server 2003

Chapter 9
Expanding the Windows Small Business
Server 2003 Network

Chapter 10
Installing and Configuring Windows
Server 2003

CHAPTER 3
Analyzing the Existing Environment

Perform a Needs Assessment

Have you ever gone on a vacation without planning where to go, what mode of transportation you would use, or what activities you would enjoy once you arrived at your destination? Probably not. Most likely you carefully planned every step of the way, imagining and envisioning what your vacation would be like, giving a lot of thought to how to get the most for your money, and perusing brochures and web sites for a variety of entertaining activities.

If you ever planned a vacation like this, you have already performed a needs assessment and created a solution!

A business has to follow the same steps in planning for the future, given that assessing technical needs is a bit more complex than planning a vacation, but basically follows the same outline. As the administrator or consultant you will have to evaluate the technical tasks, functions, and capabilities currently in place (current state) and compare those to the vision (preferred state) of the organization (regardless of whether they are realistic or affordable). The difference between the current state and the preferred state is then considered a "need."

To assess technical needs requires a complete review of the current state and is best established in a technology plan. This plan details all the resources currently in place and what resources will be needed to achieve the preferred state. Granted, a technology plan for a small business will be simple compared to an enterprise. This is certainly the case with Windows Small Business Server 2003 (SBS) customers.

Among many things, the technology plan should also cover:

- User account management

- File sharing and storage

- Printer sharing

- Database storage

- Centralized backup

- Fax server

- Web access

- E-mail access

- Remote access

- Hardware

- Software

It helps to draw up a network diagram and document configuration, gather performance information, and review recurring costs associated with each component of the current state. Make sure to document everything in the technology plan and use it as the basis for the overall business picture. After having documented the current state, you must then identify and analyze the current "pain points" that are plaguing the business.

Identify and Analyze Business Problems

Having done your homework you are now ready to find the gaps between the current state and the preferred state and articulate a business goal. Business analysis starts with identifying the business goals of the implementation project, also referred to as "happily ever after."

Begin by interviewing the stakeholders (business owners, partners, and managers) who have a vested interest in a successful implementation. Be prepared to tolerate a few war stories from the owner as part of the interview process. Ask about the business challenges and future requirements, and observe business processes. Identify the business technology services that execute and support the business mission. Services include:

- Topology

- Network services

- Database management systems (DBMS)

- Application programming interfaces (APIs)

- Security

- Operating systems

IMPORTANT: Small business technology consultants are uniquely qualified to serve small businesses. That's because small business technology consultants are themselves a "small business" and can relate well to their customers.

Look for inefficiencies in the current state—processes that consume an excessive amount of resources, such as effort, time, equipment or money.

Make sure you understand what is critical to the business, its objectives, and its long-term goals. You must understand its success factors and your client's expectations. To properly evaluate and identify the requirements of the business, you must understand what makes it succeed.

Real-World Example

So here is a great example that relates to the 70-282 exam. A small design studio has four designers, a sales person, a receptionist, and an accountant on staff. The business started out small with just two partners, so the peer-to-peer network was sufficient to support the initial business needs. Now that the business has grown, even though one computer is supposed to house all the files, each staff member still keeps part of her projects and data files on her local machine. Staff members share their drives with other staff members. There is one color laser printer connected to the sales person's computer that everyone prints to, and the receptionist has a ring binder appointment book at her desk that everyone uses for scheduling. Once a week, a staff meeting is held to bring everyone up to speed on the status of current design projects. Some staff members would like to be able to access both their e-mail and data in the office while they are traveling or working from home, which they currently can't do. Bummer!

No doubt you can easily identify several problems hampering business performance; two examples are the intranet is not being utilized and information is poorly organized. Given the technology available today, this setup is an efficiency nightmare.

When considering a solution, you will want to encompass (Granted, some of these are ten dollar words!):

- Functionality
- Efficiency
- Total cost of ownership
- Availability
- Reliability
- Security
- Flexibility
- Ease of manageability

These considerations should be added to the technology plan under a heading called "Business Requirements" and show how implementing each would address the business needs. The technology plan is basically a business problem statement—a platform on which you build your case for implementing the project.

Once all the pain points are identified and mapped out, other critical factors must be considered into the solution leading to the preferred state.

Critical Considerations

There could be several *business constraints* that limit your ability to achieve the preferred state and business goals. Business constraints can play a significant role, and meeting the business requirements within those constraints is the key to a successful implementation. Make sure to factor in these critical considerations:

Time Frame: The time frame or schedule could affect decisions. If the schedule is too aggressive, you may have to scale back goals, change priorities, or change your approach.

IMPORTANT: In a small business, there is never really enough "time" and sometimes decisions appear to be made in haste. Welcome to the real world!

Budget: The budget should always be considered in the design phase, starting with the cost of completing the project and including continuing costs for the resources required to maintain the project over a certain lifetime.

Resources: Besides capital expenditures, you must consider all necessary resources for the implementation. This would include considering the existing hardware and network infrastructure as well as maintenance, administration, training, and support. Remember the "players" at a small business wear many hats!

TCO (total cost of ownership): On top of the resource expenditure, don't forget about hardware and software upgrades, unexpected out-of-pocket expenses, and other factors that affect TCO, like the cost of telecommunications or equipment leases.

Company Policy: Knowing and understanding the company's standards or policies are important factors that could play into the technical aspect of the design, method of implementation, and product selection. To be honest, many small businesses don't have written company policies. But these companies do have cultural norms that influence (and dictate) behavior.

These critical considerations should also be included in your technology plan to encompass the full scope of the project.

In the end, the technology plan describes the current state of the business and its solution requirements. You will have gathered data on:

- Business success factors

- Size, type, and scope of the business

- Required software applications

- Current applications and required access to them

- Required number of computers, printers, and other devices

- Current hardware

- Amount of anticipated network traffic

- Network security level

- Critical constraints

- Anticipated change in business process or structure

- Plans for growth

Now you have a blueprint for designing a business network solution. Next you want to focus on identifying and selecting the appropriate hardware and software for the implementation.

IMPORTANT: Take a bow! You've just completed an MBA-like management consulting engagement. Good work. More management consulting stuff can be found in the *Small Medium Business Consulting Best Practices* book (SMB Nation Press).

Identifying and Selecting Appropriate Hardware and Software for the Environment

The right computer hardware will enable a business network to run efficiently and function effortlessly. SBS 2003 requires a server and network components equipped to meet the unique requirements of the business and preferred state.

Equally important is the business having the right software tools to resolve those gaps and issues that have been identified. You must ensure that the software applications are compatible, and were designed and tested on Windows Server 2003 and the respective client operating systems.

There are also considerations about the client hardware, the network cabling, routers, switches, mobile devices, and type of Internet connection. To get the best performance out of the entire network, all components must play together like a well rehearsed orchestra. Having one component out of tune will affect the performance of the entire opera.

Hardware Functionality and Effectiveness

Regardless of what brand computer you buy, with all the different models, options, and components available, some key components will have a fundamental performance impact. These components are the motherboard, processor, memory, and hard disks. To ensure that these components work with SBS 2003, you should check the Windows catalog at www.microsoft.com/windows/catalog before you buy.

Motherboard: Even though you could run SBS 2003 on a workstation-class motherboard, since no explicit specification exists, it is not recommended. The motherboard ties together all computer components, including the processor, memory, hard drives, and other peripherals. You should get a server-class motherboard to achieve the best performance base for SBS 2003.

Processor: The main processor consideration is the clock speed at which it operates, measured in MHz (megahertz) or GHz (gigahertz). The clock speed determines how fast the server can perform computing tasks. Windows Small Business Server 2003 supports up to two physical processors and can support up to four logical processors using hyper-threading technology. If you will be putting a large load on the server and using it for line-of-business (LOB) applications or communication or collaboration, we recommend using two physical processors at the highest clock speed your budget will allow.

Memory: Memory measured in MB (megabytes) or GB (gigabytes) can have a dramatic impact on server performance. Physical memory, also referred to as RAM (random access memory), determines the amount of data the server can manage simultaneously. Installing RAM is easy and cost effective.

Hard Drives: Several options and configurations are available that allow you to match the disk storage to the small business needs. You can choose from three interfaces: integrated development environment (IDE),

Serial Advanced Technology Attachment (SATA), and Small Computer System Interface (SCSI). All drives come in ranges from 36 GB to 300 GB, and a server can hold multiple hard drives that can be used to create fault tolerance (RAID). We will discuss backup and recovery options in Chapter 8, "Supporting and Maintaining Windows Small Business Server."

Network Adapter: Network Interface Cards (NICs) come in different speeds of 10 Mbps, 100Mbps, and 1 Gbps. Even though there are different types of networks, Small Business Server 2003 is designed to work on an Ethernet network and I always recommend using two NICs for Network Address Translation (NAT)-ing functionality.

Hubs: Don't buy a hub; buy a switch. Switches are able to operate in duplex mode, meaning they allow a client to send and receive at the same time.

Switches: Switches can be considered faster than hubs. They route traffic directly between ports instead of broadcasting traffic across all ports, meaning that each port on a switch gets dedicated bandwidth. This can make a big difference when transferring large files between multiple computers.

Routers: A router performs additional logical functions over a switch, enabling Internet access to the network. Often routers are configured to also act as a hardware firewall and help secure the network.

Firewall: SBS 2003 Premium Edition comes with ISA (Internet Security and Acceleration) Server, which is an enterprise-level firewall product. Windows Small Business Server 2003 Standard Edition comes with a basic firewall software using Routing and Remote Access (RRAS) and NAT. You could also purchase a hardware firewall appliance; most DSL modems and broadband modems come with an integrated firewall as well. More on firewalls in Chapter 6, "Securing Windows Small Business Server 2003."

Modem: You will need a modem, either a DSL or a broadband modem, to connect to the Internet. SBS 2003 allows users to "dial in" to the network using a secure virtual private network (VPN) connection. This lets users connect directly to the network. You can also use a conventional dial-up modem for Internet connectivity, but with the difference in speed and price, it wouldn't make sense unless you don't have any other choice— like if your business is located near the North Pole. See the chart below for Internet connection types and average speed.

Table 3-1

Internet connection types and associated speed

Type of Connection	Download Speed	Upload Speed
Dial Up	28.8 – 53 Kbps	28.8 – 40 Kbps
ISDN	64 -128 Kbps (one channel or two)	64 – 128 Kbps (one channel or two)
ADSL	256 Kbps – 8 Mbps	128 Kbps – 1 Mbps
IDSL	128 – 144 Kbps	128 – 144 Kbps
SDSL	128 Kbps – 2.3 Mbps	128 Kbps – 2.3 Mbps
Cable	128 Kbps – 8 Mbps	128 Kbps – 1 Mbps
Frame-Relay/T1	56 Kbps – 1.54 Mbps	56 Kbps – 1.54 Mbps
Microwave Wireless	256 Kbps – 10+ Mbps	256 Kpbs – 10+ Mbps
Geosynchronous Satellite	150 Kbps – 3 Mbps	33.6 Kbps – 128 Kbps

Fax Modems: Besides providing an Internet connection, a fax modem will allow you to send or receive faxes from SBS 2003. This will require a separate phone line, but is so much cooler than receiving faxes on the old standalone fax machine. With the built-in fax module in SBS, you can receive a fax in a central folder on the network or in a fax folder in SharePoint services, or route a fax into the Outlook 2003 e-mail client of specific users. Users can also fax directly from their desktop. More on configuring the fax service in Chapter 7, "Configuring Windows Small Business Server 2003."

Wireless Access Points: Currently you can choose from three different wireless standards: 802.11b, 802.11g, and 802.11a.

- 802.11b: Very inexpensive now, but also the slowest of the three with a speed limit of 11 Mbps (5 Mbps real-world). Supports a maximum of 32 connections per access point and up to three non-overlapping channels, allowing for three separate wireless networks. Operating at the 2.4 GHz band, it is very susceptible to radio frequency (RF) interference from cordless phones.

- 802.11g: Slightly more expensive, but backward-compatible with 802.11b. Throughput is 56 Mbps (11 Mbps real-world) and supports a maximum of 32 connections per access point and three non-overlapping channels. Operating at 2.4 GHz, it is prone to the same interference issues as 802.11b.

- 802.11a: Most expensive, but also the fastest standard at 54 Mbps (19 Mbps real-world). Operating at 5 GHz, with twelve separate non-overlapping channels, allowing twelve access points set to different channels in the same area without interfering with each other. This is a great solution for a dense user area that requires a high throughput. Beware: Due to the higher frequency, the distance is limited to about 80 feet.

Printers: It makes sense to purchase one $300 network printer instead of three individual $100 printers. SBS 2003 makes sharing printers easy. However, before purchasing a printer you want to share on the network, make sure it is designed for network use . Many network printers today have their own NIC that supplies the Ethernet connection. Make sure the printer you choose will work with the Windows Server 2003 operating system and supports the TCP/IP protocol. A nice feature is a web-based management interface so you can check the status from a remote location. See Chapter 7, "Configuring Windows Small Business Server 2003," for configuring printers.

Client Computers: This is easy. You want a client system whose hardware supports fast connectivity and performs well on the SBS 2003 network. Consider the key components—Processor, memory, hard drive and CD-ROM/DVD-ROM, and a NIC card—and get the best money can buy. Windows XP Professional is the recommended choice as the client operating system. Minimum hardware requirements are shown in Table 3-2.

Table 3-2
Minimum hardware requirements

Requirement	Minimum	Recommended
Processor	233 MHz	1 GHz or faster
RAM	128 MB	256 MB or higher
Hard Drive	4 GB	40 GB
NIC	10/100 Mbps	10/100 Mbps

IMPORTANT: As of this writing, the 70-282 exam does not include references to Windows XP Service Pack 2.

Laptops: Most laptops come with built-in wireless networking. You want to make sure they are equipped with a card that is compatible with the wireless access point you plan to use.

Mobile Devices: SBS 2003 has special features included to ensure that mobile devices—like Smart phones and Pocket PCs—can take advantage of the remote access features such as accessing your e-mail and schedule. For more information on mobile devices, see Chapter 7, "Configuring Windows Small Business Server 2003."

Additional Servers: Depending upon the purpose of your second server, you will need to consider the type of hardware it will require, as it represents a completely separate undertaking from your SBS 2003 server. Also, your second server will need to use a Windows Server 2003 operating system edition other than SBS 2003, such as Windows Server 2003, Standard Edition, since you can only have one SBS 2003 server running in a network. The second server will require one Client Access License (CAL) to access the Small Business Server.

IMPORTANT: In *Advanced Windows Small Business Server 2003 Best Practices*, you'll find richer discussion on licensing (Chapter 3) and hardware (Chapter 4).

Software Efficiency

It is possible to run client operating systems such as Windows 98, Mac OS X, and Linux on a SBS 2003 network, but you will lose out on the "SBS experience" and on support for automatic application and service pack installations as well as shared fax and modem services and Outlook 2003.

Windows XP Home is not supported on the SBS network because it is designed to be a home user system and cannot be joined to a domain.

Windows 2000 will take advantage of the SBS 2003 features, but the preferred choice is Windows XP Professional, which is designed to work with the SBS 2003 network environment. It adds security, reliability, performance, mobility and functionality to the local network for all users.

Practice Questions

Question #1

As the IT admin at your company, you must select a new server from the following choices. Considering resources, what is the best option?

A. A server with one Pentium III 500 MHz processor, 256 MB RAM, a 4 GB hard drive and two NICs

B. A server with three Pentium III 300 processors, 1 GB RAM, two 20 GB hard drives, one NIC

C. A server with two Pentium III 500 MHz processors, 512 MB RAM, two 8 GB hard drives, one NIC

D. A server with two Pentium III 300 processors, 512 MB RAM, two 8 GB hard drives, two NICs

Question #2

You are the IT admin at a small interior design firm. There are six Windows 98 computers and four Windows 95 computers on a peer-to-peer network.

Data files are spread out over the individual computers. There is a shared broadband connection. Users have POP3 e-mail accounts to retrieve their e-mail. Your employer wants you to implement centralized storage for the data files. He also wants to start using the company's domain name, Spacedesign.com, for e-mail, and give users the ability to send and receive faxes from their desktop. You are to implement the most effective and least costly solution. Which steps should you take? Choose all correct answers.

A. Install a modem on each client computer.

B. Upgrade client computers to Windows XP Home Edition.

C. Purchase a low-cost fax application and install on each client station.

D. Install a modem on the Small Business Server.

E. Install Small Business Server 2003, Standard Edition.

F. Upgrade client computers to Windows XP Professional Edition.

G. Install Small Business Server 2003 and Exchange 2003.

H. Purchase a low-cost fax application and install on the Small Business Server.

Question #3

Springers Ltd. currently has three Windows 2000 computers and three Windows XP Professional machines. The company uses a peer-to-peer network. Because they have recently hired additional staff, the owner has ordered four more Windows XP Professional computers. Springers Ltd. will also be purchasing a proprietary application that requires its own server. As the admin, you suggest implementing an SBS 2003 server and purchasing a second Windows Server 2003 to host the proprietary application. You are thinking about going with the device licensing model. How many client access licenses must Springers Ltd. purchase on top of the five licenses that come with SBS 2003?

A. 0

B. 5

C. 10

D. 15

Question #4

You are the administrator for Springers Ltd. and manage a Small Business Server 2000 domain with 15 Windows XP clients and eight Windows 98 clients. Your boss finally coughed up the bucks to purchase an SBS 2003 upgrade. The SBS 2000 server machine has two 36 GB hard drives with two FAT32 partitions each. You plan to do the upgrade over the weekend and want to perform for the upgrade with minimal effort. Prior to installing SBS 2003 on the current domain controller, you should:

A. Move all data onto one drive and create a mirror for redundancy.

B. Convert the system partition to NT file system (NTFS).

C. Run chkdsk on drive 0.

D. Format the system partition with NTFS.

E. Convert both drives to NTFS.

Question #5

Heartland Tractor Supply has called you to provide an assessment of their needs for a new platform to operate their business upon. Their parent company has told them that NT 4 will no longer be supported, and they must move to a new operating system. Before they invest any money, they want to be sure that whatever they chose will meet their needs. They currently have three locations with 45 employees. You discover during the interview process that they spend a significant amount of time each month trying to keep the line of business parts application updated. Each location currently has a NT 4.0 server that is used to run this LOB app. They receive a DVD set each month which must be loaded onto each location's server. This can take four to eight hours per machine, as their existing servers are old and slow. They also struggle to maintain the remote machines and their part-time IT manager spends hours driving back and forth to the remote locations to fix minor issues. They mentioned a desire to bring their e-mail in house, as their ISP has not been reliable in providing mail services. They have decent connectivity via a VPN between locations, but don't really use it for more than connection to the LOB app. Based on these facts, what do you do?

A. Recommend they continue to use NT 4.0, as it has worked for them for years and provides a source of regular support revenue for you

B. Recommend a Windows 2003 server replace of each of the NT 4.0 servers to bring them up to a current platform

C. Recommend replacing the individual NT 4.0 servers with three SBS 2003 servers

D. Recommend a single SBS 2003 server with a second Windows 2003 server running terminal services at the head office location

E. Recommend a single Windows Server 2003 server with a second server running terminal services at the head office location

Question #6

You receive a call from an accounting firm regarding some network issues. You determine they need to upgrade their NT 4.0 operating system to be able to operate the new tax software they purchased. Upon review of their situation, you discover there are five people in their main office, four people in a remote office, and two part-time users who operate from their homes. The tax software vendor has recommended SBS 2003 Premium edition, which you agree is the best solution. During most of the year, only eight people need access to the network. Only during tax season do all 11 need network access. You will configure the network with a VPN connection between the two offices and VPN access from the two part-time work-at-home users. How would you quote the licensing for SBS 2003 to this accountant?

A. Purchase SBS Premium 2003 with 5 CALs, and 4 additional CALs to cover the full-time workers

B. Purchase SBS Premium 2003 with 5 CALs, and 6 additional CALs to cover all the staff

C. Purchase SBS Premium 2003 with 5 CALs, and 1 additional 5 pack of CALs to cover the full-time workers

D. Purchase SBS Premium 2003 with 5 CALs, and 2 additional 5 packs of CALs to cover all the staff

E. Purchase SBS Premium 2003 with 5 CALs and ignore the remote workers

Question #7

You are called to provide advice to a prospective customer about what solution he should install in his business. Since you are a long way from this prospect, you ask him to send you an e-mail with some basic information you can use to put together an interview to define the solution. Which of the following pieces of information gives you enough information to begin formulating a recommendation?

A. One dedicated fax line that is not currently in use

B. An Internet connection

C. Three computer workstations

D. Pentium 4 – 2.4GHz server with 40 GB hard drive

E. 70 employees

Question #8

Your local chamber of commerce wants to be able to generate marketing information and communicate better with its members. Tim, the chamber director, comes to you for help in making this happen. They have a small office of six people, some of whom work from home part-time. From the following possible scenarios around SBS, which would give the best functionality for the feature it describes:

A. Purchase a color inkjet to connect to each workstation.

B. Install a 56K internal fax modem in the server

C. Talk to the ISP to set up e-mail accounts

D. Configure a remote Web workplace for outside access

E. Use file shares on local hard drives to allow others in the office to get to files

Question #9

One of your existing customers is running a single Linux server using Samba to provide file sharing for the 12 Windows XP Pro SP2 workstations they have. They also use the same server to host a simple web server with four static pages. They would like to have a shared calendar solution as well as publish the web site. They have also expressed some interest in working from home. They currently have a 512K up/down DSL connection to the Internet with static IP address. They back up the Linux server to one of the XP workstations using the built in Windows XP backup. The Linux server is a P4 2 GHz machine with 1GB RAM. What solution best fits their needs? Budget is a major concern for this project.

A. Replace the existing server with a new Small Business Server 2003 Premium Edition.

B. Back up the Linux server. Run the Small Business Server Wizard to upgrade the Linux server to Small Business Server 2003.

C. Back up the Linux server. Load Small Business Server Premium on the existing server, then create the users and file shares and restore the data from the backup.

D. Have them use the existing Linux server and install Exchange Server 2003 on it.

Question #10

A new startup company, The Recycle IT Co., receives various pieces of electronic equipment from people who do not want them anymore and do not want to just throw the equipment in the Dumpster. They do a good job of stripping equipment and recycling the parts. Recently a large firm upgraded an entire department and sent Recycle IT several servers. They would like to start keeping track of the equipment they receive; they also want to be able to receive and send faxes from their desktops. They currently have three Windows XP workstations with Office 2003 Standard on each and a dedicated fax machine. They do not have any type of network currently, so any documents they create they save to a USB memory stick then run it to the other computers.

They were also recently at a training center and received a free five-user version of Small Business Server 2003 Standard. The following is a list of four servers they received that might be used. Which machine will be able to run SBS 2003 Standard without upgrading? Select all that apply.

A. Compaq Proliant 1000: Pentium 90MHz, 128MB, RAID 5, four 2GB drives

B. Dell 4400: PIII 500 MHz, 512MB, 4GB drive (400MB used for diagnostic partition)

C. Whitebox: PII 300 MHz, 384MB, two 10GB drives

D. Dell 4400: PIII 500 MHz, 2GB, no hard drive

Answer Key

Question #1: Answer: C

The minimum system requirements to install Small Business Server 2003 are a 300 MHz CPU speed, 256 MB of RAM, and a 4GB hard disk. Answer C is correct because it offers the most resources: two CPUs and 512 MB of RAM. Answer A would work, but is incorrect because this solution does not have the most available resources. Answer B is incorrect because Small Business Server 2003 can only accept a maximum of two CPUs. Answer D would work, but has fewer resources than Answer C.

Question #2: Answer: D, E, F

The correct steps would be to install Small Business Server 2003 Standard Edition, which already includes the full version of Exchange 2003 Standard and Microsoft Shared Fax Services. You would not have to purchase a separate copy of Exchange Server, nor a third-party fax application. You would have to install a fax modem on the server to receive the faxes, but would not have to install modems on the client machines, as SBS will allow you to send and receive faxes in your Outlook client on each individual workstation routed through the SBS server. You would want to upgrade client machines to Windows XP Professional, since the Home version does not support being joined to the domain.

Question #3: Answer: C

The correct answer is ten. Ten more CALs need to be purchased on top of the five CALs that come with SBS. There are a total of ten client machines and one member server, which brings the device number on the SBS network to 11. Since licenses come in packs of five, you would have to purchase two five-packs, bringing you up to a total of 15 CALs.

Question #4: Answer: B

Windows Small Business Server 2003 requires NTFS for Active Directory and Exchange 2003 and, therefore, you must convert the system partition to NTFS. Moving all data to one drive and creating a mirror for redundancy or running chkdsk will not convert the FAT32 partitions, so you could not do the upgrade. Formatting the system partition with NTFS would erase all data. (Hey, nothing like starting out with a clean system!) Converting both drives (even that would be the better choice) would not meet your objective of "minimal effort."

Question #5: Answer: D

The need for e-mail in a company with 45 employees makes SBS a logical choice. Coupled with the fact that they want to reduce maintenance of their LOB app and remote desktops, a terminal server running as a member server provides them a very manageable platform that achieves the customer needs. Answer A is incorrect because NT 4.0 is no longer a supported application and should be replaced to provide a stable platform to build their business upon. Answer B is incorrect because simply replacing the current servers with updated ones does not address their need for mail or management of the remote sites. Answer C is incorrect because you cannot have three SBS servers on a single domain. Answer E is incorrect because it does not address the mail issue. SBS is the most cost-effective way to provide mail to this client, as well as providing a number of other valuable features they will enjoy.

Question #6: Answer: D

SBS 2003 Premium comes with five CALs, and additional user CALs are sold only in five-packs. Each person who will authenticate to the SBS server must have a CAL. All other answers are incorrect because they either do not cover all the users or are not legitimate ways to purchase CALs.

Question #7: Answer: A

This is the only piece of information complete enough to provide guidance. Answer B is incorrect as you do not know whether the connection is dial-up, DSL, cable modem, or a dedicated line of some sort. It also may be part of some frame network from another source. Answer C is incorrect as you do not know the operating system of the machines or their specifications. Answer D is incorrect because of a lack of specifications. RAM would be the first area to probe. Answer E is incorrect because you are unsure how many of these employees are actual users of the network. It is possible that the actual network users may only be a fraction of the entire employee count.

Question #8: Answer: B, D

The fax modem will allow for group faxing and an easy way to route incoming faxes. Option D allows users to work effectively from home. Answer A is incorrect. Inkjet printers are costly to use, and on a network, a better use of funds would be to purchase a color laser printer for output. Answer C is incorrect. SBS comes with Exchange for e-mail. While an ISP could do this for the Chamber, it would not provide the best functionality for their work. Answer E is incorrect. All data files should be maintained on the server to make sure they are backed up and protected. At a minimum, shared folders should be created on the server. The best solution would be to use SharePoint for this, as it is designed as a perfect collaboration tool for this type of situation.

Question #9: Answer: C

Answer A is not a good solution because of the budget constraints. Answer B is not correct because there is no direct upgrade migration. Answer D is not correct because Exchange 2003 cannot be run on Linux.

Question #10: Answer: C

Answer C meets all the minimum requirements. Answer A does not meet the RAM or processor requirements. Answer B does not have enough free space on the hard disk. Answer D has no hard drive, so cannot be installed.

Summary

In this chapter we:

- Analyzed the existing environment.

- Took a closer look at how to perform a needs assessment by identifying and analyzing business problems.

- Pointed out critical considerations that cannot be ignored when designing a technology plan.

- Learned about selecting appropriate hardware and software for an SBS 2003 server.

- Learned about the functionality and effectiveness of the SBS 2003 server.

The new Small Business Specialist program is the talk of the town at the Microsoft Worldwide Partner Conference 2005

Chapter 4
Designing a Business Technology Solution for a Small- or Medium-Sized Business

Howdy! Welcome to follow-on tasks from the prior chapter where you established the technology plan as a blueprint. You are now ready to fill the gaps (needs) and start designing solutions. In Windows Small Business Server 2003, several Windows Server 2003 technologies have been leveraged and packaged particularly to respond to small business needs.

Design a Messaging and Collaboration Specification

A couple years back, just when SBS 2000 had made its debut, I met with a client to discuss small business technology solutions. This client—an accountant who shall remain unnamed to protect the innocent—had done his own business analysis and figured out that he was in desperate need of communication solutions.

This Old House

The client's office is located in an older building that is two stories tall (see Figure 4-1), and the way the staff communicated was by either picking up the intercom or yelling up the stairs. Needless to say, clients did not find his bellowing "Hey you!" very professional.

Figure 4-1

The real-world client used in this example. Be sure to treasure your real-world experiences as one study method to pass the 70-282 exam.

Back in the SBS 2000 era, we installed new server hardware, a real Internet connection (the client used dial-up until then), and immediately started using the simple messenger application. The client and staff loved the company folder on everyone's desktop and proceeded to stick every thinkable document, application, picture, and who knows what in it. Even though we had the fax module, the client didn't trust it and proceeded to use the old fax machine. Such was life for that customer in the SBS 2000 time frame. But stand by, as things change for the better.

> IMPORTANT: Let's talk about modularity. Microsoft Learning uses some time-tested education models that are very sound. Modularity is a key methodology used by Microsoft Learning. It means:
>
> • A student could take a Microsoft Office Curriculum (MOC) course, assuming all prerequisites have been met.

- A student would be able to complete the exercises.

- The exercises would be self-contained (e.g., all keystroke procedures start with a logon command and end with a log-off command).

So, in the spirit of modularity, you do not need to have working knowledge of SBS 2000 (the prior SBS release) to pass the 70-282 exam. The 70-282 exam uses SBS 2003 as its baseline and makes no assumptions and has no expectations about your SBS 2000 legacy wisdom. This is an important tip to help keep you focused on passing 70-282. Please see the other IMPORTANT item at the end of the chapter (right before the questions).

SBS 2003 to the Rescue

With the introduction of SBS 2003, we finally made the big step and fully integrated all the features available in SBS. The client was ready to elevate and better exploit the technology prowess of the SBS 2003 bundle. The following sections show how the client utilized the communication capabilities of SBS 2003.

Fax

Faxes are now being delivered to two employees' Outlook clients as well as a shared folder on the network. With the ability to remote into the desktop via Remote Web Workplace (RWW) as well as to check e-mail through Outlook Web Access when needed (and view the faxes), the owner finally understood the value of the integrated fax module and gave up the old fax machine, which is now seldom used. To fax out material, we are discussing the addition of a high-speed scanner, which could be used to also route documents to fax, but that is another discussion. Note you can also store inbound faxes in Windows SharePoint Services.

Real-Time Communications

Messenger is still the number one inter-office communication tool and the way you instant message (IM) in SBS 2003. The receptionist now quietly IMs the owner and two other employees from the first to the second floor and there is no longer a need to yell up the stairs in front of the customers. It's worth mentioning that some customers in the real world are questioning whether instant messaging is used strictly for business purposes.

> IMPORTANT: SBS 2003 removed Exchange-based instant messaging functionality.

Exchange Server 2003

Exchange-based e-mail and other services have been implemented and we finally got rid of the POP3 accounts at the Internet Service Provider (ISP). The customer was so amazed by how fast his e-mail was working—we could almost consider it real-time communication. I won't forget the big smile on his face when he told me that he was conversing with another accountant on the other side of the USA and it was just as fast as using IM. I guess the best part, with them being tax people and all, and having to work very hard during the first four months of the year, was implementing remote procedure call (RPC) over HTTP where they could receive their e-mail at home without having to use a virtual private network (VPN) connection. Almost all communications with their clients takes place via e-mail now, and Exchange has become a pivotal point in productivity. Anything and everything you need to know about Exchange Server 2003 can be gleaned from Chapter 6 of *Advanced Windows Small Business Server 2003 Best Practices*.

Windows SharePoint Services

And what do you think happened to the Company Shared Folder? It went away. Why? Because Windows SharePoint Services (WSS) is being positioned, whether it likes it or not, as the document and data store of choice. Back at the customer site, we finally got things organized and set up document libraries in WSS. We very much have a business focus and restrict uploading to business documents. Even though the client is using a proprietary accounting solution for the bulk of the transactions, WSS has taken on the important role of catch-all that doesn't fit into the accounting software. It also serves as a discussion and transaction history tool, keeping track of goings-on with client files that need to be documented and retained for future use. One of the great productivity features is the ability to set "Alerts"—an advisory to a user that there has been a change made to a document—without anybody needing to pick up the phone or send an e-mail. Everyone is on the same page on all projects, and all information is kept neatly in one place. WSS is discussed further in Chapter 7 of this book and in much more detail in Chapter 7 of *Advanced Windows Small Business Server 2003 Best Practices* and Chapter 7 of *Windows Small Business Server 2003 Best Practices*.

Shared Resources

The default shared folder on an SBS 2003 network is called "Users Shared Folders" with the share name USERS. The company folder no longer exists, because the SBS development team received feedback that the customer was confused in the SBS 2000 time frame when there were both Users and Company Shared Folders. There are no shared folders on any of the workstations by default, and all data is kept on the server (in Chapter 7 you will learn there is a MyDocument redirection setting that moves all of the workstation data to the Users Shared Folders on the network—an administrator's dream!).

> IMPORTANT: At the customer site in my example, there IS ACTUALLY a Company Shared Folder on the SBS 2003 network. How could this be? This occurred because the SBS 2000 server machine was upgraded to SBS 2003 and the Company Shared Folder was retained. However, a fresh install of SBS 2003 would not have a Company Shared Folder.

Recently a high-speed color laser printer was purchased, which is shared on the network and available for everyone to print to. This addition is already saving money for the company by eliminating the need for individual color printers, ink, and maintenance.

> IMPORTANT: For this part of the 70-282 exam, you need to have your design thinking intact and view yourself as an architect. In that paradigm, kindly consider the following bit of history. In the earliest days of the local area network (LAN), when disciples kissed the Token

Ring and surfed ArcNet (two legacy networking standards), traction was gained because a LAN offered great cost efficiencies in a business via shared resources. The early printers cost a great deal of money, so clearly a small business couldn't afford to place a dot matrix or a laser printer on each worker's desk. However, a LAN allowed a small business to have everyone share one printer. Brilliant!

So when designing a small business network and taking the 70-282 exam, you'll never go wrong by returning to your roots: shared resources are the driver for many small business network implementations.

Design a Connectivity Specification for Networking and Remote Connections

One of the reasons this particular client had a dial-up connection when I first started working with him was really to save a penny. It took me awhile to convince him that he would be able to use high-speed Internet access and still come out better on the cost/benefit equation.

Broadband

SBS 2003 is easily implemented on a broadband connection, using either a dynamic or static IP address. I always recommend using the static IP, especially if you are running the Exchange server as your primary e-mail solution and want to make good use of the RWW. While using the Configure E-mail and Internet Connection Wizard (CEICW) "for a direct broadband connection," you will be given the choice of either using a dynamically assigned Internet Protocol (IP) address or entering a static IP as your broadband connection option. This will be performed for the network adapter on the server that will oversee the external connection. Note that once a small business person uses a high-speed broadband connection, it is unlikely she will return to a modem connection (or anything slower). This is a design consideration: Speed is addicting!

There are two traditional methods of broadband connectivity: digital subsciber line (DSL) and cable. DSL is preferred by many small businesses, as it's a service typically provided by the telephone company and oriented toward business use. DSL is usually offered with a static IP address (but you'll see the exception to this in a moment). Cable is more consumer-oriented and typically uses a dynamic IP address, but in some cases can be much faster than DSL. So there are truly two choices here.

Back at the customer site, we ended up purchasing a DSL line, because we were only 300 feet from the central office. DSL can be easily set up with the CEICW since it includes the option to set up "a connection that requires a user name and password" (PPPoE—Point-to-Point Protocol over Ethernet). This is the "exception" the last paragraph hinted at and thereby we were obtaining a dynamically assigned IP address. This scenario required two network adapters—one for the local network and one for the Internet, and the server would provide routing and network address translation (NAT) services. But I'm starting to jump the gun on a few technologies that will be detailed later in this book. However, the design phase must necessarily incorporate some technical considerations at this early stage.

Local Router with Static IP

At another customer site, we ordered a static IP address and therefore used the static setup option in the CEICW titled "a local router device with an IP address." This is the SBS way for connecting a static IP DSL router, dial-on-demand router, or ISDN router. The static IP address is supplied by the ISP on the external network adapter card or interface. If the connection requires authentication information, you must configure the router with a user name and password, even if your router supports Universal Plug and Play (UPnP). UPnP is a standard that allows SBS 2003 to easily configure the router device.

Remote Web Workplace

Bingo! Going back to the cost/benefit equation, here is where the client can definitely see the benefits, which are usually hard to establish in IT. In our case, we had a pregnant mother who had difficulty climbing the stairs in the office.

We set her up with a workstation at home and registered a .com name in domain name system (DNS) for RWW, which I showed her how to use. She then was able to use RWW connecting from the comfort of her own home to her XP client workstation at the office. She continued managing her daily tasks without a dip in productivity. That is what I call a win/win situation.

> IMPORTANT: Be sure to build in training time for the customer to learn how to use the SBS 2003 network. Customers gladly pay for training time to learn features such as RWW, which is an SBS 2003 portal for supporting the mobile worker.

More RWW information may be found in Chapter 8 of both SBS 2003 Best Practices books from SMB Nation Press.

Design the Application Specification

Unfortunately, clients rarely give you much choice on this, as they usually have already purchased the software with little thought about the hardware or operating system it will be running on and expect you to make it all work. One of the most overlooked issues concerns application compatibility.

Application Compatibility

Occasionally you will have the client who will have purchased SBS 2003 and new server hardware only to find out that his old proprietary application—for which he refused to pay the upgrade five years ago—will not be supported by the system. In this case you can always use Virtual PC for the legacy application and still bring the rest of the network up to SBS 2003 and Windows XP SP2.

SQL Server 2000

When installing SQL Server 2000, you will be offered the opportunity to add a password for the system administrator (SA) logon. This is presented for backwards compatibility of earlier SQL versions and disabled while Windows authentication mode is used. Make sure to set a very strong SA logon password if SQL is configured for mixed-mode authentication. Mixed-mode authentication enables the SA logon, which uses a blank password by default.

IMPORTANT: Review the premium technologies setup documentation found on Disc 5 of the SBS 2003 premium product. Print it out and spend 10 minutes reviewing it at a high level so you have an appreciation for the design issues surrounding SQL Server 2000 and ISA Server 2000/2004.

Backup

SBS 2003 contains a much improved backup solution (which is featured in Chapter 8 of this book). However, if you decide to purchase a third-party backup program, make sure that it supports VSS (volume shadow copy service) so it can take advantage of VSS and use it to back up open files. Veritas Backup Exec 10 robustly supports SBS 2003 and addresses VSS and other features.

Utilities

Make sure to examine existing technologies before acquiring and deploying workstation and server utilities, base applications, infrastructure services, network connectivity components, and platforms. To be honest, you can find this out by joining some of the public newsgroups and posting a question about utility compatibility. See Appendix A for a list of these types of SBS resources.

Third-Party Applications

SBS 2003 provides a stable and secure infrastructure to run small business applications, such as an accounting system or industry-vertical specific application. Before purchasing a third-party application, ensure that you have enough disk space and check for application compatibility and any application dependencies. If you have a specialized third-party line-of-business application (LOB), you may opt for getting a second server and using Terminal Services in application sharing mode, which will then be solely dedicated to the LOB application.

IMPORTANT: One thing you WILL NOT find on the 70-282 exam is direct references to specific third-party backup solutions, utilities, and applications. Back in Redmond, Microsoft Legal would never allow it (trust us on this one). So with our third-party mentions above, we've gone further than the scope of the 70-282 exam, which we are trying really hard to stay focused on in this book. But for the

70-282 exam, you'd need to have on your "radar screen" the conceptual and planning issues surrounding third-party applications and utilities. The aforementioned SMB Nation Press books about SBS 2003 delve deep into third-party interaction points with SBS 2003.

Design a Management and Operations Specification

Another client I work with also came from a peer-to-peer environment. Users had different e-mail accounts and shared resources, which were scattered amongst several workstations and difficult to locate and access. Some PCs with Internet connectivity had shared resources accessible by "Everyone," allowing full access and no password protection. Calendars and schedules were kept individually. After an SBS 2003 installation, many clients wonder now how they used to manage this way.

So, before proceeding any further, let me tell you the first thing we did for the client: We implemented centralized storage on the server, which has made it easy to locate and access resources. This early win allowed the client to gain confidence in SBS 2003. It's always good to have an early win when introducing technology in the small business.

> IMPORTANT: Expectation management. Once SBS 2003 technology is introduced into a small business that previously lived in the Dark Ages, you can anticipate a gusher of requests as the business and its culture will seek to "leap frog" and exploit more of SBS 2003 sooner rather than later. So you should consider a deployment schedule that appropriately introduces increased SBS 2003 functionality over time at a rate that allows the client to digest all this cool stuff! If you throw too much technology at customers too fast, they become overwhelmed and build up resentment! So, be disciplined in your plan and introduce technology to the small business in phases.

E-mail, Networking, and Internet Connectivity

Exchange Server 2003 allowed centralizing e-mail services, calendar, and resource scheduling at the customer site. The above-mentioned client is now using the same e-mail address for both internal and external e-mail communications. And even though this office already had a hardware firewall/Internet router, having the built-in firewall in SBS 2003 adds an extra level of protection.

Active Directory

Using Active Directory allowed the client to centralize security and authentication. Now users have to remember only one username and password for the entire network instead of using multiple usernames and passwords for different resources (e-mail, file shares, etc.). What we're really talking about here is the single sign-on experience on the computer network. When taking the exam and trying to recall some of the benefits of Active Directory, which provided directory services to the SBS 2003 network, remember "SSO" for "single sign-on."

> IMPORTANT: Little ditties, rhymes, acronyms, phrases, and the like should be considered your certification testing buddies. This is a well-known memorization technique when trying to recall someone's name. For example, you might sing "Mary had a little lamb" every time you see coauthor Harry Brelsford and can't remember his name. Why? Because Mary rhymes with Harry! You get the point. So try this on for size: "Ho ho, SSO!"

Server Administration and Management

With the preconfigured management consoles in SBS, you have a set of management tools for network management, allowing the delegation of basic tasks to power-users. They can add additional users and groups and perform basic tasks managing printers, shared folders, and faxes. Central to managing SBS 2003 is the Server Management console, shown in Figure 4-2.

Notes:

Figure 4-2

The Server Management console should be completely explored on a live server prior to taking the 70-282 exam. Drill down into each component and "look and see."

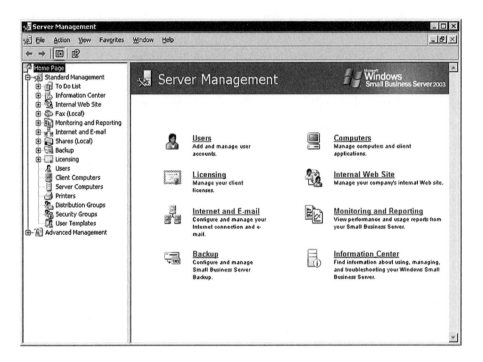

Easy Setup of Client Computers

You can anticipate positive leverage in the deployment and administration phase of the SBS 2003 life cycle because of wizards. Deploying applications and adding client computers to the network is easy when using the integrated wizards. By doing so, we were able to configure settings for an entire group of computers and push out applications to all computers instead of installing them one at a time. So you're really talking about "doing more with less," which could be less time, less money spent on consultants performing routine tasks, etc. Consultants are now freed to work on more meaningful tasks. And don't forget that major Microsoft branding themes, like "doing more with less," have a way of weaving themselves into Microsoft certification exams. Microsoft will, in crafty ways, assure itself you're onboard with its corporate messaging and ways of thinking. So, when in doubt, think the "Microsoft way" on an exam.

IMPORTANT: Consoles and wizards are central to the SBS experience and you can expect to be held accountable for having sufficient knowledge of these two features. Don't you think that Microsoft, rightfully proud of its SBS consoles and wizards, would want to test you on these? You betcha.

Monitoring and Reporting

SBS 2003 has rich monitoring and reporting capabilities you can see from the Monitoring and Reporting link under Standard Management in the Server Management console. In the real world, being able to receive performance and usage reports has really made my clients feel more comfortable knowing what is going on with the network. Usually I forward a copy of the user usage report with comments as well as an occasional performance report so my clients know they are under watch 24/7. Proactively monitoring a customer's SBS 2003 site and communicating about potential issues sooner rather than later reflects the maturity of a successful small-medium business consultant, the type who would be welcomed into the Small Business Specialist program! Chapter 8 of this book explores the monitoring and reporting area in greater depth, as do Chapter 12 of *Windows Small Business Server 2003 Best Practices* and Chapter 13 of *Advanced Windows Small Business Server 2003 Best Practices*.

IMPORTANT: You can also view the design of an operations and management plan testing section from a different paradigm: TIME and DURATION. In Chapter 11 of *Windows Small Business Server 2003 Best Practices*, administrative tasks are presented from a daily, weekly, and monthly viewpoint. These are the chores that an SBSer would perform on a regular basis to keep an SBS 2003 network happy, healthy, and wealthy. You can probably guess what some of these are: backup, virus protection, spam blocking, spyware removal, and others along these same lines.

Notes:

Design a Disaster Prevention and Recovery Specification

Having a business in Florida makes you think twice about disaster prevention and recovery. Why? Because the winds are known to blow hard in Florida during the "mean season." Well, we already know that disasters like the occasional hurricane cannot be prevented, but you can definitely prepare for them and undertake risk mitigation and plan for business continuity. Disaster prevention must take many various possibilities into consideration, from natural (hurricanes, fire, and flood) to manmade (power grid brownouts, worms, and hackers) to personal (vindictive employees and unscrupulous competitors) to political (terrorist acts and government interference). The point is not only to fully recover from a disaster, but to be able to continue business operations despite a disaster.

Integrated Backup

SBS 2003 allows you to fully recover from a disaster with its integrated Backup Solution. It is easy to schedule and implement daily full server backups using the Backup Configuration Wizard. The Backup Configuration Wizard is a reliable way to back up your entire system including the system state, registry, data files, and Exchange store. Again, backups are explored in much more detail in Chapter 8.

Storage Devices and Media

Your small business client is going to tell you that he doesn't have the money to purchase a tape drive, tapes, or other media solutions for the data backup. When you run into this type of situation, you may want to ask the customer how much money he will lose if the business suffers X amount of inoperable hours due to the loss of its infrastructure.

Storage technology is rapidly changing, and in addition to tape drives there are so many other options, like using USB external hard drives, backing up to workstations across the network, burning data to a DVD, or performing a nightly backup across the Internet. These are all viable solutions, and you must take into consideration the cost of the media, extensibility, speed, and reliability.

Checking Backup Status

There are two ways to check the backup status in Small Business Server 2003.

- Have the report e-mailed to you, with the backup log files attached

- Check the last 10 backups for success or failure in the Manage Backup taskpad in Server Management

To receive the status reports by e-mail, you must first run the Monitoring Configuration Wizard from the Server Management console. I highly recommend that you do keep an eye on the backups and log files and do periodic test restore of individual files. (That means once a month!)

Landing on Your Feet

If you plan for a disaster and adhere to a rigid backup schedule and test restores, you will be prepared when disaster strikes and land on your feet. It is a good best practice to document the recovery steps, including information on server hardware, such as disk size, controllers, and motherboard chipsets, as well as partition or volume information and drive letters. Document, label, and plan. Then review your recovery plan every three months and perform a test restore at least once a month, and you will be well prepared.

> IMPORTANT: Chapter 1 mentioned training via hands-on labs as one study approach for test-taking. In the spring of 2005, I had the pleasure of being one of the USA instructors for a three-part advanced SBS 2003 hands-on lab. One segment focused on disaster recovery, in part because of the recent Florida hurricanes!

Design a Hardware Specification

Hardware specifications will depend on the load that will be placed on the Small Business Server 2003. If you currently are running on an existing server and have to design a specification for a migration to a new server, you could sample performance on the existing server. For 70-282 examination purposes, remember the following mantra, which will be reiterated in the next couple of chapters:

> *Go with Microsoft's hardware specifications for SBS 2003. What Microsoft posts on its public-facing SBS 2003 Web site is gospel on the 70-282 exam regardless of how you personally feel.*

With your architect hat on, think about the best time to baseline the current performance so you get a data point to track the SBS 2003 network over time. A baseline would be performed during times of heavy usage—for instance, when everyone logs in first thing in the morning and checks their e-mail and the morning news and launches their applications that connect to the database on the server. That's when the network is most heavily taxed and stresses will be revealed.

The next three sections view hardware by usage classification.

Database Server

If your SBS server will mainly be used as a database server, you want to take a close look at the storage and memory subsystem. Take into consideration the number of hard drives you should use to get the best performance. You may want to consider placing the database log files on a separate hard drive from the data files if you plan on running SQL server for performance and recovery reasons.

File Server

If your SBS server will be used as a departmental file server—for instance for a company that works with larger files like AutoCAD (Architects) files or multimedia files (Photo Studio) that easily average 30 MB and more—consider faster disk drives and a gigabit network card. Remember that the file server function is historically one of the reasons folks implemented local area networks.

E-mail Server

Running Exchange on the SBS server will use storage, memory, and some CPU cycles. Just as we recommended for the database server, placing the log and data files on physically separate hard drives is a good idea.

So consider the following test-taking tip in the design context: Knowing the role of the server will help you determine the appropriate hardware requirements.

Notes:

Fault Tolerance Considerations

Having covered disaster prevention and recovery using the Backup Configuration Wizard and available media options, let's not forget additional hardware options available to us based on the Windows Server 2003 operating system.

If you are able to purchase more than one hard disk, you can implement a RAID (redundant array of independent disks) solution to the point where you could continue operating despite a single hard drive failure.

Mirrored Drives (RAID 1)

This is a simple solution requiring at least two hard drives. As the name states, one disk drive is the exact mirror of your currently working disk. If the working disk should fail, you have fault tolerance with the second disk and the system will continue to operate using the unaffected disk. You can create a mirrored drive set in the Disk Management console. Usually the write-performance takes a hit with RAID 1, due to the controller having to write the data to two disks simultaneously.

RAID 5

This requires at least three disks and uses intermittently striped data and parity for fault tolerance. Parity is the information that allows you to re-create a single failed disk based on the data information of the remaining two intact disks. If two disks fail simultaneously, you will not be able to recover. RAID 5 volumes are created on dynamic disks and cannot be extended or mirrored. If you use hot-swappable drives, you will be able to remove the failed disk while operations continue (at a decreased speed, since the remaining two disks have to create the data of the third missing disk), and then swap out the failed disk with a healthy disk, and the RAID array can rebuild the data without interruptions to your operation.

If They Let You...

If you have a client who sees the value of continued business, and she follows your advice and lets you implement the best solution, I recommend a system with a minimum of five drives: two for the system partition, which should be mirrored, and the remaining three as the data partition in a RAID 5 array.

It is possible to partition a RAID5 array. This can be beneficial, as you can separate your mission-critical data files from the users shared folders and also separate application files. You could run a separate additional backup on just the mission-critical data to make sure you have additional redundancy on top of your regular full SBS backup.

The above solutions can be implemented by using built-in tools in the Windows Server 2003 operating system, meaning that these are software solutions. These solutions, since they are software-driven, will impact the performance on the server. You could choose to use a hardware solution, using a hardware drive controller. That would cause a higher initial outlay, but would not use system resources since the read/write operations would be performed by the hardware controller and not the system.

> IMPORTANT: I promised another important tip and here it is. DO NOT OUTSMART YOURSELF on the 70-282 exam. If you are an SBS 2000 and SBS 2003 guru, it might be easy to become confused about which version of SBS contained which feature. It's kinda like taking classes in college. When you have a full schedule of classes, you might use a word differently in one course versus another. For example, the word "risk" can have different meanings in your real estate class versus your finance class. And when you have to define risk on the respective exams for each course, you might get confused and transfer the definitions inappropriately. Ergo—while honoring your SBS 2000 legacy expertise, keep a keen focus on SBS 2003 for the 70-282 exam. Case closed.

Practice Questions

Question #1

Springers Ltd. has three traveling sales managers that use Windows 98 on their laptop computers. The sales managers each also have a desktop computer at work with Windows 2000 Professional installed on them. Springers is on an SBS 2003 network and as the administrator you are asked to implement a low-cost remote access solution. What are the least costly remote access implementations? (Choose two.)

A. Add a member server to the network.

B. Install terminal services on the SBS 2003 server.

C. Enable remote desktop administration.

D. Configure Remote Web Workplace.

E. Install terminal services on the member server.

F. Upgrade the Windows 2000 Professional machines to XP Pro.

G. Configure SharePoint services.

H. Upgrade the Windows 98 machines to XP Pro.

Question #2

SpaceDesign, Inc., will be implementing an SBS 2003 network that consists of 40 Windows 2000 Professional computers and a domain controller with four SATA hard drives. The DC will be used as the file server and needs to be continuously available. How should you configure the hard drives? (Choose two.)

A. Create a system partition on one disk.

B. Create a RAID 1 volume and use one disk for shadow copy.

C. Create a spanned disk set with three disks.

D. Mirror the system partition and create a two-disk RAID 5 volume.

E. Create a RAID 5 volume with three disks.

Question #3

Schnitzelbank, Inc., is a prestigious law firm located in Paris, Texas, that plans on opening an additional office in Chicago, Illinois. Both offices will have a high-speed Internet connection and will be equipped with an SBS 2003 network. The paralegals at each location must be able to securely retrieve confidential client information at the other office. As the consultant, you are asked to implement an inexpensive, efficient, secure, and reliable solution with low administrative overhead. You propose to:

A. Install member servers with Terminal Services at each office.

B. Configure clients at each office with the "Connection Manager."

C. Install PC Anywhere.

D. Configure a router-to-router VPN.

E. Enable Remote Desktop.

Question #4

A bank officer at a small regional bank calls and asks for an assessment of their upgrade options. They are currently running on a competitive platform and want to consider options for migrating to a Microsoft Windows solution. They are concerned about security and how they can comply with the Gramm Leach Bliley Act (GLBA) regulations in the banking industry. (The GLBA is a comprehensive law requiring financial institutions to protect the security, integrity, and confidentiality of consumer information.) They connect to a larger bank system to have their data processed. Because this connection is currently across a dedicated T1, which is cost-prohibitive to continue, they want to evaluate options for making a secure connection to their processing service center via the Internet while still remaining compliant and secure. There are 30 employees in their bank, all of whom use an office suite and some bank-specific applications. They access the processing service center for account information and balances across their connection. Based on discussions with the vendors, you determine that all their applications will run on the Windows platform. As their partner and consultant, you have been asked to lay out a plan that will meet these requirements and concerns. Which of the following actions do you take? (Select all that are appropriate.)

A. Recommend that they install SBS Premium immediately and run ISA for security.

B. Sit down with the IT manager and management team to lay out a long-term plan for the bank.

C. Recommend that they upgrade their current competitive platform to keep it simple.

D. Schedule a meeting or conference call with their host bank to determine what connectivity options are available.

E. Research local ISP providers and the prices and plans offered.

Question #5

A small business owner who works out of his home calls after attending a Microsoft event that featured SBS. He describes his situation as a two-person company, just he and his wife, selling pet health care products. They have been doing this successfully, using a printed catalog and receiving most of their orders via the fax in their home. He wants to upgrade to a web-based business to expand his ability to take orders and make it easier for his customers to do business with them. He also wants to secure a domain name so they can have e-mail. He currently has one computer on which he runs a simple personal accounting system. He and his wife fight over who can get to the computer to do their part of the accounting entry. He is convinced he wants to set up an SBS-based network so he and his wife can become web-enabled. They have access only to a dependable low-speed connection. Based on this information, you recommend that they:

A. Install SBS and set up a web site to be hosted on it along with e-mail and network faxing.

B. Sell them a second PC and create a peer-to-peer network.

C. Install SBS and set up e-mail and network faxing, but recommend they host their web site at an offsite hosting service.

D. Tell them to continue to do business the same way, since they have been getting along just fine.

E. Sell them a laptop and wireless access point so they can work in different rooms.

Question #6

Al, a local contractor, has just experienced a server failure and lost data due to poor backups and data management. He calls you to help configure a new server to meet his needs with a special emphasis on data security. He never wants to experience this loss again. You have determined that SBS is the appropriate operating system for his business and now need to recommend some ways to safeguard his data. He wants optimum data security. Cost is a secondary concern. You recommend these as good solutions:

A. Manually copy all the data from his server to a CD each evening.

B. Create a backup rotation using a tape drive with daily, weekly, and monthly tape rotations and store the tapes offsite each day.

C. Configure his server using RAID 0.

D. Subscribe him to an offsite backup service over the Internet.

E. Configure his server using RAID 5.

F. Purchase SBS-specific backup software.

Question #7

Sally Smith calls you from her clothing store and wants your help in putting in a server to manage her company. She has attended one of your SBS seminars and believes that is the correct product based on the features she has seen through the demonstrations and talking with one of your sales people. You drop by the store to evaluate the equipment she has accumulated to see what might integrate with the new SBS server she is purchasing. During a discussion with her, you learn the following: 1) it will be running a LOB clothing application requiring SQL; 2) she is very interested in knowing what her employees are doing on the Internet during work hours; 3) she wants to use the fax services in SBS; and 4) simplicity of install and ease of management are important. Based on this information, which of the following items could be implemented or utilized with the SBS Premium server?

A. Hardware-based firewall, which you will configure to sit behind ISA, and split to a separate server.

B. Old fax/scan/print device with no drivers past Windows 98.

C. New laser printer with drivers for XP.

D. Hardware-based firewall, which you will configure to sit ahead of ISA on the SBS server.

E. Macintosh notebook running OS 10.

F. Linux machine running spam filter software.

Question #8

The ABC Records Company warehouses paper records for several local firms in the area. Each customer has a separate space; the location of each file box is marked with the date of arrival. Currently they have high-speed Internet access in the office and use an Excel spreadsheet to keep track of the location of each file box. They have five Windows 2000 desktop machines and a single NT 4.0 server that is used for file and print services. The owner would like to have secure remote access from home to the server. The four office workers currently open and close the Excel spreadsheet and save it. The office workers would like to be able to share the information and be able to look back at the changes made to the spreadsheet and know who made them. They recently have had to restore the Excel spreadsheet from tape backup and had to key back in the entire day of recent arrivals. The owner wants to implement the most cost-effective solution. What would solve both issues?

A. Replace the NT 4.0 Server with Server 2003 Standard Edition.

B. Replace the NT 4.0 Sever with SBS 2003 Standard and configure SharePoint.

C. Replace the NT 4.0 Server with SBS 2003 Premium and configure SharePoint.

D. Setup SharePoint and Routing and Remote Access Service (RRAS) on the NT 4.0 Server.

Question #9

The local police station has a small network comprised of two Windows 2000 Pro workstations, three XP Pro workstations, and one XP home laptop workstation the chief uses. They have a 1.5MB Internet connection and a DSL modem shared by one of the XP workstations. They have been asked by the state to secure the network and been advised that the current method is not acceptable. They need to have a true firewall. They must also be able to log all the login activity to the network. The chief mentions it would be nice if they could have their own e-mail there. He says he has changed Internet providers three times in the last year and each time has to set up new e-mail accounts. He also tells you that he only has 30 days to comply with the rules or his office will be fined $1000/day. What solution makes the most sense?

A. Put in a new SBS 2003 Standard Server. Upgrade his XP home laptop to XP Pro. Join all the machines to the new domain. Set up SharePoint.

B. Put in a new SBS 2003 Premium Server. Upgrade his XP home laptop to XP Pro. Join all the machines to the new domain.

C. Set up Server 2003 with ISA 2004. Upgrade the XP home laptop to XP Pro. Join all the machines to the new domain.

D. Set up SBS 2003 Premium Server. Join the machines with Pro to the new domain and tell the chief he needs to buy a new laptop.

Question #10

You are the consultant for Chelsea, Inc., a Title company. Chelsea, Inc. requests a proposal for implementing a client server network; specifically, they need to implement fault-tolerant document sharing. Users need to access shares from any location within the network without having to remember drive letters or share locations. Chelsea, Inc. uses a third-party application that only works with UNC path names. You propose Small Business Server 2003 and a second Windows Server 2003 file server. For the requested shared solution, what do you propose? (Select the best choice.)

A. Configuring Windows SharePoint Service

B. Configuring a stand-alone distributed file system (DFS) root

C. Configuring a domain-based DFS root

D. Configuring RAID 1

E. Configuring RAID 5

Notes:

Answer Key

Question #1: Answer: D, F

The least costly implementation would be to upgrade the Windows
2000 Professional desktops in the office to XP Pro and run the CEICW
to configure Remote Web Workplace. Adding a member server to the
network and installing terminal services would be much more
expensive. You cannot install terminal services on the SBS domain
controller. Upgrading the Win98 laptops to XP Pro does not help the
solution. You can access Remote Web Workplace from most Internet
browsers regardless of the operation system. Configuring SharePoint
will not allow remote access.

Question #2: Answer: A, E

You should create a system partition on one disk and create a RAID 5
volume using the other three disks. In a RAID 5 array, you can continue
working without interruption when one disk fails. Creating a RAID 1
volume and using shadow copy on another disk will still cause
interruptions in the workflow by taking time out to break the mirror
or having to restore from shadow copy. A spanned disk set offers no
redundancy. It takes at least three disks to create a RAID 5 array.

Question #3: Answer: D

Installing a router-to-router VPN allows secure communications where
authorized routers have to identify themselves when initiating the
connection. Installing member servers and terminal services would be
a more expensive solution. Using the Connection Manager icon on each
client workstation creates more administrative overhead than using one
router-to-router VPN and is not as efficient. Enabling Remote Desktop
would not be as efficient or secure as the router-to-router VPN. PC
Anywhere? Remember this is a Microsoft exam. And in the real exam
this would never even be given as an option.

Question #4: Answer: B, D, E

These three are needed to provide solid direction to the bank. Answer A is incorrect since you do not have enough information to make that recommendation. It may well become the solution, but before you can make a recommendation you need to get the facts. Answer C is incorrect for the same reason.

Question #5: Answer: C

Without a dependable high speed Internet connection, web hosting would be a mistake. It is not a best practice to host a web site on a single SBS server even with a high-speed connection. Network faxing would be beneficial to handle the continuing orders that come by fax, and e-mail can be effective even across low bandwidth connections. The other answers do not achieve the goals expressed by the customer. The key to successful assessment is listening to the customer and meeting or exceeding his expectations.

Question #6: Answer: B, D, E

Answer B is correct in that some sort of removable backup solution is critical to protect loss of data. Tape- or disk-to-disk solutions are effective. Answer D is a good solution for those customers who are paranoid about data protection and want another level of offsite backup protection. This requires an Internet connection with adequate speed to transfer the data. Answer E is the best configuration to provide the highest level of data security in his SBS server. Answer A is too labor-intensive and not practical, although it would work. Answer C is a legitimate solution, but not as effective as RAID 5. Answer F is not necessary unless his environment contains multiple servers that need to be backed up to his SBS server.

Question #7: Answer: C, D, E

The laser printer will work fine. A hardware firewall can effectively be used in front of an ISA server to provide depth of defense for security. A Mac with a current operating system will attach to an SBS server. Answer A is incorrect. You cannot split ISA from the SBS server. Answer

B is incorrect. You would not be able to support this fax as a solution in your SBS environment. Driver issues will prevent it. Answer F is incorrect. With the new filtering available in Outlook and Exchange, it is unlikely you need the Linux solution. It would add much complexity to the environment and would not significantly reduce spam.

Question #8: Answer: B

This will allow secure remote access via VPN from the owner's home to the server and SharePoint will fulfill the team collaboration needs of the office workers. Answer A is incorrect because it does not address all issues. Answer C would not be the most cost-effective solution. Answer D is incorrect because SharePoint is not supported on NT 4.0

Question #9: Answer: B

Answer A is not correct because it does not resolve the main problem of firewall. Answer C is not correct because it does not cover the e-mail issue. Answer D is not correct because there is no need to buy a new laptop.

Question #10: Answer C

Configuring a domain-based DFS root will allow for fault tolerance and does not require users to know where the actual share is located. The domain-based DFS root stores information in Active Directory, which will automatically be replicated. In Answer A, SharePoint Service would almost work, except shares were requested and the third-party application is dependant on a UNC path name which would not work with WSS. In Answer B, a stand-alone DFS root keeps information stored in the registry and would therefore not be fault tolerant. Answers D and E make for fault tolerance but do nothing for sharing data.

Summary

This chapter explored the upstream design function associated with planning for and deploying SBS 2003 networks. Context is king in understanding that, on the 70-282 exam, there is clearly a design section that has you thinking like an architect. This chapter touched on the major design areas and incorporated the "specifications" as the end product for the designing and planning tasks. Areas covered included:

- Messaging and collaboration
- Connectivity
- Applications
- Management and operations
- Disaster prevention and recovery
- Hardware

And all this was presented to you in the context of the REAL WORLD with client war stories. Good stuff!

CHAPTER 5
Installing Windows Small Business Server 2003

This chapter discusses the installation of a Windows Small Business Server as a first-time installation as well as upgrading from Small Business Server 2000, migrating from Small Business Server 4.5 or an NT 4.0 Server to Windows Small Business Server 2003 (SBS 2003).

Deployment Planning

Preparing for an operating system installation requires many steps and in-depth planning. You need a fundamental understanding of Windows SBS 2003 and its features, and you must decide which of those features to deploy that make an appropriate fit for the business. Knowing how to take advantage of technology is the key to increase productivity, reduce total cost of ownership (TCO), and improve workflow processes. Deployment planning works from the ground up, so let's get started with the basics.

> IMPORTANT: Microsoft's product documentation that ships with the SBS 2003 product (Quick Start Guide) and numerous other goodies can assist you in understanding the Microsoft view of the world with respect to deployment planning. Part of passing an exam, as you may well recall from grammer school, is to appreciate the intent of the teacher. In this case, the teacher is Microsoft.

In particular, see the resources listed at http://www.microsoft.com/windowsserver2003/sbs/techinfo/planning/default.mspx which includes (as of this writing) two documents especially applicable to this chapter: *Selecting Hardware Guide* and *Getting Started Guide*.

System Requirements

First we need to ensure we have a sufficient hardware level to support the Windows Small Business Server minimum requirements, as shown in the Tables 5-1 and 5-2.

Table 5-1

SBS 2003 Standard Edition system requirements

Requirement	Minimum	Recommended
CPU speed	300 MHz	550 MHz or faster
RAM	256 MB	384 MB or higher (4 GB max)
Hard disk	4 GB of available hard disk space*	8 GB of available hard disk space*
Drive	CD-ROM	CD-ROM or DVD-ROM
Display	Super VGA, 256-color monitor and video adapter (800 x 600 or higher resolution)	Super VGA (800 × 600) or higher-resolution monitor
Other devices	•Hardware that supports console redirection •Ethernet network interface card	•Keyboard and Microsoft Mouse or compatible pointing device •Two Ethernet network interface cards

Notes:

Table 5-1 (continued)

Requirement	Minimum	Recommended
Additional items and services required for Internet access	•Some server functionality requires Internet access and payment of a separate fee to a service provider; local and/or long distance telephone charges may apply. •Broadband or high-speed modem Internet connection	•Some server functionality requires Internet access and payment of a separate fee to a service provider; local and/or long distance telephone charges may apply. •Broadband or high-speed modem Internet connection
Additional items required for networking	•Dedicated Class 1 fax modem to use fax service	•Dedicated Class 1 fax modem to use fax service •Pocket PC Phone Edition 2003 or Smartphone 2003 for Outlook Mobile Access •Windows XP Professional or Windows 2000 Professional for client operating systems

*Actual requirements will vary based on your system configuration and the applications and features you choose to install.

Table 5-2

SBS 2003 Premium Edition system requirements

Requirement	Minimum	Recommended
CPU speed	300 MHz	550 MHz or faster
RAM	256 MB	512 MB or higher (4 GB max)
Hard disk	5 GB of available hard disk space* (only 2 GB required if upgrading from Small Business Server 2000)	8 GB of available hard disk space* (only 2 GB required if upgrading from Small Business Server 2000)

Table 5-2 (continued)

Requirement	Minimum	Recommended
Drive	CD-ROM	CD-ROM or DVD-ROM
Display	VGA or hardware that supports console redirection	Super VGA (800 × 600) or higher-resolution monitor
Other devices	•Hardware that supports console redirection •Ethernet network interface card	•Keyboard and Microsoft Mouse or compatible pointing device •Two Ethernet network interface cards
Additional items and services required for Internet access	•Some server functionality may require Internet access, a Microsoft Passport account, and payment of a separate fee to a service provider; local and/or long-distance telephone toll charges may apply. •Broadband or high-speed modem Internet connection	•Some server functionality may require Internet access, a Microsoft Passport account, and payment of a separate fee to a service provider; local and/or long-distance telephone toll charges may apply. •Broadband or high-speed modem Internet connection
Additional items required for networking	•Dedicated Class 1 fax modem to use fax service	•Dedicated Class 1 fax modem to use fax service •Pocket PC Phone Edition 2003 or Smartphone 2003 for Outlook Mobile Access •Windows XP Professional or Windows 2000 Professional for client operating systems

*Actual requirements will vary based on your system configuration and the applications and features you choose to install. Additional available hard-disk space may be required if you are installing over a network.

IMPORTANT: These tables were obtained from Microsoft and reproduced here. There is an important reason for this apparent copy-and-paste operation (and not just to spare the author from typing it out!). When you take the 70-282 examination, it's essential to recite "chapter and verse" the system requirements AS UNDERSTOOD AND STATED BY MICROSOFT.

You likely have formulated your own opinion as to what makes an optimal system baseline for running either Standard or Premium Edition SBS 2003. Right on! However, your own opinion, while reflecting your own personality and professional experience, might not make for a proper answer on the 70-282 exam. Avoid being the test taker who is "too smart" for the exam and views potential correct exam answers as "I don't do it that way." Such an attitude results in retakes!

FYI – Chapter 2 of *Advanced Windows Small Business Server 2003 Best Practices* (SMB Nation Press) has an excellent real-world hardware chapter written by systems guru and columnist Chris Angellini in which he discusses at length both the Microsoft stated system minimums and the "real world," and how the two paradigms are dramatically different.

FYI 2 – More real world SBS hardware discussions may be found in the Small Business-related solution accelerators from Microsoft (written by a segment team that has more editorial freedom than a product team). Visit www.microsoft.com/partner, click Products and Solutions, and then select Microsoft Solutions for Small and Medium Business.

Network Interface Cards

At least one NIC (network interface card) is required for the Small Business Server to function. We recommend installing two network cards so the server can take advantage of the basic firewall included in SBS (NAT firewall).

Disk Partitions

A single disk partition is required. There is no requirement to create multiple disk partitions, but if you chose to do so, there are several ways this can be done. When you partition a disk, each section functions as a physically separate disk. It is a good idea to decide where you would want to place Windows Small Business Server 2003 components prior to the server installation.

Dividing up the storage makes sense even if you are using RAID hardware. By dividing the disk space into logical partitions, you can distribute the data, such as operating system files, continuously changing data files, and static storage —i.e. program files—onto different logical disks which will allow for backup segregation and easier disaster recovery.

- You can create partitions during the text-mode setup of the server installation. Minimum recommendation is at least 4 GB, but real-world experience recommends at least 10 GB or more if you have enough drive space available.

- To setup software RAID, create the set after the setup process has completed.

- For a mass storage controller, such as SCSI, hardware RAID, or a Fibre Channel adapter, you might need to hit the F6 key at the beginning of the text-mode setup and then insert the manufacturer's floppy with the driver files when prompted, or setup will not see any mass storage controllers and the install will be halted. You will know this when your first setup pass fails because the storage was not detected.

Due to NT file system (NTFS) files system dependencies, Active Directory and Exchange 2003 components will only function on Windows SBS 2003 if the system partition, as well as the partitions holding transaction logs, the database and binary files are formatted with the NTFS.

IMPORTANT: You should always choose NTFS as the file system for all partitions to receive the benefits of shadow copies, disk quotas, and encryptions in addition to NTFS permissions.

Also, beware of tricks on exams where blatantly false answers are provided to mislead you. For example, if you were to see a file system answer referring to HPFS (high performance file system), you would know this was a false answer on the 70-282 exam because HPFS is an OS\2 concept (IBM's legacy operating system from the 1990s) and hasn't been available on Microsoft network operating systems since the Windows NT Server 3.51 era.

First-Time System Installation

A first-time system installation is the best scenario you can wish for. After you have gathered all the information on the business and conducted the needs analysis and finished your technology plan, you can plan and design the server to exactly the specifications that will best support the preferred state of the business.

IMPORTANT: Specific step-by-step setup procedures are revealed in *Windows Small Business Server 2003 Best Practices* (SMB Nation Press) where you will learn the SBS 2003 standard installation for the retail SKU is 42 steps when followed without customization.

To prepare the server for a first-time installation, ensure that you have:

- Adequate hardware for the load you are going to place on it. (See minimum system requirement above)

- The latest system BIOS

- Set the boot order in the BIOS to boot from the CD-ROM first

- All driver files for SCSI, Fibre Channel, RAID (if needed)

- HAL (Hardware Abstraction Layer) drivers for custom hardware

- Disconnected UPS devices (may cause Setup to fail)

Now you are ready to begin the installation and boot the server with the SBS 2003 Disc 1 CD-ROM. Upon boot, you will be prompted to press any key to start the installation and enter into the first phase of the Setup mode.

IMPORTANT: For security reasons, it is recommended to disconnect the server from the Internet during installation. This prevents slippery worms like BLASTER from sneaking in!

Setup Modes

There are two parts to Setup: the first phase is completed in Text-mode Setup and the second phase in GUI (Graphical User Interface) mode setup.

Text-Mode Setup

- Loads the Windows Small Business Server operating system

- Starts the Setup Wizard

- Loads drivers and detects storage devices

- Enables creation of new partitions

Text-mode Setup starts the program for the SBS operating system and prepares the computer for the rest of the installation process. At the end of the Text-mode Setup, the server will reboot into GUI mode Setup.

GUI Mode Setup

In GUI mode, the wizard:

- Detects and installs devices found on the computer

- Configures each device

- Installs and configures networking components

- Copies installation files that were not copied during Text-mode Setup

- Installs any additional components

- Writes the Setup log files to the installation directory

IMPORTANT: Microsoft's SBS development team is GUI-centric, so when you engage in "Microsoft-think" to guess at what types of anwsers are being sought on the 70-282 exam, think about the pride the team takes in the SBS GUI (setup, administrative, troubleshooting phases). Hey—if I had created all the GUI to create the "SBS experience" as we know it, I'd sure want it "tested" by Small Business Specialist candidates!

In the GUI-mode Setup, the wizard completes the installation of the Windows SBS 2003 operating system. Here you will specify license information, computer name, server components and network settings.

> IMPORTANT: If the server does not support booting from the CD-ROM (like a non el-torito compatible CD drive), insert a start-up floppy disk with CD-ROM drivers and navigate to the CD-ROM drive letter, run i386\winnt.ext to start copying the installation files.

Small Business Server Component Installation (Standard Edition)

After the GUI-mode setup is completed, the server will reboot and the Windows SBS Setup Wizard will launch the first time you log in. Before proceeding with the SBS Setup, make sure you:

- Check that NICs are installed and functioning properly

- Plug in the UPS

- Plug a cable into the NIC for the internal network

Do not customize your server until you are done with the entire Windows SBS 2003 installation.

> IMPORTANT: When adding the domain name, accept the default of .local or choose another extension like .prv or .internal to keep your internal domain as secure as possible. (Do not use .local if you are using Mac OS X clients on the network.) This way your internal network will stay isolated from the Internet.

At this point you can proceed with the SBS Setup Wizard. If setup requirements are not met at any time, a Setup Requirements page will launch, advising you of the issue so you can correct it before proceeding with the installation.

The Setup Wizard will now install the Server tools and applications that are listed on the Components screen. These are applications typically used by small businesses and selected by default. They are:

- Intranet

- Monitoring

- Networking

- Administration

- Client Deployment

- Exchange Server

- Fax Services

Components are installed to the default location at C:\Program Files\Microsoft Windows Small Business Server.

You can also define the location of various data folders at this point, like users shared folder, Exchange database, SharePoint, and fax folders. If you have several drives in your server, I recommended you choose different partitions for data applications and users shared folders.

The complete install at this point can take anywhere from one hour (unlikely) to several hours (most common) depending on your hardware. If you are installing SBS from the CD Disc set, you will be prompted several times to insert different CDs. If you are installing from a DVD, you may as well go get a big cup of coffee or take a nap for a while.

After the SBS 2003 installation is completed, the server will reboot and come up with the "To Do List" upon logging in.

> IMPORTANT: Once Windows SBS Setup has run, you are not able to change the computer name. The SBS tools and applications are configured to work with the full domain name system (DNS) name for the internal domain and the NetBIOS name. To change the server name, you would have to reinstall Windows SBS 2003.

Small Business Server Component Installation (Premium Edition)

ISA Server 2000, SQL Server 2000 and Microsoft FrontPage are included in the Premium Edition of Windows SBS 2003, but do not get installed as part of the core SBS setup. In effect, you install the premium components after completing the SBS 2003 Standard Edition deployment steps.

First, follow the install steps for the SBS 2003 Standard Edition. After having a successful SBS install, you can then insert the Windows Small Business Server Disk 5 CD-ROM (Premium Disc) and a new install splash screen will launch, prompting you to install the premium components.

> IMPORTANT: Read the setup discussion accessed from the "How to Install" link on the Disc 5 splash screen to both set up the premium components correctly and prepare for the 70-282 exam.

Installing SQL Server 2000 with SP3a

Insert the Premium Disc into the server and a Premium-related technolgies install screen will appear. Click on "Install SQL Server 2000" to launch the install. A dialog box will warn you that SQL Server 2000 SP2 and earlier versions are not supported. Acknowledge that and continue to the SQL Server Installation Wizard. Follow the default screens, choosing the name of the local server and then choose to create a new instance of SQL server.

Continue through the default screens, adding company information and license code. On the Setup Type screen, select your preference, and on the Services Account screen, choose to use either the Windows Administrator account or a SQL admin account specifically created for SQL. Using a separate SQL administrator account is more secure. SQL will start to copy files. Click Finish. Go back to the Premium Technologies CD install screen and install Service Pack 3a for SQL.

Upgrading SharePoint

SharePoint is included with SBS 2003 using the MSDE (Microsoft SQL Desktop Engine), and even though the 2 GB size limit and maximum user restriction of five have been removed from the MSDE, you should upgrade SharePoint to use a full instance of SQL server.

When installing SQL server for SharePoint, make sure you

- Stop the MSSQL$SHAREPOINT Service

- Select UPGRADE when prompted (do not install a new instance)

- Choose SHAREPOINT from the upgrade box (do NOT upgrade SBSMONITORING)

- Install SQL SP3a after the SQL upgrade

- Check that the MSSQL$SHAREPOINT Service started

IMPORTANT: SQL Service Pack 3a must be installed on every single instance. If you install a new instance and upgrade SharePoint to use a SQL instance, you must install SQL SP3a for each individual instance.

Installing ISA Server 2000

Just like installing SQL, installing ISA Server 2000 is an easy task to complete. To properly perform the installation, you must use the setup bootstrapper by clicking on the Install ISA Server 2000 icon presented after the premium technologies disk is launched.

IMPORTANT: Remember that, as of this writing, the 70-282 exam is based on ISA Server 2000. At a future date, you can expect this exam to be updated for ISA Server 2004.

During installation you will be given three choices for installation:

- Caching

- Firewall

- Caching & Firewall

Most businesses would choose the Firewall mode only, but if you have users who are going to the same web sites during the day, you want to choose caching and firewall, so web pages will be cached.

IMPORTANT: It's important to occasionally suspend your belief system when taking the 70-282 exam to answer the question properly. I've hammered on this theme earlier about not outsmarting yourself on this test. Here is what I mean. Perhaps you view ISA Server 2000 as a capable firewall application. However, Microsoft is also proud of its caching capabilities and won't hear otherwise. Guess you should honor that fact when taking the 70-282 exam, eh? ISA Server 2000 provides additional functionality beyond a mere firewall.

After installation is completed, ISA will not appear in the Server Management console, but will be available separately and can be accessed by:

1. Log on to the SBS 2003 server machine as **Adminstrator**.

2. Click **Start**.

3. Click **All Programs.**

4. Click **Microsoft ISA Server** followed by **ISA Management**.

Completing Post-Installation Tasks (To Do List)

The To Do List is a great tool containing a collection of tasks that must be undertaken to finalize the Windows SBS Setup. Here you can connect your server to the Internet, create user accounts, connect printers and workstations, and perform all tasks that will allow a small business to have a fully functional network.

The To Do List is broken up into two sections:

1. Network Tasks

   • View Security Best Practices

   • Connect to the Internet with the CEICW (Configure E-mail and Internet Configuration Wizard)

   • Configure Remote Access

   • Activate your Server

   • Add Client Licenses

2. Management Tasks

   • Add a Printer

   • Add Users and Computers

   • Configure Fax

- Configure Backup

- Configure Monitoring

The To Do List is shown in Figure 5-1 below.

Figure 5-1

The To Do List is central to the SBS experience and representative of the SBS culture about using the GUI to complete tasks.

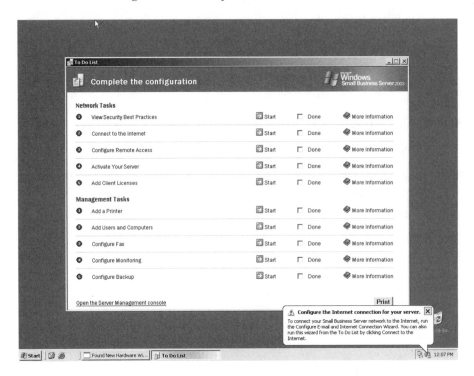

These are the choices the To Do List tasks will offer after a successful clean installation. If you did an upgrade, there will be other tasks listed depending on the setup variation.

The benefits in the real world for the task lists are multiple. If you are an administrator or consultant for a small business, you can set up the server offsite and install the required applications. Then you can bring the server online onsite and migrate data, connect to the Internet, set up users, etc., in short order. This really cuts down the time spent in another crammed closet all weekend.

We will be covering the To Do List in more detail in Chapter 7, "Configuring Windows Small Business Server 2003."

> IMPORTANT: Even though it is recommended to complete the To Do List in order, it can be completed in any order. The list can be accessed from the Server Management console.

Upgrade and Migrations

This section discusses upgrade and migration approaches applicable to the 70-282 exam. It is recommended you read this carefully!

> IMPORTANT: In the real world, it is important to note that alternative, more in-depth and more sophisticated migration approaches exist. For example, Jeff Middleton (SBS-MVP) detailed his "Swing Migration" approach in Chapter 15 of the *Advanced Windows Small Business Server 2003* book (SMB Nation Press). His detailed analysis is excellent but is in some ways beyond the scope of the 70-282 exam.

In-Place Upgrade from SBS 2000 to SBS 2003

An in-place upgrade to SBS 2003 can be done from:

1. Windows SBS 2000

2. Windows 2000 Server

3. Windows Server 2003

Coming from Windows SBS 4.5, NT 4.0 or another operating system would be considered a migration and not an upgrade.

Upgrading a server is much less complex than performing a migration, less disruptive, and less expensive. On the other hand, when you perform an upgrade, you will retain junk data, forgotten accounts, incorrect settings and the family pictures of someone who quit the company three years ago.

Performing an in-place upgrade to SBS 2003 is easy and will take little time if planned and implemented properly.

Microsoft has "official" upgrade information on its public-facing Upgrading page at http://www.microsoft.com/WindowsServer2003/sbs/upgrade/default.mspx.

Preparing the Server

To ensure a smooth and painless upgrade, there are several items to be considered and steps to be taken. Prior to the upgrade you must:

1. Meet or exceed the minimum system requirements

2. Have an additional 2 GB hard drive space for temporary Setup files

3. Install all necessary Service Packs and updates

4. Clear all fax and e-mail message queues

5. Run Disk Clean-up (cleanmgr.exe)

6. Run Disk Defragmenter (Dfrg.msc)

7. Log on as the administrator using the built-in Administrator account

8. Ensure you have SBS 2000 SP1 installed (if coming from 2000)

9. Check for updated and compatible drivers

10. Check the latest BIOS

11. Disable the external NIC

It is imperative that you plan and document the steps prior to the upgrade. Skipping steps and not taking the time to prepare the server properly can result in a fatal outcome. It will be helpful to prepare a disaster recovery plan ahead of time. Choose a time for the upgrade where downtime will create minimal disruption to the business.

> IMPORTANT: It is recommended that you anti-virus scan all files and drives, except for the M:\ drive (Exchange) and perform a full, complete backup of the System State, data, and Exchange and verify the backup integrity. (Test restore.)

I'll have more information about backup and restore in Chapter 8.

When checking for compatibility issues, consider:

- Third-Party Applications – check with the manufacturer

- Device Drivers – replace aging devices that are not supported by SBS 2003

- Client Computers – Windows 95 clients and older should be axed

You must also remove discontinued Exchange components like:

- Microsoft Exchange MSMail Connector

- Microsoft Exchange Connector for Lotus cc:Mail

- Microsoft Exchange Instant Messaging Service

- Microsoft Exchange Chat Service

- Microsoft Exchange Key Management Service

Removing Exchange components can be done in the Add/Remove Program panel by selecting Microsoft Small Business Server 2000, then choosing Change/Remove and running the SBS Setup Wizard to remove the Exchange components.

Now that you have prepped the server, let's take a look at the clients.

> IMPORTANT: Since SBS 2000 does not have Shadow Copy, boot into safe mode to run the backup. Fewer files will be in use and there is a greater chance of a successful backup.

Preparing the Client for an In-Place Upgrade

In an in-place upgrade scenario, Windows XP Professional and Windows 2000 Professional clients will not require any preparation. If you have a Windows 95 or an NT 4.0 workstation and your boss just can't live without them, you could tell him that these operating systems just don't communicate well with SBS 2003. If that doesn't work, you could:

1. Bite the bullet, and

2. Install the Active Directory Extensions (dsclient.exe) located on the SBS 2003 Disc 1 on the Windows 95 client, and

3. Install Windows NT 4.0 Service Pack 6a, IE6 and dsclient.exe on the NT 4.0 workstation. The Windows NT 4.0 Service Pack 6a essentially supports legacy workstations.

IMPORTANT: Besides preparing the server and clients, it is a good idea to prepare the end users as well. Advise them of the network upgrade and how they will benefit from it.

Performing the Upgrade

Now that you have prepped the server and client workstations, you are ready to proceed with the actual upgrade. Windows SBS 2003 upgrades the system by first upgrading the operating system, then configuring the operating system for Windows SBS 2003, and performing the actual upgrade last.

Once the system has been upgraded to Windows SBS 2003, you will have to rerun the To Do List and fulfill several other tasks.

Before we get to this point, there are some final steps to take prior to the upgrade:

1. Disconnect UPS

2. Disable third-party disk utilities

3. Disconnect from the Internet

4. Disable anti-virus programs

Log on as the built-in administrator and launch the SBS 2003 Disc 1. Follow the on-screen instructions, which will appear very much like the first-time install.

Once the upgrade has been completed and the system rebooted, you should complete the tasks in the To Do List in the order represented. Make sure to run the Change User Permissions Wizard, of all things, to ensure that users get their permissions migrated and are able to properly access all resources on the domain.

Notes:

Migrating from SBS 2000, SBS 4.5, or NT 4.0 to SBS 2003

Migrating vs. upgrading will involve moving the entire SBS installation from the source (old) server to the destination (new) server. A migration, generally referred to as a painful process, exposes large amounts of useless and irrelevant data that has been hanging around for eons. If you already have an existing network infrastructure in place, don't want to interrupt the flow of business or upset end-users, but still continue with identical operations after moving to new hardware, a migration is the only way to go.

There are slight differences between migrating from a SBS 2000 domain (AAD—After Active Directory) and migrating from SBS 4.5 or an NT 4.0 server (BAD—Before Active Directory). The procedures follow the same logical steps, and we will point out the differences on the way.

Preparing for the Migration

To have a successful migration, on the **source server** you should:

1. Record all information on the source and destination servers
2. Record the location of any shared folders
3. Record the LOB data location
4. Record general user data that is not located in a shared folder
5. Record POP3 mailbox account information – needs to be reconfigured on the destination server
6. Ensure SBS 4.5 and NT 4.0 servers are running SP6a
7. If running Exchange 5.5. or 2000:
   - Record distribution lists
   - Record Custom recipients
   - Record Public folder custom permissions
   - Export public folders to .pst files
   - Export the administrator account mailbox and rules

8. If running SQL 7.0, check the SQL version number 7.00.1063 and make sure SP4 is installed

9. Record custom server setting for:

   • SMTP connector

   • DHCP scope options

   • DNS records

   • RRAS service settings

   • GPOs

   • ISA settings

   • Custom IIS Web sites

10. Verify that hardware drivers and software are supported

11. Ensure the source server is running the latest service packs

12. Do a full system backup on the source server including system state and Exchange

13. Back up and create ERD (Emergency Repair Disk) for SBS 4.5 and NT 4.0 Server

Carefully heed the following section and its words of wisdom. You should be aware that the migration has a high probability rate for failure if you don't follow the rules listed below, starting with:

1. The source and destination servers must have different internal DNS and NetBIOS names

   • This does not affect your external DNS name

2. The source and destination server computer names must be different

   • Beware of client PCs using UNC paths; ensure you remove any references to the source server on the client machines

3. The DHCP service on the source server must be disabled

- The DHCP service must be running on the destination server, so you must disable the source server's DHCP service to avoid contention between them

4. Use the Active Directory Migration Tool (ADMT) to migrate user, group, and computer accounts

   - This will preserve the SIDs (Security Identifiers)

5. Use the Exchange Migration Wizard

   - The Exchange Migration Wizard is the successor to ExMerge and a more simplified and reliable method of moving mailboxes. Beware it does not export mailbox rules or migrate the administrator account mailbox or rules on public folders. (You could use ExMerge to export public folders and the administrator account.)

6. Custom server settings must be configured manually on the destination server

   - SMTP connector

   - DHCP scope options

   - DNS records

   - RRAS service settings

   - GPOs

   - ISA settings

   - Custom IIS Web site settings

7. Create DNS forwarders on the source and destination server

   - ADMT requires those to work with the source and destination servers

Okay, so the good news is that desktop profiles on Windows 2000 and Windows XP machines are preserved during the migration. Yeah!

IMPORTANT: Ensure that user folders do not exceed 1 GB. Disk quotas are enabled by default on the partition where the users shared folder is located. While in the real world you might know of ways to work around this disk quota matter, accept this as GOSPEL on the 70-282 exam.

Configure the Destination Server

First you must install SBS 2003 on the destination server (See section "First-Time System Installation" in this chapter.) While filling out information for server setup, make sure you:

1. Enter a different DNS and NetBIOS name than the source server

2. Have DHCP disabled on the source server

3. Enter an IP address on the same subnet as the source server

4. Install ADMT on the destination server—the ADMT is located on Disc 1 on the SBS 2003 disk set at *D*:\I386\Admt\Admigration.msi (where *D* represents the drive letter)

5. To configure ADMT, you must run this in the command prompt:

```
Net Localgroup "Pre-Windows 2000 Compatible Access" Everyone /Add
Net Localgroup "Pre-Windows 2000 Compatible Access" "Anonymous Logon" /Add
```

6. To migrate user accounts, you must also run

```
Runas  /Netonly  /user:SourceDomainName\Administrator   "Mmc
\"%ProgramFiles%\Active Directory Migration Tool\Migrator.msc\""
- replace SourceDomainName with the desitnation domain name.
```

This will cover Windows 2000, as well as SBS 4.5 and NT 4.0 servers.

IMPORTANT: Account names are automatically truncated if they are longer then 20 characters and will cause migration errors.

Prepare Clients for Account Migration

There are a few steps that need to be performed on the client machines to prepare them for the account migration.

1. Ensure that the Domain Administrator group from the source server is a member of the local built-in Administrators group

2. Disable any personal firewalls

   • Disable Internet Connection Firewall in IE

   • Do NOT disable the ISA 2000 firewall client

3. NT 4.0 workstation and NT 4.0 member servers must have SP 6a installed

4. Users should export their mailbox rules

5. Delete desktop shortcuts to the Company folder and User's shared folder

6. Delete printers and faxes that point to the source server

7. Delete all Favorites that reference the source server

   • Microsoft Small Business Internet Services

   • Microsoft Small Business Server Web site

   • My E-mail

   • SBS User Guide

   • Small Business Server Administration

8. Disable real-time virus protection on each client and run a virus scan

9. If migrating from an SBS 4.5 or NT 4.0 server, remove the following applications

   • WinSock Proxy Client

   • Fax Server Client

   • Modem Sharing Client

10. If migrating from SBS 2000, remove the Modem sharing client

11. Release and renew the IP address

When performing the account migration, be aware that the ADMT has a differential treatment depending on the OS. The migration treatment of different client operating systems is shown in Table 5-3.

Table 5-3

ADMT and client operating systems

OS	Tool
Windows XP Professional Windows 2000 Professional Windows 2000 Server Windows 2003 Server NT 4.0 Workstation	Can be migrated by using the ADMT
Windows 98 Windows 95 Windows Me	Must be configured manually for the destination server

Ensure that you have a CAL (client access license) for each client machine and member server on the destination server.

> IMPORTANT: If you have a second Domain Controller that is a Windows 2000 Server, you must run **dcpromo** to remove AD and then migrate the computer account to the destination server.

Performing the Migration

Ensure that the Domain Administrator group is a member of the built-in administrator group on the local client machines. Also, double-check that you are not running anti-virus software on the source or destination server.

You will first launch ADMT and then migrate the following accounts:

1. User accounts

2. Group accounts

   - To migrate group accounts, you will have to run the ADMT Group Account Migration Wizard twice. You will separately migrate

      - Security Groups

      - Distribution Groups

3. Computer accounts

   Before migrating computer accounts, be sure to wait at least 15 minutes after the source server reboots so that the DNS records can be updated or the client configuration for the destination domain will fail.

4. Change mailbox quotas on Exchange if client mailboxes exceed 200,000 KB (default limit) or clients will not be able to send or receive e-mail.

5. Move the users' Exchange mailboxes

6. Move the users' shared folders

7. Move the Company folder to the SharePoint Site

   • Files larger than 50 MB will be blocked

   • Files with extensions like .exe and .vbs will be blocked

8. Move SQL server databases

9. Move LOB data

10. Move any other data folders

11. Remove the DNS forwarder used for the migration

12. Remove any permissions used for the migration

```
Net Localgroup "Pre-Windows 2000 Compatible Access" Everyone /Delete

Net Localgroup "Pre-Windows 2000 Compatible Access" "Anonymous Logon" /Delete
```

13. Uninstall ADMT

14. Connect to the Internet and create the DNS forwarder

    Having migrated all the user, group, and computer accounts, you must still perform some final configuration on the destination server to ensure that users have the appropriate permission to access the new SBS 2003 network.

15. Assign new permissions to migrated accounts (run the Change User Permissions Wizard on all the SBS 2003 templates on each user account migrated from the source server.)

16. Complete all steps of the Management tasks on the To Do List (covered extensively in Chapter 7) in the order presented, including:

   • Assigning applications

   • Adding printers

   • Configuring fax

   • Configuring monitoring

   • Configuring backup

17. Re-create custom settings from the source server on the destination server

18. Configure distribution lists

19. Configure custom recipient policies

20. Configure POP3 e-mail accounts (if used)

21. Copy any custom logon scripts you used on the source server

IMPORTANT: Log on to a client machine (after it has been configured to work with the destination server) as the administrator and import the mailbox and rules to the destination server.

You are almost done! At this point you can disconnect the source server from the network and focus on some final tasks to be completed on the client side.

22. Disconnect the source server

23. Install DSclient.exe (Active Directory Client Extension) for Windows 9x, Me, or NT 4.0 Workstation. (These are two different clients, one for NT 4.0 and the other for Win9x and Me, available for download from the Microsoft site.)

24. Ensure clients can log on to the domain

25. Remove the ISA Server 2000 firewall client if you previously used ISA Server 2000 and migrated to the SBS 2003 Standard Edition

26. Install the ISA Server 2000 firewall client if you are using the Premium Edition

27. Ensure all proxy settings are configured properly

28. Install applications if needed

29. Install Outlook 2003 (it will auto-configure for the profile)

Now that you have finished the migration, it is recommended that you be on-site the first day users will be working on the newly migrated network—or be very, very far away, without a cell phone and having forgotten to let anyone know your whereabouts. Just kidding on that last point.

> IMPORTANT: Don't forget that you should actually install SBS 2003 a few times before you take the 70-282 exam. It's one thing to read this chapter and answer the questions that follow. But there is nothing like the active learning experience gained from deploying and using the SBS 2003 product in the real world. Don't kid yourself! It's not wise to "read" yourself into sucessfully passing the 70-282 exam — use our words of wisdom to supplement your real-world experience.

To get a free 180-day copy of SBS 2003 Standard Edition, you can acquire it a couple of different ways:

- SMB Nation Press starter kits and resource kits: www.smbnation.com

- Microsoft trial software: http://www.microsoft.com/windowsserver 2003/sbs/evaluation/trial/default.mspx

Practice Questions

Question #1

As the administrator of AdvantaCorp., you manage a SBS 2003 server and 35 client workstations with XP Professional. Every year, AdvantaCorp hires 5 college students to help over the summer and also hires students throughout the year. Students usually stay on for specific assingments only. Since the students are temporary, you want to secure and only allow the minimum access to folders that is required, as well as enforce disk quota limits. What would be the most efficient way to do this?

A. Create a user account using the Add User wizard. Create a security group called "SummerHelp" and enter quoata limits. Set this user account up as a template.

B. Create a user template and create a security group called "SummerHelp." Add quota restrictions. Use the Add User wizard to create the new accounts.

C. Create a security group called "SummerHelp" and add a quota. Use the Add User wizard and assign the new user to the security group.

D. Create a user template and create a distribution group called "SummerHelp." Add quota restrictions. Use the Add User wizard to create the new accounts.

Question #2

You are the new administrator at AdvantaCorp. The company has a SBS 2003 server and two member servers and 35 client workstations running XP Pro. The company uses shared folders and mapped drives. Users connect to a member server to which you just installed Terminal Services. About four months later users can no longer gain access to the terminal server. What should you do?

A. Deploy Terminal Server licensing server on the member server in per user mode.

B. Push out terminal server user licenses with a GPO

C. Add terminal server user licenses on the SBS server with the Add license wizard

D. Deploy an activated terminal server domain license server on the SBS server

Question #3

Springers Ltd. consists of an SBS server, a Windows 2000 member server, 5 NT 4.0 workstations, 4 Windows 2000 Professional and 7 Windows XP Pro clients. Springers uses software that requires clients to communicate using NetBIOS names. You also need to be able to use FQDNs. You want to make sure you have fault tolerance for the

FQDN and NetBIOS name resolution. How can you implement this? (multiple choice)

A. Configure each client as a proxy client

B. Configure the member server as a proxy client

C. Configure the member server as a DNS server

D. Configure the member server as a WINS server

E. Configure SBS 2003 as a proxy client

F. Configure SBS 2003 as a DNS server

G. Configure SBS 2003 as a WINS server

H. Configure the DHCP scope on the member server

I. Configure the DHCP scope on SBS 2003

Question #4

DentalTech.Inc is hiring you to perform an upgrade of their current SBS 2000 server to SBS 2003 Standard Edition. The company is using Exchange to host their e-mail and ISA 2000 as a firewall. In preparation for the upgrade you should: (multiple choice)

A. Scan the M:/ drive

B. Install ISA Service Pack 1

C. Remove discontinued Exchange Server components

D. Uninstall ISA

E. Disable the external NIC

F. Reformat the system drive

Question #5

You are the administrator of Kabrifam, Inc and just installed a new SBS 2003 server. There are 20 users on the network using XP Pro machines. In the past, users have inadvertently overwritten or deleted documents which were stored in the My Documents folder. You want to implement a fault tolerance solution and an easy retrieval method for files and folders stored in the My Documents folder by users. What should you do?

A. Enable shadow copies

B. Run the "Configure My Documents Redirection" wizard on the clients

C. Use a GPO to redirect the folders to the user shares on the SBS server

D. Run the "Configure My Documents Redirection" wizard on the server

E. On the client machines, go to the My Documents folder properties and change the target folder.

Question #6

Kabrifam, Inc just completed an upgrade from SBS 4.5 to SBS 2003. There are 12 XP Pro clients, 4 NT 4.0 workstations and 4 Windows 98 clients. After the upgrade users on the NT workstations and Windows 98 machines complain that they cannot logon to the network. You should:

A. Make the SBS 2003 server a WINS server

B. Release and renew the IP address on the NT 4.0 and Windows 98 clients

C. Type *flush dns* on the command prompt on the NT 4.0 and Windows 98 clients

D. Install Dsclient.exe on the NT 4.0 and Windows 98 clients

E. Configure DNS recursion

Question #7

Kabrifam, Inc. has a SBS 2003 server called Kabri1. The company has been expanding and decides to add another server to the network. Kabrifam purchases a Windows 2003 server license and has the local computer store build a white box server. After installing the server operating system and naming the server Kabri2 you want to join the new member server to the domain. What steps do you have to perform? (multiple choice)

A. Run the client computer wizard and add the server to the domain

B. Run the server computer wizard and add the server to the domain

C. Run http://kabri2/connectcomputer on Kabri1

D. Run http://kabri1/connectcomputer on Kabri2

E. Run dcpromo on Kabri2 and opt to become a child domain

F. Run dcpromo on Kabri1 and join Kabri2 to the SBS domain

Question #8

The Legal Aid non-profit group currently runs on a SBS 2000 server and seven Windows 98 client computers. Even though funding is short, due to compliance regulations they are forced to upgrade the server software to a new operating system. Currently the server has 256mb RAM and a Pentium 450 mhz processor and a 4 GB hard drive. There is no funding for new hardware in sight and the non-profit has to choose the best option, but does not want to lose the e-mail and fax capabilities. What should you upgrade to?

A. Upgrade the server to Windows XP Professional

B. Upgrade the server to Windows SBS 2003 Standard Edition

C. Upgrade the server to Windows SBS 2003 Premium Edition

D. Upgrade the server to Windows Server 2003

Question #9

You are the administrator of SMB Nation and have just purchased the upgrade CD from Windows SBS 2000 to SBS 2003 Standard Edition. Currently you are running Exchange Server 2000, IIS, ISA Server 2000, Terminal Server in Application Sharing mode DHCP and DNS. You plan to perform an in-place upgrade. What must you do to ensure a successful upgrade? (select all that apply)

A. Exmerge all mailboxes from Exchange and export all mailbox rules

B. Uninstall ISA Server 2000

C. Uninstall IIS

D. Disbable DNS and DHCP

E. Uninstall Terminal Server

F. Uninstall Exchange Server components that are incompatible with SBS 2003

G. Install Windows SBS 2000 SP1

Question #10

Trial Attorneys, Inc. just purchased a new server and would like SBS 2003 Standard Edition installed. The server contains four disks and you have to think of the best fault tolerance option for the attorneys. When attorneys prepare for trial, there cannot be any interruption or slow down on the system. After formatting all four drives with NTFS, you decide to use disk 0 as the system partition and use the remaining three disks for fault tolerance. What should you do? (select all that apply)

A. Configure two disks to a RAID 0 volume

B. Configure two disks as a RAID 1 volume

C. Configure three disks as a RAID 1 volume

D. Configure two disks as a RAID 5 volume

E. Configure three disks as a RAID 5 volume

F. Convert all disks to dynamic disks

G. Configure one disk as an extended partition

H. Configure one disk for Volume Shadow Copy repository only

Answer Key

Question #1: Answer B

The most efficient way to set up new user accounts that have the same security groups and disk quotas is by creating a template and then using the Add User wizard to create the account.

Answer A will work but is not as efficient to set up. Answer D would not work because distribution groups do not have the right to log on to the domain, only to receive e-mail.

Question #2: Answer D

When TS is installed, unlicensed clients can access the server for a 120-day evaluation period. Then TS will deny client access until it finds a TS license server to issue licenses. The TS server license service should not be installed on the TS server itself, but can be installed on the SBS server.

Question #3: Answer C, D, F, G

In order to have fault tolerance for NetBIOS and FQDNs, you have to configure WINS and DNS (DNS resolves FQDN queries and WINS resolves NetBIOS queries) on the SBS 2003 server and the member server. In this case, if one is taken down for maintenance, the other server will continue to provide name resolution for both types of requests. Configuring clients as proxy clients would not create any type of fault tolerance. Configuring the DHCP scope does not provide fault tolerance.

Question #4: Answer C, D, E

In order to prepare the server for an upgrade, you should remove discontinued Exchange Server components (Microsoft Exchange MSMail Connector, Connector for Lotus cc:Mail, Instant Messaging Service, Chat Service and the Key Management Service.) You should disconnect the external NIC and uninstall ISA2000.

The M:/ drive contains the Exchange database and should not be antivirus scanned. Installing ISA SP1 would not apply; this application must be removed because you are upgrading to SBS 2003 Standard Edition which does not include ISA. Since SBS is a bundled package, ISA 2000 should be removed. Reformating the system drive will turn this upgrade into a clean install.

Question #5: Answer D

Shadow copies are enabled by default on SBS 2003. Running the "Configure My Documents Redirection" located on the server under Users AND Backup Links will change the target folder on all clients to point to a share on the server. Shadow copy will take two snapshots daily, one at 7 a.m. and one at 12 p.m.. Shadow copy is only enabled by default on the system drive; if you choose to use it on other drives, you must manually enable shadow copies there.

Question #6: Answer D

You must install Dsclient.exe on the Windows 98 and NT4.0 workstations. The dsclient.exe is a free download from Microsoft. There is one dsclient.exe for each operating system respectively, in order for the clients to communicate with AD. All of the other answers are nonsense in this case.

Question #7: Answer B, D

To add a member server to an SBS 2003 network, you must run the Server Computer Wizard and add the server name and IP address, and then run: http://SBSservercomputername/connectcomputer on the member server. You cannot add a server through the client computer wizard. Running dcpromo and creating a child domain will fail because you cannot have child domains on an SBS 2003 network. Running dcpromo on the SBS server would only give the option to demote the DC and cannot be used to add an additional server to the network.

Question #8: Answer B

SBS 2003 Standard Edition will be the least expensive ($599) operating system and still support e-mail and faxing. Answer A. Windows XP could not manage e-mail. Answer C. SBS 2003 Premium is more expensive ($1499 retail). Answer D. Windows Server 2003 would require purchasing Exchange server as well as being more expensive.

Question #9: Answer B, E, F, G

Upgrading from SBS 2000 to SBS 2003 Standard Edition requires you to uninstall ISA Server 2000 (that is a Premium Edition component), uninstall Terminal Services, which is no longer supported in SBS 2003 (requires separate server) and uninstall all incompatible Exchange Server components (MS Mail connector, connector for Lotus mail, Instant Messaging Service, Exchange Chat Service and Exchange Key

Management Service). You must have Windows SBS 2000 SP1 installed before performing the upgrade. Answer A. Exmerging mailboxes does not contribute to a successful upgrade, but it would be a good measure in case the upgrade fails (but that is not the objective in this scenario). Answers C and D. There is no need to uninstall IIS or stop DNS or DHCP service.

Question #10: Answers B, F, H

You would first convert two disks to dynamic disks and then create a RAID 1 volume (mirrored disks). In a RAID 1 volume, one disk is duplicated to the second disk, which will slow down write performance. But the trade off is that if one disk fails, the other disk will not be affected and the system will keep functioning at the same speed. You should configure the third disk for Volume Shadow Copy repository so users can restore documents on the fly. Answer A. Raid 0 does not provide redundancy. Answer C. RAID 1 cannot be created with three disks. Answer D. RAID 5 cannot be created with two disks. Answer E. This would be an option, but not the desired option in our scenario since we do not want to experience any slow down. When a RAID array loses one drive, it slows down while recreating the missing data from the two other disks, while it is rebuilding the third disk. Answer G. An extended partition would not meet any of the objectives.

Summary

This important chapter covers the fundamental SBS 2003 deployment and setup discussion as it relates to the 70-282 examination. You were schooled in matters surrounding the underlying system requirements, first-time installations, and upgrades and migrations. The "wrapper"around this chapter was to keep you focused on the 70-282 examination. The next chapter focuses on securing SBS 2003.

CHAPTER 6
Securing Windows Small Business Server 2003

We could have started this chapter on security for Windows Small Business Server 2003 (SBS 2003) and written all the way to Timbuktu about it, there is so much to say about this topic alone. Not only that, but the topic of security presents a particular challenge because the body of security knowledge changes daily. Bad guys and gals are constantly seeking to impart evil on computer networks and thwart the effective, efficient, and honorable use of technology for peaceful and profitable businesses. It's a dark side of an otherwise sunny SBS 2003 disposition! So let's be upfront and honest here. This book is very much an "exam cram" for the 70-282 test, and as such, our focus must be firmly affixed. Manage your expectations from the start and enter this chapter with an open mind toward answering the 70-282 exam questions the "Microsoft way."

> IMPORTANT: We're not trying to play "duck and dodge" by reeling in what you can expect from this security chapter. We just want to stay focused on the goal of passing the 70-282 exam so you acquire the prerequisite certification credential to become a Microsoft Small Business Specialist. So knowing that many readers have eager minds and are seeking ever-more security knowledge, we invite you to read Chapters 5 and 13 in the introductory/intermediate *Windows Small Business Server 2003 Best Practices* and Chapters 11 and 12 in *Advanced Windows Small Business Server 2003 Best Practices* (the latter chapter written by this book's coauthor, Beatrice Mulzer),

both from SMB Nation Press. You are encouraged to also view the SBS resources in Appendix A of this book for SBS blogs, like the one by Susan Bradley that presents the most current security information on Planet Earth! And we support our friends Dr. Thomas Shinder and Roberta Bragg, both excellent security authors!

Also—because the 70-282 exam is focused on ISA Server 2000, we keep the discussion at this release level. Even though ISA Server 2004 has shipped, ISA Server 2000 is still the way the 70-282 exam presents security. Check www.smbnation.com for an updated chapter you can download that will feature ISA Server 2004 when the 70-282 exam is updated.

Many small businesses today are using IT and rely heavily on the Internet for all aspects of communiction—from simple e-mail to e-commerce transactions to Voice over Internet Protocol (VolP)—and sensitive information is constantly crossing networks. Most small businessees keep their data on a single server (or workstation) and don't recognize the value of their data until it has been compromised. Vulnerabilities are numerous, from viruses and drive-by browser jackers to full-blown security breaches, and it's beginning to feel like a Mad Max movie out there.

To protect your network from frailty, SBS 2003 comes equipped with default security features like firewall capabilities, an encrypting file system, access security authentication, enforceable policies, network protocol security and authentication, and certificate services.

Focusing on external threads, let's not overlook internal security measures and consider how authenticated users can be managed. Starting with NTFS permissions and using the principle of the least privilege, we can configure domain user accounts and set appropriate rights and permissions.

Notes:

Configure User Accounts and Permissions

Configuring user accounts and permissions is generally done using security groups in SBS 2003. You can control what users can or cannot do on a network by simply placing or removing their user accounts in specific security groups.

User Rights and Permissions

Managing users and groups can appear to be a daunting task, but as an administrator you have two friends called:

- User Rights

- User Permissions

User Rights

User rights are defined by the capabilities, like performing a task. In general, user rights apply to the entire system. There are two types of user rights:

- Privileges

  - Allow a user to perform actions like running a backup or a security audit

- Logon Rights

  - Allow a user to access the computer in a certain way

User Permissions

Permissions dictate access to a particular object (files, printers), allowing the user to interact with the object in a certain way (read, write, print). As shown in Figure 6-1, you can view NTFS permission settings. Looking at the folder name, of course, should teach you to never let new techs have access to the server. But besides that, notice that the Domain Users Group here has Read and Execute, List Folder Contents, and Read permissions inherited by default.

Figure 6-1

NTFS permission settings on a folder

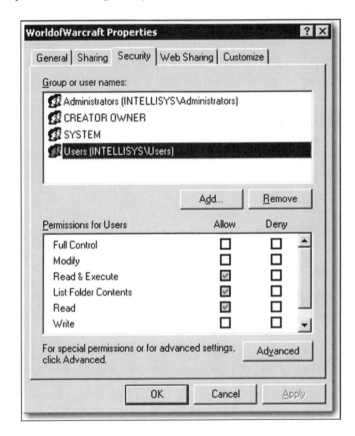

Security Groups

SBS 2003 has built-in security groups that have already assigned rights to simplify administration. You can place a user into the Fax Operators group (which has specific fax-related rights assigned), and the user will be able to manage fax queues and cover pages. This is a time-tested network administrative practice of using security groups to manage permissions.

SBS User Templates

The "SBS experience" is kinda like a popular USA beer commercial: "Tastes great and is less filling." SBS has been maligned in the haughty enterprise community because it looks like a toy and it's too easy. However, don't let the pretty SBS interface fool you. Some very sophisticated concepts (that's the "tastes great" part of the beer commercial) are being applied via simple-to-use (and we state MUST USE) SBS-specific tools. One such tool set is the SBS User Templates, which contribute favorably to the SBS experience (and make it easier to use). This section discusses default user templates and custom user templates.

Default User Templates

User Templates, selected from the Template Selection screen of the Add User Wizard (Figure 6-2), specify many account properties and permissions when selected for the user you are creating. There are four user templates by default in SBS 2003, defined in Table 6-1. With the default four user templates, all properties like group membership, SharePoint site groups, and disk quotas have already been set. Remember that the Add User Wizard is launched from the Add Users and Computers link from the To Do List (accessed via the Server Management console).

Figure 6-2

Observing user templates

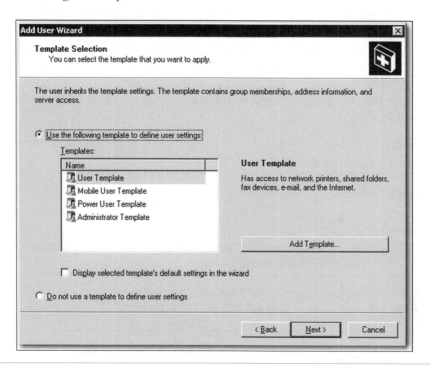

IMPORTANT: There is really no need to go into Active Directory via the Active Directory Users and Computers snap-in to create users and apply settings. SBS proudly uses Active Directory and you can certainly use all the Active Directory snap-ins to "see Active Directory." However, we're here to discourage you from such under-the-hood shenanigans unless specifically called for by a guru or Microsoft Product Support Services (PSS). Consider this to be our "safe sex" initiative in the context of SBS. Play safe with SBS!

Note that you might encounter small business technology professionals and customers who are—how can we put it mildy?—freaked out about Active Directory. When it launched Windows 2000 Server in February of 2000, Microsoft did a great job of touting and branding Active Directory because it was responding to Novell's NetWare Directory Services (NDS) product. This era of Active Directory noise had the effect of causing some people to ask whether they need to MASTER the Active Directory area to run SBS. The answer is no. The good news is that you don't need to master Active Directory to pass the 70-282 exam, so don't waste your time here.

We talk more about Active Directory interaction points in Chapter 8 in the Group Policy discussion.

The four user templates defined in Table 6-1 represent the different levels of resource access.

Table 6-1
User templates defined

User Template	•Internet •E-mail •Shared folders •Printers and faxes •Remote Desktop on an XP Pro client machine, but not the server
Mobile User Template	•All User template permissions •VPN access permissions

Table 6-1 (continued)

Power User Template	•All permissions of a mobile user template •Log on remotely to the SBS server, but no log on locally (Can only use Server Management console) •Perform delegated tasks
Administrator	•Unrestricted system access

IMPORTANT: As shown in Figure 6-2, you may select the **Display selected template's default settings** in the wizard checkbox to show how all of the above settings are applied. Very cool. You may also select the **Do not use a template to define user settings** radio button to effectively add a user the non-SBS way. Very uncool! Also something that is very uncool: If you add a user directly to Active Directory, you do not participate in the SBS user template concept.

Custom User Templates

You can create your own custom user templates by clicking the **Add template** link while completing the Add User Wizard or by going to User templates and clicking the **Add template** link, which will launch the Add Template Wizard. The use of custom templates is very exciting and very powerful. Why? Let's answer this question with a tad of Texas story-telling by the campfire. Back when knights were bold and Microsoft blue badges owned ALL the gold, there was a redhead (NetWare) on the block that was a huge threat. There were more Certified NetWare Engineers (CNEs) than Microsoft Certified Professionals (MCPs). What all CNEs knew to do was create the "perfectly" configured account (e.g., ACCT) for a department (e.g., Accounting) and then disable the account. When the customer hired a new employee in the accounting department, the ACCT account was copied over for the new user and renamed (e.g., Brisker Brelsford). This was the user template concept in its early format. Today, with SBS, you have a pretty interface to accomplish the same effect. And guess what? The user templates in SBS 2003 are nothing more than disabled user accounts.

So you would want to create custom templates that meet your needs like the accounting example. You might have a template designed for each department. You can even export templates between customer sites by selecting the Export

Templates link under Migrate Server Settings under Advanced Management in the Server Management console. This would be really cool if you were the reseller of a line-of-business (LOB) application (e.g., Microsoft Small Business Financials) and your directory permissions were the same at each client and the "accounting" template could be used at any client site. You get the point!

Use templates to make changes to a user's permissions. This is good for updating a user as needed or updating a user account that was migrated over from SBS 2000 and doesn't have the full SBS 2003 experience going for it yet! That is, if you followed the migration approaches discussed in Chapter 5, the user account brought forward would not have an SBS 2003 user template applied to it (shame and lame!). So, when launching the Change User Permissions Wizard, you can apply a template to already existing user accounts.

> IMPORTANT: Once again. Use User templates at all times if possible. This way you will have consistent permissions assigned across all user accounts, whereas assigning them manually leaves great room for error. And a big hint—certification exams tend to favor consistency.

Securing File, Folder, and Printer Objects

Now that we have established what rights and permissions are, let's take a look at how these affect securing objects on the network.

Share Permissions

In terms of "Microsoft think" on the 70-282 exam, you should always secure objects that are shared on the network. That could be folders, printers, and other devices and applications. For other users to gain access to the shared resource, it must be shared out. By default, shares allow access to Everyone (yes, there is an "Everyone" group) and assign read permissions. Once the resource is shared, you could remove the Everyone group (do not apply Deny or you will deny everyone, including you) and just add the security groups that should have Read, Change, or Full Control permissions. Share permissions apply to folders (not files) and will be inherited from subfolders. They are displayed in Table 6-2.

Table 6-2

Standard Share Permissions

Read	Allows viewing the folder, subfolders, and all files contained in them; allows running programs
Change	Allows Read access; allows changing data in files, adding and deleting files; allows creating documents and subfolders
Full Control	Allows Change permissions access; allows changing permission settings on the folder

IMPORTANT: What Microsoft doesn't offer (but NetWare did) is the hidden share permission attribute as a permission selection. But have no fear. It can be re-created by appending a share name with a dollar sign. (Granted—this is a very American way to hide something and probably is culturally offensive to the international readers of this book.) To illustrate my point, a share named HARRYB$ would not be visible from the network. Hidden share questions have been known to appear on Microsoft certification exams.

IMPORTANT: Share permissions are only effective across the network. If a user logs on locally or via terminal services, share permissions will not be effective. On the other hand, Windows Server 2003 (and SBS 2003) now has all default share permissions set to READ only for the Everyone Group as shown in Figure 6-3. You should change permission settings to be more generous (in many cases) or otherwise a user will encounter a "read-only" condition when working with document. Another example is a line-of-business application. If you set up a database for sharing, users will encounter errors when trying to work with the database application.

Notes:

Figure 6-3

Default share permissions set to READ only for the Everyone Group! In prior SBS releases (SBS 2000), this was Full Control.

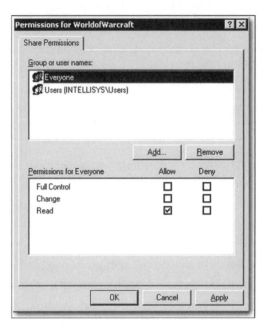

NTFS Permissions

NTFS permissions use ACLs (Access Control Lists) that are checked against the access token assigned to the user when logging into the domain. (For more information on ACLs and other related concepts like DACLs and SACLs, go to **http://msdn.microsoft.com/library/default.asp?url=/library/en-us/secauthz/ security/access_control_lists.asp**.) NTFS can be configured on files AND folders and allows for greater control than share permissions. If share and NTFS permissions are applied to the same folder, the more restrictive rule will apply. NTFS permissions are effective across the network and locally.

At a minimum, you need to memorize the following NTFS permissions: Read, Write, List Folder Contents, Read and Execute, Modify, and Full Control. Then, once you've memorized these, you should seek to understand how the core NTFS permissions are made up of a set of special permissions as shown in the following table. You might consider this "extra credit," but fully understanding Table 6-3 below can really help you in a pinch on the 70-282 exam. Suppose, for the sake of argument, things aren't going well on the exam. Perhaps you're on the borderline of failure (e.g., one wrong question away from failing), and then you get an in-depth NTFS question. Think how great you'll feel, all because you took the time to know your NTFS permissions!

Table 6-3

Deep dive into NTFS permissions

Special Permissions	Full Control	Modify	Read & Execute	List Folder Contents	Read	Write
Travers Folder/ Execute File	X	X	X	X	-	-
List Folder/ Read Data	X	X	X	X	X	-
Read Attributes	X	X	X	X	X	-
Read Extended Attributes	X	X	X	X	X	-
Create Files/ Write Data	X	X	-	-	-	X
Create Folders/ Append Data	X	X	-	-	-	X
Write Attributes	X	X	-	-	-	X
Write Extended Attributes	X	X	-	-	-	X
Delete Subfolder and Files	X	-	-	-	-	-
Delete	X	X	-	-	-	-
Read Permissions	X	X	X	X	X	X
Change Permissions	X	-	-	-	-	-
Take Ownership	X	-	-	-	-	-

Note that the Modify permission in the above table only has three less permissions than the Full permissions (see gray boxes). This is a MAJOR HINT!

IMPORTANT: An interesting question that has emerged in the SBS community concerns NTFS folders versus Windows SharePoint Services (WSS). In a sense, NTFS and WSS compete with each other because they are used to store information like files inside folders. As you seek to understand the SBS product en route to becoming certified on the 70-282 exam, you'll appreciate this cultural debate. NTFS, being based on ACLs, has a very rich set of permissions. WSS, being based on four roles, has a limited set of permissions it can apply to objects like files and folders. However, WSS has version control and alerts, something missing from NTFS. So both approaches, NTFS and WSS, have strengths and weaknesses and are present on the 70-282 exam.

Here is another test tip you'll want to memorize. NTFS permissions are either explicit or inherited. When you see a permission box grayed out on the security tab under file or folder properties, you know this is an inherited permission, whereas explicit permissions are set when you create a new folder.

Permissions and Volumes

Be aware how copying and moving files or folders on or between NTFS volumes can affect the original permissions, as seen in Table 6-4:

Table 6-4

Actions affect permissions

Action	Within NTFS volumes	Between NTFS volume
Copy	Inherits permissions of the destination folder	Inherits permissions of the destination folder
Move	Retains original permissions	Inherits permissions of the destination folder
Users who copy files or folders become owners of the new copies		

- When using both NTFS and shared permissions, the most restrictive permission will rule

- Share folders provide less security then NTFS security configured folders

- You can apply different NTFS permissions to subfolders of shared folders as well as files within them

IMPORTANT: Here's a little ditty that might help you memorize the difference between change and move actions with respect to permissions. Copy = changed permissions. Move = retained permissions. Hum that bar a few times and you'll certainly recall this factoid on the 70-282 exam. Silly!

Configuring NTFS Permissions to Files and Folders

To configure permissions on a folder, go to the folder in Windows Explorer and right-click the folder. Click **Sharing and Security** and then click on the **Security** tab in the **Properties** box. Here you can add users and groups from the SBS domain as well as set their permissions.

Configuring NTFS Permissions for Printers

Setting NTFS permissions for printers is essentially the same as for files and folders. You right-click the printer, go to **Properties,** and then select the **Security** tab. You can add users and groups here as well as set printing permissions. Table 6-5 outlines the level of access associated with print permissions.

Table 6-5

Printer permissions

	Print	Manage Documents	Manage Printers
Print	x		x
Manage Printers			x
Manage Documents		x	
Read Permissions	x	x	x
Change Permissions		x	x
Take ownership		x	x

Note that Manage Printers has all permissions but one (see gray box).

It is easy to adopt a pious attitude toward printer devices when studying for a certification exam, believing you already know all about printers. But Microsoft has historically asked printer questions on its certification exams. We believe printer questions are asked not because you'd truly be concerned about intense printer configuration questions on an SBS network, but because this testing content area is a way to fail and disqualify unworthy SBSers from obtaining a passing mark on the 70-282 exam. So, take printer matters seriously even if you believe printers are "baby simple."

> IMPORTANT: Just remember, to keep it easy and not get into a permission mess, use only NTFS permissions and assign groups instead of users to files, folders, and printer objects. The Microsoft TechNet discs, part of an annual subscription, have excellent NTFS resources down to the developer level. Visit TechNet at www.microsoft.com/technet.

Security Guidelines

If you take a look at the first step in the To Do List—the "View Security and Best Practices" task—you will find it is comprised of security best practices covering topics from protecting your server from external AND internal vulnerabilities to security issues monitoring. Want a hint? Read the To Do List!

General guidelines for securing your SBS server include:

- Keeping your antivirus application up-to-date

    - Keep the AV signatures updated as frequently as possible, as the virus epidemic has gotten out of hand.

- Using a firewall (covered later in this chapter)

- Not downloading and running programs from untrustworthy sources

    - Malicious programs resemble trustworthy software and could initiate identity theft, data destruction, and DoS attacks. Software should only be obtained from legitimate sources.

- The principle of least privilege

- A beautiful thing for administrators to use on end-users, but this should also apply to themselves. Use an account with limited permissions to handle nonadministrative tasks and use the "runas" command for administrative tasks.

- Enforce strong passwords

  - Use complexity rules and enforce a minimum of seven characters using special symbols and mixed case.

- Apply the latest software patches

  - Use Software Update Services (SUS) with Group Policy Objects (GPOs) (explained below)

- Use group accounts to manage users

  - This will be much easier than managing individual permissions.

- Do regular backups

  - Use the Small Business Server Backup Configuration Wizard or use the Automated System Recovery feature (ASR). Hang on to your hats until Chapter 8 when you'll have the opportunity to read expanded backup discussion. We even throw in a few real-world war stories for giggles.

- Restrict physical access to the domain controller

  - This is a high-level risk. Secure your server and network hardware; you never know when an employee gets disgruntled.

For more security information check out http://www.microsoft.com/security/default.mspx.

Configure Software Update Service

One of the most important steps you can take in securing your SBS 2003 network is downloading Windows updates. Patches and fixes can be downloaded as soon as they are made available. Of course, you could set each client machine to download Windows updates automatically, but that would create a lot of traffic at once. You can centralize updates by using SUS.

Working with SUS

SUS is a free download from http://www.microsoft.com/sus and provides patch, scanning, and installation services. When installing SUS, you can choose whether you want the SUS server to download the required patches from Windows update or host all patches on the SUS server. If you decide on the latter, ensure you have at least 6 GB of space on the host machine.

> IMPORTANT: For SBS 2003 Premium Edition, ISA 2000 users: For clients to update successfully, you must host updates locally or configure ISA Server not to require authentication.

Approving Updates

Before patches are rolled out to clients, they must first be approved by the SUS administrator. You can access SUS over a Web interface at http://servername/SUSAdmin, where you click on the **Approve Updates** link. Select one of the update choices and then click the **Approve** button.

History

Consider the following historical element as SBS and 70-282 wisdom. A long-time SBS development team member named Erin moved from the SBS team to the SUS team right before the release of SBS 2003. Erin was very influential and we believe her direct interest in SUS resulted in this section being placed on the 70-282 exam. While SUS is really cool, most SBSers don't use SUS, and it is not a huge part of the 70-282 exam.

Notes:

Configure ISA Server 2000 and Firewalls

When delving deep into ISA Server 2000 and the firewall discussion, step back and consider one approach used in assessment testing. Vendors love to test their stakeholders on the new delta features or the changes since the last release. That is a major paradigm that many exam writers adhere to: "...let's make sure our partners know about these new features!" So, if you agree, you'd want to approach the ISA and firewall discussion with that thinking, including it in your analytical attack strategy. How does ISA Server 2000 differ in SBS 2003 from SBS 2000 (which also contained the same ISA Server 2000 version)? Two differences we found were packet filters and attitude.

- **Packet filters.** In SBS 2000, if you drill down into the ISA Management console to the Pack Filters folder, you would see heaps of BackOffice Predefined packet filters that were created for you, including the HTTPS Port 443 filter. But in SBS 2003, at the same location in the ISA Management console, there are no BackOffice Predefined packet filters. In fact, there are significantly fewer ports open by default, which leads to our next point. By the way, can you guess why SBS 2003 Premium Edition doesn't have a Port 443 packet filter with ISA Server 2000? See the sample question at the end of this chapter to find out!

- **Attitude (get secure, stay secure).** In the SBS 2003 release time frame, Microsoft's shift to emphasizing security in its software was at full throttle! If you understand where Microsoft was coming from when it was developing the 70-282 exam and SBS 2003, that'll yield tremendous dividends when you are flat-out stuck on a security question on the 70-282 exam. If you must guess, remember that Microsoft was just starting to enter a very conservative era relating to its security practices when the 70-282 exam was created, so you'd want to answer the Microsoft way. In that case, the best answer would be the most restrictive and conservative, all things being equal.

IMPORTANT: Again, remember that the 70-282 exam was written with ISA Server 2000 in mind, not the newly released ISA Server

2004 product. So you might actually need to build a test SBS 2003 network with legacy ISA Server 2000 installed so you THINK like the 70-282 exam!

So let's dive into ISA Server 2000 and firewalls at an appropriate level for a 70-282 exam-cram book. There are many ways to configure individual settings in ISA Server 2000 and its firewalls. ISA Server 2000 controls the firewall by way of access rules, the firewall clients that use them, and policy elements. The policy elements cover bandwidth, destination sets, client address sets, schedules, protocol definitions, content groups, and dial-up entries. Policy elements allow values to be set on rule properties that are defined beyond the scope of the rule itself.

Regardless of whether you install ISA Server 2000 in firewall mode or in integrated mode, you must specify the local address table (LAT). The LAT is a table of all internal IP address ranges used by the internal network behind the ISA Server 2000. ISA Server 2000 uses the LAT to control how machines on the internal network communicate with external networks. All of these elements—the LAT, access rules, client types, and policy elements—play into configuring ISA Server 2000.

Configure Access Using NAT

Small businesses use private networking as a tool for sharing resources, such as an Internet connection. SBS 2003 has built-in NAT functionality called a "Basic Firewall" that is enabled through the Routing and Remote Access Service (RRAS) and requires two NICs to make NAT functional. The Premium Edition comes with ISA Server 2000, which uses a SecureNAT client.

How NAT Works

A user on the network requests information from the Internet. The computer will send TCP/IP or UDP datagram packets that contain information about the computer (source) to the destination server, so the destination server knows where to send back the requested information. Before the datagram packet leaves the network, the SBS server will change the outgoing packet header and change the address of the source to point to the SBS server. This way, SBS hides the real source, and by using only its own IP address, appears to be the only computer at that location. When the destination server returns the requested data packets, the SBS server receives the packet and remaps it back to the client. The server running RRAS acts as a network address translator and allows for all client commuters to share a single IP connection, shielding their true identity from the Internet.

Configuring NAT

NAT comes with both SBS 2003 Standard and Premium Edition (in Premium you would use ISA Server 2000). Even though NAT is configured by RRAS, in SBS 2003, you enable NAT by running the CEICW (Configure E-mail and Internet Connection Wizard). When configuring the CEICW, you will get to the Firewall Settings screen. By selecting the **Enable Firewall** radio button, you will enable NAT. At this point, a pop-up window will appear and advise you that it is stopping services to configure ISA Server 2000 before you continue with the CEICW.

> IMPORTANT: For NAT to create the Basic Firewall, you must have at least two NIC cards installed.

ISA Firewall Clients

Firewall clients redirect outbound Internet traffic through the firewall. ISA Server 2000 can support three firewall clients, each of which are discussed in this section:

- SecureNAT

- Web Proxy

- Firewall

ISA Server 2000 client functionality is dependent on the proper configuration of the ISA Server 2000 server machine itself. If ISA Server 2000 has difficulty resolving hostnames or reaching the Internet, so will the clients. Since ISA Server 2000 operates in conjunction with Windows 2003, the internal and external DNS server names should be provided. The proxy service is enabled on all of the ISA Server 2000 internal IPs by default at port 8080, including 127.0.0.1, the localhost IP.

SecureNAT

SecureNAT clients, which are essentially handled by the firewall service, benefit from:

- Application filters that can modify the protocol stream to allow handling of complex protocols

- Site and content rules that can be applied by way of the firewall service that passes all HTTP requests to the Web Proxy Service

Client computers that do not have firewall client software are SecureNAT (secure network address translation) clients. SecureNAT clients benefit from many features of ISA Server 2000, including most access control features, except for high-level protocol support and user-level authentication. SecureNAT clients do not require special software, but should configure the default gateway to point to ISA Server 2000.

Web Proxy

Web Proxy clients are computers that have a web browser application, which complies with HTTP1.1 and is configured to use the web proxy service of ISA Server 2000. Web browser settings on the client can be configured manually on the client or automatically by installing the firewall client and configuring the Web browser through the ISA Management console. There you can configure:

- The ISA Server 2000 and port to which the client should connect

- Automatic discovery

- Computers that the Web browser should access directly

- A backup route if the ISA Server 2000 server machine is unavailable

Firewall

Firewall clients are computers with the firewall client software installed and enabled.

Firewall clients use WinSock (Windows sockets) applications that use the ISA firewall service. When a firewall client requests an object from a computer, it uses a WinSock application and checks its copy of the LAT to see if the specified computer is in the LAT. If the computer is not found in the LAT, the request is sent on to the firewall service. The request will then be handled by the firewall service, forwarding it to the right destination if permitted.

Firewall client software can be installed on Windows ME, Windows 95, Windows 98, Windows NT 4.0, or Windows 2000. Sixteen-bit WinSock applications are supported, but only on Windows 2000 and Windows NT 4.0. Unlike SecureNAT, the firewall client service can send user information required for authentication to ISA.

Table 6-6 compares and contrasts all firewall client methods.

Table 6-6

Firewall client details

Feature	SecureNAT client	Firewall client	Web Proxy client
Installation required	Some network configuration changes are required	Yes	No, requires web browser configuration
Operating system support	Any operating system that supports Transmission Control Protocol/ Internet Protocol (TCP/IP)	Only Windows platforms	All platforms, but by way of web application
Protocol support	Requires application filters for multi-connection protocols	All WinSock applications	Hypertext Transfer Protocol (HTTP), Secure HTTP (HTTPS), File Transfer Protocol (FTP), and Gopher
User-level authentication	Some network configuration changes are required	Yes	Yes
Server applications	No configuration or installation required	Requires configuration file	N/A

IMPORTANT: A favorite test-writing technique is to invoke the compare-and-contrast method used by stern composition teachers in grammar school assigning essay homework! So make the table above your test-taking buddy and understand that a compare-and-contrast viewpoint, as expressed above specific to firewalls, is a popular exam question construct and can rear its ugly head on any 70-282 testing subject!

ISA Server 2000 Firewall Access Rules

As you will read in this section, you can configure access policies in ISA Server 2000 that consist of protocol rules and content rules.

Protocol Rules

Protocol rules define the protocols that can be used for communication between the local network and the Internet. Protocol rules are processed at the application level, allowing clients to use protocols like HTTP, HTTPS, and FTP. You can configure protocol rules to apply to all IP traffic, a specific set of protocols definitions, or to all IP traffic except for selected protocols. When clients request objects using a specific protocol, ISA Server 2000 checks the protocol rules. If there is a protocol rule specifically denying use of the protocol, the request is denied.

Site and Content Rules

Site and content rules define what content clients can be accessed on what Internet sites. Site and content rules are processed at the application level, allowing or denying clients based on the content of a web site and specific protocols used to access that web site. When clients request objects, ISA checks the site and content rules. If a site and content rule specifically denies the request, access is denied.

IMPORTANT: So how can you truly commit to memory what protocol rules and site and content rules are and how you might use them? Try this on for size. These rules prevent good girls from behaving badly (kinda sounds like an Internet web-cam site, eh?). Many faiths believe that humans are basically good, not evil. But there are temptations out there in the world that challenge the angelic behaviors of the best of us! So sometime we need a roadblock to prevent us from driving on the road to ruin. These site and content rules, when applied, can serve as that roadblock and prevent kind souls from becoming evil by visiting naughty Internet locations. Consider this akin to your buddy throwing a body block so you can't hurt yourself!

In all seriousness, one SBS site at a sheriff's department for a small county outside Denver, Colorado, uses the rules discussed in this section. Because of the nature of law enforcement work, it's essential that all employees operate and conduct their affairs in a manner above reproach. So the protocol, site, and content rules prevent employees from engaging in potentially embarrassing acts. Anything less would be criminal.

Practice Questions

Question #1

CoolBeans, Inc. is expanding their office space from 6 Windows XP Pro SP2 desktops and adding 8 new hires and Windows XP Pro SP2 workstations. The network has a single SBS 2003 server and a hardware firewall. The office is set up in an old building where you have to traverse several corners and hallways to get to the individual offices. In the past, the administrator didn't mind manually updating the workstations, but realizes that this is becoming too much work and wants to automate the Windows Update process. Client workstations need to receive their updates in a timely manner and should not receive patches that are not necessary. CoolBeans, Inc. is on a metered Internet connection and wants to use the least amount of bandwidth. How should the administrator implement this?

A. Set all client workstations to automatically download all new patches in the Security Center every night at 3 a.m. and select "download updates for me, but let me chose to install them" and then remote to the system once a week and approve the downloads.

B. Configure Automatic Updates on the SBS 2003 Server and select "notify me but don't automatically download or install them," and approve the updates once a week.

C. Install SUS on the SBS 2003 Server, set it to download the updates locally and edit the GPO for the client computers to download updates from the SBS Server.

D. Install MBSA (Microsoft Security Baseline Analyzer) and configure it to run the Security scan once a day and to automatically download required updates. Edit the GPO for the client computer to download updates from the SBS server.

Question #2

You are the administrator for a national defense contracting firm. The firm uses Windows SBS 2003 Premium. There are 15 Windows XP Professional computers in the office and 43 Windows XP Professional laptops. Your firm got a new contract and the server now contains highly sensitive data and all communications should be secured when needed. How should you configure the server? (select all that apply)

A. Assign the Server IPSec (Request Security) policy to the server

B. Assign the Secure Server IPSec (Require Security) policy to the server

C. Assign the Server IPSec (Request Security) policy to the client computers

D. Assign the Client IPSec (Respond only) policy to the client computers

E. Assign the Client IPSec (Respond only) policy to the server

Question #3

You administer an SBS server for a small travel agency in town. There are 60 Windows XP Professional computers, 3 Windows 2000

Professional machines, a color laser printer and 12 black and white laser printers. The travel agency is run by the owner, who employs several travel agents, three professional ad writers, and two marketing people. The owner doesn't want the travel agents using the color laser printer, but uses it for herself, the ad writers and marketing people. How will you configure printer permissions on the color printer?

A. Create a color printer security group. Add the owner, ad writers group and marketing group to the color printer security group. Grant the Allow Print Permissions to the color printer group and select Deny for the Everyone group.

B. Create a color printer distribution group. Add the owner, ad writers group and marketing group to the color printer distribution group. Grant the Allow Print Permissions to the color printer group and remove the Everyone group.

C. Create a color printer security group. Add the owner, ad writers group and marketing group to the color printer security group. Grant the Allow Print Permissions to the color printer group and remove the Everyone group

D. Create a color printer security group. Add the owner, ad writers group and travel agents group to the color printer security group. Grant the Allow Print Permissions to the color printer group and remove the Everyone group

Question #4

The Sinclair Group uses SBS 2003 Standard edition, and the office manager is in charge of managing the server. There are 23 Windows XP Professional computers on the network and employees are split up into different security groups. There are some folders that the office manager wants to be accessible by everyone, but only he should be able to add, remove or edit files in those folders. The office manager creates the "Company" share and wants to assign only the least required permissions. The office manager user account is in the office manager group. Which share permissions should be assigned?

A. Assign the Allow – Full Control permission to the Office Manager group for the Company share. Assign the Allow – Read permission to the Everyone group for the Company share.

B. Assign the Allow – Change permission to the Office Manager group for the Company share. Assign Allow – Read permission to the Everyone group for the Company share.

C. Assign the Allow – Full Control permission to the Office Manager group for the Company share. Assign the Allow Read & Execute permission for the Company share.

D. Assign the Allow – Change permission to the Office Manager group for the Company share. Assign the Allow – Read & Execute permission to the Everyone group for the Company share.

Question #5

You manage an SBS 2003 server for a small medical office. Due to government regulations that need to be complied with, you are now asked to install ISA Server 2000. The medical office is running a custom application that allows access to a special medical database over the Internet. This custom application uses port 4008 (TCP) to communicate. You install ISA Server 2000 and lose the ability to communicate with the remote database server. What should you do? (select all that apply)

A. Create a port proxy rule for access though port 4008

B. Create a protocol rule for access through port 4008

C. Create a port protocol definition

D. Create a port proxy forwarding definition

E. Create an IPSec policy for the custom application

Question #6

You manage a network consisting of a SBS 2003 server and 43 Windows XP Professional client computers. You check the security log in the event viewer and see several endless denied log on requests on a valid user account. This appears to be the work of a malicious intruder, attempting to gain access to the network. The user account "lsmith" belongs to Linda who should never be prevented from logging on to the network, even after you implement new security measures. You want to accomplish this with the least amount of administrative effort on your part. What should you do?

A. Set the Account Lockout Policy to 5 failed logons

B. Delete Linda's user account and create a new user account for her

C. Rename Linda's user account to "l_sm1tH"

D. Disable Linda's user account and have her use your account until the failed attempts stop.

Question #7

You are the administrator of a small law firm. The firm has an SBS 2003 Server and 12 Windows XP Professional laptops. There are 15 Windows XP workstations used by paralegal staff. Several attorneys travel nationwide for high-profile cases and are out of the office for weeks at a time. The owner of the firm does not allow the use of Remote Web Workplace. Attorneys need to have secure access to data on the server. You ran the Remote Access Configuration wizard, but attorneys with their hectic schedule don't want to be bothered with client VPN installation instructions. You have enabled Outlook Web Access and RPC over HTTP. The attorneys need to have access ASAP. What will be the easiest way with the least amount of effort for the users to install the VPN connection?

A. Run the Assign Applications wizard and assign the VPN client to the laptops. Next time when users are in the office, the client will automatically be pushed out.

B. Run the Create Remote Connection Disk in Server Management. Copy the file to a zip file and e-mail it to the attorneys

C. Run the Create Remote Connection Disk and overnight the floppy to the attorneys

D. Create a GPO that will assign the VPN client automatically next time an attorney connects their laptop in the office.

Question #8

You are the consultant at a non-profit research group. The non-profit has nine Windows XP Professional computers in a peer-to-peer configuration and will be adding four additional computers. Staff usually spends numerous hours on the Internet conducting research. They have a dial-up connection. Security is not a concern as much as being able to retrieve Internet research pages as fast as possible. Their budget was not approved for a faster Internet connection, but was approved for SBS 2003 Premium Edition and several hours of your consulting service. What would benefit the non-profit most?

A. Join the computer to the domain, install ISA 2000 in firewall mode on the SBS 2003 Premium Server, and install the firewall client on the server and the client workstations.

B. Join the client computers to the domain and install ISA 2000 in caching mode and increase the HTTP caching TTL on the SBS Premium Server.

C. Join the client computers to the domain and install ISA 2000 in caching mode on the SBS 2003 Premium Server and install the caching client on all client computers.

D. Join the clients to the domain, copy the ISA 2000 CD into a shared folder in clientapps\ and run the Assign Applications wizard.

Question #9

Your company has one SBS 2003 server, 17 Windows XP Pro SP2 client workstations, and 11 laptops with Windows XP Pro SP2. The laptop users bring their laptops to office meetings at least twice a month. You have configured SUS for Windows Updates and want to ensure that users do not download updates themselves; you especially want to prevent the laptop users from downloading and installing security updates that are not tested and approved. You decide to use Group Policy to ensure this policy. Where do you configure these settings?

A. Open the User configuration\Administrative Templates\Windows Components\Windows Update and enter the URL of the SUS server under **Specify intranet Microsoft update service location**

B. Open the Computer Configuration\Administrative Templates\Windows Components\Windows Update and enter the URL of the SUS server under **Specify intranet Microsoft update service location**

C. Open the User configuration\Administrative Templates\Windows Components\Windows Update and select and enable **Configure Automatic Updates** with automatic updating set to 5.

D. Open the Computer Configuration\Administrative Templates\Windows Components\Windows Update and select and enable **Configure Automatic Updates** with automatic updating set to 5.

Question #10

Realty Inc. has SBS 2003 that is being used for faxing, e-mail, printing, file server and has the real estate LOB application installed on it. There are 40 agents in the office who use Outlook 2003 and 30 agents who remote in with their laptops. Most of those agents use Outlook Express for e-mail, but some use Outlook Mobile Access on their SmartPhones. Users have also been told that they can access Outlook Web Access by typing http://www.realtyinc.com/exchange in any browser. You just purchased a new hardware firewall and must ensure security but more importantly, that e-mail workflow will not be interrupted. What ports should be opened on the firewall? (select all that apply)

A. 80

B. 25

C. 110

D. 443

E. 4125

Answer Key

Question #1: Answer C

Installing and configuring SUS to download locally will require only one download to service all client computers. You can edit a GPO to force the clients to update from the local source instead of the Windows update site. That would be the most efficient solution. Answer A. would have client workstations do individual downloads taking up more bandwidth, and remoting into the client would create more work for the administrator. Answer B. would only download updates to the server and not the clients. Answer D. The MBSA can be used in conjunction with SUS, but cannot be set to download updates automatically on a schedule.

Question #2: Answer B, D

The Secure Server IPSec (Require Security) policy ensures that communication with the server is protected. The client IPSec (Respond only) policy is a good choice for computers that do not need secure communications the entire time. With this policy applied, the client will only use secure communications if another computer requests it. Answer A. This would allow unsecured communication if the client computer does not have IPSec enabled. Answer C. Assigning this policy to the clients would make the client request secure communications and not the server. Answer E. This is only for computers to respond to requests for secure communications. We want to ensure that the server only uses secure communication, and this answer would not achieve the objective.

Question #3: Answer C

You should create a color printer group and add all groups that should have print permissions for the color printer. You must assign print permissions to the color printer group and remove the Everyone group, which has printer permissions by default. This way the rest of the travel agency employees will not be able to print to this printer. Answer A. would not work because when you set Deny permissions for the Everyone group, that will deny everyone from printing to this printer, including the color printer security group since a deny will overwrite everything else. Answer B. Distribution groups cannot be assigned permissions, they are merely for e-mail purpose. Answer D. This solution will also allow the travel agents to print to the printer and would not meet the objective.

Question #4: Answer B

There are two types of permissions: share and NTFS permissions. The share permissions are Read, Change and Full Control. Since we only want to use the principle of least permissions, the office manager should have change permissions and not full control permissions. The Read permission allows limited access, to view files and folders in the share, but will not allow adding, deleting or modifying folders. Answer A. This gives Full Control to the office manager and would not follow the principle of least amount of permissions. Answer C and D. Read & Execute is a NTFS permission and not available under the share options.

Question #5: Answer B, C

In ISA Server 2000 you should first create a protocol definition for the protocol and then create the protocol rule that will allow the custom protocol port to be used. Answer A and D. There is no such thing as a port proxy rule or definition in ISA. Answer E. Creating an IPSec policy will not open ports.

Question #6: Answer C

You should rename her user account to make it harder on the person attempting to access her account. Answer A. If you set the account to lock out, this will lock out Linda as well. Answer B. Creating a new user account will require migrating her profile settings and creating additional administrative effort and she would not keep the exact settings that she has now. Answer D. Disabling the account will not allow Linda to have access to the network.

Question #7: Answer C

Running the Create Remote Connection Disk wizard will create a floppy disk that will just have to be inserted and the executable sbspackage.exe launched. This will be the easiest way for attorneys to set up the VPN client. Answer A. You cannot only assign applications with the Assign Applications wizard; it will not configure the VPN client. Answer B. This would require the user to unzip the file and save it to a folder in the laptop. Way too many steps! Answer D. You would have to create a script and place it in the GPO, which is too much administrative effort on your part, plus, the client needs access ASAP.

Question #8: Answer B

Install ISA 2000 Server in Cache mode to facilitate accelerated Internet browsing. This way, the server will cache recently accessed Internet sites and if several users request the same site or page, will be served up from cache instead of having to request the data across the Internet. Increasing the HTTP TTL (total time to live) will allow you to keep cached information longer in Cache. Answer A. Do not install the firewall client on the ISA 2000 Server. Ever. Answer C. There is no such thing as a caching client. Answer D. This is a server product designed to be installed on a server operating system and not to be pushed out to clients.

Question #9: Answer B

To set the client computer, you must go to Computer Configuration/ Administrative Templates/Windows Components/Windows Update/ Specify intranet Microsoft update server. There you specify an intranet server to host updates from the Microsoft Update web sites. You can then use this update service to automatically update computers on your network. This will allow you to test updates first and then approve them on the SUS server. Laptop users will only be able to get updates when they are connected to the SUS server. Answer A and C. There is no setting for SUS under User configuration. Answer D. This selection would allow the local admin to choose the configuration modes and would not achieve the objective.

Question #10: Answer B, C, D

Port 25 is SMTP and needed to send e-mail. Port 110 POP3 is needed for the Outlook Express clients to download their e-mail. Port 443 HTTPS is needed for Outlook Web Access and Outlook Mobile Access. Answer A. Port 80 is not called for in this scenario, which would be for browsing the internet. Answer E. Port 4125 is for Remote Web Workplace, which is also not called for.

Summary

This chapter should not be taken lightly! Obviously, you were presented with appropriate 70-282 exam discussion that focused on security in the context of permissions, ISA Server 2000, and firewalls. Equally important, we pulled the drapes back on several occasions to allow you to "think" like Microsoft about security in the SBS 2003 world. If you somehow missed that, stop and reread this chapter prior to proceeding to Chapter 7 (or going out for a beer or café latté!). This topic area is also one on which you should conduct some outside research before you take the 70-282 exam; several other books focus strictly on some of the security technologies (but without our 70-282 test-taking thinking). So consider this: Your journey toward understanding security in the world of computing and SBS 2003 has now gotten off to a good start, but it is by no means over!

Authors Harry and Beatrice sign books at the HP booth during the Microsoft Worldwide Partner Conference 2005

CHAPTER 7
Configuring Windows Small Business Server 2003

Congratulations! You have just been given the Key to Life. Other administrators have to spend their entire weekend configuring remote access, e-mail, and Web services, adding users, setting permission, creating security groups, and contending with other odds and ends, while the SBS consultant can accomplish the same tasks with the same outcome and still have time to spend the weekend with the kids. And that is the Key to Life! I have gotten so comfortable doing SBS installs that I schedule some installs during the week after working hours, knowing that I can still get home at a decent time and long before daybreak.

Create and Configure User Groups and Group Policies

Configuring user groups? Now that is a trick question in SBS, because many groups have already been preconfigured for you! And based on what user template you use, permissions will then be assigned based on the template settings. But, more on templates in a bit; let's take a closer look at the groups at hand. First of all, there are two user group *types*:

- Distribution groups

- Security groups

Distribution groups facilitate communication by making it easy for you to reach all the recipients in a specific group using only one e-mail address—say, for example, everyone in the accounting department could be reached via a distribution group titled ACCOUNTING (Humor Zone: Kindly ignore the fact that this isn't the type of group you would want to spend a rollicking New Year's Eve with as accountants are known for being somber). Distribution groups can include mail-enabled contacts, which are user accounts created to be available in the contacts list and receive e-mail at an external mail account. Mail-enabled users are not domain members, like a vendor with whom your company works. They should be included in all e-mail communications with a particular department or group and show up in your GAL (Global Address List)

> IMPORTANT: You can set up mail-enabled contacts with or without an Exchange mailbox. A mail-enabled contact is usually a member in a distribution group and cannot log on to the domain.

Security groups are exactly what their name states: a group that has certain rights and permissions assigned to them that dictate how different objects on the domain can be manipulated. Creating a user group and then placing the user accounts into the security group streamlines the administrative burden and simplifies user management. Even in a small business environment where you may only have five user accounts, it is good practice to use security groups instead of assigning user accounts individually to resources. (More on this embedded security stuff in a moment under the Group Scopes section.) When creating new groups in SBS, you should always use the **Server Management Console** and use the **Distribution Group** and **Security Group** links.

To simplify administration even more, you can employ Group Policy management to manage security groups. Group Policy Objects are covered later in Chapter 8.

> IMPORTANT: Security groups may have an e-mail address (technically a Simple Mail Transfer Protocol (SMTP) e-mail address). The members of the security group would receive the e-mail that is sent to said security group (sounds a lot like a distribution group, eh?). So sometimes, a security group can act like a bucket that holds permissions plus assume the behavior of a distribution group.

Creating and Configuring Domain Groups

You can create and configure domain groups through the use of two links of the Server Standard Management console, the **Security Group** and **Distribution Group** link. There is no need to venture into Active Directory Users and Groups; again, wizards are available to make this an effortless experience.

What should be pointed out here is that the SBS Security and Distribution Groups are located in Active Directory under yourdomainname.com, **MyBusiness** organizational unit **(OU)**, **Distribution OU**, and **Security OU**. It is important that you use the Standard Management console links to create your new Security or Distribution groups, because the newly created accounts will be placed into the proper OU in Active Directory this way.

Group Scopes

This is where the fun starts—that is, at the evil enterprise-level (pardon the SBS humor about our big league brothers and sisters). But even though we are in a single domain and shouldn't have to worry about the intermingling of group scopes, I still need to shed some light on those. There are three different types of group scopes:

- Domain local

- Global

- Universal

The **Domain local** group can be used for assigning permissions within the local domain only. A domain local group can contain user accounts and global and universal groups from any domain and other domain local groups from the same domain. A domain local group can be changed to a universal group only if it does not have other domain local groups as its members.

Global groups can contain accounts and other global groups from the same domain in Windows Server 2003 server and Windows 2000 server in native mode. The global group can be used for assigning permissions throughout the entire forest. A global group can only contain user accounts and global groups from the same domain the global group is in. A global group can be changed to a universal group if it is not a member of another global group.

A **Universal** group in Windows 2003 server and Windows 2000 server in native mode can be used for assigning permissions throughout the entire forest. A universal group can contain user accounts, computer accounts, and global and universal groups from any domain in the forest. Opposite to domain local and global groups, universal groups are replicated to every global catalog in the entire forest. A universal group can be changed to a domain local group at any time. A universal group can be changed to a global group only if it does not have other universal groups as its members.

Okay, enough forestry for now. Let's look at how this affects SBS. Since SBS uses a single domain model, we don't need to worry about universal groups and domain functional levels, unless you are adding a second domain controller (DC) to the domain that is running Windows Server 2000, which should then be raised to native mode.

All security groups in SBS have universal group membership by default when they are created, which means they can be placed into any domain local group. In reality, we only need domain local groups and global groups, because we will never be replicating to another domain.

Group Strategies

There is only one acronym that comes to mind—AGDLP—that is the user and group management strategy model recommended for single domains. Let me explain this more in detail:

- Put user accounts (A) into global groups (G)

- Put global groups (G) into domain local groups (DL)

- Grant permissions (P) to the domain local group (DL)

All right, I know this looks somewhat confusing at first, so let me elaborate. Say you have a client site with 40 users, 10 of them work in a call-center processing orders over the phone, 5 are in charge of creating marketing material, and the other 25 are down in the warehouse packing and shipping orders. All employees must have access to the order/processing application and be able to print reports. There are several printers in the business, two high-speed color laser printers, two black-and-white laser printers, and the rest are older inkjet printers.

The owners want only the marketing team to use the high-speed color printers. The call-center is to use the black-and-white laser printers and the shop floor is to use the older printers.

In this case, you should create three separate security groups, and call them **Marketing**, **CallCenter,** and **ShopDudes**.

1. On the high-speed color laser printer, select **Properties,** then **Security.** Add the **Marketing** security group and assign them **Print and Manage Printers** and **Manage Documents** permission.

2. Remove the **Everyone** group from the group names dialog box.

3. Follow the same procedure for the black-and-white laser printer, adding the **CallCenter** group and removing the **Everyone** group.

4. Follow the same procedure for the older printers on the shop floor, adding the **ShopDudes** group and removing the **Everyone** group.

5. For the order/processing application, create an **OrderProcessingGroup,** then add all three **Marketing, CallCenter,** and **ShopDudes** groups into this group. Configure the NTFS permission on the folder where the application is housed for access by the **OrderProcessingGroup**.

Now you have ensured that everyone can print only to those printers they should have access to and all have access permission to the order/processing application. You may think creating the security groups is a lot of work. However, you just organized the permission structure in a way where you have only to place people in one group and they will automatically get all appropriate permissions assigned. Then when someone switches departments, leaves the company, or comes on board, you just have to add their user account to the appropriate security group, instead of assigning the user account to each individual resource, which will make life as an administrator just that much easier.

> IMPORTANT: Having a simple acronym such as "AGDLP" committed to memory will help you recall a complex study topic during the heat of the battle when taking the 70-282 exam. It's a time-tested trick for passing exams.

Using the Group Policy Management Console

With Windows Server 2003 and Windows XP, the list of Group Policy settings just keeps growing. If you make one wrong turn in configuring Group Policy and policies conflict—even on a single domain like SBS—you could have the entire office sending you death threats. So don't leave your lunch out in the open.

Now there is an easy way to figure out how policy settings affect client computers with the Group Policy Management Console (GPMC), which can be installed on a Windows Server 2003, a Windows XP SP1, or a later machine. Even though you can manage a Windows Server 2000 with the GPMC, you cannot install it on one. For information on using the GPMC, see "Using the Group Policy Management Console" in Chapter 8.

Configure Windows SBS 2003 for Networking and Remote Connectivity

Configuring a server for secure remote access sounds like a gargantuan task—and it could be if it were not for the smart wizards included in SBS.

Using the To Do List

What would SBS be without the To Do List? The To Do List, first shown to you in Chapter 5 as Figure 5-1, is the epitome of simplicity and I like it! The first thing that will pop up on the server after a new installation will be the To Do List. Basically this list is a collection of tasks to be performed to finalize the SBS setup. Funny enough, the To Do List has checkboxes so you can mark what "To Do" tasks you have already performed. I always use the checkboxes when I am at the client site setting up a server, as there are always interruptions. Checking off the tasks completed means I have one less thing to remember when I come back to the server.

Connecting to the Internet

And who is the baddest wizard of all? Of course, the CEICW (Configure E-mail and Internet Connection Wizard). Speaking of the power of wizards, at one time I spoke to another technician who told me that he could just not get OMA (Outlook Mobile Access) to work on a recently installed SBS machine. He had checked all white papers, the Exchange chat room, TechNet, and other resources and had edited and tested and spent hours, all to no avail. I asked him whether he had enabled the OMA checkbox in the CEICW, which he couldn't remember whether he did or not. So he called back to the office and had someone go through the CEICW just to find the OMA checkbox, which was not checked. Needless to say, about ten minutes later, the tech was able to receive his e-mails on the PocketPC. That is the power of CEICW.

So the first thing to do to keep the rowdy office crowd in check is to establish an Internet connection. You do this by way of the CEICW, which configures the following four components:

- Networking

- Firewall

- Secure Web Site

- E-mail

At any time you need to reconfigure a setting, you can rerun the CEICW to make changes. Settings that shouldn't be changed can be bypassed, and there is no need to reboot the server after making configuration changes.

Networking

First you will be asked to choose your connection type, which could be:

- **Direct Broadband connection**—Requires a DSL or cable modem that does not have an IP assigned to the modem. Requires two NICs on the server.

- **Local Router**—Requires a router, typically hardware-based (not another computer) with an IP address assigned by the ISP. Can be configured with one or two NICs on the server. This is Microsoft's support for having SBS 2003 use a single NIC and using a hardware-based firewall to provide Internet security and firewall protection.

IMPORTANT: So the cat is out of the bag here. Microsoft indeed supports hardware-based firewalls in the SBS 2003 product. It's not readily emphasized in the Microsoft marketing messaging because Microsoft would rather have you use two NIC cards with its built-in SBS 2003 firewall components. So for 70-282 exam purposes, it's important to honor the local router selection, but not dwell on it.

- **Broadband connection requiring a username and password**—Also called PPoE, requires authentication information and uses a DSL or cable modem which does not have an IP assigned to the actual modem. Requires two NICs on the server.

Make sure you have the IP address information from your ISP ready when starting the CEICW. Depending on your Internet connection device, you will be prompted to fill out information on the IP address, subnet mask and preferred domain name system (DNS) servers before you can continue on to configure the firewall.

SBS has support for UPnP routers and the CEICW will configure the ports for you upon detection. This is very cool and a new feature in the SBS 2003 time frame. UPnP routers do not require user name and password authentication on the LAN port and that allows the CEICW to open the ports you have elected to open as part of the wizard process.

Firewall

In the Standard Edition of SBS, the CEICW will configure a stateful firewall that monitors all communication transactions and, therefore, provides a security system preventing unauthorized access. This will be done by using Routing and Remote Access Service (RRAS) under the hood and configuring NAT if you have two NICs on the server. If you do not have two NICs, make sure to use a hardware firewall device or you will be completely vulnerable on the Internet.

In the Premium Edition of SBS, you are using ISA Server 2000. The CEICW will configure ISA for you at this point. A warning message will appear stating that services are being stopped and then restarted in order to configure ISA Server 2000.

Here are some examples of commonly used ports that can be configured:

Service	Port
SMTP	25/TCP
POP3	110/TCP
VPN	1723/TCP
Terminal Services	3389/TCP
FTP	20/TCP & 21/TCP
TelNet	23/TCP
HTTP	80/TCP
HTTPS	443/TCP

Secure Web Site

The CEICW can also configure Secure Web Site services allowing or denying access to users coming from the Internet through the firewall. Secure Web Site services include:

- Outlook Web Access (OWA)

- Remote Web Workplace (RWW)

- Performance and Usage reports

- Outlook Mobile Access (OMA)

- Windows SharePoint Services (WSS)

You could also choose to allow access to the entire web site from the Internet, which exposes the entire default web site on the Internet, including all services listed above as well as any additional web sites you created in the default web site.

The CEICW can create a Web Server Certificate for the services that require Secure Sockets Layer (SSL) to communicate. This is effectively having SBS 2003 create a self-signed certificate for SSL communication. Small business customers can reduce the cost of deploying SBS using the self-signed certificate option because the customer does not need to buy a certificate from a public certification authority (CA). You could also choose to use a certificate signed by a CA and browse to the location of the certificate file. Verisign is one such third-party CA provider.

> IMPORTANT: The self-signed security certificate discussion is new for many SBSers as it's a new capability in SBS 2003. And if Microsoft is pretty proud of this capability, don't you think it's a distinct possibility it could appear on the 70-282 exam? You bet.

E-mail

If you installed Exchange on your server, the CEICW can configure the SMTP connector required for Exchange and specify how to send and receive e-mail. Here you would choose the DNS delivery method, either **Use DNS to send e-mail** or **Forward all e-mail to an ISP**.

If you use POP3 mail at the ISP, you can configure the POP3 connector to route the e-mail to individual mailboxes and select:

- **E-mail from the Internet is delivered directly to my server**

- **E-mail from the Internet is held at my ISP until my server sends a signal**

If you choose the latter—holding the messages at the ISP—you have to decide to either use **TURN after Authentication** (requires user name and password) or **ETRN** (requires a static IP). You still have to have Exchange installed for the POP3 connector to work, and this gives you the added benefit of using all the Exchange features and being able to access your e-mail via OWA or through RWW.

I eventually move clients who come off a peer-to-peer network with POP3 accounts over to use the Exchange server only. It looks much more professional to have your own domain name than an e-mail address like Joe@somebigISPname.com

There Is More

The CEICW also configures DNS settings for the server, allows you to strip e-mail attachments based on the file extension, and sets up OWA and Outlook over the Internet (RPC over HTTP) if you select to do so.

If you had to configure all these services manually, you would spend a couple of hours doing so. With the CEICW you are done in less than five minutes. Like I said, it's the baddest wizard of all.

Configuring Remote Access

Another favorite of mine is the Remote Access Wizard. I call it the "three-click wizard" even though it really takes five clicks, but who's counting? The Remote Access Wizard configures:

- Dial-in access

- Virtual Private Network (VPN) connectivity

Dial-in access requires a modem and phone line and is seldom used anymore in my neighborhood. But many International readers continue to use dial-in access so it's a topic that can appear on the 70-282 exam.

VPN allows access through a secure Internet connection. To take advantage of the Download Connection Manager (available in RWW), you must configure the server name for the VPN using the FQDN (fully qualified domain name). This way, users can just connect to RWW and click on the Download Connection Manager link, installing a shortcut icon on their desktop from which they can launch the VPN connection. Voila! No more client-side configuration needed.

There are five PPTP ports configured for VPN and you could also enable support for L2TP/IPsec, which would require manual configuration steps in RRAS. If you find that you are in need of more than five VPN ports, you can add additional ports in RRAS by selecting the PORTS node. Go to **Properties,** click on **WAN Miniport (PPTP)**, and then click on **Configure** and increase the amount in the **Maximum ports** box.

Configure Faxing

And would you believe it, despite all Internet e-mail and scanning capabilities, faxing remains a core business service to this day, especially in worldwide markets. The fax module in SBS is a robust one and the best part about it is that you have so many choices of where to receive the faxes.

Options on Inbound Fax Routing include:

- **Route through e-mail**—You have the option to route faxes to a single e-mail address or distribution list by simply typing someone@some-where.com

- **Store in a folder**—Simply browse or type in a shared folder location on the network

- **Store in a document library**—This routes the fax to a document library in WSS. By default, the document library is located at http://servername/companyweb/faxes

- **Print**—Print faxes to any network attached printer

IMPORTANT: A really cool new feature in SBS 2003 is the ability to store faxes in WSS. And because it's new and groovy, it's likely to appear on a product-based exam such as 70-282.

Adding Users and Computers

Another goody on the To Do List is the Add User Wizard. Here you walk step by step through setting up users. Not only can you set up one, but you have the option to bulk-add users, which makes setting up a new server—one with, say, 20 clients—very easy.

The Add User Wizard will create a

- Mailbox

- Home folder

- Group membership

- Access to SharePoint services

- Computer account

All this will be based on the User Template you choose, which contains group membership, address information, disk quotas, and the level of server access. Once you have chosen the user template, you will have the option to add the computer account to the domain as well. You can bulk add the client machines or just add one, and then select the applications you would like to deploy to the client machines.

By default, the Client Operating System Service Packs, Internet Explorer 6.0, Microsoft Office Outlook SP1, and the Shared Fax Client are selected. You are able to add/remove and edit applications through the Add User Wizard as well, which makes it a snap to set up user accounts and their corresponding client computers and required software.

User Templates

I can't imagine things getting any easier than this. SBS comes with four preconfigured user templates that determine the user rights and permissions. Just in case they do not work for you, they can be easily modified or you can create a new user template by using the User Template Wizard to fit your organization's needs. But let's take a look at the four basic templates first:

- **User Template**—Allows access to network printers, shared folders, fax devices, and e-mail

- **Mobile User Template**—Has all the permissions from the user template, plus can connect to the server over dial-up or VPN connections

- **Power User Template**—Has all the permissions from the mobile template, plus can manage users, groups, printers, shared folders, and faxes. Power users can log on remotely to the server, but cannot log on locally

- **Administrator Template**—Well, guess what, this one has unrestricted access to the server and the domain.

User templates can be migrated by using the Export Templates link and then imported at another site with the Import Template Wizard.

Users should be managed with the Change User Permission Wizard, which changes permissions by assigning a new user template to a user. When assigning permissions with this wizard, you remove all previously assigned permissions from the user account and grant the new permission settings, which encompass changes to the security group membership, distribution group membership, access to WSS, and disk quotas. (User templates were covered extensively in the first part of Chapter 6.)

> IMPORTANT: Only a domain administrator can create and modify existing User Templates. However, when creating user accounts, you can assign Power Users the right to create a custom template.

Activate the Server and Add Licenses

As you are cruising through the To Do List, you will encounter the Activate License Wizard. This wizard enables you to activate the SBS client access licenses (CALs) online. During the activation process, the product key is combined with a coded number to create the Installation ID. This ID represents the hardware components in your computer. Once activated, you cannot use the key to activate other computers.

Internet Activation

The SBS 2003 server can be activated over the Internet, where a confirmation ID is sent back to your computer, or you can call Microsoft and activate over the phone. There is a 30-day grace period; once it expires, however, you will no longer have access to core functionality of the server until it is activated.

CAL Types

Every device or user that connects to the server requires a CAL. CALs can be added as per-user or per-device CALs. The first five CALs are generic and can be either/or. When you select the per-user option, every user will need a CAL to access the server.

Notes:

IMPORTANT: Here is a trick for understanding SBS 2003 CAL types: These CAL types are exactly the same as the underlying Windows Server 2003 licensing! This is the first SBS release where the underlying licensing is exactly the same. It's true and it's money in the bank when you take the 70-282 exam and encounter a question on CAL types.

Add License Wizard

You can use the Add License Wizard to add or reactivate CALs either over the Internet or over the phone. CALs can be purchased in 5 and 20 packs and then be activated over the Internet using the Add License Wizard.

Transfer License Wizard

With the Transfer License Wizard, you can reactivate CALs after you've made significant changes to system hardware or reinstalled the server software on another computer. You will have to telephone Microsoft to get the license reactivated. The Transfer License Wizard cannot be used to transfer ownership of CALs, as resale is not permitted per license agreement.

License Backup/Restore

You can back up your CALs with the License Backup Wizard and, in case the license files get corrupted or lost, you will be able to easily recover the licenses with the License Restore Wizard.

IMPORTANT: Licensing is an exceedingly popular topic during the worldwide one-day SMB Nation Summit workshops. Here are two free resources for you to improve your understanding of SBS 2003 licensing for both the real world and the 70-282 preparation:

- Chapter 3 in *Advanced Windows Small Business Server 2003 Best Practices*. The good news is that this is the free chapter and can be downloaded from www.smbnation.com.

- Microsoft's SBS licensing page: http://www.microsoft.com/ windowsserver2003/sbs/howtobuy/CALs.mspx.

Configure DHCP and IP Addressing

SBS 2003 automatically installs the DHCP (Dynamic Host Configuration Protocol) server service during setup at mid-point when a screen titled **Windows Components** is displayed. DHCP simplifies the administration of IP address assignments to client computers on the local network. If an existing DHCP service is detected, you are prompted to choose whether you want to use the existing service (say on your hardware-based router) or disable the service and use the DHCP Server service provided with SBS. It is recommended that you disable the existing DHCP service (again—on your hardware-based router as an example) and utilize the DHCP service in SBS. This way you ensure that the DHCP settings for your local network are properly configured. During setup, if you leave the default settings in the SBS Setup Wizard, SBS creates an IP Address scope of 192.168.16.1 to 192.168.16.254. Addresses from 192.168.16.1 to 192.168.16.9 are excluded from DHCP assignment.

> IMPORTANT: The default private IP address range is 192.168.16.x in SBS 2003. However, you could utilize another private IP address range such as 10.0.0.x without any major drama on your SBS 2003 network. You would make this type of private IP address range decision when you encounter the Local Network Adapter Configuration screen (technically Step 29) during the SBS 2003 setup process. It is important for 70-282 testing purposes to understand that different private address ranges are allowed.
>
> Old-timers will remember that the 10.0.0.x was the default private IP address range in the SBS 4.x era that lasted up until February 2001, when SBS 2000 was released and 192.168.16.x become the new default private IP address range and has been ever since!

To view the DHCP scope:

1. Go to **Start**.

2. Click **Run**.

3. Type **dhcpmgmt.msc** and hit **Enter**.

Configuring an Existing DHCP Service or Firewall Device

Time to get manual, baby! If you have an existing device on the local network that assigns IP addresses to client computers using DHCP, it must be configured with the necessary settings for your local network. If the device supports Universal Plug and Play (UPnP), Setup will prompt you to configure the device automatically. If the device is not a UPnP device, you will have to configure it manually. In this case, settings have to be configured as follows:

Default Gateway

1. If the SBS 2003 Server has two NICs, enter the internal NIC IP address as the default gateway.

IMPORTANT: Now is as good a time as any to slip in this SBS DHCP factoid! This is fair game on the 70-282 exam, so please read and heed. The external NIC card on an SBS server machine in a two NIC card scenario may receive its external address from an external source. Whoa—slow down, pardner, and repeat please.

Try this on for size. Imagine your ISP is a cable company in the good old US of A. In that situation, the cable company would most likely want to dynamically assign your external NIC card an IP address. This is allowed in SBS 2003, the details of which are provided in Chapter 4 of the *Windows Small Business Server 2003 Best Practices* book (SMB Nation Press).

2. If the SBS 2003 Server has one NIC and you are using the router device to connect to the Internet, use the IP address of the router's internal interface as the default gateway.

Domain Name Server

DNS provides clients with name resolution services for the local network, so you must use the IP address of the internal NIC of the SBS server.

DNS Domain Name

DNS Domain Name provides client computers with the fully qualified domain name. Therefore, you must enter the full DNS name of your local network like DomainName.local, if you used the default DNS for the internal domain.

Windows Internet Naming Service (WINS)

WINS provides local network name resolution for computers running NT 4.0 and Windows 98 and earlier. Specify the IP address of the SBS server in the WINS server option of the DHCPserver/router device.

WINS node type

If the DHCP server/router device has an option to set the WINS server, specify the node type as hybrid or h-node (0x8) to prevent unnecessary broadcast traffic.

Using the DHCP Server service provided with SBS ensures your DHCP settings are properly configured for your server. However, do not disable the existing DHCP server until after Setup prompts you to do so. Otherwise, Setup will not be able to determine the IP address range currently used by your local network.

Configure the Domain Naming Service

The DNS server included in Windows Server 2003 provides name resolution for TCP/IP-based networks. SBS configures DNS automatically during setup to listen to the local network only. The DNS server is not bound to the external NIC, and in the CEICW you will configure it to use forwarders and Preferred DNS servers, which are your ISP's DNS servers. This way you effectively shield your network and enable the use of private IP addresses. The DNS server information is given to the clients via DHCP. When a client requests an external Web address, the request first goes to the SBS DNS server; if the request can not be resolved, it gets forwarded to the preferred DNS server at your ISP, which will either resolve the query or forward it on to the next DNS server up the line.

By default, DNS is an Active-Directory Integrated-Zone and there should be no additional configurations required unless you decide to, say, host your own Internet-accessible DNS server, which is not recommended. To Access the DNS management console and view settings, on the run command type **dnsmgmt.msc** or go to **Administrative Tools, DNS**.

> IMPORTANT: Across the pages of this book, there are passing comments about the merits of having an additional server on an SBS 2003 network (to support a line-of-business application, support mobile workers with Terminal Services, have a second domain controller).
>
> But if you add a second server machine running SBS 2003 as a domain controller, DO NOT add the DNS server service on this second domain controller. It causes "confusion" and is not recommended by Microsoft Product Support Services (PSS). Don't believe that? One of the authors did indeed install a second domain controller with the DNS server service on the SBS 2003 network and things got all screwed up. So that'll help you answer any test questions correctly on that topic, eh? And who was that brilliant author who made this faux pas? You'll just have to guess!

Configure Terminal Services

In SBS, Terminal Services is available only in remote administration mode and enabled by default for access by two administrators for server administration purpose only. This occurs when the Windows Component screen is displayed during SBS setup (Step 29).

Any member of the Administrators group with access to the Terminal Service's administrative utilities can remotely manage all aspects of the SBS server. However, a user created with the Power User Template may log on remotely via Terminal Services to the SBS 2003 server machine (say from a remote location like a hotel room) and perform administration tasks ONLY from the Server Management console. This "power user" can not access other parts of the server machine interface and is not allowed to log on locally to the server machine (at the server machine console back at work).

> IMPORTANT: The above paragraph offers a great opportunity to discuss specificity and attention to detail. Did you notice the very detailed differences in Terminal Services usage for a user created with the Administrator Template versus the Power User Template? And that the user created with the Power User Template can only log on to the server machine remotely? These are fine points, and your ability to think at this granular level will have a direct bearing on your success on the 70-282 exam. Passing a certification exam isn't so much about the 50,000-foot CEO vision thing. It's more about the down-and-dirty day-to-day thing! DETAILS…DETAILS…DETAILS!

For more information on Terminal Services, see the section "Configure and Troubleshoot Terminal Services" in Chapter 8.

> IMPORTANT: You cannot convert Terminal Services to Application Sharing Mode on the SBS 2003 server machine. Okay, once more with feeling: **It cannot be done**. So, don't be duped into believing it can by a tricky question on the 70-282 exam. If you want a Terminal Services Applications Sharing Mode scenario, you'd want to perform such feats on an additional server machine (either domain controller or our preferred member server approach).

Manage Networks Using Simple Network Management Protocol

Use of the Simple Network Management Protocol (SNMP) goes way back. This is an industry standard for talking to and managing devices on a network and includes devices beyond the server machine such as switches, routers, firewalls, and the like. SNMP management software is used to monitor any device configured with SNMP agent software. The SNMP agent, which is an optional component of Windows Server 2003, interacts with third-party SNMP software to enable the flow of network status information between monitored devices and applications and the management systems that monitor them. SNMP traps are the "messages" sent that communicate performance information.

To be brutally honest—SNMP is beyond the scope of a "day in the life of an SBSer" and, as such, doesn't demand much of your attention in preparing for the 70-282 exam. SNMP environments typically have hundreds or thousands of nodes that would be difficult or costly to monitor.

> IMPORTANT: To learn more about SNMP in your free time, visit Microsoft TechNet at www.microsoft.com/technet and search on the keyword "SNMP" and you'll have over 500 hits returned. The following title is very detailed and highly recommended: How SNMP Works—Networking Services: Windows Server 2003 (Windows Server 2003 Technical Reference). You can also subscribe to the monthly Microsoft TechNet Disc library. TechNet is a great 70-282 exam preparation resource!

Okay, let us also give a tip of the hat to the instant gratification crowd. Whereas this book has a laser focus on the Small Business Specialist Community and the 70-282 exam in particular (as it should), here is an instant treat for you! If you want to see how the SNMP area applies in the REAL WORLD to the small and medium business space, visit these two SMB- and SBS-friendly independent software vendors (ISVs) and read about their management services and monitoring products:

- Level Platforms: www.levelplatform.com

- HyBlue: www.hyblue.com

It is here you can observe real world SNMP applications in the SMB and SBS areas.

Be sure to read Appendix B: More SNMP Stuff!

Notes:

Configure Messaging and Collaboration

There is an old saying in the SBS community: You already know more about Exchange Server 2003 than you think you do. How can this be? Several ways:

Exchange Server 2003 is essentially installed and configured for you when you deploy SBS 2003. Its configuration level out of the box will likely meet 90 percent of your needs with the product. End of story. (Well, actually, there is more to the story. You can find in-depth info on Exchange Server 2003 technologies in Chapter 6 of *Advanced Windows Small Business Server 2003 Best Practices*.)

The remaining 10 percent of Exchange Server 2003 that you "don't know" out-of-the-box is something you likely don't really need to know for the 70-282 exam. There are parts of Exchange that really don't relate to the SBS space, such as site connectors to link multiple Exchange locations together.

As brazen as this sounds, if you're an experienced SBS user of Exchange Server 2003 and there is something you don't know, you probably don't need to know it for the 70-282 exam. But, don't take that last comment as a license to cut your 70-282 studies short. Rather, stay focused on knowing what makes the most sense for the 70-282 exam. You only know what you need to know with Exchange for a reason.

Experience counts for something in the worlds of SMB and SBS (thank goodness) and this really manifests itself in Exchange Server 2003. More than other SBS components, there is nothing like Exchange Server 2003 experience to prepare you for the 70-282 exam.

> IMPORTANT: Be discerning in the amount of information you are prepared to digest in preparation for the 70-282 exam. Sure, you could do a deep dive into the Exchange Server 2003 internals for the sake of satisfying your own interests. However, that would be INEFFICIENT from a 70-282 exam preparation time management point of view. Rather, using your very best judgment, ask critically, "Do I really need to know that?" We like data dumps as much as anybody, but find a balance that prevents brain freeze due to overload.

One bona fide Exchange Server 2003 tip to impart at this juncture that you might not know and need to know relates to the number of Exchange servers and stores allowed on an SBS network. Briefly:

- Multiple Exchange server machines are allowed on an SBS 2003 network, assuming you purchased the extra Exchange products.

- Only one store is allowed on the Exchange version (standard edition) contained in SBS 2003. With the Exchange enterprise edition, multiple Exchange stores are allowed.

Outlook Web Access

OWA is one of the coolest features that just works straight out of the box in the SBS 2003. In case you've been living in a cave along the Tex Mex border and don't know about OWA, it's a rich web page that allows you to check your Exchange-based mailbox. It's popular with everyone on Planet Earth who uses SBS 2003. There is no server-side configuration required except:

- Using the user templates to assign a mailbox in the Add User Wizard. This will assign appropriate permissions to user accounts for OWA access.

- Running the CEICW and selecting **Outlook Web Access** under **Allow access to only the following Web site services from the Internet** on the **Web Services Configuration** page.

There is no configuration required on the remote client site (e.g., hotel business center). It is recommended that you use at least Internet Explorer (IE) 5.01 or later. Macintosh and UNIX operating systems and browsers are supported by OWA. For UNIX users, OWA is the primary solution for e-mail, calendar, and collaboration.

OWA comes in two versions:

Outlook Web Access Basic

Hey, if you are used to the old version of Outlook, it's okay to use OWA Basic, especially if you have a slow Internet connection. OWA Basic was designed to work in browsers that support HTML 3.2 and the European Computer Manufacturers Association (ECMA) script standards. It provides a subset of the features available in OWA Premium that allow you to read and send messages as well as access some parts of your calendar and your contacts. If you are accessing OWA using Windows 98 or NT, Outlook 2003 will not install and you will have no choice but to use the basic version of OWA.

Outlook Web Access Premium

OWA Premium has an enhanced user interface and several new features, including the new enhanced features for Exchange 2003. This includes a server-side spellchecker, Quick Flags, and Personal Tasks, allowing attachments to be opened from the reading pane, auto signatures, public folders displaying in their own window, two-line view, meeting requests that can be forwarded, access to GAL property sheets within an e-mail message, and numerous other improvements. However, some of the features will not work unless you are using IE 6.0.

If you log on to OWA through RWW, you automatically get the premium version of OWA. Or, if you have forms-based authentication enabled in your browser when you access OWA directly over the Internet, you will be given the choice of using either the Premium or basic version, where Premium is selected by default.

> IMPORTANT: Because OWA is so cool and so popular, it just makes sense that you can anticipate a few questions on this feature. So since we're here to support you all the way to Small Business Specialist success, let me point you to a free, kick-ass resource that goes into painful detail in describing OWA and the two versions: download the free Chapter 8 of *Windows Small Business Server 2003 Best Practices* from www.smbnation.com. You read it here first. Who loves ya?!?!

Configure Outlook Web Access

OWA is easily configured by running the CEICW and checking the Outlook Web Access checkbox on the Web Services Configuration screen. SBS will automatically make the web services available to host the OWA site and users with access permissions will be able to access OWA over the Internet.

> IMPORTANT: In the SBS 2003 time frame, OWA now operates under HTTPS over Port 443 to create a more secure session. Contrast this

with prior SBS releases when OWA could run over Port 80 (HTTP) with less security.

Configure Windows SharePoint Services

WSS is the intranet (intraweb) of the company and is automatically installed during the SBS installation. The WSS site is a collaborative platform that allows businesses to organize and manage information in a browser-based and office-integrated environment.

Understanding WSS

Central to understanding WSS are the following high-level concepts:

- **WSS replaces the COMPANY share.** Older versions of SBS had a network shared folder called COMPANY (the path was <drive letter>:\Company Share Folders). Now, in the SBS 2003 time frame, you are directed to place your bona fide company-related documents and data in the WSS repository. The WSS repository is a SQL Server-type database file and isn't part of the NTFS storage system (NTFS can be thought of as the "yellow folders" you are familiar with from MyDocuments or Windows Explorer).

- **WSS has alerts and NTFS does not.** Something you will want to configure in WSS is the alerting capabilities to advise you when documents have been checked out, help desk tickets entered, etc.

- **Full Search.** SBS 2003 Standard Edition uses the Windows MSDE engine to manage WSS. SBS 2003 Premium Edition uses the MSDE engine from SQL Server 2000 to manage WSS and has superior search capabilities.

- **More than a document management system.** In the real world, it's easy to view WSS as only a document management system (and a darn good one for free out-of-the-box in SBS 2003). However, that is not the only way MICROSOFT VIEWS IT (remember the 70-282 exam is based on Microsoft viewpoints). In fact, you won't even see the words "document management" on Microsoft's SharePoint page at www.microsoft.com/sharepoint. Here is the current WSS description from Microsoft's site:

Windows SharePoint Services is a collection of services for Microsoft Windows Server™ 2003 that you can use to create team-oriented Web sites to share information and foster collaboration with other users on documents. You can also use Windows SharePoint Services as a development platform for creating collaboration and information-sharing applications.

- **Different strokes for different folks.** There are numerous ways to access WSS (and that is fair game on the 70-282 exam):

  - CompanyWeb. This is the default home page in Internet Explorer for a client computer connected to an SBS 2003 network. See Figure 7-1.

  - My Network Places. WSS folders can be published as network places.

  - File, Open. Office 2003 applications can directly open and close documents in WSS.

  - Shared Attachments. A new form of e-mail attachment interacts directly with WSS. Very cool!.

Notes:

Figure 7-1

CompanyWeb is the WSS starting point. Use it, get to know it, and modify it before taking the 70-282 exam.

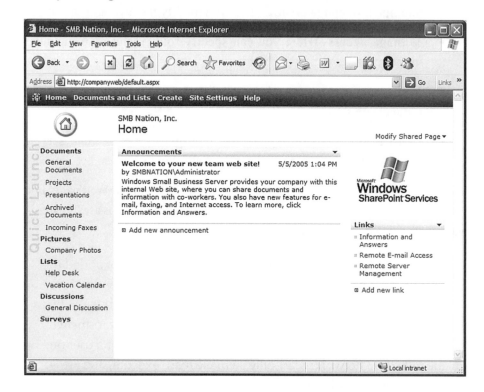

Configuring WSS

There are several customizations you can perform after installation to make the intranet more useful for your clients and/or organization. WSS is comprised of different web parts that can be modified, moved or removed, and added.

You can configure WSS by using **Tasks** located in the **Server Management** console under the **Internal Web Site** link where you can manage:

- **Importing files**—Using the Import Files Wizard, files, and subfolders can be moved into the SharePoint site from shared folders

- **Add link**—Allows you to add an internal or external link to the company's intraweb site

- **Change name**—You can change the name of the intranet displayed on the intranet site

- **Change homepage layout**—Lets you modify the layout of the site

- **Manage access**—Here you can specify roles for users to manage user access

- **Manage your company's internal web site**—Where you can manage intranet site settings

- **Central administration**—Used to configure server, virtual server, security, and component settings for SharePoint services.

You may also configure WSS in other ways from the CompanyWeb page. For example, you can create sub-webs from CompanyWeb. Sub-webs are like mini-web pages created to collaborate on a specific project.

IMPORTANT: WSS has very generous permissions. A user added to the SBS 2003 network is given the second-highest level of permissions in WSS: Web Designer. This allows users to create sub-webs by default and enter Help Desk tickets. Contrast that with the restrictive default NTFS shared network folder permission setting for a user on the SBS 2003 network: read-only (actually read, execute, and list—but effectively read-only).

The above comparison of WSS and network share permissions is presented to touch on two points in the 70-282 exam. WSS is considered cool by Microsoft and will certainly be on the exam. And I've offered you a security example. Microsoft takes security very seriously.

So the WSS section ends with a couple of homework assignments. First, use WSS as experience and you will find no better teacher for this section of the 70-282 exam. Second, read the WSS chapters in the other SMB Nation Press books (Chapter 7 in both *Advanced Windows Small Business Server 2003 Best Practices* and *Windows Small Business Server 2003 Best Practices*). Third, visit www.sharepointknowledge.com. And fourth, look for postings on the SBS newsgroups (detailed in Appendix A) from SBS-MVP Chad Gross.

Configure Real-Time Communications

Small businesses expect to have real-time communication capabilities just as seen in the enterprise. With SBS, you can offer mobile solutions that allow for increased productivity, collaboration, and communication. These solutions are enabled through core services of Windows Server 2003 and taken advantage of by SBS in different forms.

> IMPORTANT: Beware of semantics and "plays on words," as we say in the Western world. Microsoft removed the built-in Instant Messaging (IM) communications from Exchange Server 2003 in the SBS 2003 time frame (IM was available via Exchange 2000 Server in the SBS 2000 time frame). Microsoft replaced the IM functionality for SBS 2000 owners who purchased its Software Assurance prior to October 1, 2003 by giving these select owners a free copy of its Live Communications Server (http://www.microsoft.com/office/livecomm/ prodinfo/default.mspx). Here is my concern. It would be easy from the above section headline (taken from the 70-282 exam objectives) to infer that Microsoft might test you on this very limited offer to restore IM functionality via the Live Communications Server product. And it's even easier to assume that all this somehow relates to configuring real-time communications in the context of the 70-282 exam. Such is not the case. You are not tested on IM functionality and Live Communications Server on SBS 2003. Whew!

Recommend and Implement an E-mail Solution

E-mail access can be configured in many different flavors in SBS. If you installed Exchange, you have a robust e-mail solution that can be extended beyond receiving messages at the desktop. The default approach is to have SMTP-based e-mail, which is discussed above and in other book sections. But even if your client or organization still uses POP3 as its primary e-mail retrieval method, which many small businesses prefer, you will be able to take advantage of all the features that Exchange has to offer.

Configure the POP3 Connector

SBS can automatically download messages from POP3 e-mail boxes and deliver them to the proper Exchange mailbox with the Microsoft Connector for POP3 mailboxes.

The POP3 connector is disabled by default and the Microsoft Connector for POP3 mailboxes service does not start until you add the first POP3 mailbox through either the CEICW or the POP3 Connector Manager in the Server Management/Advanced Management node. You can add, remove, and edit POP3 e-mail boxes in the POP3 Connector Manager and set delivery schedules.

The Exchange server supports one single global POP3 mailbox that allows all e-mail sent to your domain to be delivered to a single mailbox managed by your ISP. You do not need to assign individual POP3 e-mail boxes to individual user accounts.

When you add POP3 mailboxes to the POP3 connector, you tell the e-mail server to retrieve from a POP3 domain (e.g., Pop3.atsomedomain.com) and add the POP3 username and password to be able to access the e-mail at the ISP. You then fill in the Mailbox information for Exchange choosing **User Mailbox** as the type and then selecting the user account that should be receiving the e-mail. You continue adding individual POP3 mailboxes in the POP3 Connector this way until you have entered every user account that should receive messages.

When the POP3 Connector retrieves e-mail from the ISP's POP3 mailbox, it will automatically distribute e-mails to the appropriate Exchange mailboxes.

> IMPORTANT: The POP3 Connector cannot deliver e-mails to a Public Folder in Exchange even though a Public Folder has an SMTP e-mail address. Why, you ask? Because a Public Folder is not a real Active Directory object, but merely a mailbox. It's these little tricky tidbits (and thinking about tricky tidbits) that will help get you over the passing bar on the 70-282 exam.

Migrating Mailboxes from POP3 to Exchange

If you have been using the POP3 Connector, mailboxes don't really get migrated from POP3 to Exchange. You already have an Exchange e-mail box and you are really just changing the e-mail retrieval method to an e-mail delivery method. To do this:

1. Configure the **CEICW**.

2. Select **Enable Internet e-mail**, then the e-mail delivery option.

3. Uncheck the **Use the Microsoft Connector for POP3 Mailboxes** checkbox.

Outlook Web Access

As discussed earlier, OWA allows remote access to Exchange Server 2003. But here is another take on OWA. Besides having an improved User Interface (UI), OWA has undergone several improvements in functionality and security. Some security enhancements include:

*   S/MIME (Secure Multipurpose Internet Mail Extentions) support (Internet Explorer 6 and Microsoft Windows 2000 or later is required)

*   Spam beacon-blocking to help protect your e-mail address privacy from spammers

*   A hidden destination site to help protect your privacy when viewing a URL from a message in OWA

*   Attachment blocking so you can selectively disable attachments being viewed from outside the firewall. You can also prevent sensitive documents from being downloaded outside your network

*   A session inactivity timeout using forms-based authentication that enables support for a timed log off after a period of inactivity; OWA enables you to log off securely even if the browser is left open with a current session to the server

Performance improvements include the choice between basic and premium versions of Outlook and a choice between the basic client version from the forms-based authentication logon page when you use Netscape and IE5.01 and earlier. Other substantial performance improvements have been made for dial-up, low-bandwidth wireless networks, and when using SSL after enabling GZip compression.

Cell Phones and Mobile Devices

Cell phones and connected mobile devices are starting to make inroads to small business and have support through OMA for use of PDAs (personal digital assistants), Pocket PCs, or SmartPhones.

OMA

Exchange 2003 supports Wireless Application Protocol (WAP) 2.x and XHTML browser-based devices, and has support for full HTML browsers as well as i-Mode devices such as mobile phones and PDAs. Mobile phone browsers in Japan can now access servers running Exchange Server by using compressed HTML (CHTML) on i-Mode devices.

Active Sync

Exchange Active Sync allows Pocket PCs, Pocket PC Phone Editions, and Windows Mobile-Based SmartPhones to stay in direct contact with the Exchange 20003 server. This means you have the capability to:

- Synchronize your e-mail messages, calendar, and contact list.

- Receive SMS (short messaging service) messages from the Exchange Server.

- Select your synchronization method from on-demand or scheduled sync. Coupled with OMA you can also get your tasks list and GAL.

IMPORTANT: As mentioned in this book a couple of times, mobility is HOT in the SBS 2003 time frame and you will most certainly be held accountable for it on the 70-282 exam. The free Chapter 8 from *Windows Small Business Server 2003 Best Practices* (visit www.smbnation.com) explores OMA and the Small IT Solution for Mobility (a cool solutions accelerator) at https://partner.microsoft.

com/global/products solutions/smbsolutions/ really explore the topics in great detail!

Outlook 2003

Outlook 2003 client comes included with SBS, and there is no reason why your clients or organizations shouldn't be using it. All I have to say is "Hey, its free!" Besides being free, Outlook 2003 also provides an integrated solution for managing and organizing e-mail messages, schedules, tasks, notes, contacts, and other information. Often end-users find Outlook so feature-rich they are scared of it and ask to keep Outlook Express. Of course, as a sensible consultant, I don't allow that on any network.

There are so many benefits to using Outlook 2003, I don't know where to start. Always focusing on the client side, I first point out that you can:

- Manage all e-mail in one place

- Easily organize the Inbox

- Access calendar, tasks, and contacts quickly in one location

Outlook also integrates with WSS and has the junk folder and search folder options. One really cool item is being able to restore deleted items directly from the Outlook client. By going to **Tools/Recover Deleted Items**, users can bring back deleted items from as far back as you set the deleted item retention in the Configure Backup Wizard.

> IMPORTANT: The best way to answer any Outlook 2003 question on the 70-282 exam is to simply use Outlook 2003 in your day-to-day life. Seriously—it's not necessary to read a big, thick book on Outlook 2003 for the 70-282 exam. Simply use it, try new things, and poke around. You'll do fine on the exam section.

IMAP4

Exchange 2003 supports IMAP4 (Internet Message Access Protocol Version 4), allowing clients to access messages in public and private folders on the server. Users with IMAP4 clients are able to retrieve their e-mail without downloading the entire mailbox to their computer. With IMAP, a client can retrieve specific messages or portions of a message like an attachment.

IMAP does not send mail—that is handled by SMTP. The difference between IMAP and POP3 is that IMAP allows you to access and manage e-mail on the server, where POP3 is a retrieval method that downloads e-mail to an Inbox.

Implement a Web Site Hosting Configuration

First of all, I want to let you know that hosting a web site on your SBS server will put you at greater risk to be attacked by hackers, script kiddies, and other malicious thingamajiggies floating around on the Internet. You have just placed your server out there and said, "Come hit me!" The only way I would personally host a web site off my SBS domain would be by using a second server hosting the site and using ISA server to take the brunt of the attacks. Hosting will require having your server patched and locked down at all the times. I'd rather pay someone else who does web site hosting for a living to have all the headaches. So the moral of the story is: Do not host a public site on your SBS machine!

So why would this topic be on the 70-282 exam if knowledgeable SBSers are opposed to hosting a public web site (even Microsoft itself discourages hosting public web sites on an SBS 2003 server)? Because some line-of-business applications require a public-facing web site on an SBS server using Port 80. Small businesses, advised of the problems of hosting a web site on the SBS server (security risks and performance concerns), may elect to host a public-facing web site to support its beloved line-of-business applications.

Granting Non-Admin Access Permissions

You decide to go ahead and create a new web site in IIS (Internet Information Services) and set it to allow Anonymous Access. Anonymous Access is enabled by default when you create a new web site in IIS. To observe or change the settings in IIS:

1. Go to the **Server Management** console and expand **Advanced Management.**

2. Expand **Internet Information Services,** expand **ServerName,** and then expand the **Web Sites** node.

3. Right-click on the **SiteName,** then click on **Properties**.

4. Click on the **Directory Security** tab, then on **Edit**. You should see that **Anonymous Access** is enabled by default.

You can use the **Authenticated access** section in the dialog box to choose another method for client authentication and uncheck the **Enable anonymous access** box.

IMPORTANT: You can fine-tune Anonymous Access permissions by configuring the NTFS permissions of the folder that holds the web site files.

1. In **Windows Explorer**, go to the folder and select **Properties**, then the **Security** tab.

2. Click the **Advanced** tab and the select the **IUSR_USER** and click on **Effective Permissions**.

Configure Firewall Settings to Publish the Web Site

To open up the SBS firewall to host the web site, you must run the CEICW again and choose to **Enable Firewall** on the firewall page. Then on the Web Services Configuration page, select **Business Web site (wwwroot)**. You can select this individually or select the radio button to **Allow access to the entire Web site from the Internet**. If you do so, when you click **Next**, you will be warned that you are exposing the entire web site and allowing users to gain access to all the web site directories on the server's default web site via the Internet. Not a smart thing to do!

Configure the File Transfer Protocol

There once was the client who tried to send 10 MB-size e-mail attachments to her clients and complained that the e-mail never made it. After receiving a lengthy explanation as to why she shouldn't send such a big file attachment, the user retaliated a week later by trying to send out an e-mail to three recipients with an 18 MB-size attachment, inadvertently crashing the Exchange server. Clearly a better approach would be to use the File Transfer Protocol (FTP).

Installing the FTP Service

The FTP service is not installed by default and it is not managed out of the Server Management console, but directly from the IIS console. To install the FTP service, you must first:

1. Go to the **Control Panel** and click **Add or Remove Programs**.

2. Click **Add/Remove Windows Components** in the left pane and se-lect the **Application Server**.

3. Click **Details** and select **Internet Information Services**.

4. Click **Details** and select the **File Transfer Protocol (FTP) Service** checkbox.

5. Click **OK** twice and then click **Finish** (you may get prompted for the SBS installation CD, so have it ready).

6. IIS then installs the default FTP site to C:\Inetpub\FTProot.

IMPORTANT: Once FTP is installed, you must rerun the CEICW to allow access for external users and open the firewall. If you have a separate hardware firewall, be sure to open Port 21. If you have a UPnP hardware firewall, SBS will configure the port for you.

Configure FTP Permissions

Once you have installed the FTP site, you may want to add a welcome or exit message for the external users or some different directory security settings. This must be configured from the IIS management console.

1. In the **Server Management** console, expand **Advanced Management,** expand the **Internet Information Services**, expand your **ServerName,** then **expand** the **FTP Sites** container.

2. Right-click the **FTP Sites** container, then click **Properties**.

3. Click the **Security Accounts** tab and select the **Allow only anonymous connections** checkbox. This prevents users with valid accounts from sending their credentials in clear text to increase security.

4. Click the **Messages** tab to enter a Welcome or Exit message.

5. Click the **Home Directory** tab to choose the FTP files folder location.

6. Click the **Directory Security** tab and select either **grant** or **deny** for specific IP addresses. This is useful if you want to enable only certain users and you know their IP addresses.

IMPORTANT: If the FTP site will not be used for periods of time, it is a good practice to stop the FTP site by right-clicking the site in IIS and choosing **Stop.** Start it up again when it is needed.

Configure Resource Sharing

Ah, the heart of the matter. Let's embrace the SBS-ology of sharing and controlling resources on our network. Resources can easily be viewed and configured, either in the Server Management console or Server Management for Power Users console. Network users can share printer and fax resources. Administrators can add, remove, and configure network printers directly from the preconfigured management consoles. It is easy to access and modify printer settings like port assignments, security, sharing, and other printing options, such as page separators. You can also use the Server Management console to view pending jobs, change the order of print jobs, pause, resume, or cancel print jobs currently in the print queue.

IMPORTANT: Microsoft products, especially Windows operating system-based products, offer about seven different ways to do a task. In fact, I recall a Windows 95 assessment exam that actually tested on the different ways to perform a simple task (command line, GUI, control panel, etc.). So it's an established Microsoft testing paradigm to test your recall of keystrokes and mouse movements. Don't fret too much over this observation, but do ask yourself, "Are there other ways to accomplish this task?" More important, ask yourself, "What is the SBS way to accomplish this task?"

Configure Print Servers

When you connect a printer to the SBS server with a USB or IEEE1394 (Firewire) cable, Windows automatically detects and installs the necessary drivers. You can also attach printers with built-in NICs to the SBS network. SBS supports TCP/IP network printers using LPD, JetDirect, and Intel NetPort. To set up a network printer:

1. Attach the printer to the network and assign it an IP address (any available address from 192.168.16.3 to 192.168.16.9 found on the exception DHCP scope)

2. In the **Server Management** console, click on **Printers**.

3. Click **Add a Printer**, click **Next,** and on the Local or Network Printer page, select the **Local Printer attached to this computer** option, then uncheck the **Automatically Detect and Install My Plug and Play Printer** checkbox. Click **Next**.

4. Select **Create a New Port** on the **Printer Port** page and choose **Standard TCP/IP Port** from the drop-down list. Click **Next**.

5. On the **Add Standard TCP/IP Printer Port Wizard**, click **Next** and enter the **Printer Name or IP Address** and **Port Name**. Click **Next**.

6. The wizard will try to connect to the printer, and if it fails, display the **Additional Port Information Required** page. Select the printer from the standard list and click **Next** followed by **Finish.** Alternatively, you could select **Custom** and then choose the protocol for the printer, either **RAW** or **LPR**.

7. Leave the port number at 9100 if using RAW unless specified otherwise in the printer manual.

8. Select the SNMP protocol if the printer supports SNMP and type the community name.

9. Click **OK** and then **Finish.**

Configure File and Folder Objects Sharing

Files and folders can be shared over the network by granting users access to shared folders. Before these are shared, however, make sure to set the proper NTFS permissions on the folder. (NTFS permissions are discussed in Chapter 6 in the section "User Rights and Permissions.") You can manage shared folders in the Server Management console from the Manage Shared Folders taskpad. You can:

- Add a shared folder

- Change shared folder properties

- Configure MyDocuments Redirection

- Stop Sharing folders

- View Connected Users

- View Open files

You can use a command line tool to view information on shared folders:

- **Net share** – Displays information about all shared resources on the local computer

- **Net session** – Displays information about all open sessions between the local computer and other computers on the network

- **Net file** – Displays information about all open files on shared resources

SBS also has the ability to create shadow copies of shared folders, a function that acts like an automatic backup. More about shadow copies in Chapter 8 in the section "Volume Shadow Service."

IMPORTANT: Files cannot be directly shared over the network. Rather, folders containing files are shared.

Configure Disk Quotas

Beware that SBS enables disk quotas on the volume or partition where the Users shared folder is located by default. Disk quotas are not enabled on other volumes or partitions unless you turn them on. Quotas can be assigned only to volumes that have a drive letter. Quotas can be set for individual users or groups or enabled for all users.

By default, quotas are set to 1GB and send a warning message to the users at 900 MB. When quotas are enabled, you can set or modify different options from:

- Deny disk space to users exceeding quota limit

- Limit disk space to ... (you can specify the limit)

- Set warning level to ... (you can specify the warning level)

- Log event when a user exceeds his quota limit

- Log event when a user exceeds his warning level

Disk quotas do not apply to administrators, unless you explicitly set them so.

> IMPORTANT: Avoid setting individual quotas. It is better to manage quotas for all users unless you absolutely have to single out an individual.

If you have special quota settings, like the boss gets more room than others or certain groups get a different amount of disk space, and you find yourself having to implement or move them to a different volume, you have the ability to import and export quotas.

You can also create quota reports on the fly by simply dragging them from the quota entries window into an Excel spreadsheet.

Create and Configure Public Folders

Public Folders is a feature of Microsoft Exchange Server that provides an effective way to collect, organize, and share information with others. Typically, public folders are used by project teams or user groups to share information on a common area of interest. Public Folders appears in the Outlook Folder List, can be managed from Outlook, and can contain messages, appointments, contacts, tasks, journal entries, notes, forms, files, and postings. You can also add a shortcut to any public folder to the Favorites folder under Public Folders.

Creating a Public Folder

You can create a public folder by creating a distribution group with the Add Distribution Group Wizard and choose to send all e-mail messages to the public folder. If you select the **Create a public folder to archive all e-mail messages sent to this group**, a public folder with the DistributionGroupName Archive will be added as a member to the group.

If you check the box **Enable this Group to receive e-mail message from users outside of your network**, the distribution group will be able to communicate with users outside the network. If the group is to be used internally only, clear this checkbox.

You can also manually create a public folder:

1. Go into the **Server Management Console**. Expand the **Advanced Management** node, click the **Exchange** node, and expand **Folder**, then **Public Folders**.

2. Right-click **Public Folders** and select **New, Public Folder**. Type a name into the **Name** box.

3. Click **Apply** and **OK**.

Configuring Public Folders

Now that you have created the new public folder, you want to configure permissions for who can create and read items in the public folder. To specify different access permissions:

1. Right-click the folder and select **Properties**.

2. Click the **Permissions** tab and you will be able to configure **Client Permissions**.

Practice Questions

Question #1

You administer an SBS 2003 network for a call center that sells logo wear and other printable marketing items. There are 21 Windows XP Pro computers and 10 Windows 2000 Professional computers. Besides phone calls, the call center receives several hundred fax orders a day. Too many times the fax machine has run out of paper or orders were neglected because there was no one there to manage the fax. The company hires two new staff people just for the purpose of handling the fax orders. Faxes should be received and processed on the desktop, but only by the two new hires. You create the new user accounts with the Add User wizard. What else should you do?

A. Create a security group called "FaxPersonnel" and add the user accounts of the new hires to the new security group

B. Create a distribution group called "FaxPersonnel" and add the user accounts of the new hires to the new distribution group

C. Run the Configure Fax Service and select the "Use the Route through e-mail routing method"

D. Run the Configure Fax Service and select the "Use the Route through distribution group method"

Question #2

You administer an SBS 2003 network for a small doctor's office in town. The server is configured with two NICs and there are seven Windows 2000 Professional and four Windows 98 computers on the network. Due to regulatory compliance regulations, you decide to add a UPnP hardware firewall to the SBS installation. After you add the UPnP hardware firewall device, users are no longer able to log on to Remote Web Workplace and internal users can't update their medical application which uses port 4008. To fix this with the least amount of administrative effort, what should you do? (select all that apply)

A. Access the firewall interface and open port 4125, 1723 and 4008

B. Run the CEICW and when prompted that there is a UPnP firewall device detected, let the CEICW configure it

C. Access the firewall interface and set port forwarding for port 80 to port 4125

D. Run the CEICW and in the Web Server Certificate screen, add a certificate

E. Add port 4008 in the Services Configuration screen in the CEICW

F. Access the firewall interface and set port forwarding for port 4008 to the SBS server

Question #3

You installed an SBS 2003 network at a paper recycling plant. There are 15 Windows XP Professional computers and the server has a proprietary recycling software solution installed. You, the office manager and the owner have the ability to administer the server from remote locations. You get a call from the plant and remote into the server, to find after logging on that you get a blue desktop background but no icons or start bar and are unable to manage the server. You drive over to the plant and find two disconnected sessions from the office manager and owner. What can you do to ensure this won't happen again?

A. Install Terminal Services on the SBS 2003 Server

B. Add additional user accounts to the Remote Desktop Administration on the SBS 2003 Server

C. Configure the server to "set a time limit for disconnected sessions" to 5 minutes

D. Configure the server to allow "automatic reconnection"

Question #4

You are the consultant for XYZ Title Company. XYZ runs an SBS 2003 server, one Windows 2003 Server and 14 Windows XP Professional computers. XYZ has grown its client base and its folder structure on the server to a point where collaboration and a document repository needs to be implemented. You suggest SharePoint as a solution. XYZ tested SharePoint with several individual client files before deciding to go ahead and move all the documents in existing shares from the two servers. What will take the least administrative effort to upload the documents into SharePoint?

A. Instruct users to create their own sites and upload all the files they are responsible for using the Upload Document button

B. Migrate the files with the SharePoint migration tool

C. Use the Import File Wizard

D. Move the files using the stsmigrate.exe command line tool

Question #5

You are the consultant for ASAP, an auto supply and parts distribution center. ASAP has an SBS 2003 server and six client computers. The SBS server has two NICs, one fax modem and an external backup tape drive. Currently ASAP is getting inundated with fax orders and customers are complaining about having to do numerous re-dials before the fax goes through. Users send and receive faxes from their desktops acknowledging orders and faxing shipping information. ASAP purchased a competitor and expects to receive double the amount of orders than it is currently receiving within the next couple of months. How can you set up ASAP to be able to manage the increasing fax demand with the lowest expenditure and fewest changes to their business processes so users do not need to be retrained?

A. Purchase two new standalone Fax machines that are capable of high-volume faxing

B. Set up an Internet Fax service to manage the fax volume and forward the faxes by e-mail to your business

C. Add three additional fax modems to the SBS machine

D. Add one additional fax modem the SBS machine

Question #6

You administer a SharePoint site for New Construction, Inc. on a SBS 2003 Server with ISA installed. The company has ten Windows XP

Professional computers in the office and has numerous contractors on job sites that are required to have Windows XP Professional SP2 computers with Microsoft Office 2003 loaded on them. The construction company wants contractors to be able to access the SharePoint site for specific projects and be able to discuss, add, edit and delete items on the lists. They should not be able to create their own lists or modify existing lists. You already have a user account template setup for contractors. What group should also be assigned to the contractor's template and how should you change permissions on existing contractor accounts? (select all that apply)

A. Distribution

B. Reader

C. Contributor

D. Power User

E. Run the Change Permission wizard

F. Add the appropriate Group through the users account properties tab in Active Directory

G. Create a Group Policy that assigns the appropriate access to the Contractors Security Group

Question #7

Callaway Antiques is a new client of yours that already has SBS 2003 server installed. There are two existing Windows 2000 Professional computers and the owner purchased two new Windows XP Pro computers he would like to add to the network. He also wants Office 2003 Professional installed on the new computers and would like to be able to backup MyDocuments data for all users in a central location. He wants you to spend the least amount of time and effort implementing a solution. What should you do?

A. Configure a GPO under Computer Configuration\Software Settings and add a software installation package for the Office 2003 installation. Configure the MyDocument redirect GPO and configure NTbackup to run a nightly backup of the Users Shared folder.

B. Insert the Office 2003 CD into the Server CD tray and share the CD. Run the Configure My Documents redirection wizard and run the Configure Backup Wizard.

C. Copy the Office 2003 CD into a folder in the clientapps folder and share it. Configure the Assign Application wizard and run the Configure My Documents redirection wizard. Configure the Configure Backup Wizard.

D. Copy the Office 2003 CD into a folder in the clientapps folder and share it. Run the Configure My Documents redirection wizard and run the Assign Application wizard and add the Office 2003 files. Configure the NT backup wizard to include the system state.

Question #8

You are the IT manager for a local delivery company Express, Inc. Express Inc. just purchased SBS 2003, 13 Windows XP Professional computers and 10 PocketPCs with Windows Mobile for PocketPC2003 installed. Express Inc. has a registered domain name. The delivery staff is constantly on the run and you would like to implement the PocketPCs to synchronize e-mails and schedules without having the delivery staff constantly calling the office. You run the CEICW and enable OMA and a self-signed Web Server certificate. You run the Assign Application wizard and add Active Sync 3.7 to the assigned applications and then join the new client computers using the Network Connection wizard. What are the next steps you should take to configure the PocketPCs?

A. Set the PocketPC into its cradle and let it sync with the Windows XP computer; when prompted to sync with the local computer or Exchange, select Exchange.

B. Set the PocketPC into its cradle and let it sync with the Windows XP computer; when prompted to sync with the local machine or Exchange, select the local computer.

C. Set the PocketPC into its cradle and let it sync. Copy the SBS Web Server certificate onto the PocketPC and then go to Settings\Connections and add the URL for the SBS server.

D. Set the PocketPC into its cradle and let it sync. Go to Settings\ Connections and add the URL of the SBS server. Install the SBS Web Server certificate over the wireless connection when prompted.

Question #9

Your company is moving from a peer-to-peer network to SBS 2003. Currently the e-mail accounts are held at the ISP and downloaded with POP3 clients. There are 23 Windows XP Pro computers on the network. The owner wants to be able to use calendar sharing features in Exchange, as well as OWA, but does not want to change the POP3 accounts at the ISP. How can the administrator implement that?

A. Install the POP3 connector from SBS Disc #4 to the server and set the client machines to pull their POP3 e-mail from the server. Have the ISP push out the POP3 e-mail to the SBS server.

B. Run the CEICW and select the "POP3 connector" box in the e-mail configuration screen. Add a POP3 connector for each individual user and point it to the appropriate Exchange mail account.

C. Run the CEICW and select the "POP3 connector" box in the e-mail configuration screen. Add the mailbox retrieval information for each individual POP3 account and point it to the appropriate Exchange mail account.

D. Run the CEICW and select the "POP3 connector" box and de-select the Exchange Server box in the e-mail configuration screen. Configure clients to retrieve their e-mail from the SBS POP3 connector.

Question #10

Magic Inc. uses an SBS 2003 server as their e-mail and file server. Magic has 30 actors working for them who are constantly on the road. The actors expressed that they would like to receive their e-mail on their SmartPhones and PocketPCs. The actors would also like to have a central scheduling method and secure access to the main office. As the consultant you want to guarantee secure access using certificate services in the most cost-effective manner with the least amount of administrative effort. What should you configure? (select all that apply)

A. Purchase a commercial certificate and install it through the CEICW

B. Select the Outlook Mobile Access checkbox in the Web Services Configuration screen in the CEICW

C. Set up an Enterprise Certificate Authority (CA) on the SBS server

D. Install the Enterprise CA on the client computer

E. Add the commercial certificate in the Web Services Configuration screen in the CEICW

F. Configure the CEICW to use a self-signed certificate

G. Select the enable Outlook Mobile Access check box in the Mobile Services Properties in Exchange

Answer Key

Question #1: Answer B, C

You want to create a distribution group since this is just for the purpose of distributing e-mail to the members of the group. The two new hire user accounts belong in this group since they are the only ones to receive faxes. Then run the Configure Fax Services wizard and select "Use the Route through e-mail routing method" and add the distribution group name as the recipient (Faxpersonnel@ mycompany.com). Answer A. A security group is not needed since this requires a group for distribution only and user accounts have already been created so the new hires can log on to the domain. Answer D. There is no such option.

Question #2: Answer B,E

The CEICW will automatically configure the ports on the UPnP firewall device for you. Any additional services should be added in under the Services Configuration screen in the CEICW, and the CEICW will configure SBS and your UPnP device appropriately. Answer A. Would work but also opens additional unused ports and would create more of an administrative burden. Answer C. That would not work. Answer D.

That adds a certificate, will not configure the router. Answer F. The server itself would still block port 4008, so use the CEICW.

Question #3: Answer C

Select the GPO to "set a time limit for disconnected sessions" in Computer Configuration\Administrative Templates\Windows Component\Terminal Services\Sessions to automatically log off a disconnected session after the time of your choice. SBS Remote Desktop allows only two sessions at a time. If users disconnect, the session continues to run indefinitely. Answer A. You cannot install Terminal Services on an SBS server. Answer B. Adding additional user accounts will not fix the disconnect issue. Answer D. Setting "Allow Automatic Reconnection" will reconnect a disconnected session, but not fix the issue.

Question #4: Answer C

The Import File Wizard allows importing files and folders into a document library from a network drive. Answer A. That would be a mess and would take a huge administrative effort to fix. Answer B. There is no SharePoint migration tool. Answer D. The stsmigrate.exe tool is a command line tool used to migrate existing SharePoint sites to a different server and could not be used in this scenario.

Question #5: Answer C

You can install up to four modems into the SBS server that will support simultaneous faxing. Since the one modem currently is not handling the load, and the load will double in a short period of time, you should install at least two additional modems and may end up adding a third modem to a total of four, based on the volume later on. Answer A. Purchasing a stand-alone Fax machine could be more expensive and would change the way users manage faxes, which they now send and receive from their desktop. Answer B. This could also be more costly in the long-term and would require users to be trained on the Internet faxing software. Answer D. One additional fax modem (bringing the total to two) would not be able to manage the anticipated fax load.

Question #6 Answer C, E

Being a member of the Contributor Group allows users to discuss, edit, add and delete items in the list and view document libraries. The appropriate SBS way to change permissions on existing user accounts is by using the Change Permission Wizard. Answer A. The distribution list is an Exchange group that would not affect SharePoint access. Answer B. Readers can view the list and document libraries, but not discuss, add, edit or delete items. Answer D. Power users will automatically be added to the Administrator site group and would be able to create and modify lists, which is an option that should not be available to contractors in this scenario. Answer F and G. You cannot manage site group membership in Active Directory; you can manage site groups either in the HTML Administration pages or the command line administration tool.

Question #7: Answer C

This answer does it all, with the least amount of effort. Also, by placing the office files in the client apps folder and adding those to assigned applications will make this install available for future use without any additional steps required. Answer A. This answer works, but requires more administrative effort. Answer B. Only shares, but does not install the application. Answer D. Again, would require more administrative effort.

Question #8: Answer A

What a beautiful thing! A no-brainer. Set the PocketPC in its cradle, and sync with Exchange. This will transfer the certificate AND configure the server settings on the PocketPC. Remove from cradle and move on with your life. Answer B. Do not set it to sync with the local computer; it must sync with the Exchange server. Answer C. No. Answer D. No.

Question #9: Answer C

It only requires one POP3 connector in SBS, and it will handle the distribution of all downloaded e-mail to all mail box-enabled user accounts. By default it downloads e-mail once every hour but you can set it to 15 minutes increments. Answer A. The POP3 connector; is installed during the SBS Installation Setup. POP3 is an e-mail retrieval method and can not push mail out. Answer B. There is only ONE POP3 connector, it will distribute all POP3 mail to the appropriate Exchange mail boxes. Answer D. This doesn't work; the POP3 connector needs to have Exchange to distribute e-mail into mail boxes. Also, this would not allow for calendar sharing or Outlook Web Access.

Question #10: Answer B, F

You can select to create a self-signed SSL certificate in the Web Server Certificate screen in the CEICW. This will require you to type in the full Internet name of the server. The certificate, SBScert.cer will be placed in the Clientapps\SBSCert folder so it can be deployed to client computers by the Client Setup Wizard. You must also run the CEICW and select Outlook Mobile Access to configure the server. Answer A. This would not be the most cost-efficient manner since you can create your own certificate in the CEICW. Answer C and D. This would not fit the "least amount of effort" objective of the SBS methodology. Answer E. That again would have required purchasing a commercial certificate, which is not cost effective. Answer G. When will you learn to just do things using the wizard?

Summary

That was one monster-length chapter. No SBS technology was left untouched if you think about it. We started with domain groups and moved on to SBS networking technologies. Included in the look at SBS networking, we took a look at the "SBS way," including walking through much of the To Do List and a few special wizards. The networking section ended with a look at specific networking components like DHCP and DNS. Terminals Services followed, with a tip of the hat to SNMP. Then an important area of discussion was presented: messaging and collaboration. The chapter concluded with a discussion of Web hosting, FTP, and resource sharing. It was a grand chapter, but don't ever lose sight of the fact that all this information was presented in the context of successfully passing the 70-282 exam. That's why we're here. Onward to Chapter 8.

CHAPTER 8
Supporting and Maintaining Windows Small Business Server 2003

Managing Windows Small Business Server 2003

Well, is it really about just managing the SBS server, or is it about managing the desktops? Should we manage users? Server management is not only about the server, but the entire network and its user culture. Therefore, server management requires a holistic view including client computers, network connections, and users.

The SBS management console reveals the most excellent management tools, but let's not forget that we are sitting on top of a Windows Server 2003. To not just get a piece of the pie but the whole thing, it is imperative you brush up on your Group Policy Object (GPO) knowledge. To achieve a well-balanced network environment, happy users, desktop security, and a healthy server, you need to employ all the tools you can get.

Using the Server Management Console

The Server Management console is the portal from which all SBS management-related tasks are performed. The Server Management console first appears automatically after the initial install of SBS opening the To Do List; it will always open up by default when you log on as the administrator as well. If it does not launch for you automatically, go to **Start** and on top of the Start bar, and click **Server Management.** In one view, you are presented with the Server

Management Home Page and its individual nodes, the **Standard Management** node and **Advanced Management** node, and shortcut icons to manage the most common management tasks for administrators.

Standard Management Options

The Standard Management node includes most actions that are **task based,** and unless you require special configurations, you will be able to perform most tasks here. The Standard Management node has a plethora of tasks that will surprise you. So, before you go about using the native Windows Server 2003 tools, make sure to check for hidden jewels in the Server Management console. Need strong Texas talk to get the point? Always use the Server Management console! The Standard Management node is broken down into several taskpads. Since there are so many options, the combined taskpad functions and tasks are shown in Table 8-1 for a quick overview.

IMPORTANT: It's reasonable to assume the 70-282 exam will highlight the Server Management console. Spend 30-minutes working through Table 8-1 by actually clicking through the Server Management console.

Table 8-1
The Standard Management Taskpads, Tasks, Tools, and Links

Standard Management		
Taskpad	**Tasks**	**Tools & Links**

To Do List	•Network Tasks
	  - View Security Best
	    Practices
	  - Connect to the Internet
	  - Configure Remote Access
	  - Activate your Server
	  - Add Client Licenses
	•Management Tasks
	  - Add a Printer
	  - Add Users and Computers
	  - Configure Fax
	  - Configure Monitoring
	  - Configure Backup
		All items listed here are tasks, which means that a wizard will be opened up to assist you in completing the task. The To Do List contains the first tasks you should complete, preferably in the order listed. If you did an upgrade vs. a clean install, tasks will display different options. After an upgrade you will also have a **change users permissions** task.

Table 8-1 (continued)

Taskpad	Tasks	Tools & Links
Information Center	• Downloads and Updates • Documentation • Community Web site • Technical Support	The Information Center contains quick links to facilitate administration.

Internal Web Site	• Import Files
	  - Performs file import from anywhere into the Share-Point file library. This is very useful when you want to copy entire folders of shared drive locations into SharePoint.
	• Add Link
	  - Creates a New Item Link in SharePoint
		Here you will also find tools that allow you to configure or have access to:
		• Change Name
		• Change Homepage Layout
		• Configure Alerts
		• Manage Access
		• Manage Your Company's Internal Web Site
		• Central Administration

Fax (local)	• Configure Fax Services - This wizard helps you configure SBS to send, route, and receive faxes to fax routing groups (into Outlook 2003 e-mail in boxes), a SharePoint fax folder, or a shared folder on the network.	Here you will also find tools to: • Manage Fax Jobs • Manage Cover Pages ...and links to: • Configure Phone and Modem Options • Manage Printers
Monitoring and Reporting	• Set Up Monitoring Reports and Alerts - This wizard assists in setting up scheduled server reports, configures alert notifications that will be sent to you by e-mail, and enables application logging.	In this category you will also find tools to: • View Services • View Event Logs Open Task Manager • Change Server Status Report Settings • Change Alert Notifications ...and a link to: • View Usage Report

Notes:

Table 8-1 (continued)

Taskpad	Tasks	Tools & Links
Internet and E-mail	• Connect to the Internet - Launches the Configure E-mail and Internet Connection Wizard discussed in detail in Chapter 7 under *Connecting to the Internet.* • Configure Remote Access - Launches the Remote Access Wizard discussed in detail in Chapter 7 under *Configuring Remote Access.* • Create Remote Connection Disk - This wizard assists in creating a floppy disk with a setup.exe file that, once executed on the client, configures the remote computer for remote access.	There are several additional tools found here to manage the Internet and e-mail. With these tools you can: • Synchronize E-mail • Change Server IP Address • Change Broadband Connection Password • Change Dial-up Connection Password • Change E-mail Password • Configure Network Connections • Configure Phone and Modem Options ...and links to: • Manage POP3 E-mail • Manage Distribution Groups
Shares (local)	• Add a Shared Folder - The Share a Folder Wizard shares a folder on the Server computer and sets the appropriate client access permissions on the folder.	Tools include: • Configure MyDocuments Redirection ...and links to: • View Connected Users • View Open Files
Backup	· Configure Backup - This wizard assists in configuring back up to tape or a hard disk (or other location), allows you to specify excluded folders, defines a backup schedule, selects a user to manage backup media, and sets deleted item retention and the space allocated for VSS snapshots.	Here you will also find tools to: • Configure MyDocuments Redirection ...and the link to open up Help files to: • Learn How to Restore the Server • Restore Individual Files • Restore SharePoint Files

Table 8-1 (continued)

Taskpad	Tasks	Tools & Links
Licensing	•Add Licenses - With this wizard you can add client access licenses to the server. You should already have the license codes on hand and will be able to activate client access licenses over the Internet.	There are also tools to: • Back up Licenses • Restore Licenses • Transfer Licenses ...as well as links to: • Purchase Licenses • Print License Information • View License Agreement • View Privacy Policy
Users	•Add a User - Launches the Add User Wizard to add a single user as discussed in detail in Chapter 7 under *Adding Users and Computers* in the *Using the To Do List* heading. •Add Multiple Users - Launches the Add User Wizard with the bulk-add tool as discussed in Chapter 7 under *Adding Users and Computers*.	Additional tools listed here allow you to: • Change User Permissions • Configure Password Policies • Configure MyDocuments Redirection • Change Mailbox and Disk Quota Limits • Offer Remote Assistance
Client Computers	•Set Up Client Computers - This wizard creates client computer accounts and assigns applications to client computers. •Create Remote Connection Disk - This wizard assists in creating a floppy disk with a setup.exe file that, once executed on the client, configures the remote computer for remote access.	Here you also find tools to: • Assign Applications to Client Computers • View Computer Settings • Set Up Client Applications • Offer Remote Assistance ...as well as links to: • Manage Users • Manage Server Computers
Server Computers	•Set Up Server Computers - This wizard creates a server computer account and configures a static or dynamic IP address for the Server.	There is also a link to: • Manage Client Computers

Table 8-1 (continued)

Taskpad	Tasks	Tools & Links
Printers	•Add a Printer - This wizard assists in installing a printer and making printer connections. If you are using a USB, IEEE 1394, or infrared printer, you will not need to use this wizard. Attach and turn on the printer and Windows will install it.	There is a link provided to: • Manage Fax Printers
Distribution Groups	•Add a Distribution Group - This wizard assists in adding a distribution group and defines the group membership.	There are links to: • Manage POP3 E-mail, and • Manage Security Groups
Security Groups	•Add a Security Group - This wizard assists in adding a security group and defines the group membership.	There is a link to: • Manage Distribution Groups
User Templates	•Add a Template - Launches the Add Template Wizard discussed in detail in Chapter 6 under *Small Business Server User Templates.* •Import Templates - This wizard imports templates. •Export Templates - This wizard exports templates.	There is a link to: • Manage Users

Even though the Server Management console is represented in a combined view here, there is no comparison to actually going to, clicking around, and looking at all the tools and tasks named above.

You may have noticed some tool and link repetition in different nodes. At times we need to engage several different tools, and the links make it easier to follow the logical order. In the next release of SBS, it would be nice to see one wizard where you can just add tools and tasks as needed without having to leave the wizard.

Tools are differentiated from **tasks** in that they open directly into a utility window so you don't have to rerun an entire wizard. An example of this is the Change Server IP Address under the Internet and E-mail node. This will save you time from going through the entire Configure E-mail and Internet Connection Wizard (CEICW) again.

> IMPORTANT: You should use tools whenever you can. A good example is the Change Server IP address tool. Run this instead of manually changing the IP on the Server Local Area Connections Properties page, because it will reconfigure all network services for the SBS server to work with the new IP address, instead of just changing the NIC properties.

Each node also lists a **More Information** link that will open the SBS online Help on the specific subject. Don't ignore the online Help; there are some real nuggets of wisdom at your fingertips and this should be your first avenue for finding valuable information for all things SBS before you spend hours scavenging the Internet.

Another way to complete some tasks is by clicking on the node. An example of this is **Client Computers;** click the **Action** command in the tool bar. Point is, the Server Management Console is very feature-rich which, even though it appears simple at first, is surprisingly well thought-out and capable of managing most common tasks very efficiently.

Advanced Management Options

Now that we've covered Standard Management options and acknowledged that these are task based, let's look at the Advanced Management options, which are tool based. The Advanced Management node gives fast access to management tools listed here in order:

- Active Directory Users and Computers

- Group Policy Management

- Computer Management (local)

- Exchange System Manager

- POP3 Connector Manager

- Terminal Services Configuration

- Internet Information Services

- Migrate Server Settings

Interestingly, when you click on some nodes, the right pane will display shortcut options, like in Standard Management, as well as the full native option, so take your pick. At times you just want to dive down and check a specific setting, especially Exchange and IIS settings, and this lets you drill down without having to leave the Server Management Console. The Advanced Management tools give you the same shortcut options as the task-based tools, except they are organized by application.

One tool to focus on, though, is **Migrate Server Settings**, which not only has the Import and Export Templates option for SharePoint, but also has additional configuration options like:

- **Import Health Monitor Configuration** –This is helpful if you have several SBS server installations and you want to standardize Health Monitor across all your client locations. You would first configure settings as desired on one SBS server, then export the settings to a file to import them at another SBS server as needed.

- **Export Health Monitor Configuration** – After you create the perfect configuration, use this wizard to export configured settings to a floppy disk or USB key for later import at another server.

- **Migrate E-mail and Internet Connection Settings** – Provides steps on how to modify config.vbs, which is the script that runs the CEICW. It is located in the Program Files\Microsoft Windows Small Business Server\Networking\ICW folder. This is useful if you want to migrate Internet connection settings to another computer running SBS.

Whew, lots of options here. It will take a while for you to get used to using the Server Management Console and not reaching for native tools, but once you get the hang of it, you'll never go back. After you've set up your server, there should be little need for special configurations outside the Server Management Console. You'll even become accustomed to using the Group Policy Management node out of the Advanced Management node—hey, it takes seven clicks to open it the native way: **Start**, **Administrative tools**, **Active Directory Users and Computers**, right-click the domain, **Properties**, **Group Policy** tab, and click **Open**. Forget that—I get a cramp in my finger just thinking about it.

Using the Group Policy Management Console

Windows Server 2003 includes the new Group Policy Management Console (GPMC) from where you can manage all Group Policy tasks. If you have not acquainted yourself with this yet, it is high time. Even though the GPMC is meant to manage a collection of GPOs and multiple domains and forests, it is also useful to manage our lonely SBS domain. To manage the content of a single GPO, you still use the Group Policy Object Editor, formerly known as GPedit.

With the GPMC you can:

- Drag-and-drop (cool)

- Backup

- Restore

- Import

- Copy

- Run GPO reports

The GPMC runs only on a Windows 2003 Server operating system and can also be installed on a Windows XP SP1 machine.

Applying and Configuring Group Policy Using the Group Policy Management Console

Before we even go there, I would like you to be keenly aware of where your SBS organizational unit (OU) is actually located. Figure 8-1 shows the MyBusiness OU being used for all things SBS in the left pane. A word to the wise: Do not move users or groups outside this OU. You can create users in the regular user container in AD then move them into the MyBusiness OU, but

never, **ever** move them out. Better yet, just get into the habit of creating user accounts using the SBS templates. Okay, off the soap box and on with life...

Figure 8-1
> *MyBusiness OU*

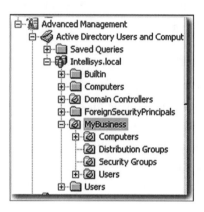

GPO settings can only be applied if the GPO is linked to a site, domain, or OU. In Figure 8-2 you can see the GPMC tree view with GPO links displayed as child nodes under the domain. For instance, you can see a SUS policy under the GPOs, but the SUS GPO does not show up in the left pane under the domain node. SUS in this case is linked to the MyBusiness OU as shown in Figure 8-2.

Figure 8-2
> *Linking in the GPMC*

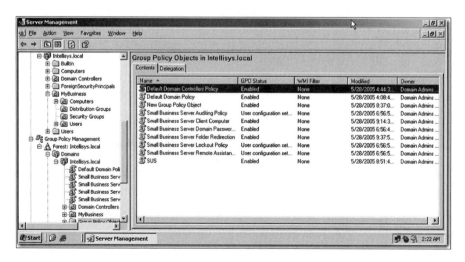

So, for you to apply a GPO, it must first be created and then **linked** to the site, domain, or OU. This can be achieved easily in one step by right-clicking **the object** of your desire (site, domain, or OU) and then choosing **Create and Link GPO here.** This is analogous to clicking **New** in the old Group Policy before GPMC.

Okay, the cool part is the drag and drop functionality. You can grab any GPO from the **Group Policy Objects** node and just drag it over to the site, domain, or OU.

Editing Group Policies

Initially, when a new GPO is created, it has no settings defined. You can edit a GPO by right-clicking the **GPO** in the GPMC and selecting **Edit.** This opens the **Group Policy Object Editor** displaying the Computer Configuration and User Configuration. At this point you just have to path your way to the object where you want to edit the setting and choose:

- Not Configured

- Enabled

- Disabled

Not Configured means exactly that, and when GPOs are processed, the settings will not conflict with any other setting. The **Enabled** setting allows the GPO setting to be processed, whereas a **Disabled** setting will not process the GPO. It is recommended to switch all unused objects to **Disabled** instead of leaving them on **Not Configured** to speed up processing.

Not that you will be using this in an SBS environment (but you never know) and just in case you encounter this in the exam, let's touch on inheritance for a moment.

GPO Inheritance

When studying to become a Microsoft Certified System Engineer (MCSE), you had to repeat the mantra of site, domain, and OU (SDOU) in just that order—which is the way group policy is applied. First the local computer policy is applied during logon. Then the computer checks for site policies, then domain, and then OU. The last policy applied (OU in this case) would overwrite previously applied policies. Then came **Block** and **Overwrite** into the equation, which was not a hard concept to grasp but could be tricky especially if you were working in an enterprise environment where multiple GPOs would be applied across sites and domains and issues arose and you had to start sifting through the policy quagmire.

The default inheritance behavior is altered by several Group Policy options:

- **Link Order** – The GPO with the #1 under the **Link Order** has the highest precedence, then #2, and so on.

- **Block Inheritance** – Allows an OU to block inheritance from a parent container. This will prevent domain GPOs from being applied to an OU, for instance, unless the domain GPO was set to **Enforced.**

- **Enforced** – Previously known as "Overwrite," this will enforce the GPO on an OU or domain, regardless of whether the domain or OU is set on **Block Inheritance**.

- **Link Enabled** – Since GPOs must be linked to a site, domain, or OU for settings to be applied, you could also choose to uncheck the **Link Enabled** setting when right-clicking a **GPO**. This will exclude the GPO from being processed.

Configuring Folder Redirection

In SBS you can redirect the MyDocuments folder of all clients (Windows XP and Windows 2000) to a single shared folder on the server or a network share with the **Client Document Redirection** tool. It is recommended that you choose the **Redirect all My Documents folders to the default shared folder for users on the Small Business Server** for numerous reasons including:

- Folders are automatically included in the SBS Backup

- Deleted files can easily be recovered through Volume Shadow Service

- If users log on to another machine on the network, their documents will always be available.

When you redirect the My Documents folder, it will still appear as a local folder on the user's desktop, but the target path will point to the **Users Shared Folders** folder on the SBS server.

IMPORTANT: Folder redirection is cool and you should anticipate 70-282 exam questions in this area.

Disk quotas are enabled by default on the same volume where the **Users Shared Folders** folder resides and default settings are both:

- Quota limit: 1 GB

- Warning level at: 900 MB

Essentially, the MyDocuments redirect tool configures the **Small Business Server Folder Redirection** GPO, linking it as a node in the domain container and pointing the root path to *SBSServerName*\Users.

To manually create this policy setting, you would have to go to the Advanced Management tasks and create and link a GPO in the GPMC to the domain or OU container. You would then drill down under the **Users Configuration** to the **Windows Settings** and expand **Folder Redirection,** right-click **My Documents**, click the **Properties** tab, and in the **Target** tab manually enter your preferred settings.

Resultant Set of Policies (RSoP)

Resultant Set of Policies (RSoP) is an addition to Group Policy that simplifies GPO troubleshooting. RSoP consists of two modes:

- Planning Mode

- Logging Mode

The **Planning** mode simulates the effect of policy settings that would be applied to computers and users and the **Logging** mode reports on existing policy settings for computers and users currently logged on. RSoP helps determine a set of applied policies and the order in which they are applied (precedence). It details settings including:

- Administrative Templates

- Folder Redirection

- Internet Explorer Maintenance

- Security Settings

- Scripts

- Group Policy Software Installation

You can run the wizard by right-clicking the **Group Policy Results** folder in **Group Policy Management** (see Figure 8-2). RSoP needs a Windows Server 2003 or Windows XP machine to run. It cannot retrieve Windows 2000 Group Policy data, but this can be simulated with Group Policy Modeling.

> IMPORTANT: For a deeper dive on GPOs, see the books by Jeremy Moskowitz, who is slated to speak at the SMB Nation 2005 Conference (www.smbnation.com).

Manage and Troubleshoot Small Business Client Computers

SBS has come a long way since its first inception way back when. I remember looking at the SBS 4.x console, observing the meager choice of management tools and deciding to skip the entire console altogether and just going about my business with the NT 4.0 native tools—essentially breaking the SBS console and disliking it even more and insisting that it did not function. I call that MCSE job security!

Today, when you open the Server Management Console, the Home Page displays several "most common tasks" icons in the right pane, and in the left pane you have all the taskpads at your fingertips. From the **Manage Client Computers** taskpad you can create computer accounts to assign applications, view event logs, and perform other advanced tasks. You can also find help for troubleshooting the most common SBS 2003 issues. The SBS server tools no longer break if you use native tools, but at this point the question is: Why bother? You can perform just about any client management task right from here.

Adding and Removing Clients

If you remember the dark days of the magic disk, fear no longer because here comes http://*SBSServerName*/connectcomputer—and it works! This is about the easiest way to join clients to a domain if you are coming from a peer-to-peer network. If your client is coming from another SBS domain or domain in general, we'll cover that one in a minute.

First of all, the question arises: What client operating systems are supported on the SBS network? Well, since we are dealing with Active Directory, the easiest client operating systems to join to the network are:

- Windows XP Professional

- Windows 2000 Professional clients

We can do so by running http://*SBSServerName*/connectcomputer in the browser UI of the client to be joined. And even though they are not really supported by Active Directory, you can also join the following:

- Windows 98

- Windows Me

- Windows NT 4.0 SP6a / IE4.0

- Mac OS X clients

Do we recommend this? Well, NO...but if you *have* to go this route you can. Just be prepared to perform several manual steps along the way. So let's get started and look at the easy way first.

> IMPORTANT: the 70-282 exam tends to emphasize the easy way, which is the Microsoft way of thinking.

> IMPORTANT: On the 70-282 exam, assume it is nearly always correct to try to upgrade legacy clients to Windows XP Professional if the budget allows.

Small Business Server Network Configuration Wizard

Once again, you can type http://*SBSServerName*/connectcomputer into the client workstation Internet Explorer browser address bar to initiate the Small Business Server Network Configuration Wizard. This is the simplest way to establish a network connection and join a **Windows XP Professional** or **Windows 2000 Professional** workstation to the domain after you created a computer account with the Set Up Computer Wizard. This wizard will join a **workgroup** client to the SBS domain. During the process of joining the client, the wizard will:

- Make the workgroup computer a member of the SBS domain

- Migrate existing local user account profiles

- Install operating system service packs (optional):

  - Shadow Copy client

  - Internet Explorer 6

- Install the Outlook 2003 client (optional) and configure Outlook Profile settings

- Install the Shared Fax client and configure fax settings (optional)

- Install printer drivers (optional)

- Install printers (if published in Active Directory)

- Install additionally assigned software (optional)

- Configure Remote Desktop Assistance and enable Remote Desktop

- Add the selected user account (for the specific computer) to the local administrator's group

- Set the Internet Explorer Home Page to http://companyweb (pointing to the internal SharePoint site)

The "Other" Clients

When joining Windows 98, Me, or NT 4.0 SP6a / IE4.0 clients, you do not have to create the computer account with the Set Up Computer Wizard. You will have to manually join the client to the domain since the http://*SBSServerName*/connectcomputer method would not work here. Also, you will have to manually install the client applications located at the *SBSServerName*\clientapps folder. This folder includes:

- Shadow Copy client located in *SBSServerName*\clientapps\ShadowCopy (only works with Win98 SE and Me)

- Shared Fax client located in *SBSServerName*\clientapps\faxclient

- Outlook 2003 (will not install on Win98 or NT4.0)

- SBScert

- Connection Manager

- Internet Explorer 6 client located in *SBSServerName*\clientapps\ie6

- If running ISA, the firewall client located in *SBSServerName*\mspclnt

Client files will have to be manually installed and configured; shared printers need to be added as well.

Windows 98 and Windows Me require the Active Directory client extensions. You will find the files on any Windows Server 2000 CD in the \Clients\Win9x folder.

NT 4.0 SP6a requires the files for NT 4.0 on the SBS Disc #3 in the \SBSSUPPORT\ADCLIENT folder. The Active Directory client provides:

- Support for DFS (Distributed files system)

- NTLM ver.2 (stronger authentication)

IMPORTANT: Remember that data stored on Win98 is available to anyone who has physical access to the Win98 machine. If security is an issue, it is better to upgrade to Windows 2000 Professional or Windows XP Professional and use NTFS permissions and EFS (Encrypted File System) for file encryption.

The client extensions also DO NOT support certain Active Directory features. For instance, there is no support for:

- Kerberos, which requires kernel-level extensions for security and is only available in Windows XP and Windows 2000 clients.

- Group policies, which cannot be created or deployed to computer objects with client extensions.

  - Windows NT 4.0 clients will need to use the NT administrative templates (.adm files) and the NT system policy editor (poledit.exe)

- Windows 98 clients need to be manually managed with system policy editor

- IPsec and L2TP. This requires an upgraded network stack, which is available in Windows 2000 and later. Client extension cannot provide this functionality. However, there is a separate Microsoft client for IPsec and L2TP connectivity for legacy clients.

A Special Word About Macs

Be aware that when you connect Mac OS X clients, they do not get along with the .local DNS extension that SBS uses by default for the internal domain name. Windows systems use SMB (Server Message Blocks) as the default file sharing protocol and Macs have an issue with that unless you are running Mac OS 10.4 or OS 10.3 with special configurations for Active Directory Access and disabled SMB encryption. Another way around this is to either choose a different DNS name extension, like .prv or .office, or not to join the Mac to the Windows domain at all. Mac clients will still be able to access shares and happily participate on the network, unless you are running ISA. And this is where the discussion ends today.

Migrating Profiles

Yes, migrating profiles still is a lively topic at many SBS meetings, and even though Microsoft recommends using the Files and Settings Transfer Wizard included in XP, it will not preserve all user settings of the domain account nor will it pick up certain files you would think should be included, like the .pst file. You have to be sure and specifically tell the Files and Settings Transfer Wizard which file extensions to transfer. For more information on the Files and Settings Transfer Wizard go to: http://www.microsoft.com/technet/prodtechnol/winxppro/deploy/mgrtfset.mspx.

One workaround when moving from an old to a new domain, is to create a separate local user account with administrative rights on the computer and then copying the domain profile of the old user account into a specific folder using the **Control Panel\System Tools\Advanced\Settings and Copy to Profile** option. You then go to the **Local Users and Groups Console**, right-click the newly created user account, click the **Profile** tab, and type the path to the folder holding the copied **Profile** into the **Profile Path** box. You then switch the computer from being a domain member to a workgroup computer and join it to the SBS domain using the newly created user account.

> IMPORTANT: For a total deep dive on migrations, see Chapter 15 of the *Advanced Windows Small Business Server 2003 Best Practices* book (SMB Nation Press).

Removing Clients

Removing clients from the network is rather simple. In the **Standard Management Console**, go to the **Client Computers** container, right-click the computer object you want to delete, and select **Delete**. This will remove the computer account from the Active Directory domain. Don't forget to disjoin the client from the domain and revert it back into a workgroup.

Assigning Applications to Clients

Assigning applications is one of the easiest tasks in SBS. If you don't want to dabble with GPO application deployment, you can just use the Assign Application Wizard and be done with it. Of course, experienced admins can still use GPOs; just make sure to stick with one way or another to standardize the deployment procedure and not have a hodge-podge of methods.

SBS uses the SBS_LOGIN_SCRIPT.BAT logon script that is automatically assigned to all domain user accounts. When a user logs on, the script launches Setup.exe in the *SBSServerName*\Clients\Setup folder. Setup.exe parses the Apps.dat file in the *SBSServerName*\Clients\Response*ClientComputerName* folder that contains the information of each setup program for an assigned application.

Assign Application Wizard

Once you've launched the Assign Application Wizard from the link located in the Client Computers container, you will be presented with default available programs:

- Client Operating System Service Packs

- Internet Explorer 6

- Microsoft Office Outlook 2003

- Shared Fax Client

These are all located in the \Clientapps folder. If checked, these applications will automatically be installed when a user logs on to the client computer. You can also add your own additional applications here by selecting the **Edit Applications** button, which will launch the Set Up Client Applications Wizard. It makes sense to place your application into its own shared folder in the \ClientApps folder to keep all applications together.

Administrative Install

If you are deploying Microsoft Office, make sure to do an administrative install by using **setup.exe /a** to extract the .cab files into a shared folder before you launch the Set Up Client Computer Wizard. Note: if you use the administrative install, make sure to always patch the clients from the same location using the full Office patches, which are entire file replacements, and disallow clients to patch through Windows Update, which are only binary patches. If you mix and match these patch files, you will get funky Microsoft Office behavior. Also do not remove the original install files from the shared location or you will lose the resiliency of the self-repair function since clients have the source install path hard-coded in their registry and will check this location to repair damaged files.

Additional applications assigned in the Assign Application Wizard will appear as a desktop shortcut icon on the user's computer the next time she logs on. The user will then have to initialize the install by clicking on the icon (it will have a UNC path to the executable). The disadvantage here is that you cannot control if and when a user installs the application or decides to simply delete the desktop icon.

On the same screen, the **Advanced** button allows you to configure Internet Explorer settings, Outlook 2003 profile settings, Desktop settings, Fax printer and Fax settings as well as Fax configuration information, and Remote Desktop.

As shown in Figure 8-3, there are also two checkboxes:

- **During client setup, allow the selected applications to be modified** allows a user who is installing applications to change the default application installation location or to deselect applications

- **After client setup is finished, log off the client computer** will log off the client workstation after the installation and prevent other users from accessing the computer.

Figure 8-3

Assigning Applications with the Assign Applications Wizard

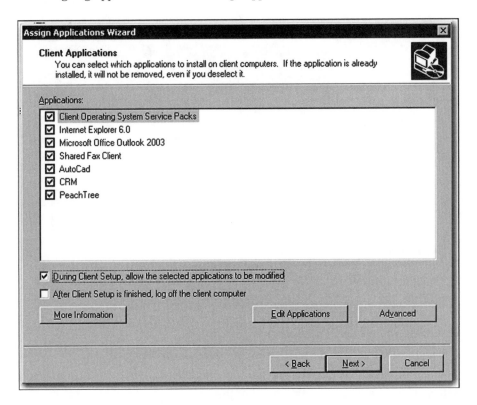

Managing Assigned Applications

A quick and easy way to view and modify assigned applications is by using **View Computer Settings**. You just have got to love this! Go to the **Client Computers** container and click on the **View Computer Settings** link. You will get a display with all client computers and can expand each node to access the **Assigned Applications, Client Setup Settings,** and **Client Setup Configuration Options** (as shown in Figure 8-4). You can expand each of those nodes and then just right-click on a setting or option displayed to change it.

Notes:

Figure 8-4

Viewing and modifying assigned applications in the Server Management Console

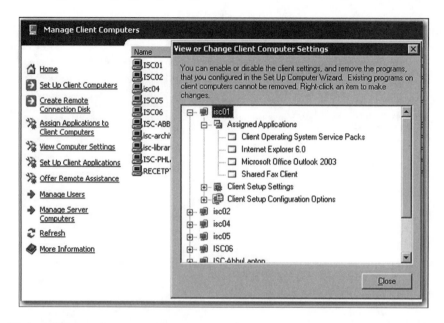

GPO Assigned vs. Published

If you use a GPO to deploy software packages, you can force an application installation based on a user configuration policy or computer configuration policy. The installation can be forced in the:

- **Computer configuration** by choosing the **assign** option for an application, whereas under the

- **User configuration container**, you have the option to either **publish** or **assign** the application.

When **assigning** an application, it will be **automatically installed** the next time the user or computer logs on. When an application is **published**, the icon will be **made available** in the Add/Remove Control Panel and under the Programs Menu, but the application will not be installed until it is actually required. The install can be triggered by either clicking the application install option in **Add/Remove Programs**, or by a user clicking on a file extension that calls for the program (i.e., clicking on a file with the .xls extension that will trigger the install of Excel).

The nice thing about GPO deployments is that you can also push out patches and updates via GPO, as well as remove the application if it is no longer needed.

Setting Up a Client Computer

Setting up the client computer account in SBS is done through the Server Management Console with the Set Up Computer Wizard. Launch the wizard from the **Standard Management Console**, click **Client Computers,** and click the **Set Up Client Computers** link. The wizard will launch and first ask you to specify the name for the client computer account.

- In the **Client Computer Names** screen, you can add multiple computer accounts at once. This is called the **bulk-add tool**. Adding computer names here will create a machine account in Active Directory.

- In the **Client Applications** screen, discussed in the section above, you add or edit client applications.

- In the **Mobile Client and Offline Use** screen, you can select to:

  - **Install Connection Manager** to create the download Connection Manager in Remote Web Workplace (RWW) for easy client VPN configuration. More on this topic is provided in the following section.

  - **Install Active Sync 3.7,** which will push down the Active Sync application to the client computer during the network join process. This will allow devices such as SmartPhones and PocketPCs to synchronize with the client computer and SBS. In fact, if you have a PocketPC with the 2003 OS version, when setting it in the cradle to sync the first time, set it to sync with the Exchange server and it will be automatically configured for wireless access. If you are using General Packet Radio Service (GPRS) or Wi-fi, you will be able to sync your e-mail, contacts, and schedule from wireless.

IMPORTANT: The 70-282 exam, as of this writing, assumes Active Sync 3.7 (even though SBS SP1 upgrades this component to version 3.8).

At this point you are done setting up the client computer and are prompted to go to the client machine and type http://*SBSServerName*/connectcomputer into the browser to launch the Network Configuration Wizard.

Now that you have typed http://*SBSServerName*/connectcomputer into the browser on the client computer, the process of physically adding the client computer to the domain will initiate. You will see the following screens:

- **Network Configuration screen**, which will ask you to **Connect to the Network Now** and then give you a Security Warning dialog box if you want to install the SBS Network Configuration Wizard.

- The first page that appears will be the **Assign users to this computer and migrate their profile** page, where you have the choice of adding **local user accounts** to the **Users assigned to this computer** box. You can assign more than one user to the computer. On this same page you choose to **preserve existing settings** by selecting the assigned user and pairing them with **current user settings.** This is how the local profile gets migrated into the domain profile.

- The next page will be the **Computer Name** screen, where you select the computer account name for the client machine. If the machine currently has a different computer name, it will be renamed.

You then complete the Network Configuration Wizard by clicking **Finish.** The client machine will reboot and go through an automatic logon using the **sbs_netsetup** profile, joining the client to the domain, and boot again.

At this point you can log on with the designated user account for this client machine. When you log on, you will be prompted to install the assigned application packages or to postpone installation until later. During the application install, Outlook 2003 will be installed and automatically configured, so when the user clicks on the Outlook icon, he will be presented with a fully configured e-mail client.

Setting Up Server Computers

Yikes! Turns out there is a lot to these wizards. Learning to trust and use them to your advantage will make your life so much easier. Recently I developed a training course for an enterprise-level class using Windows Server 2003

Enterprise, and it made me realize how much I have become accustomed to the SBS way of doing things. Even though there is the Add Server Roles Wizard in the "other" Windows server versions, it doesn't have anywhere near the ease of setup and management that you have with SBS.

A word about joining additional servers to the SBS domain. I can't tell you how many times I was told that after joining a server to the domain, people experienced somewhat funky server behavior ranging from permission problems to plain odd intermittent connectivity issues. Every time when I asked how the second server had been joined to the domain, it turned out that the Set up Server Wizard had not been used. No comment.

Setting up a server to be joined to the domain is very similar to joining a client and will be covered in Chapter 9, "Expanding the Windows Small Business Server 2003 Network."

Configuring Remote Client Computers

SBS is all about mobility and remote connectivity. Setting up a remote client and configuring a VPN connection or RWW access is easy. Note: Do not try to join remote clients to the domain via VPN. Having to push the applications out over the VPN link would be excruciating to say the least. Best to join a client to the domain in the office, and then ship the client workstation to its final destination. If security is a concern, joining a client to the domain will support not using an L2TP VPN, since we then have computer authentication. On the other hand, if security is not a concern, there is no reason why a remote client needs to join the domain.

Regardless, whether joined to the domain or not, if you want to set up VPN connectivity, you can achieve this in two ways:

- Create a **Remote Connection Disc**

- Use the **Connection Manager** download link in RWW

To create the Remote Connection disk, click the **Create Remote Connection Disk** link in the **Client Computers** container. It will prompt you for a floppy at the finish to load the setup.exe file on. You could transfer this file to other media, like a thumb drive, burn it to CD, or e-mail it (it has a very small footprint). The setup.exe file will have to be executed on the target machine and will create an icon on the desktop that will just require the username and password to log on to the server remotely.

The **Download Connection Manager** link appears in **RWW** by selecting the **Install Connection Manager** checkbox on the **Mobile Client and Offline Use** screen in the **Assign Applications Wizard.** Well, they had to stick this somewhere and this seemed like the most logical place.

Now, none of this will allow remote access or configure remote access settings unless you run the Remote Connection Wizard, which is located on the **To Do List**, Step #3 in the Network Tasks, right below the CEICW.

> ATTENTION: To gain full functionality without having to do any client-side configuration, you must use the fully qualified domain name (FQDN) with this wizard. If you use an IP address, you will have to manually configure the VPN client. Just a minor glitch where the developer of the wizard stated, "DUH...I never thought about that..."

As you can see, even though the Server Management Console is laid out very logically, you should have some hands-on time to become familiar with the whereabouts of individual wizards and how they play together. If you are fairly new to the SBS game, I recommend reading *Windows Small Business Server 2003 Best Practices*, which is a great get-your-feet-wet SBS book that has you build a sample company for practice with super tips to boot!

Configure Offline Mail Synchronization

With the Outlook 2003 client came a new feature called **Cached Exchange Mode** that is very useful for mobile users. The cached mode creates a full copy of all the current items in the user's mailbox. It also creates an offline copy of the address book. This process is called **synchronization.** Items synchronized are:

- Utility folders
- Calendar
- Contacts
- Drafts
- Inbox

- All other folders (defined by the user)

- Sent Items

- Deleted Items

- Public Folder Favorites (added by user)

The Outlook client is set to use Cached Exchange Mode by default. You can manually turn Cached Exchange Mode on or off:

1. Go into **Control Panel**, **Mail**, and click on your current **Profile Properties**.

2. Click **E-mail accounts** and **view or change existing e-mail account**.

3. Select the **Microsoft Exchange Server** account and click **Change**.

4. On the **Exchange Server Settings** screen, under the Exchange server entry, there will be the checkbox **Use Cached Exchange Mode**.

5. Once you have verified that Cached Exchange Mode is set, you can go to **File** and deselect **Work Offline.**

The first time the inbox will synchronize, it will appear empty until the calendar, contacts, and draft folders are synchronized. Once synchronized, you can take the computer offline and all mailbox contents will still be fully accessible. When the client connects back to the network and detects the Exchange server, Outlook will detect the difference between the mailbox and the local cached mailbox and start synchronizing the changes.

Usually, Outlook 2003 configures the optimum synchronization setting based on the connection speed. You can configure them manually (as shown in Figure 8-5) and select from the following:

- Download Full Items

- Download Headers and then Full Items

- Download Headers

- On Slow Connections, Download Only Headers

Your choice will depend on whether you have a fast connection or are on a dial-up connection. Slow connections are 128 kilobits or slower.

Figure 8-5
Exchange Download Options in Outlook 2003

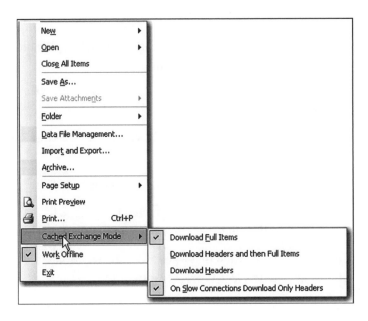

When you have a fast online connection, the e-mail headers are retrieved followed by the full contents of the message, and the OAB (online address book) is updated every 24 hours.

When you have a slow online connection, only the e-mail headers are retrieved and you will have to click **Download the rest of this message now** to download the full message from the server. The OAB is not updated.

The cached file (outlook.ost) is located at C:\Documents and Settings \Administrator\Local Settings\Application Data\Microsoft\Outlook.

> IMPORTANT: It is still a best practice to back up your e-mail inbox to .pst occasionally. In case all hell breaks loose and you find yourself having to recover e-mail from the client side, recovering them from the .ost file can be cumbersome. There is no import/export option for the .ost files as there is for the .pst file and you will find yourself looking at expensive third-party tools.

Configure SUS Using Group Policy

The automatic Software Update Service (SUS) is a free tool for deploying patches to client workstations. You can download SUS from the Microsoft web site and install and configure it to either:

1. **Host the SUS updates locally**, where the client computers get all updates installed from the local computer. This will require only a single download to patch all clients, but be sure to have at least 6 GB of space on the server. The first time you download SUS, it will take a considerable amount of time.

2. **Keep the updates on a Microsoft Windows Update Server** to which you will direct the clients. This will have each individual client connect and download, taking up considerable bandwidth, but will not take up a considerable amount of space on the server.

Updates should be checked and approved at least once a month, if not weekly. The easiest way to deploy SUS to the clients on the network is by creating a new Group Policy Object. To configure the GPO settings:

1. Go into the **Adavanced Management Console** and expand **Group Policy Management** down to the **MyBusiness** container.

2. Right-click the **MyBusiness** container and click **Create and Link a GPO Here**.

3. Give the **New GPO** a descriptive name, like SUS, and click **OK**.

4. Expand the **MyBusiness** container, right-click the **SUS policy object** and click **Edit**.

5. Go to **Computer Configuration, Administrative Templates, Windows Components** and click **Windows Update** to expand the settings.

6. Click **Configure Automatic Updates,** then click **Enable.**

In the **Configure Automatic Updates Properties,** you can now select:

• **Notify for download and notify for install** – This will create a local notification message to prompt the download and installation.

- **Auto download and notify for install -** This will automatically download updates and prompt for the install.

- **Auto download and schedule the install -** This will automatically download and install the new updates.

You can also choose the **scheduled install day** as well as the **scheduled install time**.

If you want the clients to get updated from the local SUS server:

1. Click **Next** and choose **Enabled** in the **Specify intranet Microsoft update service location Properties** box.

2. Type the address of the SUS server (http://*SBSServerName)* in both boxes and click **OK.**

SUS is continuously being improved and we are now on WUS (Windows Update Service). To get the latest information, go to http://www.microsoft.com/windowsserversystem/updateservices/default.mspx.

Resolve Client Computer Connectivity Issues

It never fails; regardless of how much you plan a new install, there will always be the oddball machine that has to act differently than any other machine on the network, and despite having the same hardware, etc., displays its own individual behavior by refusing to play nice. Or you will have an installation that has been running smoothly for the longest time and for no apparent reason (i.e., nothing obvious you can immediately pinpoint) the network connectivity has become flawed. Mostly these will be isolated incidents pertaining to individual computers, but at times it will affect several machines simultaneously, leaving you stumped and clueless as to where to start tracing the issue.

SBS comes with some troubleshooting information in the **Small Business Server Help and Information** file. In addition, at http://www.microsoft.com/sbs, there is a **Support** link that will lead you to several support choices including a **Troubleshooting** link referring to the top troubleshooting issues for SBS 2003. If none of these resolve your current issue, you need to reach for the network troubleshooting utilities.

Network Troubleshooting Utilities

There are several utilities available that help diagnose and resolve networking problems. Besides checking the above-mentioned troubleshooting help files, there is also TechNet (http://www.microsoft.com/technet) and, of course, the built-in troubleshooting tools in Windows Server 2003. You can start troubleshooting by using:

- Event Viewer

- Network Diagnostics

- Command Line tools

The **Event Viewer** records events in the Application, Security, and System logs. The SBS server will also have Directory Service, DNS Server, and File Replication Service logs. By first checking the event viewer, you can find out about possible hardware, software, or system problems that could be the cause of your network connectivity issue. Usually, the Event Viewer will provide a **Source** and an **Event ID**, which you can then use to investigate the issue on TechNet or Google. (Yes, Google is an excellent search tool for Microsoft Event IDs). More on the Event Viewer later in this chapter.

The **Network Diagnostics** tool, which is located in the **Help and Support Center**, performs a series of tests to help isolate causes of network-related issues. It will check the system for network connectivity and whether network-related programs and services are running on the computer. To access Network Diagnostics:

1. Click **Start,** then click **Help and Support.**

2. Click **Tools** and in the left pane expand the **Help and Support Center tools.**

3. Click **Network Diagnostics** in the left pane, then click **Scan your system** in the right pane. You can click **Set scanning options** to see the several choices for which Network Diagnostics will gather information.

There are too many command line tools to cover here, but you can see the entire list in the **Help and Support Center Tools** by clicking **Tools by Category** and then selecting **Network Services Management Tools.** There are some all-time favorites to help you troubleshoot network connectivity on you network, like:

- **Arp** – Arp a displays the Address Resolution Protocol (ARP) cache for stored IP addresses and their resolved MAC address.

- **Ipconfig** – Ipconfig /all displays the full TCP/IP configuration for all adapters, including subnet, gateway, and IP address.

- **Nbtstat** – Nbtstat displays the NetBIOS name resolution statistics. This requires your Windows XP machine or Windows 2003 server to be configured with WINS. Eventually, WINS should go away.

- **Pathping** – Pathping *IPaddress* will provide information on network latency and network loss between intermediate hops between the source and a destination. It will help you determine the degree of packet loss at any given router or link.

Of course, there are also Ping, netstat, netdiag, NSLookup, and Network Monitor as well as additional tools that can be installed from the SBS Disc #1 Support Tools folder or from the Windows Resource Kit. Either way, make sure to be familiar with individual troubleshooting tools including their command line switches. Please visit the list in the Help and Support Center for descriptions on command line tool switches.

> IMPORTANT: More troubleshooting and utilities discussion is presented later in this chapter and in Chapter 10.

Back Up and Restore SBS 2003

Recently I went on a 25-city Hands-On-Lab training tour that included a Disaster Recovery Session for SBS. Microsoft had wanted a bare-metal restore lab. If you have done a bare-metal restore before, you know that according to Microsoft SBS white paper ideology, you first reinstall the operating system from Disc #1 of the SBS disc set, then after the reboot of the GUI portion install, and before going into the SBS 2003 Installation Wizard, you connect your backup media device, load the drivers, and then do a full restore to the server. That of course goes with the assumption that the data on the backup media was placed there by running the Configure Backup Wizard. Now, the Configure Backup Wizard is a cool wizard to have when you don't know anything about backing up data, but as it turns out, most IT professionals choose a third-party backup solution, which was confirmed every time I posed this question.

So why is there so much discontent? The Configure Backup Wizard really uses the NTbackup utility in Windows Server 2003 (configured by the Small Business Backup.bks script located in %systemdrive%\program files\Microsoft Windows Small Business Server\Backup folder), which has had a bad rap in the past. Fickleness and oddities about ntbackup utility behavior have made this utility a great discussion topic, as well as creating many frustrated system admins.

Volume Shadow Copy technology (covered in a bit), which is new to Windows Server 2003 and being embraced by many consultants, plays a big part in the SBS data availability and recovery model.

But, to find out more about what real-life backup solutions and strategies are recommended by IT professionals, check out Chapter 14 in the *Advanced Windows Small Business Server Best Practices*. Topic by topic it is lined with genuine backup tips and information used by real-world SBS professionals.

So back to honoring the SBS Backup and Recover methodology, which should not be dissed just because it uses NTbackup. You should know about it for the exam, so lets get started.

Creating a Backup Job Using the Backup Configuration Wizard

The Backup Configuration Wizard is located under the **Backup** link in the Standard Management Console. The wizard not only allows you to make a full system backup, it also lets you set the **Deleted Item Retention** for Exchange e-mails and the size of the Volume Shadow Copy snapshot. Having all tools in one wizard follows the "keep it simple" SBS methodology—kudos to the person who thought this up. It's like having the "one-stop-backup-shop." Of course, as several Hot-Lab attendees have pointed out, there is always room for improvement, but mind you that the wizards and entire SBS methodology were designed for nontechnical people. Good thing Microsoft didn't succeed all the way, or we would be looking for work.

Backup Configuration Wizard

Once you launch the wizard, the first screen will ask in what location to place the backup data. Two choices are offered:

- Back up to a tape drive [recommended]

- Back up to a local hard disk or network share

By default, the backup wizard will back up ALL data on the server (except for default excluded files) including the System State comprised of:

- Boot files, including the system files

- Files protected by the Windows File Protection (WFP)

- Registry

- Performance counter configuration information

- Component Services class registration database

Also backed up are all other data folders, as well as the Exchange database, SharePoint database, and SQL databases, including open files with the help of the Volume Shadow Copy Service (explained more in a bit).

Exclude Folders

You can then manually select to exclude certain folders from the backup. This option is useful when you, say, have a 60 GB hard disk and only a 20 GB tape drive; you would want to exclude all the junk data (disposable data that would not have a financial or operational impact on the business if it wasn't restored immediately after a disaster) and include only the pertinent high-value (mission-critical, immediate financial, or operational impact) data folders in the backup.

Define Backup Schedule

By default, the Define Backup Schedule page starts the backups at 11 p.m. and has Monday – Friday selected. Here you can change the schedule and select a different time of day. You can only create one backup job with the Backup Configuration Wizard. If you want to set up a nightly differential backup and a Friday full backup, you will still have to use NTbackup to define a more sophisticated backup job.

Tape Changer

You have the ability to select the tape changer—no, that is not your tape backup device. In this case it will be the person designated as the official "Tape Changer" who will be in charge of manually changing the tapes in the server. Setting this option will send a reminder e-mail to the person at a designated time; you can also set it to send a monthly tape drive cleaning reminder.

> IMPORTANT: It strikes both authors that this type of oddity is the type of thing that could appear on the 70-282 exam.

Storage Allocation for Deleted Files and E-mail

Here you can set the option to **Retain copies of permanently deleted e-mail messages**, which will allow you to bring back deleted e-mails, even if they were deleted with the Shift+Ctrl keys. By default, this is set to 30 days; you can bump it up to any number of days you like. Just keep in mind that even though the deleted item does not count against your 16 GB mailbox store limit, this will take up space in the Recovery store, so you don't want to overdo it. Keep it at about 120 to 160 days. By configuring this setting in the Backup Configuration Wizard, you don't have to go into the Exchange System Manager. Deleted e-mails can then be retrieved from the Outlook client under **Tools** by clicking on **Recovery Deleted Items.**

The **Enable periodic snapshots of users' shared folders** option will let you configure the amount of space you can allocate for the Shadow Volume Copy snapshot. When you redirect the user's My Documents folder (covered earlier in the Standard Management section), this will be the amount allocated to store the snapshot. More on VSS (Volume Shadow Service) later in this chapter.

Excluded Files

Now, when we say "backs up ALL files," that is, of course, with the exclusion of "default-excluded files" like temporary files such as:

- Pagefile.sys

- Hiberfil.sys

- Win386.swp

- 386spart.par

- Backup.log

- Restore.log.

If you are backing up from a network share on a remote computer, backup skips these files if they are in use at the time of the backup.

Volume Shadow Service (During Backup)

VSS requires NTFS as the file system. VSS is a copy technology that provides an instant copy of the original volume. When the backup is initiated, a shadow copy of the volume is made even though the original volume continues to change as the process continues. The shadow copy of the volume will remain constant. Users can continue to access files while you are running the backing job. Once the data is backed up to media, the shadow copy will be deleted.

The advantages of VSS include:

- Computers can be backed up while applications and services are running.

- Files will not be skipped during the backup process.

- Files that are open at the time of the shadow copy appear closed on the shadow copy volume.

- There is no need to shut down applications or services to ensure a successful volume backup.

> IMPORTANT: **Caveat Emptor!** The NTFS volume stores the difference between the original volume and the shadow copy volume in a record, and the data on the shadow copy volume exists only while the shadow copy is being taken. There has to be sufficient disk space available for the volume shadow copy, or the service will shut down and Backup will skip the open files.

If you purchase a third-party backup solution, make sure to verify that it can register with writer interfaces and make use of the Volume Shadow Copy technology.

Volume Shadow Service (Periodic Snapshots)

Volume Shadow Copies are enabled by default in SBS. You can check the settings by going to **C:**, clicking on the local disk properties, then clicking the **Shadow**

Copies tab. Its purpose is to keep previous versions of users' files and is, therefore, called "Previous Versions." Accessing previous versions can be useful when users need to:

- **Recover accidentally deleted files**

- **Recover from accidentally overwritten files**

- **Compare different file versions**

Snapshots are taken at 7:00 a.m. and 12:00 noon, Monday through Friday, and can be manually modified to fit a different schedule. Shadow Copies will keep up to 64 versions before overwriting the last one.

The snapshot is being taken on the volume that occupies the **Users Shared Folders** by default. When you have **Client Document Redirection** enabled, documents that are placed into the MyDocuments folder on a user's computer are automatically placed in the Users Shared Folders where Volume Shadow Copies Service will take the snapshot. If a user accidentally deletes a file, he can right-click on his **MyDocuments** folder where he has the **Previous Versions** tab and be able to recover the previous version of the document from that point in time when the last snapshot was taken.

Backup Location and Media Considerations

Historically, the preferred backup location has been a tape drive, as the tape can then be moved off-site after the backup is completed. With disaster recovery becoming a more prominent item due to Health Insurance Portability and Accountability Act of 1996 (HIPAA) compliance and other legislative requirements, terrorist acts, hurricanes, and the likes, technology is switching to support not only recovery, but business continuity despite a catastrophe. There are more solutions available and affordable now with dropping hardware prices and technology improvements, allowing more small businesses to afford RAID arrays, NAS storage, and other previously too expensive solutions. Small businesses do backups using removable hard drives, DVDs, network shares, even over the web, and in general have become more sophisticated about disaster recovery and prevention.

A balance must be struck between the price of the recovery solution and the availability and cost of the backup media. There is no point to have a really inexpensive solution if it will take you days to get back to the point of being operable. In the meantime the business may have lost a million-dollar contract or was unable to deliver on a deadline. Then again, there is no point in spending dollars on having the latest high-tech recovery solution only to use it to back up not just mission-critical data, but also junk data that should have no business on the server or should have been removed eons ago.

Unfortunately, there is no one-size-fits-all formula, and considerations of media and backup location will have to be carefully weighed against the impact of financial and operational loss that will be caused due to irrecoverable data.

Restoring from a Backup Job

So the unexpected happened and you had corrupted or damaged data to the point where you have to recover the entire server. One business where I was performing a backup job got hit with the "I love you" virus just as I was running the backup. After containing the outbreak, we started to restore from the backup tape and guess what? It started all over again! Well, lucky enough, we were on a regular rotation schedule and ended up only losing one day's worth of work, but the impact could have been much worse.

In a rosy-rose world (the Microsoft exam view), you are on a regular tape backup schedule, there are no tapes that fail, and, of course, you are able to recover to the same hardware as before. So now you are ready to use the backup utility and have a backup on a tape, hard drive, or network share.

You can launch the NTbackup utility by typing **ntbackup** in the **Run** command. You want to select the **Advanced Mode** and click on the **Restore and Manage Media** tab.

Select the media you will be restoring from and decide whether to restore to one of the following:

- **Original location** – if you had to replace a failed drive for instance

- **Alternate location** – especially if you are not sure of the data integrity and only have to restore a few files, you should not restore into the original location

If the restore turns out to be bad, and you restored the entire tape into the original location, you just shot your last chance of possibly doing a last resort data recovery of the hard drive.

Before you initiate the actual restore, click **Advanced** and make sure that you have checked:

- **Restore security**

- **Restore junction points, restore file, and folder data under junction point to the original location**

- **Preserve existing volume mount points**

Click **OK** and wait and see! The restore will finish and display a message that the restore is completed. Click **OK** again. You may want to also check the Report to ensure the successful restore.

Another method for restoring individual files would be using the **Previous Versions Client** to restore individual files. Some installations will have an entire hard drive dedicated to take a snapshot of an entire volume. You can enable the snapshot by modifying the settings in the Local Disk Properties on the **Shadow Copies** tab. First disable the current snapshot, then click **Settings.** You can use the dropdown in the **Storage area** to select the drive you dedicated for the volume snapshot and set the **Maximum size** to **No limit.** Then click **Schedule** and set your preferences.

Monitor and Troubleshoot SBS 2003

SBS 2003 comes with the Monitoring Configuration Wizard from which you can set up alert notifications and enable application logging. The Monitor Configuration Wizard will configure settings in **Health Monitor** which for some reason is no longer part of the Server Management Console. To access Health Monitor, click **Start, Administrative Tools,** then click **Health Monitor**. You will have to first run the Monitoring Configuration Wizard before the Alerts show up in Health Monitor. Another great monitoring tool is the **Performance Monitor**, which will require manual configuration.

Configuring Monitoring and Alerts

You set up Monitoring by running the Monitoring Configuration Wizard, which will create server performance and usage reports that can either be e-mailed or viewed from Server Management or on the intranet. In the Server Management Console,

1. Click **Monitoring and Reporting** to launch the wizard.

2. On the **Configuration Mode** screen, select **Modify existing settings** and click **Next**.

3. On the **Reporting Options** screen, under **Performance Report,** select **Receive a daily performance report in e-mail**, and under the **Usage Report**, check **View the usage report in Server Management** and **Receive a usage report in e-mail every other week.**

4. Enter an **E-mail address** on the **E-mail Options** screen.

5. Specify who you want to have access to the usage report by adding respective user names.

6. On the **Alerts** screen, select **Send me notification of performance alerts by e-mail** and enter your e-mail address. Now the Monitor Configuration Wizard will configure the:
   - Data store
   - Data collection
   - Alert Threshold
   - Configure Reports

Performance data is collected hourly, so it will take a bit before you can view your first report. By selecting to receive the report by e-mail on a daily basis, you configured the server to send you a report every morning at 6 a.m., which is a default setting that can be changed to a different time. I do prefer the 6 a.m. schedule because this way I know first thing in the morning that the server is up and running. If there are critical events or alerts, it is still early enough for me to look over the issue and remote manage the server and not have to interrupt my clients in the middle of the day in case the server requires a reboot.

Performance, Usage, and Server Status Reports

What can I say, these are cool! In SBS 2000 we had the xml reporting tool, which provided great information but was a bit cumbersome to use because you had to save the files and, and, and—there were just too many steps involved. Being able to receive the reports now in e-mail in html format has made life as an administrator so much easier. The performance report contains detailed information about the overall health of the server. The daily server performance report includes:

- **Server Specifications** – displays information on the OS, Processor, Speed, and the amount of RAM

- **Performance Summary** – displays Memory in use, free disk space, disk busy time, CPU use, and the rate of change/growth over the last month

- **Top 5 Processes by Memory Usage** – displays the process using up the most memory

- **Top 5 Processes by CPU Usage** – displays the processes using up the most CPU cycles

- **Backup** – displays whether the Backup completed successfully or with errors

- **Auto-started Services Not Running** – displays services that are set to auto start and should be running, but are not

- **Critical Alerts**

- **Critical Errors in the Event Logs**

You can also attach event viewer log files and the backup log status to be sent with the daily performance or the usage report. To attach the files, you have to go into the **Change Server Status Report Settings** tool and select from:

- **Application Event Log**

- **IIS Log**

- **SBS Backup Logs**

- **Security Event Log**

- **System Event Log**

In a daily performance report, as shown in Figure 8-6, you first get a summary view, which, if there are any problems, lets you drill down to **Details** and provide an Event Viewer view of the log file, including Event ID and Source.

Figure 8-6
Daily Performance Report Summary View

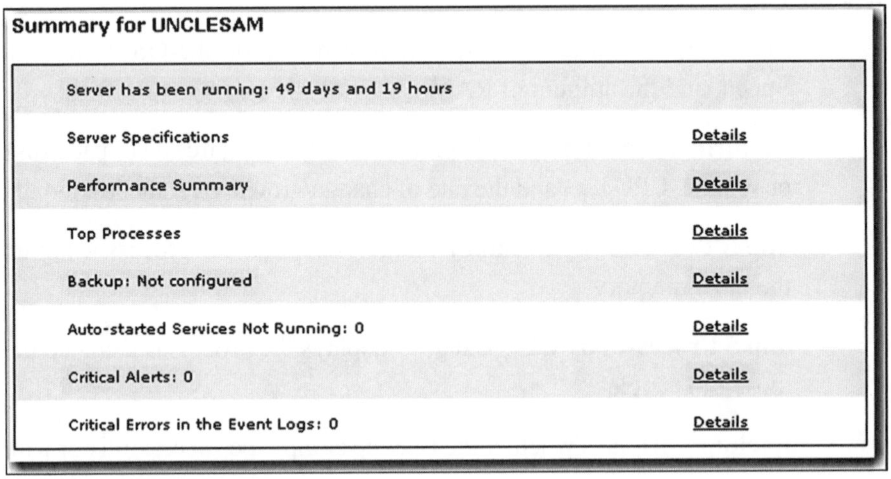

Summary for UNCLESAM

Server has been running: 49 days and 19 hours	
Server Specifications	Details
Performance Summary	Details
Top Processes	Details
Backup: Not configured	Details
Auto-started Services Not Running: 0	Details
Critical Alerts: 0	Details
Critical Errors in the Event Logs: 0	Details

Usage Reports are a great tool for business owners to get a quick glimpse of what is going on. If you have an owner who wants to know everything from web usage to applications used, I suggest you install ISA Server which is an excellent reporting tool.

IMPORTANT: Remember that reporting and configuring are not the same actions.

The Usage report is composed of

- **Web Activity by Computer** – Displays the total active and average active hours per day

- **Web Traffic by Hour** – Displays the total connection and average connections per day

- **E-mail Sent** – Displays the amount of internal and external e-mail sent, including the size in MB

- **E-mail Received** – Displays the amount of internal and external e-mail received, including the size in MB

- **Mailbox size** – Displays the mailbox starting size and ending size for the last two weeks and the rate of change as a percentage

- **Outlook Web Access Activity by User** – Displays who accessed OWA, how many visits, and the average visit per day

- **Outlook Web Access Usage by Hour** – Displays the hours of the day and total and average visits during these hours

- **Remote Connection Activity by User** – Displays the user name and total VPN connections and the average time and average connections per day

- **Remote Connection Activity by Hour** – Displays the hours and average connections per day during these hours

- **Fax Sent** – Displays faxes sent to destination, total faxes, average amount of pages, average transmission time, and average number of faxes per day

- **Faxes Received** - Displays faxes received from, total faxes, average amount of pages, average transmission time, and average number of faxes per day

- **Faxes sent by User** – Displays faxes sent by user, total faxes, average amount of pages, average transmission time, and average number of faxes per day

- **Fax Traffic by Hour** – Displays fax traffic by the hour of the day, total faxes, and average number of faxes per day

It is good business to e-mail forward the usage reports and performance reports to the business owners on a regular basis. This way your client sees that you are truly monitoring her network, as well as helping her keep tabs on employees. We recently had a case where a user started working remotely. When the first usage report came in, we discovered the user had connected only once in two weeks for less than 30 minutes! Needless to say, the employer that had been paying a full-time salary was able to take corrective action based on the report. Certainly this would have been discovered eventually, but why not find out sooner and have it documented?

Figure 8-7 shows a detail cut-out on E-mail Received, which tells us right away who is giving out their business e-mail address to Internet sites they should stay OFF! (And this is after the spam filter…)

Figure 8-7

E-mail received cutout from a Usage Summary Report over a two-week period of time

E-mail Received

User Name	Internal E-mail	Size (MB)	External E-mail	Size (MB)	Total E-mail Received	Size (MB)
James Taylor	0	0.0	690	3.6	690	3.6
Diane Welford	2	0.1	153	4.0	155	4.0
Debbie Dye	3	0.1	52	0.4	55	0.5
Tim Heffernan	2	0.1	48	1.1	50	1.2
Laura Peery	4	0.0	16	0.0	20	0.1
Administrator	2	0.1	1	0.0	3	0.2
Liz Dye	2	0.1	1	0.0	3	0.1
Lynda Pritchard	2	0.0	1	0.0	3	0.0
Andrea Wilson	0	0.0	1	0.0	1	0.0
Jennifer Walter	1	0.0	0	0.0	1	0.0
Company Total	18	0.6	963	9.1	981	9.7

Changing Alert Notifications

You can configure a change alert notification by going to the **Health Monitor** snap-in and right-clicking the **Actions** node, then clicking **New.** You will be able to configure an Action as a response to an Alert. You can configure the following Actions:

- **Command Line** – executes a file that can be run from the command line

- **E-Mail** – Sends SMTP e-mail to a specified recipient

- **Text Log** – Writes text that you specify to a specified test-based log file

- **Windows Event** – Generates an event that will be written to the application log in the Event Viewer

- **Script** – Runs a WSH (Windows Scripting Host) that you specify

An alert is generated when a defined threshold is crossed, and the action is a response to the alert.

Small Business Server Troubleshooter Utilities

SBS comes with a variety of built-in troubleshooter utilities. These utilities will help you diagnose and solve technical issues. The troubleshooters are interactive and will require you to answer a series of questions about the problems you have encountered. Each troubleshooter utility addresses a different problem, based on the answers you provide. Troubleshooters are listed in Table 8-2

Table 8-2

Small Business Server Troubleshooter Utilities

Troubleshooter	Identifies and resolves problems related to:
System Setup	Installing and setting up Windows.
Startup/Shutdown	Starting up and shutting down your computer.
Display	Video cards and video adapters, including your computer screen, outdated or incompatible video drivers, and incorrect settings for your video hardware.
Home Networking	Setup, Internet connections, sharing files and printers.
Hardware	Disk drives (including CD-ROM and DVD drives), game controllers, input devices (such as keyboards, mice, cameras, scanners, and infrared devices), network adapters, USB devices, modems, and sound cards. Also see the more specific hardware device troubleshooters below.
Multimedia and Games	Games and other multimedia programs, DirectX drivers, USB devices, DVDs, sound, joysticks, and related issues.

Table 8-2 (continued)

Troubleshooter	Identifies and resolves problems related to:
Digital Video Discs (DVDs)	DVD drives and decoders.
Input Devices	Keyboards, mouse and trackball devices, cameras, scanners, and infrared devices.
Drives and Network Adapters	Hard discs, floppy discs, CD-ROM and DVD drives, network cards, tape drives, backup programs.
USB	USB connectors and peripherals.
Sound	Sound and sound cards.
Modem	Modem connections, setup, configuration, and detection.
Internet and Connection Sharing	Connecting and logging on to your ISP
Internet Explorer	Browsing the web, downloading files, saving your favorites, using IE toolbars, or printing web pages.
Outlook Express	Outlook Express and Windows Messenger Service.
File and Print Sharing	Sharing files and printers between computers, connecting to other computers in a network, installing network adapters, logging on.
Printing	Printer installation and connection, printer drivers, print quality, printer speed, and fonts.

Troubleshoot Outlook Web Access

Remember the problem where your client accessed Outlook Web Access (OWA) one day, simply checked some e-mails, and then the next day she couldn't get into the site? You hadn't installed new service packs or applications on the server and the log files all came up clean, but OWA just decided on its own to not work that day. There are so many factors that come into play when troubleshooting OWA, from possible issues with Exchange and IIS to web browser settings and authentication methods used.

Outlook Web Access Basic/Premium

When accessing OWA, you may receive one of the following error messages:

- HTTP 401.1 – Unauthorized: Logon Failed

- Access is Denied

- Page Cannot Be Displayed

Or you can log on successfully but will be prompted to enter your credentials again. If you fail to type your user name in the **domain/username** format, you will be faced with one of the following:

- Logon failed or cancelled message

- After you provided the correct credentials, the OWA page doesn't load

- You can log on with Netscape, but not use any other browsers

Most of these issues occur if users have not been granted the correct permissions or use an incorrect authentication method. Also, a combination of IIS 6.0 on a Windows Server 2003 with Exchange Server 2003 requires entering the **domain\username**. (This has been fixed with KB831464.)

By default, Integrated Authentication is enabled in Exchange Server 2000 SP3 and later on the Outlook Web Access folder. You should try using basic authentication when:

- Integrated Windows Authentication between the client browser and the web server isn't functioning and a proxy server exists between the client browser and the web server.

- Integrated Windows Authentication fails because there is a time difference between the client and the server.

- Web Proxy clients using SecureNAT in ISA Server experience issues trying to authenticate to OWA.

There are workarounds to these issues. You could also try to:

- Remove Integrated Windows Authentication from the OWA site

- Add the FQDN, the IP address of the Outlook Web Access server, or both to the **Do not use proxy server for addresses beginning with** list in the advanced proxy settings of the LAN settings in the Internet Explorer options

- Install the ISA firewall client and add the FQDN of the OWA site to the local domain table in ISA Server

Okay, the point is—use TechNet. There are several Knowledge Base (KB) articles on troubleshooting OWA access and when I went to the KB and entered "outlook web access," it came back with 100 KBs! There is something for everyone.

OWA Client-Side Troubleshooting Remedies

If you are experiencing trouble accessing OWA, try these steps on the client first before changing any settings on the server side.

- Clear the browser cache and history. Also check http://windowsupdate .microsoft.com for critical updates for the operating system and browser.

- Delete temporary Internet files and cookies.

- Reset all Internet Explorer settings to default.

- Ensure you are using IE5.01 or later to use the premium version of OWA (some features will work only with IE6.0.).

- Set the browser to use SSL.

- Accept and install the site certificate.

- Set the browser to accept cookies.

- If OWA loads but the right pane is stuck on "loading," make sure to add the site to your trusted sites.

- If you use Windows 98 or 98SE and you are using IE6.0 and the right pane remains empty, you may need to install the Java plug-in for IE.

Troubleshoot Company Network Connections to an ISP

Once in a while you will have issues with Internet connectivity, and your ISP will tell you it's your server, at which point you have to pull out the tools to show them otherwise. We have already discussed some troubleshooting tools useful for LAN issues, and some of those tools work for Internet connectivity as well.

- GetMac – GetMac.exe is a quick way to get your MAC address.

- IPConfig – IPConfig displays the current configuration of your IP stack.

- Network Connectivity Tester – Netdiag.exe gathers static network information and tests the network driver, protocol driver, send/receive capability, and well-known target vulnerabilities.

- Nslookup – Nslookup.exe performs DNS queries and examines content of zone files on local and remote servers.

- Trace Route – Tracert.exe traces the connection pathways between the source and destination including the amount of hops and the time.

- Network Monitor – Netcap.exe monitors network traffic and captures information to a log file.

- Netsh – Netsh.exe is a command line scripting utility that displays and lets you modify network configuration.

There are several command line switches with these tools. We recommend you check them out individually by going to http://www.microsoft.com and typing each command into the Microsoft Search. Also, see the section "Troubleshooting Utilities" in Chapter 10.

> IMPORTANT: Given that a common call to SBS consultants from customers is "..I can't connect to the Internet," don't you think it's likely there would be this type of question on the 70-282 exam?

Event Viewer

When it comes to troubleshooting, the Event Viewer should always be the first tool checked for logged error messages. It will give you clues to help discover problem areas with the server as well as the applications running on it. The Event Viewer allows you to view, clear, save, filter, and find Events.

Events are broken down into Event Types as shown in Table 8-3. Each event is a particular type, and five types of events are reported. Event logs include the date, time, source, category, and Event ID.

Table 8-3

Event Types

Event Type	Description
Information	This indicates a significant, successful operation—for example, an event indicating that a service has started.
Warning	Warning events indicate problems that are not immediately significant, but could cause problems in the future. Resource consumption is a good example of a warning event.
Error	Error events indicate significant problems the user should know about. Error events usually indicate a loss of functionality or data.
Failure Audit	Failure audit events are security events that occur when an audited access attempt fails. A failed attempt to open a file (due to lack of permissions) is an example of a failure audit event.
Success Audit	Success audit events are security events that occur when an audited access attempt succeeds.

Now you open the Event Viewer and are inundated with a gazillion log entries. Don't cry; simply specify a filter that limits the type of information that you want Event Viewer to display. To filter events:

1. Click **Start, Programs, Administrative Tools**, and then **Event Viewer.**

2. In the console tree, right-click the appropriate log file, and then click **Properties**.

3. Click the **Filter** tab.

4. Type the appropriate information that you would like to filter and click **OK**.

You can filter for an event based on the five event types or by source, user, computer, or date of the event. This really helps sorting through large log files.

Now that events are filtered by your particular criteria, you may want to find an event based on a user name or computer within the filter, a category, or a source. To use the Find function:

1. Click **Start**, **Programs**, **Administrative Tools**, and then **Event Viewer**.

2. In the console tree, right-click the appropriate log file.

3. On the **View** menu, click **Find**.

4. Type the appropriate information you would like to find in the dialog box, and then click **Find Next.**

Make the Event Viewer your friend and combine it with other troubleshooting tools and the TechNet Knowledge Base, and you will rarely have to call Product Support Services.

> IMPORTANT: By the way, an old trick Microsoft Certified Partners have used to obtain an MCSE is to use one of their five free Product Support Service incidents to get the smarties at Microsoft to walk the caller through a tough exam area. That is, burn a support incident as a study tool. In your case, you might have to find a partner with support incidents left to burn. Try a local user group meeting to meet such a person.

Configure and Troubleshoot Terminal Services

At some point you will meet a business that needs the ability to host multiple, simultaneous client desktop sessions. It could be the doctor's office with eight branch offices in different suburbs seeking to keep the financial side down on the proprietary medical application while giving the branch offices real-time access to the server application and making all data centralized. Or you may have a client who needs to support a large mobile workforce where workers rarely come to the office and have no designated workstations, instead using their own laptops to connect to the office several times a day to enter data and check the latest reports.

Understanding Terminal Services

With Terminal Services you can run any installed program on the server. Because it is optimized to run Windows-based applications, you can deliver the Windows desktop itself to just about any computing device, even those that cannot run Windows. Clients connect to Terminal Services using RDC (Remote Desktop Connection), which is built into Windows XP and Windows Server 2003. Clients who do not have RDC installed can download the RDC client at http://www.microsoft.com/windowsxp/downloads/tools/rdclientdl.mspx. The client can be run on Windows 9x, Windows Me, Windows NT 3.51, NT 4.0, Windows 2000, and Mac OS-X, as well as on any Windows CE-based handhelds. RDC can also be run on 16-bit-based computers running Windows for Workgroups with MS TCP/IP-32. RDC uses RDP (Remote Desktop Protocol) to connect to the server and has support for:

- 24-bit color

- Audio redirection

- Smart card redirection

- COM port redirection

- Local network printer redirection

- File system redirection

- Disk drive redirection

- 128-bit encryption

Terminal Services cannot be installed on the SBS machine in Application Sharing Mode due to security and technical limitations, with some services competing for the same resources as the SBS services. But Remote Desktop for Administration (a.k.a. Terminal Services in Remote Administration Mode) is enabled by default on the SBS server allowing two simultaneous connections for administrative purposes. (This is not application-sharing mode.)

The client and server communicate via the RDP 5.2 with high encryption (128-bit RC4). RDP is designed to support many different types of network topologies, like ISDN, POTS, IPX, NetBIOS, TCP/IP, and other LAN protocols. The current version of RDP will run only over TCP/IP and use port 3389 by default. RDP provides 64,000 separate channels for data transmission, but is used only on a single channel for keyboard, mouse, and presentation data.

Installing Terminal Services

Terminal Services is automatically installed on the SBS 2003 server machine. But the best practice would be to add an additional Windows Server 2003 server machine to the network to host Terminal Services in Application Sharing Mode.

To install Terminal Services on a Windows 2003 Server (not the SBS server), you would:

1. Go to the **Manage Your Server** page and click **Add or remove a role**.

2. Select **Terminal Server,** click **Next**, and click **Next** on the **Summary of Selection** screen. Click **OK**.

By default, you have **160 days** before the Terminal Server requires access licenses for clients.

Configuring Terminal Services
Changing the Session Encryption Level

By default, all Terminal Services sessions connect using high encryption, which provides bi-directional security using a 128-bit cipher. However, some older versions of the Terminal Services client do not support this high level of encryption. Clients that do not support this level of encryption will not be able to connect. Therefore, the encryption level can be set to "client compatible" to provide the highest encryption level supported by the client. Both levels use the standard RSA RC4 encryption.

Changing the encryption level is performed within the Terminal Services Configuration utility, located under **Advanced Management, Terminal Services Configuration.** Right-click the **Connections** folder and click on

Properties. The **General** tab will show the Encryption dialog box where you can select:

- Low

- Client Compatible

- High

- FIPS compliant

Remote Desktop User Group

Instead of adding users to a list in the Terminal Services Connection Configuration (TSCC) program, you can simply make them members of the **Remote Desktop Users** (RDU) group. For example, the administrator can add the "Everyone" group to the RDU group to allow everyone to access the terminal server.

Maximum Connections

You may want to set the number of maximum connections; if so, best practice dictates using Group Policy. Go to **Group Policy Management** and in the appropriate container:

1. Click **Computer Configuration** and expand **Administrative Templates.**

2. Expand **Windows Components**, expand **Terminal Services,** and double-click the **Limit number of connections** setting. Click **Enabled** and enter the number of maximum connections allowed.

We recommend that you use Group Policy for Terminal Services Configuration in general. For more information on this topic, go to http://www.microsoft.com and do a search on "Terminal Server Best Practices." (The URL is too long to list here.)

Terminal Services Manager Utility

The Terminal Services Manager can be used to monitor sessions, users, and processes and to manage the Terminal Server. The utility can be accessed under **Advanced Management, Terminal Services Configuration,** and by clicking on **Terminal Services Manager** in the right pane or typing **tsadmin.exe** on the

Run command line. By clicking on **Actions** in the **Terminal Services Manager** toolbar, you can:

- **Connect** – connects a user to another session. This will disconnect the current session but not delete it. You can use this to switch between sessions.

- **Disconnect** – disconnects a user from a session. The session remains attached and currently running applications continue to run. The user will be reconnected to the session when logging back on, even when connecting from a different computer.

- **Log off users** – logs off users without warning and can result in data loss for that session. All processes will be ended and the session is deleted from the server.

- **Reset** – deletes a session instantly without warning the user, and can result in loss of data at that session. Use this if a session has stopped responding.

- **Remote Control** – allows monitoring a user's session and will interact if needed.

- **Status** – enables the administrator to monitor session-related counters, such as incoming and outgoing bytes.

- **Send Message** – allows the administrator to send a message to a session and to remotely control sessions.

- **End Processes** – allows the administrator to end a process running in a user's session.

Practice Questions

Question #1

Race Brook Publishing has 29 Windows XP Pro SP1 client computers, 10 Windows Professional SP3 computers, an SBS 2003 server and 2 Windows 2000 servers on the network. Your boss has asked you to implement standard policy across the network. There is one accounting application that should only be accessed by certain users and others need to have access to different proprietary applications and their respective files. Where can you install the GPMC (Group Policy Management Console) to manage users? (check all that apply)

A. Install the GPMC on the Windows 2000 servers

B. Install the GPMC on a Window 2000 Professional Computer

C. Install the GPMC on the SBS 2003 Server

D. Install the GPMC on a Windows XP Pro client

Question #2

As a promotional gig you give away a 20 hours of free consulting to a non-profit group in town. As you survey their network, you discover that they have ten Windows 95 computers and seven Windows XP Pro Machines. They purchased SBS 2003 Standard and expect you to help them install the server and enable the clients to communicate with the SBS domain. Currently the non-profit uses the sneaker network and wants to implement SBS as their file server and Internet connection with the least amount of your time used. What could you do? (select two)

A. Set up a separate DHCP scope for the Windows 95 clients. Install the Active Directory client extensions on Windows 95 computers and assign static addresses.

B. Set up a separate DHCP scope for the Windows 95 clients. Install the Active Directory server extensions on the Mac clients.

C. Install Active Directory client extensions on the Windows 95 machines.

D. Disable SMB signing on the SBS server.

Question #3

ABC Insurance has one SBS server located in the Headquarters office. They have four additional Windows Server 2003 servers in four branch office locations, connected with a T1. There are 15 client Windows XP Pro client workstations at each location and a backup is performed every night at the Headquarters office. You have been noticing errors in the

DNS event log and want to check the SBS 2003 server errors. Which tool should you use?

A. DNS console

B. NSLookup.exe

C. Dcdiag.exe

D. Health Monitor

Question #4

You are the consultant for Travel, Inc., a small travel agency. You just installed SBS 2003 and connected 23 Windows XP Professional workstations and 12 Windows 2000 Professional computers to the network. Employees use e-mail to communicate with clients and the Internet for research. The owner wonders if there is a way to monitor e-mail and web usage inexpensively. He also asks you to check the event logs on a daily basis. How can you configure this with the least amount of administrative effort?

A. Run system monitor and create a base line. Create alert thresholds and set the action to send e-mail when the threshold is exceeded. Write a script to send Exchange and Internet information from the collected logs to the owner.

B. Run the Monitoring Configuration wizard and create custom alert thresholds, and set the actions to send e-mail when a threshold is exceeded. Write a script to send you the daily system event log.

C. Run the Monitoring Configuration wizard and add the owner's user account to the report recipients. Run the Change Alert Notification wizard and attach the system event log files to your e-mail notification.

D. Run the Usage Report wizard and add the owner's user account to the report recipients. Run the Monitoring Configuration Wizard and attach the system event log files to your e-mail notification.

Question #5

You administer a network for a restaurant chain. The main office runs an SBS 2003 server, a Windows Server 2003 and six Windows XP Professional computers. The chain has several branch locations that feed their transactions via Terminal Services into the Windows Server 2003. The server has the restaurant point of sale system installed, and uses a SQL database. The server is configured with three disks. The system sits on disk 0, the SQL database is located on disk 1 and the transaction log is located on disk 2. You run a full backup every two hours. The last full database backup finished at 9 p.m. Transactions are continuing in this sequence:

9:05 p.m. – Transaction 313 starts

9:07 p.m. – Transaction 314 starts

9:08 p.m. – Transaction 315 starts

9:15 p.m. – A differential backup begins

9:17 p.m. – Transaction 316 starts

9.17 p.m. – Transaction 315 commits

9:21 p.m. – Transaction 317 starts

9:22 p.m. – The differential backup ends

9:23 p.m. – Transaction 313 commits

9:25 p.m. – The transaction log backup starts

9:29 p.m. – The transaction log backup ends.

Disk 1 fails at 9:24 p.m. You replace disk 1 and restore the database and transaction log. To what state can you recover the database?

A. To the state at 9 p.m. of the last full database backup

B. To the state at 9 p.m. and all transactions up until 9:24 p.m.

C. To the state where transaction 315 is committed

D. To a state where transactions 313 and 315 are committed

Question # 6

Spanferkel, Inc. is running one SBS 2003 and two Windows Server 2003 Standard Edition Servers and 35 client computers with Windows XP Pro SP2. The Internet connection is a broadband connection, there is a hardware firewall and the SBS server has two NICs installed. Due to construction in the inner city, the consultant has been having a hard time responding in a timely manner to client support requests. The consultant suggests using remote support in SBS 2003 first, before having to come on-site in person. The very next day, the consultant gets a support request call from an employee who is having trouble with his e-mail. You want to start the troubleshooting process remotely. How can remote support be initiated?

A. Ask the employee to send a Remote Assistance invitation via e-mail to your e-mail address.

B. Remote into the SBS Server and offer Remote Assistance to the employee from the Server Management console.

C. From Remote Web Workplace, use the "Download Connection Manager" to connect to the employee's computer.

D. Use PC Anywhere to connect to the employee's computer.

Question #7

Your company has a SBS 2003 server, 15 Windows XP Pro SP1 computers and 9 Windows 98 computers. There is a backup tape drive connected to the server. The Backup is set to run Monday through Thursday as a differential backup at 11 p.m. On Friday, there is a full backup at 11 p.m. On Wednesday the server gets hit with a worm at 4 p.m. Even though quickly contained, it destroys the data to a point where a recovery is the best option. What information will be lost?

A. Monday and Tuesday information will be lost.

B. Monday, Tuesday and Wednesday information will be lost.

C. Only Wednesday information will be lost.

D. Tuesday and Wednesday information will be lost.

Question #8

You are the office manager at Fishhooks, Inc. in Florida. Your company receives the latest fishing reports from all major fishing locations on a daily basis via fax. The company uses SBS 2003 primarily as a file and print server. The SBS server has a dial-up modem and two NICs installed. In the past you printed out a report for every employee and put it on their desk. At times, users would misplace their report so they had to make additional copies, which interrupted the workflow. You want to stop using all this paper and find a better solution so employees will not lose their copy of the fishing report and have it at their fingertips at any time. What would be the easiest way to accomplish this?

A. Configure the SBS fax service to route the fax to a shared folder on the network

B. Configure the SBS fax service to print the report at each user's local printer

C. Configure the SBS fax service to route the fax to the SharePoint fax folder

D. Configure the SBS fax service to route the fax to each user's My Document folder.

Question #9

You are the administrator of Stockbridge Construction Co. There are 20 Windows XP Pro clients on the network and one SBS 2003 server that is used as a file server and application server. The server has three volumes: Volume 1 holds all the by-default installed SBS shares, Volume 2 holds the applications and Volume 3 holds the Data share. In the past, users have been storing their documents in the My Documents folder on the desktop despite having been told to store documents on a network share called Data on the server. This has resulted in lost and overwritten documents that have not been backed up. You are thinking about redirecting the users' My Documents folders to a share on the server to be on the safe side. How can you accomplish this? (select all that apply)

A. Set the Group Policy in User Configuration\Administration \RedirectDocuments to point to the Data Share

B. Set the Group Policy in User Configuration\Administrative Templates\Desktop\Prohibit user from changing My Documents path to enabled and configure it to point to the Data share.

C. Run the My Document Redirect wizard in the Server Management console and select the Data share.

D. Enable Shadow Copies on the Volume where the Data share resides.

Question #10

You are the administrator of a regional start-up cosmetics sales office. The office runs on SBS 2003 server and most company staff is working outside sales and on the road most of the time. Sales agents want to be able to access their e-mail, shared folders and personal data on the server. Sales Agents want to know what the most efficient way will be to access Remote Web Workplace using a 56k dial-up modem. You recommend that:

A. Users type http://www.mycosmeticscompany.com/remote

B. Users select: Modem (56Kbps) in the Connection Speed drop down on the Remote Web Workplace logon screen.

C. Uses connect to Remote Web Workplace and select: Download Connection Manager.

D. Users de-select the "I'm using a public or shared computer" on the logon screen.

Answer Key

Question #1: Answer C, D

You can install the GPMC only on Windows Server 2003 and Windows XP Professional with Service Pack 1 (or later) For installation on an XP machine with SP1, you need to also apply the hotfix Q326469 which is included with the GPMC. You cannot install the GPMC on any other operating systems.

Question #2: Answer C, D

To enable Windows 95 clients to communicate with the SBS server, you need to either disable SMB signing on the server or install the Active Directory client extensions.

SBS 2003 server requires SMB signing and encryption to secure traffic on the network, and because Windows 95 computers do not support SMB signing you have to implement one of the two choices. None of this has anything to do with DHCP which assigns IP addresses. Theoretically Answer A could be right, but this will take more effort creating the scope and assigning static addresses (and for what reason?) Answer B. Active Directory server extensions do not exist.

Question #3: Answer C

To get a quick look at domain controller issues, including DNS in general, use the dcdiag.exe tool. Dcdiag.exe will check for LDAP/RPC connectivity, perform a basic DNS test, check DNS forwarders, DNS delegation, DNS dynamic updates and a record registration test and many more. (Check Technet for dcdiag.exe for a full list of tests performed.) The DNS console can be used as a monitoring tool for iterative and recursive tests for external DNS server verification. NSLookup.exe will retrieve zone information. The Health Monitor will give you overall server status health, not DNS issues.

Question #4: Answer C

You can run the Monitor Configuration wizard from the Server Management console and select to e-mail a daily Performance Report and a bi-weekly usage report to specific user accounts or distribution groups. You can attach log files for application events, IIS, SBS Backup, security events and system events to the performance and usage reports in the Server Status Report Properties in the Change Server Status Report Settings tool. Answer A. That would be the opposite of the least amount of administrative effort. Answer B. Same as A; and you can't create custom alert thresholds in the Monitoring Configuration wizard. Answer

D. Nonsense, there is no Usage report wizard and you can't attach system event log files in the Monitoring Configuration wizard.

Question #5: Answer D

First you would restore the full database backup from 9:00 p.m. and then restore the differential backup and all transaction logs since the differential database backup. This will bring back the committed transaction 315 from the differential database backup. Since disk 1 failed, with the database, Transaction 315 will be committed when the transaction log is restored, which is located on disk 2 and completed successfully.

Question #6: Answer B

You can use Remote Web Workplace or the TS client to remote into the SBS Server. In the Server Management Console, under the Users link, you have a link to Offer Remote Assistance. Answer A. Even though this would work, the employee is having e-mail trouble and couldn't send you an invitation. Answer C. The "Download Connection Manager" sets up client workstations with VPN connections and would not help in this situation. Answer D. Get real, this is a Microsoft Exam and third-party tools don't exist.

Question #7: Answer C

Only the Wednesday information is lost, the server can be restored with last Friday's full backup and Tuesday's differential backup. Okay, here is the refresher on differential vs. incremental. Or better yet, go to TechNet and search for: "How Backup Works – Core Operating Systems – Windows Server 2003." This will give you the low-down on the NTBackup Utility and prep you with all there is to know for the 70-282 Exam.

Question #8: Answer C

Configuring to receive the fax in SharePoint would be the answer. That would be the most convenient and efficient way, and no paper would be used in the future and the report can't get lost. The fax will display with caller ID, number of pages, time received and size of the message file. Answer A. Viewing the fax over a mapped drive is just not as pretty as in SharePoint. Answer B. That would create tons of paper and why aren't they using a network printer? Answer D. That is not an option.

Question #9: Answer C, D

You should run the My Document redirect wizard which can be found in the Server Management console under the "Backup" and under "Users" links. You then must enable VSS manually on that volume because SBS will only enable shadow copies on the volume where the Users Shared folders are located. In our case, they are part of the default installation and located on Volume one, whereas the Data folder resides on Volume three. Answer A. You can only set VSS on a Volume, not a folder. Answer B. This GPO setting will not give the option to select a folder or share to point to.

Question #10: Answer B

Selecting the connection speed at the Remote Web Workplace logon screen will make the most efficient use of the connection. Answer A. This just places you at the logon portal and does not affect connection speed. Answer C. The Download Connection Manager downloads a shortcut VPN connection to the client desktop. Answer D. This will allow the SBS server to place a session cookie on the computer, which has nothing to do with the connection speed.

Summary

This chapter presents a deep dive into SBS administration and support functions supporting the core Windows Server 2003 operating system in a small business environment. Special attention was paid to the configuration and deployment of Group Policy Objects. This is an area of much improvement in the Windows Server 2003 time frame and you should expect this to appear on the 70-282 certification examination. Traditional functions such as data protections, monitoring and basic troubleshooting were covered. The emphasis was clearly on SBS 2003 and how it interacts with the underlying Windows Server 2003 operating system.

CHAPTER 9
Expanding the Windows Small Business Server 2003 Network

Technology in the small business arena would be an oxymoron for many readers of this book if they were to step back in time about 30 years. Only the most successful small businesses, such as well-heeled law firms, had "technology" that included an expensive photocopier and a new thing called a "fax" machine. The good old IBM Selectric typewriter was the order of the day. A few years later, the local area network (LAN) concept was developed that allowed small offices to share an expensive printer and other resources. It worked well, it was simple, and sharing was the reason for being.

Fast forward to the 21st century. Small businesses are truly starting to embrace technology and trust their <u>entire operation</u> to IT infrastructure. That alone is a huge step for some SMBs, and for many of these business people, one server is enough for their immediate needs. However, as those businesses start to grow and business owners learn to take advantage of the IT infrastructure, these SMBs find the need for more flexible solutions and increased storage space. E-mail storage, proprietary line-of-business applications requiring their own server, regulatory compliance, and the 24/7 mindset of service and data availability are changing the landscape. Hardware costs have decreased dramatically, making additional server purchases a viable SMB consideration.

We have created a monster! SMBs are learning to operate with enterprise-level technology and have an elevated expectation set that they can "do more with less." And SBS delivers. SBS 2003 now has the ability to add additional domain controllers (DC) to the SBS 2003 network and in this chapter you'll learn some important reasons for doing so! Being untied from the single-server model, SBS has become a more robust computing environment, an option for some branch office solutions, and an easy way to expand and grow your business.

Add Member Servers to the SBS 2003 Domain

Member servers are historically used as file servers storing data or applications to be shared by users. Member servers, being part of a domain, are not domain controllers and do not handle any sort of logon functions. In their most pure form, they are just plain dedicated to managing file, printing, or application services.

> IMPORTANT: Time to think outside the server box! The above paragraph gives the "corporate speak" viewpoint of the generic role of a member server in a Microsoft networked environment. But there really is more you can do with a member server. A member server makes an excellent platform on which to run Terminal Services in Application Sharing Mode (discussed a tad in Chapter 7 and again in Chapter 8) and to support important line-of-business applications (discussed in Chapter 4). So, kinda like the "zen of golf," where you are advised to meditate and "be the ball," please do the following: Drop down into the yoga "downward facing dog" pose. Take a few deep breaths via your nose. Be the member server!
>
> Get excited about the possibilities of introducing a member server into your SBS network!

So, time to run for a moment before we walk. After joining a member server to the domain, you have the ability to promote the server to a domain controller and participate in Active Directory replication, make it a global catalog server, and enjoy all the rights bestowed upon a DC in a Microsoft Windows Server 2003 networked environment. However, any additional server (as either a member server or a domain controller) you join to an SBS 2003 network will necessarily assume a subservient role to the SBS 2003 server machine. That is because the SBS 2003 server machine must be the ROOT OF THE ACTIVE

DIRECTORY FOREST (yes—I'm shouting for emphasis). This was discussed in passing in Chapters 4 and 5 of this book and there are excellent references to this in both *Windows Small Business Server 2003 Best Practices* and *Advanced Windows Small Business Server 2003 Best Practices* from you know who!

Note that an additional server could be either a Windows Server 2003 Standard Edition-based or a Windows Server 2003 Enterprise Edition-based solution. It's true! There is a common belief that you would use only Windows Server 2003 Standard Edition for an additional server on an SBS 2003 network. However, one of the authors (who is a "He") had a few Windows Server 2003 Enterprise Edition SKUs lying around the office (25-user, not-for-resale editions given to SBS-MVPs), and he used one of them when he performed a migration using fellow SBS-MVP Jeff Middleton's "Swing Migration" approach (not on the 70-282 exam per se, but discussed later in the chapter). The Windows Server 2003 Enterprise Edition worked just fine! Finally—a Windows 2000 Server machine in native mode can join an SBS 2003 network.

> IMPORTANT: Take the discussion about adding a member server in the section very seriously. Microsoft and the SBS-MVPs do. You'll see a simple procedure for adding a server to an SBS 2003 domain. At first blush, the keystrokes are simple. But did you know that adding an additional server to an SBS 2003-based network is one of the top product-support issues? It's true, and that was the basis for one of the hands-on labs at the Spring 2005 USA SBS 2003 hands-on lab tour that visited over 25 cities. The hands-on lab had you add a member server to an SBS 2003 network and then promote that server to be a DC.
>
> And to add more value to this discussion, you might be interested in knowing that Harry created the add-a-server lab for Microsoft and Beatrice was the instructor. Enough said!

Adding a Server Procedure

Joining a member server can be done through the Set Up Server Computers Wizard in the Server Management Console, as shown in Figure 9-1. The two basic steps are (1) the wizard will ask for the server name and (2) either a static IP or a dynamic IP will be assigned.

Then you click **Finish** in the wizard and a dialog box will advise you to go to the server to be joined and run http://sbsservername/connectcomputer in the browser to be joined to the domain. This is the appropriate way to create a machine account in the domain and sets up the member server with the correct trust relationship. You want it to play nice with the SBS domain controller.

Figure 9-1

Adding a member server with the Set Up Server Computers Wizard.

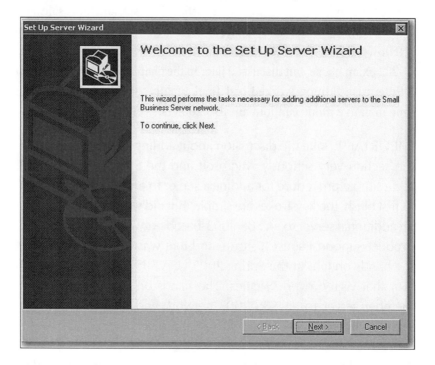

An interesting data point for you on the above discussion. When I (Harry) was reviewing this document on a dark and stormy night, I began to question the above procedure of using the Connect Computer Wizard. I started to "overthink" the issue and second-guess myself. Fortunately, I was smart enough to ask for help. SBS-MVP Susan Bradley confirmed the above is correct and pointed me to an excellent Microsoft document ("Deploying Windows Server 2003 Terminal Server to Host User Desktops in a Windows Small Business Server 2003

Environment") that does a deeper dive on this matter available at http://microsoft
.com/downloads/details.aspx?FamilyID=0a06e845-57ef-43eb-802f-
f274fd937400&displaylang=en. Enjoy it in good health!

> IMPORTANT: Two thoughts to reinforce the points made in the
> above paragraph:
>
> Don't overthink and second-guess yourself. As a general rule, on a
> test the first answer you mark on an exam question is the proper
> response. Study after study has confirmed this. You'll typically get
> into more trouble by going back and changing your answer
> (effectively from correct to incorrect).
>
> Just as important is asking for help. If you don't know something,
> don't fret over it all night. Use the resources in Appendix A, like
> newsgroups, to answer your SMB business questions and your SBS
> technical questions, and even to solve problems in your family life!
> (I've seen it done on that last point!)

Promoting Additional Windows 2003 Servers to Domain Controller Status

Now that you have joined an additional server to the domain, you can opt to
bring it up to DC status. Some small businesses with multiple locations first
build the DC server machine onsite (home office), then move the server machines
off to a branch office location, where servers are then reconnected by WAN
links. An interesting historic data point and not part of the 70-282 exam is that
the dearly departed and discontinued BackOffice 2000 product had a "branch
office setup wizard" that did exactly what we are describing herein.

When promoting a Windows Server 2003 member server to a DC, use the
Manage Your Server Wizard and choose to add the Domain Controller role
which will launch the Active Directory Installation Wizard. When asked for the
Domain Controller Type, you would select **Additional domain controller for
an existing domain** to make this a member domain controller.

If you are adding an additional server for the purpose of using Terminal Services to run in Application Sharing Mode, it is not recommended to promote this server to a domain controller, since users will have direct access to the server. Think about it. Mere mortals like Pat, the office manager, would effectively be performing a "local logon" to a DC if you ignored this advice. See Chapter 8 for more information.

Configuring Member Servers

Once you have brought your member server online, the Manage Your Server Wizard will appear and ask you to configure a server role. You could choose to add a server role as a:

- File server

- Print server

- Application server (IIS, ASP.NET)

- Mail server (POP3, SMTP)

- Terminal server

- Remote Access / VPN server

- Domain Controller (Active Directory)

- DNS server

- DHCP server

- Streaming media server

- WINS server

Not all roles would fit the SBS bill, and most realistic choices will be the File, Print, Application, Mail and Terminal Server. If you select the Mail server option and plan on using Exchange, you must have a separate license for the Exchange server as well as the Terminal server, which will require separate licenses away from your SBS Client Access Licenses (CALs).

IMPORTANT: Don't KISS me right now. No, I'm not shunning your affection, but referring to that well-known acronym for "Keep it simple, stupid." The idea is to simplify business transactions and consummate relationships. But here is the anti-KISS message relating to the above section. Wizards make life very easy for SMB consultants and the like. However, I don't feel you are well served in this situation if you use a wizard selection to define your additional server role but don't understand the underlying concept. Just picking a server role from a selection screen doesn't cut it.

Wizards are great if you know what they are doing. However, perform a "gut check" and make sure you understand each of the server roles in the above list. If not, leave right now, surf over to TechNet (www.microsoft.com/technet), and search on each of the words in the above list to learn more. We'll wait right here for you to return.

Create an Application Migration Strategy

There once was a client who had about 20 different apps on the server and insisted he used them all. My job was to move five of those critical applications to a new member server. In this case, I first inventoried the existing applications and categorized them by their relative business value and dependencies. I then called the manufacturer to find out whether there were any updates available or special considerations when moving the applications and data to a new location. (Hey, beats reading documents for three nights in a row.) I estimated the amount of time it would take to do the migration, then doubled that amount. We decided when to make the last backup of the application's data files and figured out the best time to perform the migration. I wanted to disturb the business as little as possible and choose an appropriate time frame, which meant working the weekend.

Migration Considerations

First thought is always application compatibility. Moving to Windows Server 2003 is easy. Most applications are written to support the Windows operating system, but you want to make sure they have been tested with the 2003 version and not just for Windows 2000 or NT 4.0. There is a really cool tool out—the Application Compatibility Toolkit 4.0—which is used by Microsoft developers themselves to test application compatibility. Test-driving an application with this toolkit will tip you off immediately whether there are going to be issues. The toolkit has been a real time-saver in the past. You can download the toolkit at http://msdn.microsoft.com/library/default.asp?url=/library/en-us/dnanchor/html/appcompat.asp.

You will also run into obsolete applications that require obsolete operating systems (NT 4.0) and the owners will refuse to upgrade or have a new application written. In this case you can consider moving them into Virtual Server 2005, which will allow you to continue running the aging line-of-business application on newer, more resilient hardware.

When moving shared files, consider how the folder structure could be improved for management, retrieval, and disaster recovery purposes.

Consider implementing redundancy by using Distributed files system (Dfs) or other available Windows storage features, like Volume Shadow Services (VSS), or using the File replication service (FRS) for replicating data, and set up your volumes and shares accordingly.

Consider using disk quotas and NTFS permissions to enforce appropriate usage and configure the settings accordingly on your destination server. Make sure to document your configurations.

You may want to partition drives in a manner where you keep data, application, and system files each on a separate partition. This will help mainly with disaster recovery by keeping things organized and allowing for quickly targeted backups.

Some applications require hard-coded paths to be mapped from the client, and you don't want to have to reinstall all client-side software. Then you best get with the manufacturer to find out which client-side files can be edited to save time with the migration.

> IMPORTANT: Can we speak honestly for a moment about the real world? (I even think this has planning implications on the 70-282 exam, but don't dwell on that point.) Experienced SMB consultants typically know when to call in the line-of-business application

consultants for assistance. For example, a common use for a second server is to run Great Plains Dynamics in some SMBs. But those with the newly acquired Small Business Specialist designation (that you'll earn by the end of the book and after you pass the required exams) who feel truly qualified to migrate the Great Plains Dynamics application and data aren't being very honest with themselves.

In the world of application migrations, one of the biggest considerations is to bring in an expert to assist with that phase. Case closed!

Backing Up Data Folders

Before moving application data, you should do one, no two, no three backups prior to the move. You can use the Backup Configuration Wizard to do a full backup of the source server. You should also back up the data folders separately and have them easily retrievable (DVD, network share). If it's a third-party application with its own built-in backup mechanism, use this to make the backup, then move the backup to the destination server and use the application's restore feature. Also, do not delete the data folders from the original destination until you are sure the application and data are working well in the new location.

Installing Applications on the New Server

Applications are usually not migrated, but reinstalled. When reinstalling applications, you should follow manufacturer's recommendations and ensure that all requirements, in terms of hardware and other dependencies, are met. (This is a great time to bring in a specialist for the specific application you are deploying.) Make sure you have the serial number handy beforehand. I have run into numerous instances where the owner had the media and then couldn't find the serial number. This should actually be part of the planning stage so you don't come to a grinding halt on the Sunday morning migration. After the application has been installed, and you have specified the appropriate folder locations or use the application's default storage data folder location, you are now ready to restore or move files and folders to the new server.

Moving Data Folders

For one reason or another you may decide to move data folders from the SBS 2003 server. You can move:

- Users Shared Folders

- Windows SharePoint Services databases

- Exchange databases and log files

- Sent Faxes folder

- Client Apps shared folder

Best practice dictates you always make a full backup before you undertake a move operation. For detailed steps, see the SBS white paper located at: http://www.microsoft.com/technet/prodtechnol/sbs/2003/maintain/movedata.mspx

> IMPORTANT: It's always about the DATA. Fellow author Wayne Robertson, who wrote extensively in the mid-1990s about Novell NetWare, had a catchy mantra he liked to use in speeches: "It's the DATA, stupid! That's why we're here." This is being shared with you so that when you find yourself in the heat of a certification test-taking session, you can always return to your roots: DATA. Data is truly why we're here and everything from its creation to its protection to its usage is what the solutions in this book are all about. It's what we're all about. You'll never go wrong on an exam question if you honor the DATA at the foundation level and build up from there!

Migration Open Minds

Both authors debated long and hard about adding this section, which takes you onwards from the 70-282 exam or, as Buzz Lightyear of *Toy Story* fame is prone to intone, "…To infinity and beyond!" We trust you are mature enough to handle the following and won't become so absorbed that you'll forget to manage your time and hence lose your 70-282 exam-cram focus!

The fact of the matter is that there are some excellent external migration resources out there that you should know about. These resources won't hinder your 70-282 exam preparation and should be consulted only if your time allows and you've got the emotional health and mental bandwidth to absorb more stuff! (How's that for a Surgeon General health alert?) First, take a look at Chapters 14 and 15 from *Advanced Windows Small Business Server Best Practices*, which do a deep dive on the topics in this chapter. Then, trot yourself over to SBS-MVP Jeff Middleton's SBS Migration site (www.sbsmigration.com) and do the SWING. It's NOT a dance or an alternative adult sexual lifestyle. Rather, it's the best darn tootin' guidance for helping SBSers perform real-world complex migrations beyond the scope of the 70-282 certification exam.

Practice Questions

Question #1

You are the administrator for a glass manufacturing company. You performed an upgrade from Windows NT 4.0 to SBS 2003 and added a second Windows Server 2003 server. The client computers were also upgraded from Windows 98 to Windows XP Professional. The application that runs the glass cutting equipment, which was previously installed on all the Win98 computers, has been removed and is now installed on the Windows Server 2003 computer. The client computers now use Terminal Services to access the application on the server. When clients connect to the application and try to use full-screen mode, it only opens in a small window on their monitor. You test the terminal services connection and find out that this only happens with this application, not with any others. In order for employees to effectively use the application, it must show in full screen mode. What can be done to fix this?

A. Configure the application to run in NT 4.0 compatibility mode on the Windows Server 2003 computer

B. Configure the application to run in 640 x 480 screen resolution

C. Run Terminal Services in Windows 98 compatibility mode when connecting to the application

D. Configure the application to run in 256 colors

Question #2

You are the administrator of Widgets, Inc. The network consists of one SBS 2003 Standard Edition server, a Windows 2003 server and sixty Windows XP Professional client computers. The Windows 2003 server is configured as a file server. The file server has five hard disks, Disk 0, Disk 1 through Disk 4, and runs a RAID 5 array on Disk 2, Disk 3 and Disk 4. The system partition is located on Disk 1 and mirrored to Disk 0. Each hard disk has 300 GB of space. There are sixty users on the network and you need to implement disk quotas so everyone gets the same amount of storage space on the volume. What steps should you take? (select all that apply)

A. Format the volume with NTFS

B. Enable FRS

C. Configure disk quotas to be 10 GB per user

D. Configure disk quotas to be 15 GB per user

Question #3

You are the consultant to a call center in town. The network is set up with one SBS 2003 Standard Edition server and four Windows 2003 member servers, all located in separate branch offices and connected with a 128Kbps WAN link to the main office where the SBS domain controller is located. Users come in at the same time in the mornings and complain about the time it takes to log on to the domain. How can you fix this in the most cost-effective way?

A. Create a connection bridge between the servers

B. Create a sub-site and site link for each connection

C. Add the Domain controller role to each Windows Server 2003

D. Install compression technology

Question #4

You administer a Windows SBS 2003 network for a regional sales office of herbal products. The server is configured with two NIC's and a hardware firewall. There are 34 agents out in the field with Windows XP Professional SP1 computers and 22 with Windows 2000 Professional

SP2 computers. Sales agents need to securely connect to the network for about 10 minutes a day to transfer data. Agents are calling to say that they are unable to connect via VPN to the server. There is no way of telling at what time agents will connect and you want to change current practices. How can you remedy this situation?

A. Assign Group Policy to the sales agents and specify a VPN logon time

B. Add additional VPN ports in RAS

C. Configure the hardware firewall for multiplexing

D. Upgrade the amount of bandwidth available from your ISP

Question #5

You administer a network consisting of an SBS 2003 Server Premium and four Windows Servers 2003. The SBS server is located at the main office site in Denver, CO and the member servers are located in branch offices in Orlando, Dallas, and San Jose. Users from all branch offices regularly connect to the main office Windows 2003 member server named HQ, which is configured as a terminal server to run an application. The client computers deployed all have Windows XP Professional with the latest service packs and patches installed. One new user in the Dallas office is unable to print reports from the application on HQ to his local printer. Other users do not have this problem and can print from HQ to their respective client computers. How can this be fixed?

A. Add the user to the Remote Desktop Users group on HQ

B. Configure automatic printer redirection

C. Configure manual printer redirection

D. Configure bi-directional printing

Question #6

You administer a network consisting of an SBS 2003 Server Premium and four Windows Servers 2003. The SBS server is located at the main office site in Denver together with three Windows 2003 member servers.

All Windows member servers have terminal services enabled and are frequently used by remote employees. What is the most convenient way to connect to terminal services on member servers?

A. Type *mstsc* into the command line and then enter the IP address of the server in the Remote Desktop Connection box

B. Use Remote Web Workplace and then select to "connect to my computer at work" and then select the member server you want to connect to

C. Open a remote Desktop Connection

D. Use the Terminal Services client

Question #7

You are the administrator of a small software development company. Currently there are eight Windows XP Professional computers in a peer-to-peer configuration. You decide that you will benefit greatly from a client/server environment that facilitates collaboration, e-mail and faxing. Your company develops software that needs a dedicated SQL server. How can you implement this in the most cost-effective way?

A. Install SBS 2003 Premium, Windows Server 2003 Standard and SQL 2000

B. Install SBS 2003 Premium

C. Install SBS 2003 Standard, Windows Server 2003 Standard and SQL 2000

D. Install Windows Server 2003 Standard and SQL 2000

Question #8

You are the administrator for a company with a SBS 2003 domain. The domain also has four additional domain controllers, two Windows 2003 Domain controllers and two Windows 2000 domain controllers, and 60 Windows XP Professional computers spread over four branch locations, all connected with high-speed broadband. You would like to securely manage all the domain controllers remotely from your office in one desktop monitor without having to log in and out of the remote domain controllers. Which tool will let you manage the domain controllers cost effectively and with the least administrative effort?

A. Remote Desktop

B. Remote Assistance

C. SMS (System Management Server)

D. Telnet

Question #9

You manage a SBS 2003 network with two additional Windows Server 2003 domain controllers. They are called SBS1, Server2 and Server3. Fifty-five clients use applications on all three domain controllers. You make a full backup of each domain controller every Friday and run differential backups Monday through Thursday. On Wednesday, the hard drive on Server 2 seizes. You have a spare on hand and install the new disk immediately. What will you have to do to get the server back into the most recent operable state?

A. Start Server2 in Directory Services Restore mode

B. Start Server2 in safe mode

C. Recreate all volumes as they were on the previous disk

D. Hit the F2 key in the text mode installation

E. Authoritatively restore the system state data from the full backup

F. Non-authoritatively restore the system state data from the full backup

G. Do a full restore from Friday

H. Restore the Tuesday differential backup

Question #10

You are the administrator at Paletti Bicycles, Inc. and you just added an additional Windows Server 2003 named TS1 to the network using the add Server Computer wizard to your SBS 2003 network. You install the Terminal Server role on the server and load the multi-session application. You send an e-mail to the RemoteSales group outlining the steps of connecting to the terminal server via Remote Web

Workplace. Twenty minutes later, users are calling you, stating that they get this message: "The local policy of this system does not permit you to logon interactively" and are unable to logon. What should you do to enable the RemoteSales group to log on with the least amount of permissions?

A. Add all users to the Power Users group in the Domain

B. Add all users to the Domain Admins group in the Domain

C. Add the RemoteSales group to the Power Users group in the Domain

D. Grant the RemoteSales group "Log on locally" rights on TS1 using a GPO

E. Add the RemoteSales group to the Remote Desktop Users group on TS1

F. Add the Mobile User group to the Remote Operators group

Answer Key

Question #1: Answer B

You should configure the Terminal Services to run the application in a lower resolution. On the client computer, right-click the Remote Desktop icon and click Properties and then the Compatibility tab, select Run in 640 x 480 screen resolution. When the screen displays small and centered on the monitor, it is an indication that the screen resolution is set to high to run the program in full-screen mode. Answer A. Running the application in compatibility mode is not necessary because it is functioning on the Windows Server 2003 computer. Answer C. The Remote Desktop Client comes built into XP Pro and does not need to be run in compatibility mode. Answer D. You would use the 256 color option only if the application displays the wrong color.

Question #2: Answer A, C

The volume needs to be formatted with NTFS in order to use Disk Quotas. Disk Quotas are not available on a FAT volume. Since we are running a

RAID 5 array with three disks totaling 900 GB, one third is being used for striping so we really only have 600 GB total space available. With 60 users, this makes for 10 GB per user. Answer B. FRS is used for replicating data. Answer D. If you configure 15 GB of storage per user, the volume will physically run out of space before anyone will reach their limit.

Question #3: Answer C

Adding the domain controller role to the member servers allows for logons to be authenticated locally and do not need to cross the WAN-link. This will increase logon speed. Answer A. A connection bridge allows you to bridge two subnets and would not increase logon speed. Answer B. Site links are used to control Active Directory replication between domain controllers in each site. This would not speed up logons. Member servers do not use replication. Answer D. This would require a third-party application and, thus, be an expenditure.

Question #4: Answer B

You would add additional VPN ports in the RAS console by expanding the Ports node and then click Properties, highlight the port to configure and click Configure. SBS assigns only 5 ports by default. Answer A. Using GPOs and setting a specific time will actually compound this problem because you are now narrowing down the time window when agents can connect to the network, as well as changing current practices by dictating the log on time. Answer C. Ahem, this is a Microsoft exam. Answer D. Upgrading bandwidth would not be a solution.

Question #5: Answer B

Automatic redirection is for 32-bit terminal services clients, enabling automatic printer redirection and will allow the user to print from the Terminal Service session to the local printer on his computer. This setting can be set on the user account properties in Active Directory on the Environment tab by selecting "connect client printers at logon." Answer A. The user is already logged on and working in the application, so this is not the problem. Answer C. The manual redirection is for 16-bit clients and local printers that require drivers other than those shipped with Windows Server 2003. Answer D. Bidirectional printing is not supported.

Question #6: Answer B

Using the Remote Web Workplace lets you securely connect to all available member servers running terminal services. Answer A. This option will not work because the member servers are sitting behind a firewall with private (internal) IP addresses not accessible from the internet. Answer C. Same as B. Answer D. Same as B, only this is the old client used for NT 4.0

Question #7: Answer C

The most cost-effective solution will be to install SBS 2003 Standard for the e-mail, fax and collaboration solution, and install Windows Server 2003 Standard with a separate SQL installation on it for the dedicated use of SQL server. Answer A. SBS 2003 Premium is more expensive then the SBS 2003 Standard edition. We can't use the SQL software that comes with this package since the software being developed needs a dedicated SQL server and needs to be installed on a separate server. Purchasing SBS 2003 Premium would not be cost effective. Answer B. This would not work since this would not achieve the objective. Answer D. This does not take into account the e-mail, faxing and collaboration solution.

Question #8: Answer A

Remote Desktop uses RDP 5.2 with a 128 bit encryption. It allows you to be connected to several domain controllers simultaneously by opening a new remote desktop session for each, switching between the remote desktop sessions. Answer B. Remote Assistance requires a user to be logged on locally to give you control of the desktop. That would not be a solution. Answer C. SMS would not be cost effective. Answer D. Telnet is limited and would not be a "least administrative effort".

Question #9: Answer A, C, F, G, H

After you install the new hard drive, you would first load a new copy of
Windows Server 2003 and then reboot, hit the F8 key and select
Directory Services Restore mode. You get another boot screen, press
enter, and the server gets booted into a special safe mode that will not
start Active Directory. Perform the non-authoritative restore of the full
Friday backup including the system state. Then restore the Tuesday
differential including the system state non-authoritatively. When you
reboot and bring the server online, it will replicate the most current
Active Directory data from the other DCs that has changed since it was
disconnected from the network.

Answer B. You must use DSRM (Directory Service Restore mode)
regular safe mode will not support the restore functions as needed.
Answer D. Using the F2 key is an ASR restore function. Answer E. If
you were to perform an authoritative restore, it would increment the
USN (update sequence number) by 10,000 and would therefore replicate
the older data from Server2 back to Server3 and SBS1 because of the
higher USN. That is not wanted. We want the latest AD objects to be
replicated to Server2 from Server3 and SBS1.

Question #10: Answer E

Adding the RemoteSales group to the Remote Desktop User local group
on TS1 will provide proper permissions to log on to the terminal server
and run the application. This gives the right to logon through terminal
services which is assigned to the Remote Desktop Users group. Answer
A. Adding ALL users to the Power User group would allow all users to
log on remotely. Only the RemoteSales group is to have permissions.
Answer B. Adding all users to the domain admins group would be a
bad thing. Answer C. The Power User group has the right to log on
remotely to the server, but this would mean they could also logon
remotely to the SBS server. Permissions are too lenient. Answer D.
Granting the log on locally right would also allow users in the
RemoteSales group to log on interactively to the server when in the
office. Permissions are too lenient. Answer F. Adding the Mobile Users

group to the Remote Operators group will allow the wrong group to log on remotely with terminal services.

Summary

Subliminally, this chapter is here to help you avoid developing a narrow-minded viewpoint of the 70-282 exam wherein you want to stay inside your SBS world. Hopefully, this chapter expanded your mind by getting you to think about expanding an SBS 2003 network. It's not sacrilegious to go beyond the SBS 2003 server box and there are appropriate times and places to do so.

You learned about adding a member server to an SBS 2003 network. Then you were taught how to promote the member server to a DC and what the ramifications would be. You delved into the nuts and bolts of migration strategies and execution. And, as always, the materials presented in this chapter focus on the 70-282 certification exam!

CHAPTER 10
Installing and Configuring Windows Server 2003

Now that we have been prepping for the 70-282 exam in the SBS realm for a couple of hundred pages, it should appear odd to have a section on Windows Server 2003. May I remind you that 70-282 is a Microsoft exam oriented toward a particular segment: small and medium businesses. The 70-282 exam is unique with its segment approach and isn't focused solely on a specific product. Rather, the 70-282 exam is focused on both SBS and the underlying Windows Server 2003 network operating system. Therefore, as odd as it seems, readers lucky enough to have Microsoft Certified System Engineer (MCSE) knowledge under their belts will find such knowledge helps them greatly!

Even though it's easy to read into these pages and decipher SBS speak to conclude that SBSers don't like MCSEs, I find MCSE-level knowledge to be helpful in the real world when installing SBS at small businesses. Having an understanding of the server subsystem, services, storage, and networking capabilities only contributes to positive outcomes.

> IMPORTANT: The 70-282 exam isn't just about SBS! In reality, the 70-282 exam will be very Windows Server 2003-centric, interwoven with SBS questions. So don't think that knowing all about the SBS wizards alone is going to get you through this. Be sure to have your Windows core knowledge polished as well.

Install Windows Server 2003

Insert Disc 1 and go! Hee, hee, I am just being silly, but that is how I feel about server installs. There was a time when I was installing several servers a week, and I can still remember dreaming about the text mode setup at night and visions of BSODs (blue screens of death). The installation for NT required hitting the F8 key several times before you got to the end of the End User License Agreement (EULA). Nightmares!

Much time has passed since I encountered a BSOD during an install, and the SBS install is no different. Obviously with SBS running on top of Windows Server 2003, Disc 1 of the SBS Disc Set contains all the Windows Server 2003 installation files, located in the \i386 directory. Okay, enough talk. Let's move on.

Windows Server 2003 System Requirements

Without further ado, the system requirements are shown in Table 10-1. Please don't laugh—just remember the minimum recommendations for the exam, so we made sure we got it straight from the horse's mouth.

> Remember in the SBS setup chapter, emphasis was placed on using Microsoft's version of the truth when preparing for the 70-282 exam? The same truth still holds here. Even though you might personally dispute the minimum system requirements, the 70-282 exam has no such dispute. Treat Microsoft communications, such as presented here, as gospel!

Table 10-1
Windows Server 2003 Standard Edition minimum system requirements

Component	Requirement
Computer and processor	PC with a 133-MHz processor required; 550-MHz or faster processor recommended (Windows Server 2003 Standard Edition supports up to four processors on one server)
Memory	128 MB of RAM required; 256 MB or more recommended; 4 GB maximum
Hard disk	1.25 to 2 GB of available hard-disk space
Drive	CD-ROM or DVD-ROM drive

Table 10-1 (continued)

Component	Requirement
Display	VGA or hardware that supports console redirection required; Super VGA supporting 800 x 600 or higher-resolution monitor recommended

IMPORTANT: Do not install Windows Server 2003 on a compressed hard disk unless it was compressed with the NTFS file system. Drive Space or Double Space volumes should be uncompressed before running the Windows Setup.

Preparing for the Installation

Regardless whether you have a brand new system or are recycling another system, before performing the installation you should prepare and verify several tasks to ensure a smooth install.

- Verify the hardware as listed in the Windows Server Catalog

- Verify that components meet the minimum system requirements listed above

- Format the partition file system with NTFS (NT File System)

- Decide whether to use the Per Server or Per Seat licensing mode

- Decide on installing either a workstation or domain (in our case, choose the workstation because you will join the SBS domain)

- Create the machine account in the SBS domain by using the Add Server Computer Wizard

- Create a local Administrator password

- Have the driver for SCSI, RAID, or Fibre Channel hard disks available

IMPORTANT: When you install Windows Server 2003 Standard Edition, any previous operating system must be completely removed from the partition. However, dual boot is still supported with Windows Server 2003.

Ensure that the computer BIOS is set to boot off CD-ROM and that you have an el-torito compatible drive, and you are ready to go.

Performing the Installation

There are two phases to the Windows Server 2003 installation process: the text-mode setup and GUI-mode setup. During the text-mode setup, the setup function performs the following tasks:

- Examines the hard disk

- Determines what hardware is installed

- Performs limited Plug and Play detection

- Creates registry and files systems

- Partitions and formats the disks

- Checks for minimum system requirements

- Checks for adequate disk space

- Copies minimal installation files for the GUI-mode setup

If you have SCSI, RAID, or Fibre Channel hard disks, remember to engage the F6 key at the beginning of the text-mode Setup, so you can provide the driver files.

> IMPORTANT: You can run the install from a network location from a computer that contains the Windows Server 2003 source files by running x:\386\winnt.exe (x is any drive letter)

After text-mode setup the computer will reboot and continue with the installation in GUI mode and:

- Detect and install devices found on the computer

- Configure each device, install and configure network components

- Copy installation files that were not copied during the text-mode setup

- Write the setup log files to the installation directory

During GUI mode, the Windows Server 2003 Setup Wizard will complete the installation by requiring the following steps:

- Select regional and language settings

- Provide name and organization

- Ask for the 25-character product key

- Choose a licensing mode (select Per Seat—this way clients can use the SBS CAL (Client Access License) to access the member server)

- Ask for a computer name

- Configure system date and time

- Configure network components

- Ask to join either a workgroup or domain. Often you first deploy Windows Server 2003 in workgroup mode and then make a decision about creating a domain (using the Configure Your Server Wizard discussed next, which effectively runs the dcpromo command). However, in some cases you might have the Windows Server 2003 machine join an existing domain during the setup phase. You will need to make the proper choice depending on your situation.

Configure Your Server Wizard Components

The Configure Your Server Wizard is a central location from which you can choose to install and configure many components and server roles available in Windows Server 2003. The first time you log on with administrative rights, the Configure Your Server Wizard will launch automatically.

There are several components and server roles the wizard can install and configure, as listed in Table 10-2.

Notes:

Table 10-2

Windows Server 2003 Standard Edition components and server roles

Component or server role	This wizard:
Administration across the network	Turns on Remote Desktop for Administration so this server can be administered from another computer.
A Dynamic Host Configuration Protocol (DHCP) server	Installs DHCP and starts the New Scope Wizard.
A domain name system (DNS) server	Installs DNS and starts the Configure DNS Wizard.
A domain controller (Microsoft Active Directory Service)	Starts the Active Directory Installation Wizard and effectively runs the dcpromo command.
File server	Limits the amount of hard disk space allocated, toggles indexing on or off, and installs a utility to manage folders.
The Post Office Protocol 3 (POP3) Service	Installs the POP3 Service
Print server	Starts the Add Printer Wizard and the Add Printer Driver Wizard that installs printers and printer drivers on this server.
A server running Session Initiation Protocol (SIP)	Installs SIP on this server. SIP enables communication sessions like instant messaging, data collaboration, and file transfer.
Remote access server	Starts the Routing and Remote Access Setup Wizard.
A server running Microsoft Windows SharePoint Services 2.0	Installs WSS (Windows SharePoint Services) and turns on the indexing service
Streaming media server	Installs WMS (Windows Media Services). WMS delivers real-time multimedia content or prepares and streams stored content.

Table 10-2 (continued)

Component or server role	This wizard:
Terminal Server	Installs Terminal Server. This sets up the server to process tasks for multiple clients. It does not set up the server for remote administration; use the Administration across the network role for this.
Web server	Installs IIS (Internet Information Services). You can host and manage web sites, share information on the network, and install a web user interface for web server administration
Windows Internet Name Service (WINS) server	Installs WINS, which maps NetBIOS names to IP addresses.

As you can see, there are a lot of choices for server roles. Before configuring a server role, make sure you consider the impact and effect it will have in the SBS domain and on the SBS server itself.

Troubleshooting Setup Issues

There are numerous erroneous and weird things that could happen to you during setup. If you stick with the guidelines and are not experimenting, then you should have smooth sailing. Table 10-3 contains a list of common and easily identifiable setup issues and the solutions to them.

Table 10-3

Common setup issues and their solutions

Problem	Solution
Media errors	Use a different CD. (Get a burned copy from your buddy.)(Just kidding! Call Microsoft.)
Non-supported CD-ROM drive	Replace the CD-ROM drive OR use a different install method, like across the network
Insufficient hard disk space	Create a larger partition using the setup program

Table 10-3 (continued)

Problem	Solution
Unable to contact the Domain Controller	Check the NIC first, as well as all physical connections. Check that the server running the DNS server service is online. Verify that the domain name is correct. If this is a reinstall using the same computer name, delete and re-create the computer account on the server
Failure of Windows Server 2003 family to install or start	Check that the operating system detects all hardware and that such is listed in the Windows Server Catalog
Bad device driver	A bad device driver can manifest itself in numerous ways including causing a failed setup. Ugly!

These are common setup issues you may encounter on a Windows Server 2003 build. Here are troubleshooting approaches I've used when trying to connect a Windows Server 2003 server machine to an SBS 2003 network and things weren't going my way! Try these workarounds:

- IPCONFIG /ALL and verify that you have a DHCP assignment from the server.

- Add to a new workgroup (from **Control Panel**, **Network**) and try to join the SBS domain then. Reboot twice—don't ask why (group-policy related) and try again.

- Synchronize Computer Time, a common issue on domains when clients and servers are out of sync. Set the time manually to match the SBS server.

Upgrade from SBS 2003 to Windows Server 2003

So your client with 30 users decides to partner with another company. Or the company is going to outgrow the 75 CAL limitation by the end of the year. Doesn't matter what the reason is; if there is a need to move into a full-blown "back office" solution using full server products, Microsoft has an elegant migration path called the "Transition Pack." The Transition Pack is a disc you can purchase (SKU available at http://www.mircosoft.com/WindowsServer 2003/sbs/techinfo/planning/transition.mspx, and Select the License link) that includes an Upgrade Wizard and Windows Server 2003 Standard Edition. There are really two Transition Packs: standard and premium.

With the Transition Pack, you can remove the 75-license restriction as well as the trust-relationship restriction. You will also have the rights to move core applications like Exchange Server 2003, SQL Server 2000, or ISA Server 2004 to different servers (something SBS 2003 doesn't allow). After applying the Transition Pack, you can create child domains or join other domains, just as with any fully functional Windows Server 2003 server. The nice thing about that is that you will not have to reinstall your network or make any changes, and you get to keep all the SBS wizards to boot!

> IMPORTANT: Don't get too focused on the "bits" surrounding the Transition Pack SKU. The Transition Pack is also a financial concept! The Transition Pack is sold at a price point that has three financial implications:
>
> - **Going Up To Market.** The Transition Pack effectively charges the customer the full cost of the Microsoft technologies being implemented. Basically, if you are going to go up to the full server SKUs, shouldn't you pay the cost of doing so? Read the next point for an exception.
>
> - **Rebates Are Us.** The Transition Pack is priced to effectively credit you for the original cost of the SBS 2003 product. That's a nice touch and akin to getting trade-in value on your used car when you purchase a new car.
>
> - **Rollback**. The CAL count is rolled back to five CALs and you must then "re-purchase" sufficient full server SKU CALs to become legal and compliant with Microsoft's licensing scheme. For example, an SBS 2003 site with 65 CALs that implemented

the Transition Pack would rollback to five CALs and you would need to purchase 60 new full-server SKU CALs. The good news is that Microsoft has tried to help by providing "Transition Pack CALs" at the aforementioned Transition Pack page on Microsoft's SBS site.

Enough ducking and dodging. Table 10- 4 shows the different Transition Pack SKUs, including the CALs.

Table 10-4

Transition Pack information with prices in USD

Transition Pack Standard Edition	$1,769 T72-00346
Transition Pack Premium Edition	$3,522 T75-00039
5-Pack Transition CALs	$194 Device: T74-01130 User: T74-01131
20-Pack Transition CALs	$776 Device: T74-01132 User: T74-01133

Expect to see at least one question on the 70-282 exam regarding the Transition Pack, because Microsoft thinks it's cool AND Microsoft is adamant about communicating that you're not "locked" into SBS as your firms grows! There is indeed an elegant migration path with the Transition Pack.

Upgrade Guidelines from Windows 2000 Server to Windows Server 2003

Your client just got a contract to be a vendor of a large corporation that will require establishing a trust relationship between the two networks. Your client wants to keep all his files, applications, and set preferences in place. Also, with all the new work, the office is very busy and the client doesn't want any changes made to the current environment (user settings, groups, rights, and permissions) or anything that could hinder the workflow.

The upgrade guidelines in general are:

- You are using a previous version of Windows that supports upgrades (clearly Windows 2000 Server supports this).

- You want to replace a previous operating system with Windows Server 2003 Standard Edition

- You want to keep your previous files, applications, and preferences

- You want to keep your existing users, settings, groups, rights, and permissions.

If you are upgrading from a Windows 2000 Server Service Pack 2 (SP2) or Windows NT 4.0, you must first ensure hardware and software compatibility.

IMPORTANT: Windows Server 2003 Standard Edition supports upgrading from Windows 2000 SP2 and Microsoft NT 4.0 SP5.

Ensuring Compatibility

System requirements for upgrading from Windows 2000 Server to Windows Server 2003 will be the same as the system requirements for a new installation of Windows Server 2003.

- **Run the preinstallation hardware and software compatibility check** – run the operating system disc from the command line using **x:\i386\winnt32\checkupgradeonly**. This will not begin the upgrade or installation process.

- **Check the Windows Server Catalog** – located at http://www. microsoft.com/windows/catalog/server. If your hardware is not listed in the Server Catalog, contact the hardware manufacturer to find out if there is a Windows Server 2003-compliant driver available.

- **Check drivers and BIOS** – upgrade to the latest BIOS and check that you have the latest device drivers for your hardware. You can check this at http://v4.windowsupdate.microsoft.com/en by clicking on **Scan for Updates,** then **Driver Updates**. If you cannot find a driver here, check with the device manufacturer directly.

- **Check all 16-bit or older hardware devices** – inventory your current hardware and check whether devices use Plug and Play.

Once you have verified hardware compatibility, you should check with software manufacturers to verify that your current software will be supported on Windows Server 2003. There is nothing worse than undertaking an upgrade only to find out incompatibility issues after the fact and having a Line of Business (LOB) application go belly up because someone wasn't checking.

> IMPORTANT: You must upgrade all Windows 2000 domain controllers to SP2 or later to avoid potential domain controller corruption.

Preparing for the Upgrade

There are some basic guidelines to follow when you prepare an upgrade from a domain controller in a Windows 2000 domain. The command line **adprep** tool is located on the Windows Server 2003 operating system disc in the \i386 folder. In preparation for the upgrade, you need to:

- Identify the domain controllers that hold the schema and infrastructure operations master roles

- Back up the schema operations master

- Disconnect the schema operations master from the network

- Insert the Windows Server 2003 Standard Edition CD-ROM into the drive

- Navigate to the \i386 folder

- **Run the adprep /forestprep** command to update the schema and prepare the forest

On the server that holds the infrastructure operations master role:

- **Run the adprep /domainprep** command to update object references (schema) in the domain.

> IMPORTANT: You must first run the adprep.exe utility to prepare the forest and domains within the forest on the Windows 2000 domain controllers, or you will not be able to perform the upgrade.

The key point is that Active Directory has been modified, improved, baked, and otherwise changed between the Windows 2000 Server and Windows Server 2003 time frames. That is key conceptual knowledge you'll want to take forward into the 70-282 exam.

You may have a mixed environment where there are still NT 4.0 servers, so when you prepare for the upgrade, you should:

- Have at least one NTFS partition on the NT 4.0 server (best if all partitions are NTFS for security reasons)

- Apply Service Pack 5 (SP5) or later

- Retire Windows 3.51 servers or upgrade them to Windows NT 4.0 SP5 or later (there is no direct upgrade path from Windows 3.51 to Windows 2003)

- Upgrade the NT 4.0 domain controllers to Windows 2000 to reduce the number of version differences and simplify management and troubleshooting

Upgrading a Member Server or Domain Controller

Now that you adequately prepped your Windows 2000 domain controllers, you are ready for the upgrade process. The upgrade is primarily an automated procedure for upgrading a member server. During the upgrade, Windows 2000 Server migrates the current settings of the operating system, and little administrator input is required. For a member server or domain controller in the Windows 2000 domain, you perform the upgrade by:

- Inserting the Windows Server 2003 system disc into the CD-ROM drive and the setup wizard will guide you through the steps and prompts to **Upgrade to Windows 2000** for upgrading the operating system.

- Setup will copy necessary files and start the upgrade process. The server will reboot and automatically upgrade to the Windows Server 2003 operating system based on preexisting settings from the previous operating system.

IMPORTANT: If the Windows 2000 server is a domain controller, Active Directory will automatically be upgraded to domain controller status in Windows Server 2003 Standard Edition.

Upgrading Workgroup Servers

When prepping workgroup servers, you do not have to run the adprep.exe tool, since they do not belong to a domain. Some basic steps before you perform the upgrade are:

- Verify that Windows 2000 is optimally configured

- Make a complete system backup (in the real world you might make two such backups)

- And Go! Insert the Windows 2003 system disc and follow the same steps as listed above for member servers and domain controllers.

IMPORTANT: On the one hand, you don't need to know much detail about peer-to-peer workgroup server scenarios for the 70-282 exam, as Microsoft isn't emphasizing that form of architecture for its Windows Server 2003 product family. However, Microsoft has many public-facing slide decks where it emphasizes the "opportunity" to migrate customers from peer-to-peer scenarios to true client/server solutions centered on Windows Server 2003. Because of that opportunity emphasis, you might see some exam questions weave in that opportunity logic.

Configure Windows Server 2003

Well, we've left the SBS realm completely at this point and are going to look at how configuration is managed in the Windows Server 2003 world. Even though we like to keep things simple with SBS, it is a good thing to know how the native tools work in the Windows Server 2003 environment. It just makes me appreciate the SBS wizards so much more! In classes I have taught in the past, there was confusion at times when we dabbled on the outer limits of the SBS sphere and discussed native tools and practices out of the context of SBS. So, from here on, put on your enterprise hat and don't look back and don't mix this up with SBS methodology—we are going enterprise....

IMPORTANT: For this portion of the exam, please retire the "SBS Way."

Configure File and Print Servers

File and print services are the heart of a business, regardless of its size.

Windows Server 2003 has several wizards of its own, and the most prominent one is the Manage Your Server Wizard from which you can assign server roles and configure server settings. Quite honestly, I recommend installing Windows Server 2003 in either virtual PC or on an old machine floating around in your garage (as long as it meets minimum requirements) and getting some hands-on with the product so you don't walk into the exam totally cold. It helps the confidence level to have seen and touched it. You can acquire a copy of Windows Server 2003 Standard by downloading a trial version or purchasing the Action Pack from the Microsoft Partner site.

Configuring a File Server

In the following, we walk you through the steps of setting up a shared folder, turning on the indexing service, and setting permissions on the shared folder.

1. Click **Start** and then click **Manage Your Server**.

2. On the **Manage Your Server** page, click **Add or remove a role**.

3. On the **Preliminary Steps** page, review the preliminary steps and then click **Next.**

4. On the **Configuration Options** page, click **Custom configuration** and then click **Next**.

5. On the **Server Role** page, click **File server** and then click **Next.**

6. On the **File Server Disk Quotas** page, click **Next**.

7. On the **File Server Indexing Service** page, select **Yes, turn the Indexing Service on,** and then click **Next**.

8. On the **Summary of Selections** page, review the options you have selected, and then click **Next**.

9. On the **Welcome to the Share a Folder Wizard** page, click **Next**.

10. In the **Folder path** field, type **c:\shared\projects** and then click **Next**.

11. Click **Yes** to create the c:\shared\projects path.

12. On the **Name, Description, and Settings** page, in the **Share name** box, verify that **Projects** is displayed, and then click **Next**.

13. On the **Permissions page**, click **Administrators have full access; other users have read and write access**, and then click **Finish**.

14. On the **Sharing was Successful** page, review the options you selected and then click **Close**.

15. On the **This Server Is Now a File Server** page, click **Finish**.

That was pretty simple and we managed to configure basic settings in one task. You probably noticed that we turned on the **Indexing Service**, which is a service that can scan files on servers and workstations and then build content and property indexes.

Indexing Service

The Indexing Service will allow you to search thousands of files in the index in different formats and languages by using key words, phrases, or properties. You can start a search by either clicking **Start** and then **Search** or through a **web browser**.

After the Indexing Service has been configured, its operations run automatically, including index creation, updating, and crash recovery. The Indexing Service requires little maintenance and is designed to run continuously. Indexing Service properties can be configured through the Multimedia Command Set (MMC) snap-in. It can be configured to use minimal resources for indexing, or to be a dedicated index server using all available resources.

To perform a search for a document that contains "OWA" in close proximity to "SBS," you would type **OWA NEAR SBS AND @filename=*.doc** in the Indexing Service query window.

To configure the Indexing Service,

1. Click **Start**, point to **Administrative Tools**, and then click **Computer Management**.

2. In the console tree, expand **Services and Applications** and then click **Indexing Service**.

3. On the **Action** menu, click **Properties**.

4. In the **Indexing Service Properties** dialog box, click the **Generation** tab and select the options you want:

    • **Index files with unknown extensions**. This option indexes documents with unknown extensions (those for which you do not have filters installed). Indexing Service extracts whatever content and properties it can from the documents.

    • **Generate abstracts**. This option produces abstracts of documents to present in the list of results. In the **Maximum size** box, type or select the maximum number of characters for the abstracts.

5. Click the **Tracking** tab, select the **Add Network Share Alias Automatically** checkbox if you want Indexing Service to use the share name of any shared directory as the alias for that directory, and then click **OK**.

6. On the **Action** menu, click **Stop** and then click **Start** for these changes to take effect.

IMPORTANT: To be honest, the Indexing Service typically has a supporting actor role in a small or medium-sized network. You don't really "use" the Indexing Service directly. However, the Indexing Service has a huge background role. It supports the searching capabilities of native operating system tools. But in my humble opinion, the real benefit of the Indexing Service is the supporting actor role for line-of-business applications. For example, when you install Microsoft CRM 1.2, a line-of-business application used for customer relationship management, the Indexing Services is required to be installed and properly configured. That is a key dependency you should understand.

Configuring a Print Server

A print server is a server that routes print requests and job status information on the network. This does not need to be a dedicated computer and servers usually share the printer server function with other duties.

First you would physically attach a printer to the network using the Add Printer wizard in the Printers and Faxes system folder. Needless to say, you must be an Administrator on the print server. The Add Printer wizard guides you through the steps of adding a printer for a print device that is shared on the network or directly connected to the print server.

Once you add a printer to the network and share it, you will be prompted for:

- The printer port on the server to which the print device is attached

- The printer driver for the local print device

- The printer name

- The share name that allows users to connect to the printer.

After adding the printer to the network, you must run the Manage Your Server Wizard and choose first to **Add or remove a role** and then **Print Server** role. The wizard will then guide you through the rest of the installation configuring the particular settings the printer requires.

> IMPORTANT: We can't emphasize enough the importance of exact terminology and we're starting to run out of chapters in this book to make that point! Read the following carefully, because some exam questions will invoke terminology trickery. A "print server" is a server that routes print requests and job status information on a network. A "printer" is the print device that performs the printing. A "logical printer" is the software interface on the print server.

> And don't forget that printers were the entire reason local area networks where created in the early 1980s (circa early NetWare releases). Printers where expensive and the whole paradigm was to efficiently share one printer in a small or medium-sized office. That historical context is an important way to think when taking the 70-282 exam. Kindly honor the past!

Promoting a Domain Controller

A server can be promoted to a domain controller by installing Active Directory (AD). Once promoted, the server will then contain a writable copy of the AD database, participate in AD replication and be able to control access to network resources. You install Active Directory through the Manage Your Server page and choose the domain controller role, which will then launch the Active Directory Installation Wizard.

The Active Directory Installation Wizard will ask you if you want to create a:

- Domain in a New Forest

- Domain Tree in an Existing Forest

- Child Domain in an Existing Domain Tree

The wizard will continue and ask for:

- NetBIOS domain name

- Active Directory Database and log file location

- Shared System Volume (SYSVOL) folder location

- Whether to install and configure DNS

- Permissions for user and group objects to be compatible with previous Windows versions

- Directory Services Restore Mode Administrator Password

After all the above information is provided, the Active Directory Installation Wizard installs Active Directory and promotes the server to a domain controller. The following consoles will be added to the Administrative Tools menu:

- Active Directory Domains and Trusts

- Active Directory Sites and Services

- Active Directory Users and Computers

You must restart the Windows Server 2003 after the Active Directory Installation Wizard finishes, where the server will then be converted to a domain controller and the consoles will be added.

Creating and Configuring User, Group, and Computer Accounts

Even though there have been many changes in logical and physical structure due to Active Directory, and a lot nicer GUIs, many concepts have remained the same. One of them is that since this is a domain controller, you do not have the option to create local user accounts. It has been this way since the days of Windows NT.

Let me establish one paradigm of the traditional Windows Server 2003 crowd versus the SBSers. The "traditional" crowd takes pride in using native tools and even the command line on occasion. But SBSers are spoiled, and most of what I call "grunt" tasks have the luxury of our SBS wizards. I feel much better for sharing that with you.

User Accounts and Domain Groups

Creating user accounts is easy. After you have promoted the Windows Server 2003 to a domain controller, you can now create a **domain user** account in the **Active Directory Users and Computers** console. There are some preexisting containers, two of importance, namely the Built-In container and the Users container.

The Built-In container houses the following groups, which are all domain local groups and cannot be moved to another container or OU. They are created by default in Windows Server 2003 with the following rights:

Account Operators - Members of this group can administer domain user and group accounts, log on locally, and can shutdown domain controllers. Account Operators cannot modify the Administrators or Domain Admins groups and accounts.

Administrators - Members of this group have full access to the domain or computer. By default, this group contains the Domain Admins and Enterprise Admins groups and the Administrator user account.

Backup Operators - Members of this group can back up or restore files without being limited by file permissions. Backup Operators can also log on locally and shut down domain systems.

Guests - Members of this group have the same permissions and rights as the Users group by default. The Guests user account is disabled by default. This Guests group contains the Domain Guests group as a member.

Incoming Forest Trust Builders - Members of this group can create incoming, one-way trust relationships to this forest. This group appears only in the root domain of the forest.

Network Configuration Operators - Members of this group can change the TCP/IP settings on domain controllers in the domain.

Performance Monitor Users - Members of this group can monitor performance counters on domain controllers in the domain.

Performance Log Users - Members of this group can manage performance counters, logs, and alerts on domain controllers in the domain.

Pre-Windows 2000 Compatible Access - Members of this group have read access to all users and groups in the domain. This group provides backward compatibility for computers running Windows version pre-Windows 2000, such as Windows NT 4. The Everyone group is a member of this group by default.

Print Operators - Members of this group have the appropriate rights to administer printers connected to domain controllers and shared printer objects in the Active Directory. Print Operators can also log on locally and shutdown domain systems.

Remote Desktop Users - Members in this group are granted the right to log on remotely using a terminal session.

Replicator – A system group account used for file replication in a domain, this group has no members—and you should not add them, either.

Server Operators - Members of this group can administer shared resources on domain servers, start and stop certain services, and format hard disks. Additionally, members of this group have the same rights Backup Operators have.

Users – Members of this group have sufficient permissions and rights to run certified Windows applications, but cannot run most legacy applications. This prevents regular users from making system-wide changes.

The Users container includes domain local, global, and universal groups that can be moved to other Organizational Units (OUs) if needed. A list of the groups and their rights follows:

Cert Publishers - Members of this group can publish digital certificates for users and computers.

DnsAdmins - Members of this group have permission to administer DNS.

DnsUpdateProxy - Members of this group can act as a DNS proxy for clients. A DHCP server that handles dynamic updates for DHCP clients should be a member of this group.

Domain Admins - Members of this group have full control of the domain. This group is a member of the Administrators group on all domain members including domain controller. The Administrator user account is a member of this group by default.

Domain Computers - This group contains all the computer accounts of the client and servers joined to the domain.

Domain Controllers - This group contains all domain controllers in the domain.

Domain Guests - This group contains all domain guests.

Domain Users - This group contains all domain users. When you create a new user account in the domain, it will automatically become a member of the Domain Users group.

Enterprise Admins - Members of this group have full control of all domains in the forest. This group is a member of the Administrators group on all domain controllers in the forest. The Administrator user account is a member of this group by default.

Group Policy Creator Owners – Members of this group can modify Group Policy settings in the domain. The Administrator user account is a member of this group by default.

IIS_WPG – A system group account used by Internet Information Services (IIS) 6.0.

RAS and IAS Servers - Servers in this group have access to the remote access properties of users. This group is used for Internet Authentication Service (IAS) servers that perform authentication for a collection of Routing and Remote Access Service (RRAS) servers.

Schema Admins - Members of this group can modify the Active Directory schema. The Administrator user account is a member of this group by default.

Then there are some special groups that do not belong to either container but allow you to assign permissions to users, which are:

Everyone – Includes everyone with a user account.

Anonymous Logon – Includes everyone without a user account.

Network – Includes users who are currently logged on to a computer over the network. This is the opposite of the Interactive group.

Interactive – Includes users that are currently logged on to the local computer. This is the opposite of the Network group.

Domain groups are only created on domain controller. They enable centralized administration within a domain and are used to grant users permission to resources and rights for system tasks on any computer in the domain. Considering the groups included in the Built-In and Users container, let's take another look at group scopes and what they are.

Domain local groups

This group scope in either a Windows 2000 native or a Windows Server 2003 domain can contain user accounts, global groups, and universal groups from any domain in the forest, as well as domain local groups from the same domain. In Windows 2000 mixed-mode domain, they can contain user accounts and global groups from any domain.

You can grant permissions only to domain local groups on objects within the domain in which the group exists.

Global groups

This group scope in either a Windows 2000 native or a Windows Server 2003 domain can contain user accounts and global groups from the domain in which the global group exists. In a Windows 2000 mixed-mode domain, they can contain only user accounts from the domain in which the group exists. You can grant permissions to global groups for all domains in the forest, regardless of the location of the global group.

Universal groups

This group scope can contain user accounts, global groups, and other universal groups from any Windows 2003 or Windows 2000 domain in the forest. The domain must be operating in Windows Server 2003 or Windows 2000 native mode to create security groups with universal scope. The list of universal group memberships is maintained in the global catalog. Global and domain local groups are listed in the global catalog, but their memberships are not. Each change to the membership of a universal group is replicated to all global catalog servers. By minimizing the use of universal groups, you will help reduce the size of the global catalog. This reduces the amount of replication-related traffic on your network. You can grant permissions to universal groups for all domains in the forest, regardless of the location of the universal group.

The underlying idea is to place a user account into the proper group so you have to manage the user account only once, and by association of group membership, inherits the proper permissions assigned to all resources on the domain. At this point we should be discussing group strategies, but we don't want to kill too many trees in the making of this book. By remembering the group scopes and how they relate to each other, you should be fine for the exam.

> IMPORTANT: Also revisit the groups discussion in Chapter 7 to provide "context" and to allow you to understand how groups are handled differently between SBS 2003 and Windows Server 2003.

Computer Accounts

Computer accounts are also created in the **Active Directory Users and Computers** console (the name sort of gives it away, eh?). Computer accounts are similar to user accounts whereas the computer needs to authenticate to the domain controller as well to gain access to resources. Client computers are added to the domain by going into the **System Properties**, **Computer Name** tab and use the **Network ID** or **Change** box to join the client to the domain.

You should always create a computer account within an OU for easier delegation and management. Computer accounts can be created for Windows Server 2003, Windows 2000, Windows XP, and Windows NT 4.0 clients. When a computer account is created, a Security Identifier (SID) number is created. A SID looks like a serial number (long, alpha-numeric) and is unique to the specific machine.

Windows 9x and Windows Me were never intended to be domain clients. People using Windows 98 in the enterprise and all the issues that arose (the support incidents were too numerous) brought about the restriction in the Windows XP Home edition, which cannot be joined to a domain. But a positive note (and something that is not on the 70-282 exam) is that Windows 98 machines are great for consulting with many customers. This is true because you can take your Windows 98 machine to multiple customer sites, log on to different domains to do your voodoo, and not have a bona fide domain computer account membership issue (e.g., SID for just one domain preventing you from logging on to multiple domains).

Configure Networking Hardware

The good news is that configuring the networking services and hardware components is not really much different from your learning experience early in the book.

> IMPORTANT: No, the authors are not trying to cop out on you and head to the pub early! Rather, we are subliminally trying to make a point: efficient use of leverage. Just as we don't need to copy and paste text from other chapters into this networking and hardware section to bulk out the book, you don't necessarily need to re-read something you already know. Let us further explain.

- In academic learning environments, the top students are sometime truly smarter (higher IQ). However, just as likely you will find the top students are efficient in their studies. Top students who are models of efficiency:

  - Do not spend time learning the same subject twice

  - Selectively pick which topics are important and which are not

  - Filter through much information rapidly with strong reading comprehension skills

- Have an innate sense to anticipate what content will be tested and what content will be ignored

- Enjoy a certain amount of luck! Some students, when faced with a question for which they have no idea what the answer is, luckily GUESS the proper answer. The oldest joke in test-taking is to select answer "C" in a multiple choice problem when you are guessing and don't now the answer. But there is truth in humor!

So for all the reasons stated here, I'm going to point you to Chapter 5 and Chapter 7 as primers for reviewing generic networking (DHCP, DNS, IP, WINS, etc.) and hardware (drives, memory, processors, hardware-sizing issues). Meet you back here in a few minutes after you revisit those select references, but don't spend too much time!

Secure Windows Server 2003

First install Windows Server 2003 SP1—wait, that's not included in this exam. We must focus on the pre-SP1 era and consider how to secure communications between the server and clients going out to the Internet as well as those coming in from public unsecured networks. There are numerous ways to secure and lock down the server, but let's not get away from Microsoftology and look at natively included options in Windows Server 2003.

Configure and Secure Internet Access

NAT (Network Address Translation) configured through RRAS translates private, internal IP addresses to external public IPs. This protects the private network from unauthorized access by hiding the private IP from the public networks (as explained previously in Chapter 6). To implement NAT in RRAS, you can use the Manage Your Server Wizard and follow these steps:

1. Click **Start,** then click **Manage Your Server**.

2. On the **Manage Your Server** page, click **Add or remove a role**.

3. On the **Preliminary Steps** page, click **Next**.

4. On the **Server Role** page, click **Remote access/VPN server**, and then click **Next**.

5. On the **Summary of Selections** page, review the selected options, and then click **Next**.

6. On the **Welcome to the Routing and Remote Access Server Setup Wizard** page, click **Next**.

7. On the **Configuration** page, click **Network address translation (NAT)** and click **Next**.

8. On the **NAT Internet Connection** page, select the interface to connect to the Internet.

9. Clear the **Enable security on the selected interface by setting up Basic** Firewall checkbox and then click **Next**.

10. On the **Name and Address Translation Services** page, click **Enable basic name and address services**, and then click **Next**.

11. On the summary information page click **Finish**.

This is too easy; the enterprise people are supposed to use command lines and scripts and stuff like that. Who allowed them to have wizards?

Configure a VPN Connection

RRAS not only manages NAT, but also provides VPN (Virtual Private Network) services. RRAS encrypts the data as it is sent over an unsecured network, encapsulating the data with a header that provides routing information, and acts like a point-to-point link on a private network. Even if data is intercepted, it cannot be read without the encryption key. This is also called a VPN tunnel.

There are two tunneling protocols

- PPTP (Point-to-Point Tunneling Protocol) – uses user-level PPP (Point-to-Point Protocol) authentication methods and MPPE (Microsoft Point-to-Point encryption)

- L2TP/IPSec – (Layer 2 Tunneling Protocol with Internet Protocol Security) uses user-level PPP authentication methods over an IPSec encrypted connection. IPSec requires either Kerberos, Certificates, or Shared Secret Keys for authentication.

- Used for secure communications between a remote client and a corporate network across the Internet

- Used for secure communications between branch offices

For L2TP, both the client and server must support L2TP and IPSec. Client support for L2TP is built into the Windows XP remote access client, and VPN server support for L2TP is built into the Windows Server 2003 family. The L2TP server support is automatically installed when you install RRAS. Based on your choices during the RRAS Setup Wizard, L2TP can be configured for as few as five or as many as 128 L2TP ports.

By using a L2TP enabled VPN with IPSec for authentication, data transfer is as secure as a LAN in a corporate network.

Before you can configure a VPN server role, you must:

- Identify the network interface connecting to the Internet and the remote interface connecting to your network

- Decide whether to assign IP addresses to clients through the VPN server or the DHCP server on the network

- Decide whether you want the VPN server or RADIUS (Remote Authentication Dial-in User Service) to authenticate connection requests from VPN clients.

Before being able to configure VPN, you must add the Remote access/VPN server role. You must be a member of the administrator's group on the local computer. If you are not a domain admin, you can have the domain admin add the server computer account to the RAS and IAS security server grouping Active Directory. This action can also be performed on the command line by typing **netsh ras add registeredserver smbnation server1**. This would register the server1 in the smbnation domain.

You can check whether the RAS is already registered in AD by typing **netsh ras show registeredserver smbnation server1**.

To configure RAS for the VPN connection, you would open the **Manage Your Server** console and **Add or remove a role** and choose **Remote access/VPN server**. On the **VPN Connection** page, you select the NIC that will receive the connections from the VPN clients. On the **IP Address Assignment** page, you choose to either have the server generate the IP addresses by leaving the default selection on **Automatically** or select **From a specified range of addresses** option. You then choose to use RAS to authenticate connection requests locally by using Windows authentication, and then complete the wizard.

> IMPORTANT: Ensure that you configure enough ports to support all simultaneous connections.

PPTP and L2TP ports are configured through the RAS console by expanding the **Ports** node and clicking **Properties**, highlighting the port to configure, and clicking **Configure**.

> IMPORTANT: It is easy to overthink and debate in your head and trot down the wrong test-taking path. Here is what I mean in the context of the above discussion. Many real-world SMB consultants are revisiting the assumption that all mobility must include a VPN connection. There are alternatives, such as tunneling in ISA Server.
>
> However, for the 70-282 exam, keep it simple and keep it straight! Microsoft, as you would infer from the section above, is thrilled by advances in its VPN-related capabilities. Please be sure to share the same excitement level when you take the 70-282 exam.

Manage Windows Server 2003

First off, perform the following simple task so you have an overall view of managing a Windows Server 2003 machine. In the Administrative Tools program group, open each item and poke around. Don't commit changes, but understand that a simple look-and-see exercise (also know by certification instructors as "daze and amaze") is an effective learning approach. It's uncanny that on an exam, such as 70-282, you'll say to yourself "I've seen that before!" You are able to utter such remarks and answer the test question correctly because you used playtime (that's the poking around part) as learning time. So go play and explore the items in the Administrative Tools group and return back here in one hour. Bye!

Okay—welcome back from your playtime recess hour! Let's do a deep dive into the world of group policy objects (GPOs).

From the **Manage Your Server** page to the new **Group Policy Management Console (GPMC)** and built-in **remote administration**, many improvements have been made in managing the Microsoft Server world. Managing a server is becoming easier, more mundane tasks are optimized through the use of wizards, and hey, we are getting a lot fewer blue screens and headaches. I know there are some of you out there who like to do things the old way, but the nature of IT is that it is constantly changing. I used to laugh at people when the mouse first came out, thinking they were lazy because with a mouse you didn't have to remember keyboard commands. Well, was I ever wrong! I finally accepted mouse-use and managed to move on with my life. So let this be a lesson, and embrace all the new wizards and anything that will save you time, like using the GPMC. I know—it's hard to relearn something in a different way, but truth be told, the time you spend learning a new tool vs. the time you would spend sticking with the old way will pay off hundredfold.

Managing User Environments with GPOs

If you are looking for a way to bullet-proof and lock down the environment, Group Policy is the dot on the "i" in controlling the user environment. The Group Policy feature provides powerful capabilities for automatically managing and configuring servers and workstations in distributed Windows environments. With Group Policy you can distribute software, control IE (Internet Explorer) configuration, redirect folders, and much more.

You can apply Group Policy to users and computers to:

- **Manage users and computers** – You can ensure that users get the same desktop every time they log on, even from different computers. Local folders can be redirected to a central location, where they can be backed up as well as made available to the user regardless from which computer the user logs on. Group Policy includes administrative templates that allow you to manage Shared Folders, Control Panel access, Start Menu and taskbar settings, and other computer settings.

- **Deploy software** – You can ensure all users have the software they require available for their job function, even when a user logs on from a different machine. You can also ensure that computers in a specific department have specific software available, regardless of who logs on. You can also deploy hot fixes and service packs with Group Policy.

- **Enforce security settings** – Security settings for local and domain policies can be centrally applied through Group Policy to protect the user environment. You can use it to set the minimum number of characters in a password, audit policy, user rights assignment (like load and unload device drivers), and security options (e.g., not displaying the last logged-on username).

- **Ensure consistent desktop settings** – With logon scripts you can ensure users get a specific environment, like always having the same mapped drives and printers available, regardless from which computer they log on. The logon script will run every time a user logs on to the network

By default, Group Policy settings are **not configured** and you should decide whether to **enable** or **disable** a Group policy setting.

The easiest way to configure security policy is by creating an mmc (Microsoft Management Console) and adding the Security Configuration and Analysis Snap-in and the Security Templates Snap-in.

Then you can run an analysis against your current policy settings and apply a template that is configured with the minimum security configuration settings.

Folder Redirection

Four folders that are part of the user profile can be redirected:

- My Documents

- Application Data

- Desktop

- Start Menu

By redirecting them to a centrally stored location on the network, you can ensure the folders are available regardless of the client computer the user logs on to. Since the files are stored centrally, there will be no storage space used on the client machines and confidential data will not remain on the client computer. In case of a workstation loss or the operating system on the client needs to be reinstalled, the user's files are protected and will not be lost.

These are the choices when redirecting folders:

- **Redirect folder to the following location:** all users' folders will be redirected to a common area and will be accessible by other users (not private). When redirecting, choose **Basic,** and in the **Target Folder location** field to **Redirect folder to the following location**.

- **Create a folder for each user under the root path:** all users' folders will be redirected to a private area, accessible only by the individual employee. When redirecting, choose **Basic**, and in the **Target Folder location** to **Create a folder for each user under the root path**.

- **Advanced – specify locations for various user groups:** where you can redirect folders to different locations based on the user's security group membership.

IMPORTANT: When using Folder redirection to create the folders, permissions will be assigned automatically and there is no need for manual NTFS configuration. If you create the folders manually, make sure to set the appropriate NTFS permissions.

Also note that folder redirection is often mentioned as a cool GPO in public-facing Microsoft presentations. Hint-hint!

Delegating Administration

Delegating administration of various tasks that could be performed by nontechnical personnel helps distribute the administrative workload. You could delegate less technical and more frequently used tasks to the office manager at a business. This way you can keep the support costs down and help the office function more autonomously. You would not make the office manager a member of the

Administrators group to perform this task, but set appropriate permissions. In this case you would want to make the office manager a member of the Account Managers Operators group, which is an already built-in group in Active Directory.

You can delegate administrative control by using the Delegation of Control Wizard to specify users or groups within any OU within the domain tree. Active Directory defines specific permissions and user rights to help assign the most appropriate administrative scope for a particular person. This can be assigned at the domain level, a single OU within the domain, or all OUs in the domain, or on an object within an OU.

With the Delegation of Control Wizard, you can allow a user to:

- Create, delete, and manage user accounts

- Reset user passwords and force password change at the next logon

- Read all user information

- Create, delete, and manage groups

- Modify the membership of a group

- Modify Group Policy Links

- Generate RSoP (Planning and Logging)

- Create, delete, and manage inetOrgPerson accounts. Active Directory provides support for the inetOrgPerson object class and its associated attributes.

- Reset inetOrgPerson passwords

- Read all inetOrgPerson information

IMPORTANT: Several third-party Lightweight Directory Access Protocol (LDAP) and X.500 directory services use the InetOrgPerson object class to represent people within an organization. Support for InetOrgPerson makes migrations from other LDAP directories to Active Directory more efficient.

1. Go to **Active Directory Users and Computers**.

2. **Expand** the domain node.

3. In the console tree, right-click the container or OU where you want the user or group to have control. Click **Delegate Control**.

4. On the **Welcome to the Delegation of Control Wizard** page, click **Next**.

5. On the **Users or Groups** page, click **Add**.

6. In the **Select Users, Computers, or Groups** dialog box, in the **Enter the object names to select** box, type the users or groups to whom you want to delegate authority and then click **OK**.

7. On the **Users or Groups** page, click **Next**.

8. On the **Tasks to Delegate** page, in the **Delegate the following common tasks** box, select the tasks to delegate and then click **Next**

9. On the **Completing the Delegation of Control Wizard** page, click **Finish**.

IMPORTANT: The Delegation of Control Wizard changes permissions on specified objects according to the users, group objects, and tasks that were indicated. To undo changes, the object must be modified manually. Therefore, you should use groups instead of individual users, because you can just remove users from the group and not the object.

Also, from a 70-282 testing perspective, understand that Microsoft is keenly interested in administration delegation in the small and medium networking space. It views such efficiency gains as the only way to truly grow the SMB space on a worldwide basis. Remember— for today—think like MICROSOFT!

Notes:

Protecting Against Data Loss

This section presents a discussion on protecting against data loss.

Shadow Copies

One of the cool features in Windows Server 2003 is shadow copies. Shadow copies allow users to restore their own files so they don't have to bother you and wait for them to be retrieved from a tape backup. Shadow copies come in handy for:

- Recovery of accidentally deleted or overwritten files.

- Version-checking a document.

Shadow copy will take a snapshot of the file at specifically set intervals. You must first enable Shadow copies on the server and on the client. You must copy the shadow copy client file **twcli32.msi**, from the **%systemroot\system32\ cleints\twclient\x86** folder to the client workstation.

To enable shadow copies on the server:

1. Go to **My Computer**, right-click, then click **Manage**.

2. In the console tree, right-click the **Shared Folders** and point to **All Tasks**.

3. Click **Configure Shadow Copies** and click **Enable**.

Once installed and enabled, this will create a **Previous Version** tab in the network share properties.

> IMPORTANT: To use shadow copies in Windows 2000 you must have Service Pack 3 or later installed.

Backup Utility

With the built-in backup utility (NTbackup), you can back up the entire system or choose to back up specific files and folders or system state data and schedule backup jobs. Backup uses the Volume Shadow Copy service, which is enabled by default. This allows you to back up open files and they will not be skipped.

With the backup utility, you can back up to a selection of storage media and devices, including CD-ROM, removable disks, network drives, tape drives, and logical drives.

Backup allows for five different types of backups, as shown in Table 10-5.

Table 10-5

Backup types available in the Backup Utility

Type	Description	Archive Attribute cleared?
Normal or Full	Backs up all selected files regardless of archive attribute setting	Yes
Copy	Identical to Normal except it does not change the archive attribute	No
Differential	Creates backup copies of files that have changed since the last Normal or Full backup	No
Incremental	Creates backup copies of the files that have changed since the last Normal or Incremental backup	Yes
Daily	Backs up files based on the file modification date and ignores the current state of the archive attribute	No

So what does the archive attribute setting really dictate? If you did a Normal backup each Friday, the archive bit gets reset. Then on Monday through Thursday you could create a Differential backup that does not reset the archive bit. That means on Monday you back up all changed files since Friday. On Tuesday you back up all changed files since Friday, since the Monday Differential did not reset the archive bit. So goes Wednesday and Thursday. In this case, if the server crashed on Wednesday, you would perform the restore using the Friday Normal backup tape and the Tuesday Differential tape, since the Tuesday backup contains all files changed since last Friday.

New scenario. You perform a Friday Normal backup, but make Incremental backups every night of the week. The Incremental backup resets the archive bit, which means after the Monday backup, the Tuesday backup only backs up files that have changed from Monday to Tuesday. The Tuesday Incremental backup resets the archive bit again and on Wednesday, the Incremental backup only backs up files that have changed since Tuesday. When you suffer a server crash on Wednesday, to restore you will need the Friday Normal backup and the Monday AND Tuesday Incremental backup tapes!

So all this has its pros and cons. Whereas the Differential backup will take longer to back up by Thursday, it will also restore faster compared to an Incremental backup, since it only requires two tapes (Friday's Normal tape and the Differential tape of last backup).

The Incremental backups will be faster, but the restore will take longer because we now need the Friday Normal tape and every Incremental tape up to the last backup tape.

There are numerous backup strategies and methods which are beyond the scope of this book. I recommend further reading on the Microsoft web site on the backup utility to fully understand all of its functions and capabilities.

> IMPORTANT: This is a classic certification testing area. Traditionally, Microsoft has held you responsible for a rich understanding of backup approaches. Let's just say you needed to know the "finer points" to become an MCSE!

> Here is the conceptual challenge you will face on the 70-282 exam. It is easy to think real world and say, "Oh...I always do Full backups each day." Perhaps such is the case and it makes sense because it's easy and you've got plenty of room to store backup data at the SMB level. However—the real world and 70-282 exam reality are often NOT the same. So even if you couldn't care less about Differential or Incremental backup methods, PLEASE care about these approaches for the 70-282 exam!

Automated System Recovery

The Automated System Recovery (ASR) Wizard is included in the backup utility in Windows 2000, Windows Server 2003, and Windows XP. It is an automated recovery that requires the use of the original system CD and an ASR disc. The ASR is not a Full backup and should only be used in conjunction with another Full backup.

When you create an ASR backup, it will back up:

- The system state data

- Windows file-protected files

- System services and minimal system files

The ASR does not back up data files. ASR works best with NTFS and it does not support FAT partitions larger than 2.1 GB and does not support 64 kb clusters.

When you create an ASR backup, it will prompt you to insert a floppy on which the backup will create two files:

- Asr.sif

- Asrpnp.sif

These files will contain all the disk signatures along with volume and partition information. Do not confuse the ASR floppy with the ERD (Emergency Repair Disk) floppy under NT. The ASR floppy contains enough information to restore partitions and volumes to the proper configurations, remembers the location of the last backup, and automatically connects to the last backup location pulling the backup data, all without requiring any user interaction.

To perform an ASR restore, you insert the Windows Server 2003 disk and hit the F2 key when prompted. The system restore will be automated from that point on, and when it finishes the restore, you have a fully bootable system.

Beware: Since the ASR does not back up data files, use it only in conjunction with your regular backups.

Monitoring Server Performance

It makes sense to monitor system performance on the server routinely. Best practice would have you create a baseline established over several months, giving you the ability to compare your performance data when you have to diagnose a problem. This can reveal issues, such as high demand on a specific resource, that end up creating a bottleneck. This can affect the entire system, so it is a good idea to baseline your four subsystems:

- Memory

- Processor

- Disk

- Network

Reasons for bottlenecks are:

- Insufficient subsystems, like not having adequate memory

- Uneven distribution of workload (e.g., using old parts in a new server)

- Failing subsystem—before a motherboard or hard drive fail, you will experience odd occurrences

- A runaway program or process, interfering with other application performance

There are built-in tools in Windows Server 2003 that can collect and view real-time system data in the System Monitor. The Performance Logs and Alerts allow you to configure logs, record performance data, and create system alerts.

System Monitor obtains information on how the system and applications are functioning, helping prevent bottlenecks by keeping an eye on resource usage. The collected data can be displayed in a text file or bar graph, which can be viewed in a browser, saved as an html file, or printed.

The Performance Logs and Alerts console contains the following utilities:

- **Counter Logs** – Based on performance objects and counters, these logs record data sampled from hardware resources and system services. You have the ability to set the interval time for sampling data from several seconds to minutes or hours.

- **Trace Logs** – These measure performance statistics such as disk and file input/output, page faults, and thread activity.

- **Alerts** – These logs are useful to monitor specific counters you actively monitor and will send you notification when a specific threshold value has been reached or exceeded. Alerts can be set to send a network message, run a program, or start a log file.

Please be sure to take a quick look at additional monitoring tools like Task Manager (right-click the **Start** bar to access) and Disk Defragmenter (select from the **System Tools** program group under the **Accessories** program group). A quick peek-and-poke session is all you need.

> IMPORTANT: You will like this tip! Instead of referring you to another information source for more studying, I can now say that the above discussion on performance monitoring is SUFFICIENT for your 70-282 exam preparation purposes! While I think the entire monitoring area is really cool and a service revenue opportunity for SMB consultants, the fact of the matter is that Microsoft historically does not test extensively on this topic. Personally, I think it's a bummer, but it's to your benefit for managing your study time to pass the 70-282 exam. In the old days, there was an MCSE exam that had a major testing objective focused on performance monitoring. When I took the test, there was only ONE question on Performance Monitor. What a letdown!!!

> I can't resist throwing you a performance monitoring bone to chew in your free time. For giggles and fun, install the Network Monitor sniffer from **Control Panel**, **Add\Remove Programs**, **Add\Remove Windows Components**, **Network Monitor Tools** (and install the 2.3 MB application). Then play with it and "sniff" traffic and learn to read packet details. Very cool. Use this as your reward for passing the 70-282 exam!

> And be advised you can do deeper dives on the entire performance monitoring area, including the use of native Windows Server 2003 performance monitoring tools, in Chapter 12 of *Windows Small Business Server 2003 Best Practices* and Chapter 13 of *Advanced Windows Small Business Server 2003 Best Practices* (both from SMB Nation Press, as you likely know by now!).

Microsoft Operations Manager

MOM (Microsoft Operations Manager) can centrally monitor user actions, application software, and desktop computers and servers for several thousand computers. There are several features included in MOM that allow you to manage servers and applications:

- **Alerts** – MOM rules can be configured to create specific alerts with associated severity levels. Alerts can be set to trigger e-mail messages, Simple Network Management Protocol (SNMP) traps, pages, and scripts to notify other management systems. Alert history and associated events can be traced and looked up in the Microsoft Knowledge Base (KB).

- **Rules** – Administrator-created rules allow MOM to react in a predetermined event pattern, triggering administrative alerts or specific actions. With MOM rules, events can be linked to the KB articles providing probable-cause guidance and links to additional information.

- **Distributed Event Management** – MOM uses a repository for all system and application events stemming from the Windows-based systems within a network. Events can be consolidated and specific information on a detailed event stream can be viewed in a single desktop console view.

- **Performance Monitoring** – MOM can be configured to monitor key performance thresholds. New rules can be added and existing rules can be customized to allow system and application performance to be monitored. Reports can be used for baseline reporting and capacity planning.

- **Web Reporting** – MOM can be configured to generate HTML snap shots of all generated reports. HTML reports can be exported and hosted on a Web server for browser viewing.

- **Graphical Reporting Tool** – In addition to the Web console, preconfigured performance data reports and charts can be viewed at a glance by administrators in the MOM MMC.

- **Management Packs** – There are preconfigured MOM-rule sets and Knowledge Base articles for specific applications and services. MOM Management packs are available for Active Directory, IIS, and ISA Server 2004.

Remote Administration of Windows Server 2003

The days of having to run down hallways or speed over to the client site to look at a server hiccup have long gone, thanks to Remote Desktop Administration, a built-in feature since Windows 2000. Formerly known as Terminal Services, the remote desktop protocol (RDP) still uses port 3389 for connections. RDP uses 128 bit encryption. The RDP session transmits the user interface, keyboard, and mouse clicks and has low overhead. You can connect with Remote Desktop for Administration via WAN, VPN, or dial-up connection.

The client system from which you connect has to have the remote desktop client installed (in Windows XP and Windows 2003 Server by default) to communicate. You can either type **mstsc** on the client system run command or go to **Start, All Programs, Accessories, Communications, Remote Desktop Connection** to launch the Remote Desktop Client.

Once connected to the server, you are able to perform most administrative tasks that would usually require you to be logged on locally to the system, including:

- Run batch jobs (e.g., tape backups)

- Upgrade server applications

- Promote and demote domain controllers

- Copy and move files, create shares, add users…

Okay, you get it. You can do just about anything unless it requires a physical interaction like inserting a floppy or disk.

Remote Desktop Administration is not enabled by default. To enable the remote desktop connection:

1. Click **Start** go to the **Control Panel** and click **System**.

2. Select the **Remote** tab and choose **Allow users to connect remotely to this computer** checkbox.

3. Add the remote user security group that should have remote access permissions and then click **OK**.

For more information on how RDP works, see Chapter 8!

Troubleshoot Windows Server 2003

Well, we all wouldn't have a job if this stuff would just work. So yes, once in a great while, we experience a minor glitch, weird symptoms, servers with attitude, and just plain misconfigured servers like a recent server I ran into. A client had called me in to oversee the continuing e-mail issues. They were using the POP3 e-mail retrieval method for external e-mail and also had separate internal e-mail set up—get this—by first using separate POP3 accounts at the ISP. The business was running a Windows 2000 server and—hold on to your hats—it was not being used as a domain controller. To further explain the situation, all network users had local user accounts set up on the server (since it's not running AD you can do that), and they connected using mapped drives and using ICW to get Internet access. They were using NTFS permissions, and every time someone changed their password on their respective workstation, they could no longer connect to server. Yes, the previous consultant (always the bad guy) had also enabled Group Policies, and I found some server-side scripts. To make a long story short, I sold them on SBS 2003, which will be installed in the very near future.

But back to troubleshooting a system: If it's your creation, you usually have somewhat of a clue what the issue is; if it is an adopted system, like the one I mentioned above, you cannot rule out anything. Windows Server 2003 comes with a whole barrage of troubleshooting utilities included, downloadable tools from the resource kit, as well as free third-party tools.

Troubleshooting Utilities

All right, so where do we start? There are oodles of troubleshooting tools and utilities available for Windows Server 2003 appearing in all sorts of flavors. You just have to know where to find them. We can separate Windows Server 2003 troubleshooting tools into:

- **Operating system tools** – These are installed as part of the default Setup program. You can view a list of them by going into the Help and Support Center for Windows Server 2003 and clicking on **Tools** and then on the **Command-line reference A-Z** or **Windows interface administrative tool reference A-Z**.

- **Help and Support Center Tools** – These are user-friendly trouble-shooting tools built into Help and Support Center and are designed for interactively troubleshooting problems with a remote user.

- **Support Tools** – These optional tools are not installed by Setup, but you can find them on the Windows Server 2003 Disk under **\Support\Tools\Suptools.msi**. Double-click the **.msi file** and follow the instructions to install them. This will add a Windows Support Tools folder shortcut to the Start menu.

- **Downloadable Debugging Tools** – Debugging tools are available at http://www.microsoft.com/windows/reskits/webresources. If you need to diagnose a Stop error, such as Stop 0x0000000A, IRQL_NOT_LESS_OR_EQUAL error, you can use a kernel debugger to determine the issue.

- **Windows Resource Kit Tools** – These tools are part of the Windows Server 2003 deployment kit and must be downloaded and installed separately. You can download these tools from http://www.microsoft.com/windows/reskits.

For more information on all Windows Server 2003 troubleshooting tools, I highly recommend that you do a search and download **SPTCC_TOL.doc** on the Microsoft web site. It covers many tools included with the family operating system that are distributed separately and useful for troubleshooting hardware and software problems in Windows Server 2003.

The main troubleshooting tools you will be working with most of the time are:

- **Event Viewers** – maintains the Application, Security, System, Directory Services, DNS Server, and File Replication Service log. Here you can usually get the event error code which can then be researched on the Internet (use Google—it's faster then the Microsoft site) for KB articles.

- **GPResult** – a command-line tool that can be used to view Group Policy settings on a local computer if you need to troubleshoot issues with missing or incorrectly applied GPO.

- **Performance Logs and Alerts** – discussed earlier in this chapter.

- **Program Compatibility Wizard** – a cool built-in tool that allows you to set compatibility modes if you need to run a legacy application that doesn't play quite nice in XP, for instance.

- **Runas** – Okay, so this isn't a troubleshooting tool, but it allows you to run programs using different user credentials and comes in handy when you are troubleshooting issues on client workstations, especially if they are experiencing quirky behavior when connecting to applications and folders on the server. This helps diagnose a permission issue on the fly.

- **Task Manager** – immediate information on processes, applications, and CPU statistics as well as memory utilization and process performance. Helps you weed out unwanted processes by being able to right-click them and kill the process.

- **DcDiag** – this domain controller diagnostic tool will run 27 tests (AD, DNS, NIC, etc.) against a DC and is the first tool you should run if you suspect issues on the domain controller.

- **DNSLint** – use this if you suspect DNS issues in the domain; it will return any issues related to incorrect or missing DNS records in the domain.

- **DS-tools** – Dsquery, DSget, DSadd, DSmod, DSmove, and DSrm, obviously Active Directory tools with different functions. I suggest you take time and play with all of them to get acquainted.

- **ADLB** – Active Directory Load Balancing tool, new in the Windows Server 2003 resource tool kit. This is a cool enterprise tool that handles connection objects between sites, allowing staggering replication intervals between connection objects owned by a bridgehead server.

As you can see, there are many troubleshooting tools available. I didn't even touch the tip of the iceberg here. Key is, you need to know most of these, not only for the exam, but for real-life support of your networks.

IMPORTANT: Before we leave the chapters in the 70-282 exam preparation section of this book, let's talk about performance anxiety (also known as test-taking tension). And we'll talk about it in the context of the last section on troubleshooting.

First, feeling anxious is normal, natural, and a good thing. It means you care, and it's your body's natural reaction to stress. So celebrate anxiety! You might be concerned about successfully completing the troubleshooting sections of the 70-282 exam because you are not an SBS or SMB technology guru and have limited experience. It's a completely understandable concern.

But... I've got a little secret for you. Just as you might be fretting over the troubleshooting problems on a certification exam, I can attest that the test writers STRUGGLED to write decent troubleshooting questions! It's true for many reasons. Test writers often sit around and ponder such conundrums as "How can we test troubleshooting? Troubleshooting is something you just do on a case-by-case basis." And troubleshooting lends itself to third-party interactions, like antivirus vendors, backup vendors, hardware vendors, and line-of-business application vendors. Microsoft Legal will never, ever allow third-party vendors to be mentioned in its exams, so think about the functional constraints that the poor test writers had to live under. If misery loves company, you and the test writers are soul mates!

So what can you expect in troubleshooting testing scenarios? Historically, such exam questions have been generic, high-level, and aimed at testing your conceptual thinking rather than measuring your super-deep technical knowledge. Microsoft's 70-282 exam has a strong business component and this would be the place to test your analytical reasoning capabilities. So in addition to just picking the correct answer on a troubleshooting question, think about the troubleshooting steps you are undertaking and whether they flow logically.

DETECT

A long time ago, co-author Harry Brelsford taught MCSE courses at night at Seattle Pacific University to adult learners. A favorite MCSE course in that timeframe combined performance monitoring and troubleshooting. In that course, students learned Microsoft DETECT, a time-tested troubleshooting model. DETECT stands for Discover, Explore, Track, Execute, Check, Tie up. The following list outlines the DETECT troubleshooting model.

- **Discover** the problem. Talk to users and look at the systems in question to determine what the problem is. Find out what software is running and what versions of operating systems and service packs are being used. Gather as much information as you can to figure out what the real problem is.

- **Explore** the boundaries. Determine the scope of the problem and whether it is reproducible. Does it happen only at specific times of the day? Is other software running when it happens? Is the same problem occurring in other locations on your site? And does TechNet record the problem as common and solvable?

- **Track** the possible approaches. Brainstorm—either alone or with others—to determine the possible approaches to solving the problem. Include solutions that have been tried in the past (especially if they have been successful).

- **Execute** an approach. Implement the approach that you determine is most likely to succeed. Don't forget to consider possible problems that might occur and take steps to avoid making the problem worse. If it is possible that some working system might be rendered inoperable by your changes, back up the data or disconnect it from the network. Be sure to make copies of all the files you propose to change.

- **Check** for success. Determine if your solution worked, and consider whether the solution is permanent or whether the system is likely to return to the problem state. If it is likely to reoccur, will the same fix work again, and can a user implement it?

- **Tie up** loose ends. Document your successes and failures as you work through the problem. Then gather the notes you made during the brainstorming and implementation of your solution so that you will have them for similar solutions. If you feel that the solution you used was not the best (even though it resulted in a successful repair), be sure to document that so you can try another solution next time. Also be sure that the user who placed the call (if it was someone other than yourself who discovered the problem) is satisfied that the problem is resolved; this will instill confidence in you and in your systems.

Practice Questions

Question #1

You have a client that has Windows 2003 domain controller, 7 Windows XP Professional clients, 15 Windows 2000 Professional and 9 Windows 98 clients. The business uses a third-party application that uses a small but essential database. The domain controller has one volume which is C:\ and holds all files. You set up a backup schedule with an ASR backup using the ASR backup wizard once every Saturday backing up to an external tape drive. On Tuesday your domain controller experiences a fatal crash. You perform the ASR restore and even though your domain controller boots fully restored and functional, the third-party database is missing on the restored domain controller. All the user accounts are in Active Directory and the domain controller appears to have had a successful restore. Why did the application database not restore?

A. The ASR floppy disk was corrupt

B. The ASR backup does not work properly with external tape drives

C. The ASR backup only backs up minimal Windows system files and system state

D. You forgot to hit the F2 key during the restore operation

Question #2

You are the admin for TeleNut, Inc., which has three Windows Domain controller 2003 servers named SERV1, SERV2 and SERV3. All client computers run Windows XP Professional. TeleNut, Inc., is a single domain implementation. You set up SERV3 as the SUS server since this is the only server connected to the Internet. SERV2 is also a SUS server and gets the updates from SERV3. All clients are configured to receive automatic updates from SERV2. You download the latest Windows updates to SERV3 and notice that the clients are not receiving any updates. You check all connectivity and find everything in working order. What must you do to ensure that clients receive the updates?

A. Configure clients to receive updates from SERV3

B. Set a GPO to push the updates out to SERV2

C. Install the SUS connector on the clients

D. Approve the updates on SERV3

E. Approve the updates on SERV2

Question #3

You are the outside consultant for a huge company. You help manage the Active Directory domain for the huge company. The Active Directory domain consists of four Windows 2003 domain controllers and two Windows 2000 domain controllers, and Windows XP Professional and Windows 2000 computers. You have been asked to implement a GPO for several OUs in the Active Directory structure. Before you deploy the GPO, you would like to know how it will affect the OUs. How can you anticipate this with the least amount of administrative effort?

A. Use the gpresult.exe command line utility

B. Use the RSoP MMC snap-in

C. Use the repadmin/ showreps command

D. Use the replmon.exe command line utility

Question #4

You are the administrator for Gadgets, Inc. Gadgets, Inc. consists of one Active Directory domain. The domain consists of 6 Windows 2003 domain controllers and 300 Windows XP Professional computers. Two Windows 2003 servers, DNS1 and DNS2, are the DNS servers for the domain. DNS1 hosts the standard primary DNS zone and DNS2 hosts the standard secondary zone. Both DNS domain controllers are configured with forwarders to external ISP DNS domain controllers. There have been too many requests for the DNS servers lately and requests have been forwarded to the external ISP DNS servers. You want to delegate some of the workload to another server in the domain. You create a new zone and install a new server, DNS3. How can you implement delegation with the least amount of administrative effort?

A. Set the forwarders on DNS1 and DNS2 to point to DNS3

B. Create an A record for DNS3

C. Create an NS record for DNS3

D. Run the New Delegation Wizard on DNS3

Question #5

Your company uses a SBS 2003 Standard Edition server and two Windows Server 2003 member servers to store data files. The owner of the business requests that you create a folder named Mangement and a folder named Confidential, which both should be secured and only accessible by the Managers Group and no other employees should be granted access. What technology can you use to ensure the appropriate level of security?

A. Share permissions

B. NTFS permissions

C. EFS

D. IPSec

Question #6

You administer an SBS 2003 server and two Windows Server 2003 member servers. Users report that access to one member server is very slow and you want to investigate the cause of this. You employ Network Monitor to analyze packets going back and forth from the member server and notice that there is a lot of DNS related traffic. What would be the next step to find the cause of the DNS related traffic?

A. System Monitor

B. Task Manager

C. Event Viewer

D. Netdiag.exe

Question #7

You are the IT admin at Response, Inc. You manage a network with four Windows 2003 domain controllers and two Windows 2000 domain controllers, and 350 Windows XP Professional client computers. The company has a high turnover rate and you are adding and removing user accounts on a weekly basis. Usually you do full backup on all servers on Friday nights and differentials on Saturday through Thursday. Wednesday you are adding five user accounts. The next day you realize that you accidentally deleted an entire OU with all user accounts in it. This has already replicated across the entire Active Directory domain. You want to be able to restore the OU without losing the newly created user accounts in Active Directory. What should you do?

A. Quit

B. Perform an authoritative restore of the OU only from the last full backup

C. Perform a non-authoritative restore of the last full backup

D. Perform a non-authoritative restore of the last full backup and perform an authoritative restore of the OU from the last full backup

E. Perform an authoritative restore of the last full backup

Question #8

You are the consultant for a medium-sized business that has 1 Windows Server 2003 domain controller and 70 Windows XP Professional client computers. All applications are loaded on this one server under C:\apps. The server has a single hard disk configured as drive C:\. You notice that the C:\ drive is going to run out of space before long. As a temporary fix until a new additional server arrives, you install a new drive as drive formatted with NTFS as D:\ and decide to mount a new disk to C:\apps but are unsuccessful. What can you do to remedy this?

A. Use Diskpart to move data from drive C:\ to drive D:\

B. Convert drive D:\ to a basic volume

C. Convert drive C:\ to NTFS

D. Convert drive D:\ a dynamic volume

Question #9

Your Domain Controller, which is also your GC (global catalog) server fails. What group or user can still log on to the network?

A. Power Users

B. Domain Administrators

C. Enterprise Administrators

D. Network Configuration Operators

Question #10

Your company has been experiencing unprecedented growth. The company business is of a sensitive nature and has employees world-wide that need to connect to the Windows Server 2003 and upload their findings. The owner is concerned about corporate espionage when employees connect to the network, so a new company policy has been put in place. The VPN has to be at the highest level of authentication and encryption possible without spending any additional money. What can you implement? (select all that apply)

A. PPTP

B. L2TP

C. IPSec

D. PEAP

Answer Key

Question #1: Answer C

The ASR backup wizard only backs up Windows file-protected files (WFP), system state and system services, and minimal system files. When you do an ASR restore, ASR will reformat the C drive in the process. It will restore the system files, system state and WFP files, but if you had any other files on the C:\ drive, they will not be restored. Therefore, it is important to do additional backups and only ASR as part of your disaster recovery plan. Answer A. The ASR floppy point to the location where the backup media is located. If the ASR floppy would have been corrupt, the restore would have failed. Answer B. The ASR wizard works with external tape drives, some USB drives and over a network share. Answer D. You must hit the F2 key during the text mode installation process in order to initiate the ASR restore. If you do not hit the F2 key, it would have never restored the domain controller.

Question #2: Answer D

You must use the SUS administration page (http://localhost/susadmin) to approve updates by selecting the updates and then clicking Approve. You can set up internal distribution points (in this case SERV2) for the downloaded updates. But even if all clients to SERV3, which is SERV2 and all client computers, are set to receive automatic updates, updates first must be approved before SERV2 will make them available to the clients.

Question #3: Answer B

You should use the RSoP MMC snap-in (Resultant Set of Policies) to view how the GPO will affect the OUs. RSoP is a new feature in Windows domain controller 2003. You can run RSoP in two modes, either logging or planning. In this case you would use the planning mode to see the effects of a GPO before deployment. The logging mode enables you to view current GPO settings on a specific object in Active Directory. Answer A. The gpresult command line utility will give the same results as RSoP in logging mode. Answer C. This command is used to check for replication link failure between replication partners. Answer D. The replmon command line utility is used to manage replication between domain controllers.

Question #4: Answer D

To delegate a zone, you must run the New Delegation wizard in the DNS console by right-clicking on the zone to be delegated. The zone corp.sbs.gadgets.com is a delegated zone of gadgets.com. Answer A. Setting forwarders to point to DNS3 will achieve the same result except that delegation takes precedence over forwarding and then it wouldn't be delegation, now would it? Answer B and C. The A and NS record will automatically be created by the New delegation wizard, again requiring less administrative effort.

Question #5: Answer C

Encrypted File System (EFS) can be used to secure data on NTFS. After you encrypt a file, you can go to the files property sheet, General tab and click Advanced, Details and then Add and add the users that should have access to the file. Answer A and B. NTFS and share permissions do not provide this level of security. Even if the NTFS permissions were set to Full Control for Everyone, EFS will still protect the data. Answer D. IPSec is used for encrypting data that is sent over network connections.

Question #6: Answer A

System Monitor would be the best way to identify the cause. There are about 60 DNS-related counters (too many to list here), including TCP and UDP, WINS, Zone transfers, Queries, Dynamic updates and memory counters. You can get to the Performance monitor by going to Start, Run and typing *perfmon.msc*. Right-click in the graph windows and click Add Counters. None of the other tools, even though very useful for troubleshooting, will allow for this granularity of monitoring.

Question #7: Answer D

First you would want to do a non-authoritative restore of the last full backup; this way, you will not lose the new user accounts added on Wednesday. When a restore is non-authoritative, it will be overwritten when replication occurs. Because we don't want this to happen, you use the Ntdsutil and mark the deleted OU and its contents as authoritative. When you start the domain controller and replication occurs, the OU being marked as authoritative (has a higher USN) will replicate and overwrite the information on other domain controllers. All other objects that were not marked as authoritative will be overwritten by the synchronization information from the other servers (because the USN is lower) during normal replication. The new user accounts will remain in Active Directory this way. In order to undertake this entire operation, you will have to boot one domain controller into Directory Services restore mode (Active directory will not be initialized and the server will act as a stand-alone server). You restore the system state and use Ntdsutil.exe, configure what is authoritative and what is not, and then reboot the server, which will then go about its synchronization business. Answer A. Nah, don't do that. You will just end up working somewhere else and doing the same thing. So you may as well just grin and bear it. Answer B. A deleted OU cannot be marked authoritative unless it was first restored in a non-authoritative system state restore Answer C. That only gets us halfway there—the OU would not be restored. Answer E. This way you would get the OU back and lose the new user accounts.

Question #8: Answer C

The host disk must be formatted with NTFS. The new volume must be empty. Answer A. Diskpart is used to create or delete partitions on a hard drive. Answer B and D. It doesn't matter if the new disk is a basic or dynamic NTFS volume.

Question #9: Answer B

The GC is required for authentication. Only members of the Domain Administrators group are allowed to log on to the domain if the GC failed. An exception to this rule is that if a user has logged on previously, the logon will be successful because of the user's cached credentials. If this would be the first time a user logs on, the user would not be able to log on to the domain.

Question #10: Answer B, C

L2TP and IPSec will give you the highest level of authentication and encryption. L2TP provides tunneling between the remote laptop and the server. IPSec uses Transport and Tunnel mode, encrypting the payload of the IP packet in transport mode and encrypts the header and payload of the IP packet in tunnel mode. Answer A. PPTP does not provide the security that L2TP provides. Answer D. PEAP (Protected Extensible Authentication Protocol) is currently used for securing wireless LANS and will not be available for VPN until the release of Longhorn.

Summary

This chapter brings to an end the preparation for the 70-282 certification examination. In this chapter, you were brought into the world of Windows Server 2003 stand alone edition and how it is positioned in the small- and medium-sized business segment.

To be honest, this chapter, reflecting the 70-282 examination guidelines, is a soup-to-nuts all-inclusive view of the underlying network operation system. You were schooled on installation, deployment, configuration and administration topics. The chapter ended by presenting troubleshooting topics.

A few final notes that may be helpful:

1. Both authors, upon reflection, recall more questions specific to Windows Server 2003 than might have been anticipated. Take this topic seriously.

2. Read the examination questions carefully. It was easy to overlook whether the question related to Windows Server 2003 or SBS 2003. Such an oversight could be costly and cause you to answer the question incorrectly.

3. Go and schedule the 70-282 examination right now before you forget, then return and start reading the final few chapters!

Section III
Additional Exam/Assessment

Chapter 11
Exam 74-134 -
Preinstalling Microsoft Products Using
OEM Preinstallation Kit

Chapter 12
Small Business Sales and Marketing
Skills Assessment

CHAPTER 11
Exam 74-134—Preinstalling Microsoft Products Using the OEM Preinstallation Kit

The Small Business Specialist program has a certification examination requirement, and you can choose which examination to take. As of this writing, there are two certification exams you can select one from: (1) the 70-282 exam covered extensively in this book (Chapter 3-10) or the 74-134 exam covered in this chapter. This chapter will serve as a "primer" for the 74-134 exam and point you to additional resources to properly prepare you.

> IMPORTANT: Look for updates to this book to reflect inclusion of additional certification exams that will satisfy the testing requirements of the Small Business Specialist Community. Microsoft has signaled that it intends to add qualifying certification exams to the mix over time. By registering your book, you'll be notified of this additional content.

It seemed in the early 2000 time frame that you couldn't attend a Microsoft workshop without having a PowerPoint slide deck presenting the Original Equipment Manufacturer (OEM) Preinstallation Kit, affectionately called the OPK. The OPK exists for a variety of Microsoft products spanning the underlying operating systems, etc. This set of tools helps the OEM partner or system builder automate the installation of Windows Server 2003, Windows XP, Windows

Small Business Server 2003 and other support products, saving valuable time and increasing revenue opportunities.

So what gives? Why the interest in the OPK? Microsoft is learning that the low-hanging fruit of the SMB segment has been harvested and eaten. That is, the low-hanging law firms and doctors offices are now successfully using SBS 2003 and other SMB product stack solutions. So Microsoft has turned its focus toward the system builder community, ever loyal, as fertile hunting grounds. The system builder community, a very loyal and enthusiastic group, benefits from using the OEM Preinstallation Kit tools, and passing the 74-134 exam can validate such expertise.

Steps to Passing the 74-134 Exam

This section outlines suggested steps for passing the 74-134 exam. Understand that you'll have to commit the necessary hours of preparation to successful pass the 74-134 exam. The good news is people are doing exactly that, each and every day!

Purchase Microsoft Action Pack

If you haven't already done so, as explained in Chapter 2 of this book, go purchase Microsoft Action Pack at www.microsoft.com/partner. Offered for the first year price of $299 USD, this is a library of Microsoft front office and back office software and partner guides. More importantly for system builders and relating to the 74-134 exam, Action Pack is one place to easily acquire the OPK for numerous Microsoft products.

Review the Exam Objectives

Believe it or not, as of this writing, the public-facing Microsoft web page for the 74-134 exam is actually a hidden link when you visit Microsoft Learning (www.microsoft.com/learning). So you will need to very carefully type in the following URL in your web browser: http://www.microsoft.com/learning/exams/74-134.asp and your page should look like Figure 11-1.

Figure 11-1

The comprehensive Preparation Guide for Exam 74-134

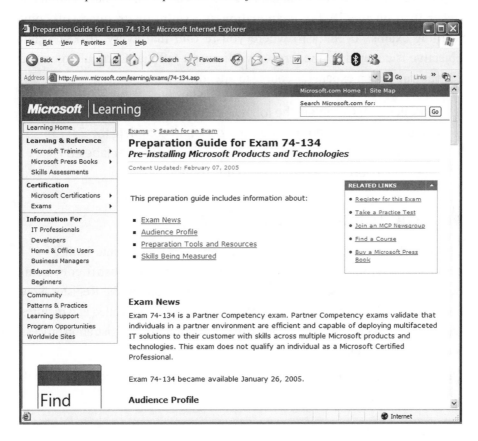

IMPORTANT: Passing the 74-134 exam does not qualify you to hold the Microsoft Certified Professional title. Passing the 70-282 exam DOES qualify you to hold the Microsoft Certified Professional title. For that reason, if you have the choice in your professional field, the authors prefer that you complete the 70-282 examination to meet the one certification test requirement to join the Small Business Partner Community.

When you review the 74-134 examination site, pay careful attention to the **Skills Being Measured** section. This is an excellent matrix that relates the exam objectives to preparatory learning resources. In effect, Microsoft tells you what's on the exam and then tells you were to go find target information to prepare for specific exam objectives. This is a very nice touch and much richer than on the 70-282 examination site (http://www.microsoft.com/learning/exams/70-282.asp) where you're told that every 70-282 exam objective is covered by the three-day Microsoft Official Curriculum course 2395a (true but an expensive course to attend).

> IMPORTANT: Complete the following step now. Print this web page and use it as your roadmap to prepare for and complete the 74-134 examination. Place the print out in a notebook or folder labeled 74-134. You'll add more resources to this shortly.

Visit the Microsoft OEM Site

Consider the following URL to be your portal for tapping into both 74-134 exam and system builder resources: http://www.microsoft.com/oem/default.mspx. Your first step here is to register by clicking the Register Now button. Much of the excellent information on this site is controlled and requires registration to access. Go ahead and do that now. I found the registration process took less than ten minutes.

Once you've registered and performed a site logon, your screen should look similar to Figure 11-2.

Notes:

Figure 11-2

Welcome to the system builder site. Take 30 minutes to explore the sub-sites linked from the left side to rapidly immerse yourself in the system builder community.

Get To Know BOB!

As you explore the Microsoft OEM and system builder site, you'll bump into the BOB team. BOB, which stands for US System Builder Technology Team, is really a group of Texans in Building 121 at the Microsoft Redmond campus. Not only are they as friendly as the day is long in Alaska in mid-June, but their hearts are truly as large as Texas. I found Steve and the other partners to be some of the most exciting Microsoft blue badges I'd met in a long while (harkening back to the early days of the SBS 4.x development team). What's important about that sage observation is team attitude speaks volumes about partner momentum. When you've got a jacked-up team behind a partner program, as is the case with system builders, it's a good trend line and suggests you should jump on board!

Be the Webcast Warrior

Educational delivery, often the subject of long-winded speeches at academic conferences and the like, is ever evolving and changing. With the higher adoption rates of broadband technology, Microsoft (like many technology vendors) is cost-effectively delivering cool content to the masses using Webcasts. The system builder program and your ability to effectively and efficiently prepare for the 74-134 exam benefit from this emerging education paradigm! And did I mention that the vast majority, if not all, of these Webcasts are FREE! (See – we just paid for the price of this book.)

> IMPORTANT: A few years ago, after gaining much weight writing books and serving a portfolio of real-world customers as an ardent SMB consultant, I hired a personal trainer to right my life and return me to good health. Steve Rhoades, this athletic angel in disguise, provided some invaluable advice on day one: sign up for as many classes at my athletic club as I could.
>
> In the same vein, I offer a similar suggestion to you. Sign up for as many system builder Webcasts as you can muster and tolerate! Not only are these Webcasts immediately applicable to your cause of passing the 74-134 exam, but you might just meet a famous author or two along the way (Hint: see Figure 11-3). The System Builder Events page, found at http://oem.microsoft.com/script/contentPage.aspx? pageid=4078 is where you join the Webcast fun.

Notes:

Figure 11-3

Look closely. Co-author Harry Brelsford presented that June 22, 2005 Webcast while traveling in Dublin with his SMB Nation Summit workshop tour. Co-author Beatrice Mulzer presented the June 29th Webcast on ISA 2004 (she wrote the ISA 2004 chapter in the Advanced Windows Small Business Server 2003 Best Practices book).

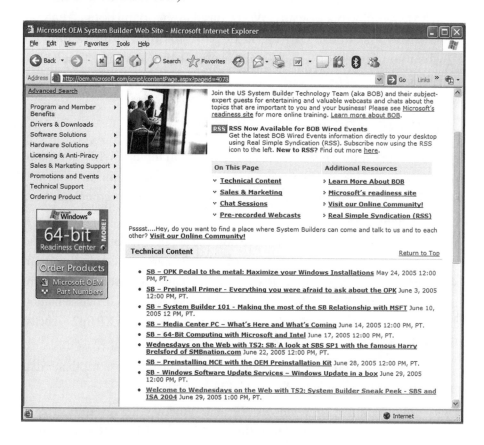

IMPORTANT: Use the system builder Webcasts wisely to prepare you for the 74-134 exam. First attend at least a handful of applicable Webcasts related to the OPK and other 74-134 exam topics. While attending, take a critical step: ASK LIVE QUESTIONS. What better way to prepare for the 74-134 exam than to have your exam-related questions answered by the Microsoft experts!

Second, view past Webcasts. Figure 11-3 displays a link for "Pre-recorded Webcasts." This is especially applicable for newcomers who missed the live delivery of important content and international readers who don't live on Pacific Standard Time (PST), which is GMT -8. Microsoft, located in PST in the Pacific Northwest, tends to have a timing bias towards West Coast USA working hours. That translates into missing a wee bit of pub time in Dublin, Ireland when you are giving a high noon Webcast on Redmond time! I speak from experience.

Complete Applicable Coursework

There are more learning resources online at Microsoft for the 74-134 exam than you can shake a stick at. If you plan to follow our advice in this section, you should budget for approximately 20-hours of study time to complete these learning opportunities.

First, let's do it by the book and observe how the applicable courses map to the 74-134 exam. To accomplish that, go to your Preparation Guide for Exam 74-134 printout and carefully review the Skills Being Measured section. Here you'll see how the XP and Server course, SBS course, OPK Documentation (discussed in the next section of this chapter) and the Windows XP Sp2 Webcast align with specific 74-134 exam objectives.

Second, peruse the following three courses listed under Course for this Exam on your Preparation Guide for Exam 74-134 printout:

- Preinstallation of Windows XP and Windows Server 2003 (http://oem.microsoft.com/downloads/ABCs_OPK/ABCs_updated/ABC'sOPK/Bin/default.hta). See Figure 11-4.

- Using the OEM Preinstallation Kit to Preinstall Windows Small Business Server 2003 (http://members.microsoft.com/partner/profile/learningcenter.aspx?courseid=442). See Figure 11-5.

- Windows XP SP2 Recorded Webcast (http://oem.microsoft.com/script/ContentPage.aspx?pageid=551604)

Figure 11-4

The Windows XP and Windows Server 2003 preinstallation learning opportunity.

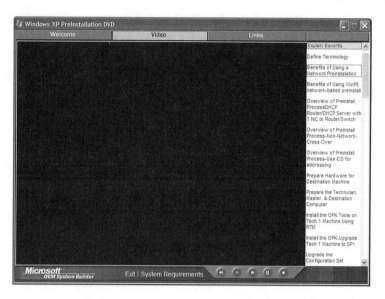

Figure 11-5

The SBS 2003 preinstallation learning opportunity.

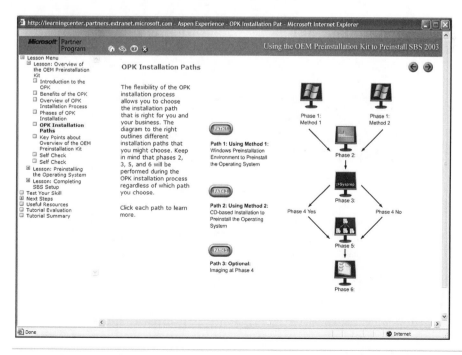

Third, complete the following learning opportunities that weren't explicitly listed in the Preparation Guide for Exam 74-134.

- Under Training and Readiness on the main Microsoft OEM System Builder site, there is a link to the Windows XP SP2 Readiness Center (http://oem.microsoft.com/script/contentpage .aspx?pageid=551796). Visit that page and peruse the Essential Information: Preinstall Windows XP SP2 PowerPoint slide deck (which has its own URL of http://oem.microsoft.com/static/Worldwide/file/OEM_ Preinstallation_ Win_XP_SP2.ppt).

- After performing a registered member logon at www.microsoft.com/oem, visit this URL: http://oem.microsoft.com/script/content page.aspx?PageID=552172, which is the System Builder Training and Readiness Center. Select the Online Training link (http://oem.microsoft .com/script/contentpage.aspx?pageid=500972) and complete the following learning opportunities, as shown in Figure 11-6.

  - Windows XP

  - Windows Small Business Server 2003

  - Windows Server 2003

Figure 11-6
A gold mine of online learning opportunities.

IMPORTANT: You do not need to complete the Windows Media Center or Office 2003-related online learning course to prepare for the 74-134 exam, but you can certainly return at a future date and do so (after you pass the 74-134 exam!).

- Complete the product-specific training courses by selecting the product of your choice on the left drop menu at Software Solutions Overview page (http://oem.microsoft.com/script/contentpage.aspx ?PageID=4022). For example, drilling down into the Servers link, Windows Small Business Server, will result in the page displayed in Figure 11-7 (found at http://oem.microsoft.com/script/contentPage.aspx ?pageid=554992).

Figure 11-7

Note the SBS-related training and hands-on lab. Complete this for SBS 2003. Complete at least the How to Install Microsoft Small Business Server 2003 course.

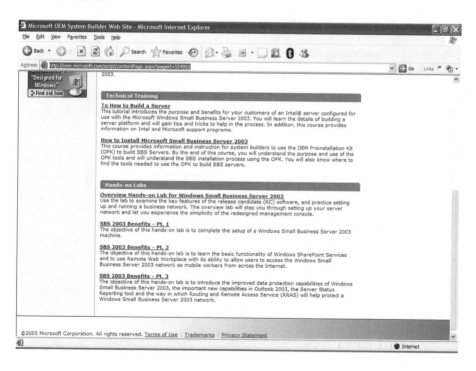

- Also complete the learning opportunities for Windows Server 2003 and Windows XP accessed at the above-mentioned site (http://oem.microsoft.com/script/contentpage.aspx?PageID=4022). Ignore the coursework for Windows 2000 products.

IMPORTANT: Here's an insider tip directly from one of the internal Small Business Specialist Community team members at Microsoft. Search on the term "OPK" at the OEM System Builder Training and Readiness site at http://oem.microsoft.com/script/contentpage.aspx?PageID=552172. This will return numerous new and updated curriculums that have emerged since this book was published. It's your way to stay current!

Well, were we right or what? That above "game plan" should have taken approximately 20 hours to complete. Trust us, though. It was time well spent!

Read OPK documentation

The cliché of a droning college professor admonishing his weary students to "…read the book" truly applies to the 74-134 exam. In this case, the required reading is the OPK documentation for Windows XP, Windows Server 2003 and Windows Small Business Server 2003, as per your Preparation Guide for Exam 74-134 printout.

There are two ways to review the all-important OPK documentation. First, you can simply access the OPK Discs contained in Action Pack and open the applicable documentation. Second, you can click over to the following links for the following readings:

- Windows XP (http://oem.microsoft.com/script/contentpage.aspx?pageid=512504)

- Small Business Server 2003 (http://oem.microsoft.com/script/contentpage.aspx?pageid=550830)

- Office 2003 (http://oem.microsoft.com/script/contentpage.aspx?pageid=550618)

IMPORTANT: Even though the 74-134 exam doesn't explicitly hold you responsible for Office 2003 matters, the above link is recommended because there is enough OPK "table talk" that you can benefit from a casual reading of that document. Note that I didn't instruct you to take the Office 2003 OEM, System Builder or OPK online courses because the time consumption outweighed the value received vis-à-vis that 74-134 exam. In an inconsistent way, I believe I'm being consistent here!

Complete Online Assessments

Ah, now for the fun part. You've meticulously followed our suggested steps and arrived at the payoff point: you get to take some sample exams.

Click over to http://oem.microsoft.com/script/contentpage.aspx?PageID =552866 (Figure 11-8) and complete the following assessments:

- Microsoft Office 2003 Preinstallation Exam (12-questions, worth a try but don't dwell on this)

- Windows Small Business Server 2003 Preinstallation Exam (12 questions, very important)

- Windows XP Service Pack 2 (SP2) Preinstallation Exam (25 questions, very important)

- Windows Server 2003 Preinstallation Exam (25 questions, very important)

IMPORTANT: Use leverage to your advantage. Earn your Microsoft Preinstallation Specialist designation too! That's right! With a few extra steps, a tad more moxie and a little bit more gumption, you can complete the online assessments and hold this title in addition to your soon-to-be-awarded Small Business Specialist Community title!

Notes:

Figure 11-8

Details of the Microsoft Presinstallation Specialist program and your access portal to the online assessment exams. These will assist you immensely in preparing for the 74-134 exam.

Finally, visit the generic Microsoft Skills Assessments site for other interesting and applicable tests: http://www.microsoft.com/learning/assessment/default.asp.

> IMPORTANT: You will notice this chapter does not contain sample questions. Please register your book with the registration form at the back of the book and we'll be delighted to provide you with some online sample 74-134 test questions on our site!

Schedule and Take Test

Time to make it happen. Register for the test. Visit the Microsoft Learning exam registration page at http://www.microsoft.com/learning/mcpexams/register/default.asp and pick from either PearsonVue or Prometric.

IMPORTANT: Schedule the exam a couple weeks out if you feel you need sufficient preparation time. The important point is to schedule the exam and put yourself under a wee bit of pressure to perform! Deadlines do wonders for writers and test-takers. Trust us!

74-134 Certification Secrets

Shhh! Don't tell anyone, but here are a few secrets to increase your odds of success on the 74-134 exam. I gained these insights from behind closed doors in Redmond, water cooler talk and whispers in the hallways. These secrets are presented here for your benefit!

- **Tools.** The 74-134 exam is very tools centric. There is little emphasis on strategy and design (which play significant roles on the 70-282 exam). Truly your best bet is to learn and use the tools. Have an appreciation for why the tools were created but don't dwell on this aspect. Rather, remain tactile (touch) rather than tactical (strategy) for the 74-134 exam.

- **Interface.** Your short-term memory will likely be tested on the 74-134 exam because a premium is placed on graphical user interface (GUI) recall. Hopefully you're fortunate to have something of a photographic memory and you can "burn" the screen images into your cerebellum. Such image recall will be immensely useful in passing the 74-134 exam.

- **Can Do. Will Do. Done!** Active learning rules! Equal with the 70-282 exam, you need to use the OPK. Want some free advice? Create a Microsoft Virtual PC environment (http://www.microsoft.com/windows/virtualpc/default.mspx) and just DO IT. Use the OPKs to install the various operation systems. Use the Action Pack OPK bits to achieve this. You read it here first!

- **Intent.** When in doubt, you can always revisit what the intent of something was to seek clarification. To assist you in using the intent framework in the 74-134 realm, remember that Microsoft wants you to "preinstall" correctly to avoid a "reinstall!"

- **Scorecard.** As long-time college instructors and trainers (both authors bring this background to the table), it was a true pleasure to bump into the OEM system builder scorecard generated when you complete the assessment path to earn the Preinstallation Specialist designation. This is shown in Figure 11-9 and provides that critical dimension necessary to any successful transfer of knowledge and assessment: FEEDBACK!

Figure 11-9

Scorecard...use it! Very cool!

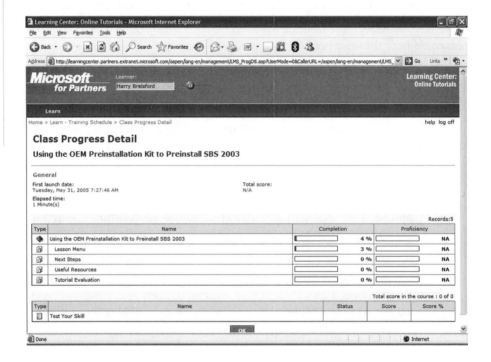

- **Read *Reseller Advocate Magazine* (RAM).** Co-author Beatrice Mulzer writes a monthly column for a leading USA system builder magazine and she and other writers share applicable community insights at www.reselleradvocate.com. Bookmark it!

- **Appendix A.** By all means, help yourself to the resources listed in Appendix A of this book to pass both the 74-134 exam and become a Small Business Specialist Community member!

Summary

Alternatives are a good thing, and it's a good thing Microsoft placed the 74-134 exam in the mix as a certification alternative for the Small Business Specialist Community program! We applaud that. This chapter provided you a detailed strategic plan to go forth with God Speed and slay (we mean pass) the 74-134 exam.

You were introduced to the OPK concept and the system builder community. Then we asked you to purchase Microsoft Action Pack. We directed you to the 74-134 exam preparation guidelines that we highly recommend you print out and use as a roadmap. Then it was time to go off and read, study and learn from a library of rich OPK resources. An assessment process followed, and then a gentle nudge to go schedule and actually take the 74-134 exam. At the end of the chapter, a few extra secrets were provided to get you over the top of the pass bar!

A roomful of engaged partners listen in as Harry and Beatrice launch the new book at the Microsoft Worldwide Partner Conference 2005

CHAPTER 12
Small Business Sales and Marketing Skills Assessment

In the past, it's been easy to criticize Microsoft and take some cheap shots about its small business segment strategy. In fact, I can recall many Windows Small Business Server (SBS) Channel Advisory Council (CAC) meetings in Redmond where attendees grumbled that Microsoft "just doesn't get it." Let's not use too much timber to debate the merits of those repetitious debates. Rather, join me in a positive paradigm shift and enter the final chapter of this book with a positive attitude and open mind!

Please indulge me, jury of readers, as I assume the position of an attorney making closing arguments: Microsoft is not guilty of neglecting the small business segment. In fact, Microsoft should be applauded for launching the Small Business Specialist community program and, as you will soon learn, incorporating business development skills into the partner qualifications.

> IMPORTANT: Full disclosure time. I almost feel like a courtroom attorney who must disclose any conflicts to the judge. I, Harry Brelsford, wrote the SMB Consulting Best Practices book (SMB Nation Press). That book (which I considered my best writing effort at the time) provides you ample opportunity (with over 500 pages) to delve deep into the very important BUSINESS discussion surrounding the small and medium business segments. I strongly encourage you to consider acquiring that book as an additional resource to supplement this chapter and your career as a Small Business Specialist community member!

Why Are We Here?

This chapter is about preparing for and passing the Small Business Sales and Marketing Skills Assessment. This is a REQUIRED competency component for gaining acceptance into the Small Business Specialist community.

> IMPORTANT: In describing the Small Business Specialist community to lay people, you will find some confusion about the examination and assessment. You can certainly revisit Chapter 2 if you've forgotten the finer points of this exciting new partnership level from Microsoft (Hint: for a quick read, see the Elevator Ride Version near the end of that chapter).

> What is the bottom line on the examination and assessment? You must successfully complete (pass) one certification examination. As of this writing, you can select from two Microsoft Certified Professional (MCP) certification exams: 70-282 and 74-134. It is important NOT to say that the 70-282 exam is required because a candidate could always select the alternative 74-134 certification exam.

> The Small Business Sales and Marketing Skills Assessment is a required assessment. In explaining the Small Business Specialist program to me, Microsoft was adamant that the Small Business Sales and Marketing Skills Assessment NOT be called a test or examination. It is an online assessment that you can attempt multiple times until you achieve a passing score.

I liken this chapter to a mini-MBA program, where you can efficiently and effectively be schooled in business fundamentals before heading out into the real world carrying the Small Business Specialist community credential.

The World We Live In

Small business technology consultants wear many hats. As a small business themselves, a small business technology consultant must perform many tasks in operating an ongoing business concern: sales and marketing (business development), management, finance and accounting functions, service delivery (actually performing the technical work for customers), and numerous other chores like cleaning the office!

Finder, Minder, Grinder

Believe it or not, there is a well-known business model that characterizes the small business technology consultant's world called Finder, Minder, Grinder.

- **Finder:** Gets the work! This is the sales and marketing function.

- **Minder:** Manages the work. This function is a combination of office management, general management, and project management responsibilities.

- **Grinder:** Does the work. This function includes designing, deploying, maintaining, and troubleshooting an SBS network.

Readers will likely agree that getting motivated to "do" the actual work (Grinder mode) is the least of our problems. In our community, getting the work and managing the work are more problematic.

A truism in the professional services community rings true with small business technology consultants: In the Finder, Minder, Grinder construct, you can reasonably expect to perform any two roles well, but not all three! That is, one person can't do it all! I concur. I can hold my own as a Finder and a Grinder, but I'm not a strong Minder. Fortunately, I've hired strong managers at SMB Nation to run things for me and to offset my weaknesses.

Go ahead, take a deep breath, and think about what your strengths and weaknesses are when it comes to the Finder, Minder, Grinder model. In just a few paragraphs, you'll complete an exercise where this information is necessary.

Notes:

Mapping to Finder, Minder, Grinder

In the last section, I left you thinking about which two out of three roles (Finder, Minder, Grinder) you perform best. In mapping the Small Business Specialist community program to the real world Finder, Minder, Grinder model, I discovered something very interesting! It only maps to two out of the three elements: Finder and Grinder. While it does a very good job of Finder and Grinder, as illustrated in Figure 12-1, as of this writing, the Small Business Specialist community program does not include a management dimension (Minder, if you will).

Figure 12-1

Mapping Finder and Grinder to the Small Business Specialist community. See the important note below for the link to the SMB Nation "SBS Franchise Kit"

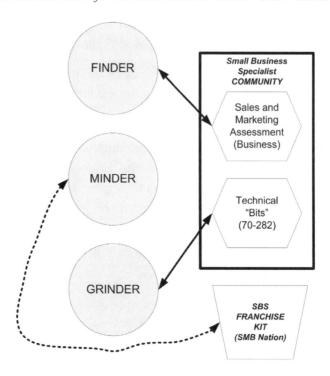

IMPORTANT: SMB Nation prides itself on being a "gap filler" in the Microsoft small and medium business (SMB) segment. Having identified that the new Small Business Specialist community program doesn't sufficiently prepare you for the management responsibilities of running a small business technology practice, we have brought to market the SBS Franchise Kit. This MBA-in-a-box allows you to dramatically boost your return on investment the old fashioned way: by operating more efficiently and effectively! Visit www.smbnation.com for more details.

Worldwide versus Domestic Perspectives

Early in this book we discussed the impact of the Small Business Specialist program on improving the lives of eager and earnest small business technology consultants around the world. I still believe that line of reasoning in this, the last chapter of the book. However, I feel we must briefly revisit this topic to understand the role of the Small Business Sales and Marketing Skills Assessment in the Small Business Specialist community program.

In many ways, wealthy Americans enjoy an economic advantage over their small business technology consultant counterparts in developing nations. If for no other reason, it's that cultural business "table talk" where Americans pick up on business norms, such as business development, that underprivileged brethren from emerging countires don't receive.

By making the Small Business Specialist community program a worldwide effort and providing business-related training and assessment opportunities, Microsoft has really reached out to the cold, starving, and homeless small business technology consultants around the world and attempted to better their lives! Think about that when you're completing the Small Business Sales and Marketing Skills Assessment!

SWOT Analysis Exercise

In the MBA world, there is an exercise called SWOT which means strengths, weaknesses, opportunities and threats. It's a valuable assessment exercise and I present it here as a tool to prepare you for the Small Business Sales and Marketing Skills Assessment that you'll take by the end of the chapter. Strengths and weakness are internal matters ("my strength is…"); opportunities and threats are external ("our competitor's new service is a threat to our livelihood"). Take up to 30 minutes to complete Table 12-1 now by applying this SWOT analysis to you individually and your small business technology consulting practice.

Table 12-1

Small Business Specialist SWOT Analysis

Strengths	Weaknesses	Opportunities	Threats
Example: Creative problem solver	Example: Weak at C# programming	Example: Merge with John's Computer Repair Shop	Example: Linux consultants calling on my SBS customers

IMPORTANT: With the above exercise, I am not only hoping to move you into the assessment mind-set; I also hope the information you provided above will be useful as you actually begin building your practice.

Think Small – Microsoft's New Partner Paradigm

There is something important to understand about large and small companies and how they work together. This is the concept of organizational size alignment. For example, in the world of legal services, clients relate best to law firms that are of a size similar to their own organization. That is, large clients like large law firms and small clients like small law firms. This organizational size alignment is consistent with you, the small business technology consultant (likely working for a small consulting practice) serving small business customers. Indeed it's a marriage made in heaven!

Understanding organizational size alignment also helps explain why it took Microsoft so long to introduce a small business partner level like the Small Business Specialist community. Heck – with over 60,000 employees worldwide and $37.5 billion USD in the bank, it's hard for Microsoft to truly understand the small business segment. I don't blame them because they're plenty smart; this is mainly an alignment issue.

But Microsoft is tenacious. It brought forth the Small Business Specialist community for the readership of this book and we applaud its recognition of small business needs. And while it might not have appeared until the eighth year of the SBS product life cycle, better late than never. And as you'll read in the next section, I think Microsoft was wise to marry the business side and the bits side to create a more perfect union!

Forced Marriage

In the early days of small business technology, you could get by with just your bits-based knowledge (read: technical skill set). That's because immature technology, like Windows For Workgroups peer-to-peer networks based on NetBEUI in the early 1990s, required your technical, not business, proficiency to function. And it's equally likely that during those days, as a pioneer small business technology consultant, you didn't need highly evolved sales and marketing skills. Your practice grew organically and you greatly benefited from word-of-mouth marketing (always a good thing).

Now fast forward to the early part of the 21st century. In developed countries, nearly all small businesses have some form of technology infrastructure in place. And the underlying technology has become much more stable and mature. Customers are now seeking business value and business results from their technology! In addition, sales and marketing to the small business segment has become much more sophisticated. In short, technology and business are now necessarily married!

Here is where the Small Business Specialist community is doing you a great favor. The bulk of this book was skewed toward the "bits" dimension in exhaustively preparing you for the 70-282 certification exam and honoring the 71-134 exam. This chapter reflects Microsoft's appreciation for your business sense, holding you accountable for your sales and marketing acumen. In this way, Microsoft has married the small business bits with sales and marketing. Bravo!

Back To School

Thoughtful study, not haste, will prove to be your ally as you prepare for the Small Business Sales and Marketing Skills Assessment. This section provides advice on properly preparing for the Small Business Sales and Marketing Skills Assessment.

> IMPORTANT: Be the life learner. Don't simply view the following study aides as required drudgery. Rather, embrace the educational opportunity to expand your horizons and increase your business development knowledge as a budding Small Business Specialist. Be the life learner!

Online Study Resources

The good news is that no trip to the book store to purchase over-priced texts is necessary. Microsoft has leveled the playing field between worldwide "haves" and "have nots" by posting many excellent study resources for immediate dissemination via no-cost downloads. That's means FREE! This table (Table 12-2) summarizes an outright orgy of knowledge tools for you to use as part of your "back to school" strategy! These resources are online courses and tutorials, online and in-person hands-on labs, or MS Official products. When you visit the Web sites, you'll be able to read detailed descriptions for each offering, the estimated time needed to complete it, and what type of resource it is (online, etc.). Apologies in advance for the gnarly URLs pasted in the table. (The Small Business Specialist Web sites, referenced in Chapter 2 and Appendix A, will have more elegant hyperlinks for you to click on <Big Grin>.)

Table 12-2
Small Business Sales and Marketing Skills Assessment Learning Resources

Category and URL	Components
Core Sales Training (See Figure 12-2) https://training.partner. microsoft.com/plc/ search_adv.aspx?ssid=D0D 896614FC14021B39F9046 D50013F5	Selling Microsoft Windows® Small Business Server 2003* Microsoft Office 2003 Sales Training for OEMs and System Builders Windows XP Professional Volume Licensing Essentials* Understanding the Value of the Microsoft Platform versus Open Source Selling Microsoft Solutions to Small Business*
Core Windows Small Business Server 2003 Technical Training https://training.partner. microsoft.com/plc/search_ adv.aspx?ssid=F43A34871 A3D481C9D74412DC69 7468F	Small Business Server 2003 – Parts 1-4 Designing, Deploying and Managing a Network Solution for the Small and Medium-size Business Implementing Microsoft Solution Accelerators for Small Business

Category and URL	Components
Core System Builder Technical Training https://training.partner.microsoft.com/plc/search_adv.aspx?ssid=141 59B2A151F4F5AA 176036D34932600	Using the OEM Preinstallation Kit to Preinstall SBS 2003
Extended Sales Training https://training.partner.microsoft.com/plc/search_adv.aspx?ssid=6B57 100CBDDD410181792F 181D883E7F	Managing Sales and Opportunity Management in Outlook for Office Small Business Edition 2003 Selling Microsoft CRM
Extended Technical Training https://training.partner.microsoft.com/plc/search_adv.aspx?ssid=E34848B31 35E4A70AEFECCAD9A3 8DD07	Featuring Security, Privacy and Data Recovery in Office Small Business Edition 2003 Exploring SharePoint Services and Integration Capabilities in Office Small Business Edition 2003 Microsoft CRM: Plan, Install, and Configure Microsoft Small Business Server Premium Supporting End Users for System Builders

Notes:

Category and URL	Components
Small Business Sales and Marketing Tools (Figure 12-3) https://partner.microsoft.com/40015982	Part 1: Identify High-Potential Sales Opportunities in the Small Business Market Part 2: Deliver a Winning Sales and Marketing Message to Small Business Prospects Part 3: Efficiently Reach Your Target Prospect Desktop Value for Small Business (Go To Market Campaign) Business Productivity (Go To Market Campaign) Servers for Small Business (Go To Market Campaign) License Renewal (Go To Market Campaign)

* Both authors strongly recommend you should complete prior to attempting the assessment. All courses are important (of course) but the asterisked selections have very specific information you will need.

IMPORTANT: Everyone knows books start to age like fine wine, starting on the publication date. So you'll appreciate that the above list of educational resources will be added to as time passes. That's great news for the life learners among us!

Notes:

Figure 12-2

Core sales training opportunities

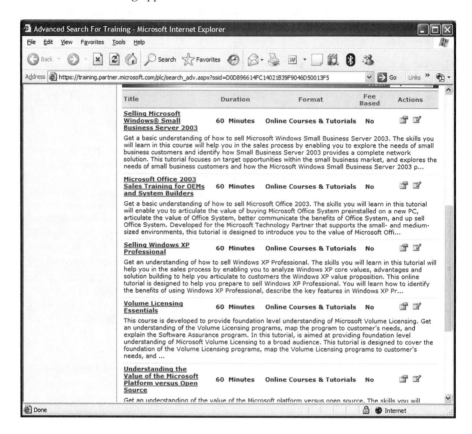

Educational Value Adds

As I prepared for and successfully completed the Small Business Sales and Marketing Skills Assessment, I identified the following two concepts that are important for successfully navigating the assessment process: segmentation and licensing.

Segmentation

MBAs and other business heavyweights love to talk about niches, categories, and segments. A *niche* might be your boutique practice in delivering SBS 2003 deployment services to small law firms in your city. A *category* is much broader and might include the deployment of front office business applications to any small business customer. A segment is a measured market "space" with well-defined boundaries. In the Small Business Sales and Marketing Skills Assessment, you will be responsible for four small business IT segments. I'll define those in Table 12-3 and send you to a Web-based resource for further study.

Table 12-3

Know Thy Small Business IT Segments

Segment	Basic Definition
IT Light	Grow revenue and profit. Reduce costs. Increase sales and better manage cash flow. Technology price, Software performance and compatibility of existing systems.
IT Basic	Grow revenue and profit. Reduce costs. Increase sales and better manage cash flow. Enhance marketing efforts. Technology price, Software performance and compatibility of existing systems. Trust of software company.
IT Dependent	Grow revenue and profit. Reduce costs. Increase sales and better manage cash flow. Enhance marketing efforts. Better tracking of costs/billable time. Software performance and compatibility of existing systems. Trust of software company.
IT Strategic	Grow revenue and profit. Reduce costs. Increase sales and better manage cash flow. Enhance marketing efforts. Better tracking of costs/billable time. Software performance and compatibility of existing systems. Trust of software company. Concern about security breaches.

As a rule of thumb, the more sophisticated the small business, the further down the segment table it appears.

Notes:

Figure 12-3

Part Two of the Small Business Sales and Marketing Tools includes a document that spends seven pages defining and detailing the IT segments.

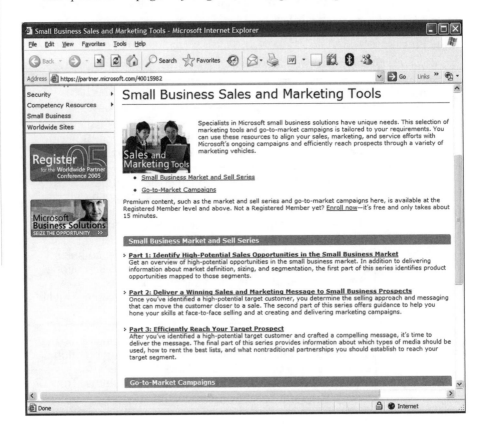

Here's a study trick that might be helpful for test preparation and memorization. It uses a simple childhood syndicated cartoon puzzle titled Hocus Focus (by Henry Boltinoff from King Features Syndicate). Syndicated in over 300 papers worldwide, this cartoon puzzle presents readers with two extremely similar looking drawings, as you can see in Figure 12-4. You must find six differences between the pictures.

Notes:

Figure 12-4

Finding the differences is a time-tested learning tool.

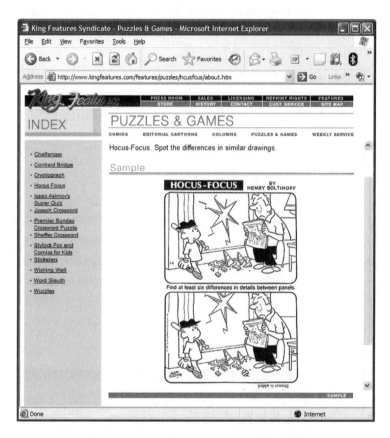

In the context of IT segments, I encourage you to find the differences between the segments. That's the information you should commit to memory. For example, the IT Strategic segment is the only segment concerned with security breaches. Take five minutes to do a Hocus Focus on Table 12-3 and return here.

> IMPORTANT: The above discussion offers a chance to revisit a discussion presented earlier in this book. Answer the question the Microsoft way. While you may have a difference of opinion on segment definitions and measurements, it DOES NOT MATTER when trying to pass the Small Business Sales and Marketing Skills Assessment. Got it?

Licensing

Make sure you are sitting down before you read the next sentence, as I'm concerned you might faint and hit your head! **Know your licensing for the Microsoft SMB product stack.** Now calm down and take a deep breath (even go for a 30-minute walk if needed and return here).

While it's easy to freak out over licensing, I have a free assessment preparation resource for you. Go to www.smbnation.com and download the free Chapter 3 on licensing topics from the Advanced Windows Small Business Server 2003 Best Practices book (we typically provide one free download chapter per book for public perusal). Spend at least 60-minutes reading this chapter.

Then go to Microsoft's Windows Small Business Server 2003 Web site at www .microsoft.com/sbs and select How To Buy on the left side. Then select Pricing from the context menu that appears. Scroll halfway down that page and observe the Open Value and Software Assurance licensing discussion and links for more information (Figure 12-5). Read and click, baby! Do a deep dive right here, right now! You might also read the April 2005 Redmond Magazine article on Software Assurance at http://redmondmag.com/features/article.asp?EditorialsID=470.

Figure 12-5

Major hint: read this licensing discussion.

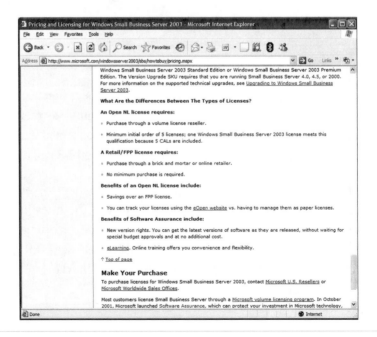

E-Mail Order Diploma

All work and no play would make Suresh in Mumbai India a dull Small Business Specialist community member! Suresh, a real small business technology consultant whom I've met at my India workshops and corresponded with over the years, is anything but dull. However, I use him as a CALL TO ACTION to have some fun. You are near the end of the book. You are almost a Small Business Specialist community member! For goodness sake – stand out on your balcony and shout something like "I'm a SBSer!"

We at SMB Nation thought it'd be fun to challenge you and reward you with an unaccredited Masters of Business Administration diploma with a Small Business Technology specialization if you complete all of the educational opportunities (coursework) in Table 12-2, send an e-mail to sbs@smbnation.com attesting that you've achieved this milestone, and request your camera-ready MBA diploma suitable for framing. Doesn't that sound like fun?

A Day in The Life

Your dedication to the study of small business technology consulting is admirable. It's now time to complete the Small Business Sales and Marketing Skills Assessment. First, trot over to Small Business Specialist community Web site and select the assessment. A back door direct link is: https://training.partner.microsoft.com/plc/register.aspx?publisher=3&courseid=542.

To walk you through this, I thought I'd give you a play-by-play day in the life rendition of when I completed this assessment.

Coffee at 7a.m.

Even after earning two degrees and a half dozen certifications, I found myself nervous and anxious about completing the Small Business Sales and Marketing Skills Assessment. I guess it's only natural; I share these words with you so you can lighten up and go easy on yourself.

I was relieved that the assessment is open book, although I didn't surround myself with any external resources. No sir. It was just me and my laptop, ready to take on the Small Business Sales and Marketing Skills Assessment!

IMPORTANT: The open book nature of the assessment signals that Microsoft wants you to be successful. You may also take the assessment multiple times if for some reason you are not successful. That is, retakes are allowed!

Starting the exam

After completing my authentication as a registered partner at the Microsoft Partner site, I proceeded to the Small Business Sales and Marketing Skills Assessment page as illustrated in Figure 12-6. A greeting screen follows (Figure 12-7), which describes the assessment and allows you to take a training path for more study. Many of the early educational resources discussed in this chapter are listed when you click the Training Path link, as shown in Figure 12-8.

Figure 12-6

Take it now!

Figure 12-7

More students fail tests, exams, and assessments because they don't read the rules (ask any college professor). Please read the assessment description here.

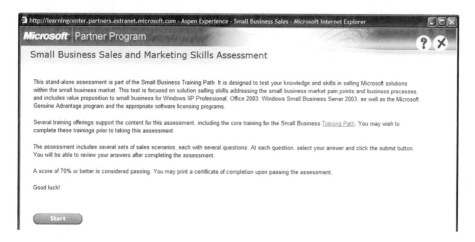

Figure 12-8

Last call for education and another chance to ride the training path!

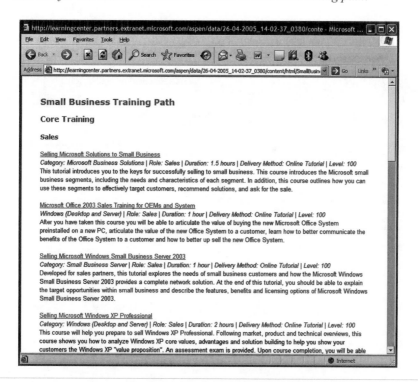

IMPORTANT: Life happens. When I was taking the assessment, I was interrupted by my lovely wife Kristen to find lunch money for Harry Jr. I turned away from the assessment, dug through my upper desk drawer for quarters so one of my heirs could have milk that day. I then refilled my coffee. When I returned to the assessment after 15-minutes, it was still there! It did not time-bomb out and terminate my session. This friendly, realistic setup proved to me that Microsoft designed the assessment to account for some "life happens" moments.

The exam questions are based on real-world scenarios. When I took it, four companies were profiled and five questions were asked about each company (for a total of 20 –questions). What I really liked about the company scenarios was I only had to read the descriptive paragraph once before proceeding to answer five follow-on questions. I felt like I was able to positively leverage my time.

With Microsoft's permission, I'm allowed to show you one assessment question so you can gain appreciation for the look and feel of the online assessment environment (see Figure 12-9). E-mails to me requesting the answer will be ignored!

Figure 12-9

A bona fide assessment question before your very eyes!

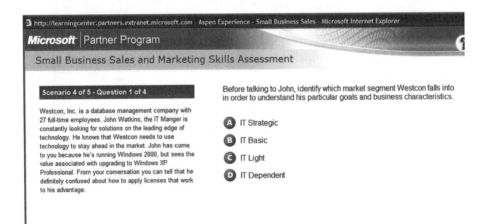

Completion

I really got into the assessment because it celebrates the marriage of technology and business in the small business segment. This assessment was the wedding ceremony! It took me about 30 minutes to complete the assessment. And now for the million-dollar question: did the author pass the assessment? See Figure 12-10 for your answer.

Figure 12-10

Success! It's a nice touch that a certificate, suitable for printing, is available.

Next Steps

So that brings the Small Business Sales and Marketing Skills Assessment story to an end. But think about your legacy. Perhaps you've turned over a new leaf in life and become a life learner. Maybe you'll take the business classes you've been interested in for all these years. The world is your oyster. Time to harvest!

Summary

This chapter is mandatory reading because it covers the mandatory Small Business Sales and Marketing Skills Assessment as part of the Small Business Specialist community program. I hopefully was able to deliver much more business context than you bargained for. It was a pleasure to dig deep into the business back office and share some strategic thinking that would cost you a lot of money to hear recited at a top-tier MBA program. And let us not forget that we prepared you for successfully completing the Small Business Sales and Marketing Skills Assessment.

You've reached the end of this book on the Small Business Specialist community program. But you've only begun your career as a Small Business Specialist community member. May your increased financial net worth going forward be outmatched only by new-found personal and professional joy and happiness!

Appendices

Appendix A
   SBS 2003 RESOURCES

Appendix B
   More SNMP Stuff

Appendix C
   Third-Party 70-282 Viewpoints

Index

Appendix A

SBS 2003 RESOURCES

This appendix lists SBS 2003 resources that will be useful in your quest to better utilize SBS 2003. Many of these resources have previously been listed in the book, but many new resources are added here as well. Bottom line: All the SBS 2003 resources you need to move forward are provided here in one easy, at-a-glance location.

Small Business Specialist Community Sites

- **Overview:** https://partner.microsoft.com/global/smallbizspecoverview

- **Benefits and requirements:** https://partner.microsoft.com/global/smallbizspecbenefits

- **Training and exams:** https://partner.microsoft.com/global/smallbiztraining

- **Readiness site:** https://partner.microsoft.com/global/smallbizreadiness

Certification Sites

- Microsoft Learning: http://www.microsoft.com/learning

- *Certification Magazine*: http://www.certmag.com

- *MCP Magazine*: www.mcpmag.com

- Transcender certification testing software. http://www.transcender.com/

- Self-test certification testing software: http://www.selftestsoftware.com/

SBS-MVP Sites and Blogs

Meet the SBS-MVPs and click over to their blogs: http://www.microsoft.com/
windowsserver2003/sbs/community/default.mspx

Microsoft Windows SBS Sites

- www.microsoft.com/windowsserver2003/sbs/default.mspx

- www.microsoft.com/sbserver

- www.microsoft.com/sbs

- Microsoft Learning SBS course: Designing, Deploying, and Managing a Network Solution for the Small- and Medium-Sized Business (three-day SBS course): www.microsoft.com/traincert/syllabi2395afinal.asp

- Exam 70-282: Designing, Deploying, and Managing a Network Solution for the Small- and Medium-Sized Business: www.microsoft.com/learning/exams/70-282.asp.

Microsoft Partners-Related Sites

- Microsoft Partner's SBS site: www.microsoft.com/partners/sbs

- Main Microsoft Partner site: www.microsoft.com/partner

- Microsoft SBS Partner Locator Tool: sbslocator.cohesioninc.com/apartnerlocator.asp

- Microsoft Certified Partner Resource Directory (how to find a Certified Partner): directory.microsoft.com/resourcedirectory/solutions.aspx

- Action Pack: members.microsoft.com/partner/salesmarketing/partnermarket/actionpack/default.aspx

Additional Microsoft or Microsoft-Related Sites

- Microsoft TS2 Events: www.msts2.com

- Microsoft Connections: http://www.microsoft.com/connections

- Eric Ligman's Microsoft Small Business Channel Community site: www.mssmallbiz.com/default.aspx

- Microsoft TechNet: www.microsoft.com/technet

- Microsoft Office templates: officeupdate.microsoft.com/templategallery/

- bCentral small business portal: www.bcentral.com

- bCentral Technology Consulting Directory: directory.bcentral.com/ITConsultant/

- Great Plains: www.microsoft.com/greatplains

- Microsoft Visio: www.microsoft.com/visio

- Asentus: www.asentus.net

- Hands On Lab: www.handsonlab.com

- Granite Pillar: microsoft.granitepillar.com/partners/

- Entirenet: www.entirenet.net/registration

- Directions on Microsoft: www.directionsonmicrosoft.com

- Microsoft Solution Selling: www.solutionselling.com/mspartners/fusion.html

- Dr. Thomas Shinder's ISA Server Web site: www.isaserver.org

- Bill English's SharePoint Web site: www.sharepointknowledge.com

Third-Party SBS-Related Sites

- Susan Bradley's Small Biz Server Links: http://www.sbslinks.com/ (and try www.sbslinks.com/really.htm for a really good time)

- Wayne Small's SBS Web site: www.sbsfaq.com

- Another SBS FAQ site: http://www.smallbizserver.net/

Newslists, User Groups, Trade Associations, Organizations

- SBS—Microsoft Small Business Server Support: http://groups.yahoo.com/group/sbs2k/

- Small BizIT "Small Business IT Consultants" newslist at Yahoo: groups.yahoo.com/groups/smallbizIT

- San Diego SBS User Group: www.sdsbsug.org

- CompTIA: www.comptia.com

- Network Professional Association: www.npa.org

- West Sound Technology Professional Association(Kitsap County, Washington): www.wstpa.org

- Adelaide Australia SBS User Group. For information, contact Dean Calvert: dean@calvert.net.au (also details at www.sbsfaq.com)

- Boston, MA, USA SBS User Group. For more information, contact Eliot Sennett: eliot@esient.com

- Cincinnati, OH, USA SBS User Group. This SBS group is a SIG that is part of a larger general user group. For more information, contact Kevin Royalty: kevin_royalty@yahoo.com

- Cleveland, OH, USA SBS User Group. For more information, visit http://www.gcpcug.org/ or contract Fredrick Johnson: fjohnson@rosstek.com

- Denver CO, USA SBS User Group. For more information, contact Lilly C. Banks: lilly@iSolutionsUnlimited.com.

- Omaha, NB, USA SBS User Group. For more information, contact Amy Luby: aluby@tconl.com. has started a user group in the Omaha, Nebraska area, 10 users

- Portland, OR, USA SBS User Group. For more information, visit http://pdxsbs.fpwest.com or contact Patrick West: patrick@west.net

- San Francisco/Bay Area, CA, USA SBS User Group. For more information, contact Ed Correia: ecorreia@sagacent.com

- Seattle, WA, USA SBS User Group. For more information, contact Steven Banks steve@banksnw.com

- Southern CA, USA SBS User Group. For more information, contact Donna Obdyke: DObdyke@prodigy.net

- Sydney, NSW, Australia SBS User Group. For more information, contact Wayne Small [wayne@correct.com.au] and visit http://www.sbsfaq.com

- Tampa/Palm Harbor/Largo, Florida SBS User Group. Rayanne M. Buchianico, rbuchianico@tampabay.rr.com, flsbsug@yahoo groups.com.

- Black Data Processing Association (BDPA): www.bdpa.org

Notes:

Seminars, Workshops, Conferences

- SMB Nation: www.smbnation.com

- Microsoft TS2 events: www.msts2.com

- Microsoft Connections: http://www.microsoft.com/connections

- Microsoft Momentum Conference: http://www.microsoft.com/partner/events/wwpartnerconference/

- ITEC: www.goitec.com

- Guerrilla marketing and sales seminars: www.guerrillabusiness.com

- Who Moved My Cheese seminars: www.whomovedmycheese.com

- Myers-Briggs Type Indicator: www.apcentral.org

- Millionaire Mind / T. Harv Eker: www.peakpotentials.com

- TechMentor: www.techmentorevents.com

- SuperConference (accounting/technology): www.pencorllc.com

Business Resources

- US Small Business Administration: www.sba.gov

- Palo Alto Software for business planning: www.paloaltosoftware.com

- PlanWare: www.planware.org

- Outsourced accounting: www.cfo2go-wa.com

- US Federal Reserve Web site: www.federalreserve.gov

- Presentations: www.presentations.com

- CardScan: www.cardscan.com

- Plaxo: www.plaxo.com

Media

- SMB Technology Watch newsletter: http://www.smbnation.com

- CRN: www.crn.com

- SBS Maven Andy Goodman posts SBS-related articles at http://www.12c4pc.com.

- Small Business Computing: www.smallbusinesscomputing.com

- PC Magazine Small Business Super Site (www.pcmag.com/category2/0,4148,13806,00.asp)

- Mary Jo Foley's Microsoft-Watch: www.microsoftwatch.com

- NetworkWorldFusion SMB portal: www.nwfusion.com/net.worker/index.html

- Microsoft Certified Professional Magazine: www.mcpmag.com

- Certified Magazine: www.certmag.com

- Windows and .NET Magazine: www.winnetmag.com

- CRMDaily: www.crmdaily.com

- TechRepublic: www.techrepublic.com

- VAR Business: www.varbusiness.com

- Small Business Technology Report: www.smallbiztechnology.com

- Win2K News: www.w2knews.com

- SmallBizTechTalk: www.smallbiztechtalk.com

- Eweek: www.eweek.com

- ComputerWorld: www.computerworld.com

- Kim Komando Show: www.komando.com

- WinInformit: http://www.wininformant.com/

- Entrepreneur Magazine: www.entrepreneur.com

- INC Magazine: www.inc.com

- Fortune: www.fortune.com

- Bizjournals: www.bizjournals.com

- CNN: www.cnn.com

- Business Week: www.businessweek.com

- CBS MarketWatch: www.marketwatch.com

- USA Today: www.usatoday.com

- Money Magazine: www.money.cnn.com

SMB Hardware & Software Companies

- HP/Compaq: www.hp.com

- ConnectWise: www.connectwise.com

- Document Locator—Small Business Server edition: www.document
  locator.com

- TimeSlips: www.timeslips.com

- QuickBooks: www.quickbooks.com

Miscellaneous

- Geekcoprs—technology volunteers enabling communities worldwide:
  www.geekcorps.com

- Google search engine: www.google.com

- NPower, not-for-profit technology agency: www.npower.org

- eBay: www.ebay.com

- GeekSquad: www.geeksquad.com

- Geeks On Call: www.geeksoncall.com

- Soft-Temps: www.soft-temps.com

- Insurance for technology professionals: www.techinsurance.com

- Robert Half International salary survey: www.rhii.com

- AOL for Small Business: aolsvc.aol.com/small_biz

- eProject: www.eproject.com

Appendix B

More SNMP Stuff

Manage Networks by Using Simple Network Management Protocol (SNMP)

SNMP is a widely used network management standard on TCP/IP and IPX networks. SNMP can manage nodes (servers, workstations, routers, bridges, and hubs) from a centrally located host. You can use SNMP to configure remote devices, monitor their network performance, detect faults or inappropriate access, and audit network usage. The centrally located host is referred to as an SNMP manager and the network nodes are called SNMP agents.

SNMP Services

Both agents and management systems (SNMP manager) use SNMP messages to inspect and communicate host information. SNMP messages are sent using UDP and IP is used to route messages between the two. The information will be contained in a management information database (MIB). Information like hard disk space is requested using messages. Message requests are sent as **Get, Set, GetNext, Getbulk** requests by the manager and agents will respond with the information. **Notify** would be the only agent-originated message if traps have been set.

The SNMP Service will first have to be installed through the **Add/Remove Windows Components** in **Control Panel** by an administrator. Once installed, the service will automatically start and can be configured for the management of computers on your system. Under the **Agent** tab in the SNMP **Service Properties**, you can select:

- **Physical** – The computer manages physical devices, such as a hard disk partition

- **Management of logical devices** – The computer uses applications that send data using the TCP/IP protocol suite. This service should always be enabled.

- **Datalink and subnetwork** – The computer manages a bridge.

- **Internet** – The computer functions as an IP gateway (router).

- **End-to-end** – The computer functions as an IP host. This service should always be enabled.

Configure Agent Properties

The SNMP agent responds to management system requests for information. Any computer running SNMP agent software is an SNMP agent. The agent responds to information requests from the management system. To configure agents:

1. Go to **Start, Administrative Tools**.
2. In the dropdown, click **Services**.
3. In the details pane, click **SNMP Service**.
4. On the **Action** menu, click **Properties**.
5. On the **Agent** tab, in **Contact**, type the name of the user or administrator for this computer.
6. In **Location**, type the physical location of the computer or the contact.
7. Under **Service**, select the appropriate checkboxes for this computer, and then click **OK**.

Management hosts and agents belong to an SNMP community. The community is a collection of hosts that is grouped together for administrative purposes. Defining communities provides security by allowing only management systems and agents within the same community to communicate. You can configure agents, traps, and security from the SNMP **Properties** tab as shown in Figure B-1.

Notes:

Figure B-1

SNMP property configurations.

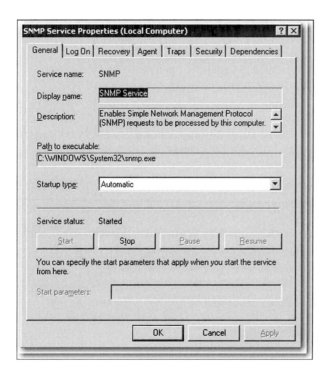

Configure Traps

A trap message is the only agent-initiated SNMP communication. A trap is an alarm-triggering event on an agent, such as a system reboot or illegal access, which provides enhanced security. To configure traps:

1. Go to **Start, Administrative tools**.
2. In the dropdown, click **Services**.
3. In the details pane, click **SNMP Service**.
4. On the **Action** menu, click **Properties**.
5. On the **Traps** tab, under **Community name**, type the case-sensitive community name to which this computer will send trap messages, and then click **Add to list**.
6. In **Trap destinations**, click **Add**.
7. In **Host name, IP or IPX address**, type information for the host, and click **Add**.

Configure Security

SNMP provides security through the use of community names and authentication traps. SNMP communications can be restricted for the agent, allowing it to communicate with only a specific list of other SNMP management systems.

There are several options that can be configured for SNMP security.

- **Accepted community names** – The service requires at least one default community name; the default of **Public** should be changed.

- **Rights** – A permission level can be selected and determines how the agent processes requests.

- **Accept SNMP packets from any host** – No SNMP packets will be rejected; all will be accepted from any name or address.

- **Accept SNMP packets from these hosts** – This is the list of hosts from which sent packets are accepted; all others will be rejected.

- **Send authentication trap** – This option is checked by default and verifies that host names and addresses are valid.

To configure security:

1. Click **Start, Administrative tools**.
2. In the dropdown, **click** on **Services**.
3. In the details pane, click **SNMP Service**.
4. On the **Action** menu, click **Properties**.
5. On the **Security** tab, select **Send authentication trap** if you want a trap message sent whenever authentication fails.
6. Under **Accepted community names**, click **Add**.
7. Under **Community Rights**, select a permission level for this host to process SNMP requests from the selected community.
8. In **Community Name**, type a case-sensitive community name, and then click **Add**.
9. In **SNMP Service Properties**, specify whether or not to accept SNMP packets from a host:
   - To accept SNMP requests from any host on the network, regardless of identity, click **Accept SNMP packets from any host**.

- To limit acceptance of SNMP packets, click **Accept SNMP pack ets from these hosts**, click **Add**, type the appropriate host name, IP or IPX address, and then click **Add** again.

Important: If you remove all the community names, including the default name **Public**, SNMP does not respond to any community names presented.

Appendix C

Third-Party 70-282 Viewpoints

Near the end of writing the book, two strong SMB consultants who focus on Windows Small Business Server 2003 stepped forward to provide some excellent content and outside context on the 70-282 exam.

Andy Goodman, SBS-MVP

It is with great pleasure that we have been granted permission by *MCP Magazine* (www.mcpmag.com) to reprint Andy Goodman's 70-282 exam review. But first things first: we revised the MCP Magazine article slightly to fit a book format. Now meet Andy in Figure C-1.

Figure C-1

Andy Goodman is a long-time SBSer!

Exam Review

70-282: Planning, Deploying, and Managing a Network Solution for the Small- and Medium-Sized Business

This exam covers Windows 2003 Server and Small Business Server 2003, including Network Planning, Security, Backup, SUS, and Maintenance Group Policies.

by Andy Goodman

February 2004 — So you've heard the rumors that there is money to be made in the SMB Space. And you're wondering how to show your knowledge fits the market. Well, Microsoft has just released a new exam to do just that.

In this review, I try to give you an idea of what to expect. Of course, I can't give you the actual questions or the answers. But I can give you an idea of what is involved.

The Main Areas Tested Break Down as Follows

Analyzing the Existing Environment

Make sure you know how to "walk the job," looking for what existing equipment and software

> **70-282: Planning, Deploying, and Managing a Network Solution for the Small- and Medium-Sized Business**
>
> **Reviewer's Rating**
> This exam is hard, especially if you have not used the product in real life. If you've just been reading about, do yourself a favor and get the trial and use it.
>
> **Status**
> Available as of December 16, 2003.
>
> **Exam Title**
> Planning, Deploying, and Managing a Network Solution for the Small and Medium-Sized Business (70-282)
>
> **Who Should Take It**
> People with real world experience, wanting to prove it, this exam is also an elective for 2003 Server MCSE
>
> **Preparation Guide**
> http://www.microsoft.com/learning/exams/70-282.asp

can be used or will need to be replaced. What licenses does the customer already have? Should you offer a software audit? Keep in mind the HCL is your friend. Where is the data stored now and what is it going to take to gather it together? Where are the bottlenecks? What is the customer's "Business Need"?

Designing a Business Technology Solution for a Small- or Medium-sized Business

This is where you will put the information gathered previously into use. Keep in mind this exam is mostly about SBS, so you should know what tools it offers and especially what tools are new to the 2003 version. What business goals does the new technology infrastructure solve? Which version is right for which customer? There is now a whole family ofWindows Servers; make sure you know the differences between them and when to use which one. You should know which products fill which customer's needs.

Installing and Configuring Windows Small Business Server 2003

Although you won't find a lot of licensing stuff, there is some. Make sure you understand the different types of licenses new to SBS. Prior versions did not have this confusion. Remember, in SBS we use the console whenever possible. There are improved tools for adding users and computers, and you should know how to use them. Make sure you know the installation limitations— what can go where. Make sure you know how to set up a user's access to the new Remote Web Workplace. Become familiar with the To Do List and the CEICW—what it does and why you need to use it. Remember, they took away some things that used to be included in SBS. You should know what's not there anymore. Know how to configure a DHCP scope, and how DNS works.

Supporting and Maintaining Windows Small Business Server 2003

The improved backup that comes with SBS is actually a functional tool now. Make sure you know how to schedule backups and do restores. Install and configure SUS on your test machine; get to know how to manage it with Group Policies. Under the hood of SBS is Active Directory and Group Policy Objects. You should understand how they work and why they might not. Study up on delegating administrative tasks and configuring a console for these limited administrators. Also, you want to clearly understand remote administration of the server.

Expanding the Windows Small Business Server 2003 Network

When the customer outgrows SBS, you need to know how to move them to the full-blown products. What are the upgrade options to get them there? Can it be done little by little or must it be all or nothing? This section seemed to be pretty light if my memory is correct.

Installing and Configuring Windows Server 2003

Whether you are dealing with an additional domain controller, a stand-alone server, or the new Web server edition, make sure you know the basics of setting up and configuring a Windows Server.

10 Things To Practice

1. Install, configure, and get to know SBS 2003!
2. Learn how to get around in the Administrator Console.
3. Learn how to set up Users and Computers correctly and how to restrict their permissions
4. Learn to create and use Group Policies to save trips to the desktops.
5. Discover the Built-in Backup Utility.
6. Learn to administer SharePoint. This is one of the two biggest things MS marketing will be pushing, so it is only reasonable they will be testing you on it.
7. Set up and use Remote Web Workplace. See Number 6.
8. Set up SUS and learn how to manage it—more trips to the desktop saved.
9. Learn how to use MBSA to scan your server and your entire network
10. Learn the Windows Server Family Product Line. It's not just one product

Okay, here's my take...

When I took the test, it was still in beta. I did it as a favor to one of the authors of the test—kind of a test of the test. I finished it in about half the allowed time and didn't find it too difficult. So, I was surprised when I talked to some of the other test takers afterwards. Many folks whom I highly respect as being SBS experts confessed they had a hard time with it; some even ran out of time before they could finish.

My theory is this: While these people have been working toward becoming SBS experts, and most are MCSEs or better, their knowledge has come from studying and taking tests. My knowledge comes from actually being in the field and tracking down reference books whenever I had to research a problem. I'm not here to say one way to learn is better than another, but I do know that on-the-job training, getting down and dirty with the product, is a great way to really learn your stuff. So, if you want to pass this test—and not just pass but *know* the material—get the demo and install it a few times. Then break it and try to fix it. Don't just do it once, but a few times. And read the marketing literature. This test is not just testing you on the technology, but whether you can sell the right product to the customer, based on that customer's needs. If you don't know the marketing hype, you won't know what to recommend when or for whom.

Final Report

This exam is tough! If you've just started to work with SBS, and especially Windows Small Business Server 2003, make sure you get some hands-on experience before trying to take this exam. Plan on going to a TS2 event (www.msts2.com), if one happening is near you. Listen to the pitch; you will find it very helpful. Good luck!

Andy Goodman, MCP, SBS-MVP, has more than 25 years of experience in computer-related fields. He's the owner of DownHome Computers, a small computer shop in Kernersville, NC, specializing in Microsoft Small Business Server. He has been involved with SBS since its initial release. He's also the online SBS Forum Moderator for MCPMag.com's "SBS Forum." He hosts a monthly technical chat on MCPmag.com about SBS with Harry Brelsford. His work can be found scattered about the Web on sites such as ServerWatch.com, SWYNK.com, and Admin911.com as well as on his own site www.SBS-Rocks.com. You can contact Andy about "70-282: Planning, Deploying, and Managing a Network Solution for the Small- and Medium-Sized Business at andy@SBS-Rocks.com or meet him face to face at a SMB Nation Event, www.smbnation.com.

Vladimir Mazek, Orlando SBS User Group Leader

Vlad has the energy found in youth that some of us can only remember! Fortunately, he has directed his energy into the small business segment where he runs an SBS user group, delivers an off-premise hosted product for small business technology consultants to resale to customers, and delivers Microsoft TS2 sessions as a contractor! Meet Vlad in Figure C-2. He can be reached at vlad@ownwebnow.com and you can visit his Web site at http://www.own webnow.com.

Figure C-2
Remember Vlad's name and face. You'll likely see him again!

Here is Vlad's opinion on the 70-282 certification exam:

Welcome to Vlad's World!

Before you read this review you should probably be aware that I do not fit the target profile Microsoft had in mind when they put together this exam. I'm already an MCSE on Windows 2003 with MCP on all core SBS components. I also just happen to run a 1200-server network with a cumulative collection of over 400 SBS systems, so I see a wizard or two every day. Why become certified on solutions for small and medium business networks? IT consultants are becoming my biggest customers, so I was very curious to see what Microsoft envisioned as a competent small business technology advisor.

The Bad

The biggest complaint I have with this exam, and nearly every other MCP exam, is that the difference between passing and failing is not in your ability to comprehend the technology, but in your ability to decipher the actual question. For example, it is not unusual to see questions where situation descriptions are twice the length of the possible answers. If you skimmed the question part, every answer provided would seem to be an appropriate solution for the given problem. Your ability to pass this exam lies in your ability to find the magic words in the question that make this problem unique. The exam tests not only your ability to deploy the solution with the least administrative effort, but also demands you to be budget-conscious and aware of all the technology used in a small- to medium-sized business network. It is difficult to shift between administration, design, and business-savvy gears, and this exam checks them all.

The Good

The biggest compliment I have for this exam is that it goes to the core of what would make a great small business IT consultant. Your understanding of basic TCP/IP essentials will be tested as you're asked not only to troubleshoot local area networks, but also problems encountered over the Internet with a wide variety of hardware. You will be expected to understand server and network design as well as the enterprise folks—redundancy, failover, and data protection are part of the IT game at every level. Finally, the licensing aspect of the exam is structured to check your ability not only to sell these solutions, but also to recommend cost-conscious migration paths to your client.

The Details

If there is one word I'd use to describe this exam, it would be "comprehensive." No, you will not be asked to write stored procedures or advanced firewall rules. Likewise, if you're solely a wizard-pusher, you will be throwing away $125. You will need to know how to design the network, server, workstation, security, and disaster recovery—and do it all within your client's budget. Essentially, you'll be expected to be good at what you do.

Consulting

The core of the consulting aspect of this exam is your understanding of how Microsoft licenses its software and the cheapest way to deploy it. There are questions that will make you pick between Windows XP Home and Professional editions, but you'll also need to know when you should recommend upgrades to the latest and greatest and where you can get by with what you already have. Just like in the real world, you will need to know when a peer-to-peer network with Windows XP will accomplish all the business needs and when the budget and requirements warrant investment in Small Business Server. The key to the right answers comes from asking yourself a few questions, such as: Is this type of problem one that can not be solved with what I already have? Does the business owner want me to just get the system working for the least amount of money, or does he want it done right?

Licensing

This is not a sales exam, so you will not be asked to put together a proposal. What you will get asked is what type of a solution your client needs to consider when migrating from peer-to-peer, third-party solutions or a previous version of a Microsoft platform. These are the same questions you've already answered a million times: Why should I upgrade to Windows XP Professional when the Home edition works just fine? Why am I going from SBS 2000 to SBS 2003 Premium? Why do we need to buy an additional server? No, you will not be asked about the MSRP of the product, but you will be expected to know which features are available with which product and, more important, which features solve the problem at hand.

Servers

If you have always accepted the "default" settings when purchasing the server, it's time to go back and read all the details. You will need to know how to design a flexible, powerful, and fault-tolerant solution for your clients. This includes reliable storage and a reliable network, but it also includes a sanity check. My buddy Greg and I always chuckle when we see a consultant stand up during the Microsoft Connections seminar and talk about the Dual Xeon with 8 GB of RAM he recommends for the SBS systems. That guy is not walking away with this certification, especially when he is tested about the bare minimum requirements. In the real world you need to be capable of designing a failover situation, but you also need to be able to get by with what you already have.

Networking

Your comprehension and knowledge of TCP/IP essentials and how the Internet works in general is absolutely critical on the 70-282 exam. You will not be asked to do subnet calculations (although the calculator is available) and you will not need to explain the seven-layer-burrito OSI model. You will need to know which protocols are used by which applications and which ports they communicate over. You will need to be able to troubleshoot the network connectivity, set up routers, and secure connections. This is a check of fundamentals. You will not be asked to find the missing set of rules in an ISA configuration, but you will need to be aware of which wizards were not completed to open required ports. Likewise, wizards-pushing alone will not get you through this exam. You need to know which wizards will configure which components, but if you do not know how they function at the networking level, you will not be able to find the answer to the question.

Taking the Test

This test is quite different from its enterprise counterparts of the MCSE track, so you need to adequately prepare yourself for it. The first and critical step in taking this exam is finding out where the testing facility is. Give yourself plenty of time to get through the traffic; if you get lost, call the center for help and more detailed directions. You'll have enough on your mind thinking about the test; driving in circles around an industrial park that has no markings or street numbers will be counter-productive.

Once you've found your exact test location and hopefully arrived a few minutes early, find a nice place with plenty of light and air conditioning (this is immensely helpful in Florida) and RELAX! I personally went back to my car and used my PocketPC to browse around the CDW site and find out which components were included in SBS 4.5 and 2000. Just a last minute step that I found comforting.

Getting Psyched

Being in the right state of mind is absolutely critical to your success with any exam, especially one sponsored by Microsoft. For years I have wondered under what conditions Microsoft puts their test writers, given some of the questions they come up with. I can almost guarantee that you will see questions that either have no answer whatsoever or all the answers are completely valid to a certain extent, but none actually answer the question.

These questions are there for one reason and one reason only: to throw you out of your comfort zone. Mark these questions for review and go through the rest of the exam. Most questions have an answer that will be immediately apparent to you. Read the question twice: First skim for the general scenario and then look for the real question. Are you trying to find a solution with the least administrative effort or a solution that will be the least expensive? Is the question asking you to fix the problem or find the cause of it? Figure out the answer you'd give to the question being asked before you look at the answer choices the exam gives you. Available answers generally go hand in hand with the overall scenario, so it will seem like all the answers are correct. They almost always are correct solutions, but you need to be able to isolate the actual problem the question asks you to solve.

Overall, this exam is testing your understanding of fundamentals and your ability to offer competent IT advice to small- to medium-sized businesses. It will quickly weed out the enterprise experts and wizard-pushers, because the right mix of technical expertise and business savvy is needed. Approach this exam the same way you approach your business: read, research, and look for the details in the big picture. Don't give the exam a chance to defeat you. Enter that testing room with a winning attitude!

Index

16 GB limit, 2-19, 8-35

A
AAD. *See* after active directory
access rules/restrictions, 6-18, 6-22
ACL (access control lists), 6-10, 6-12
Action Pack, 2-8 to 2-17
Active Directory (AD)
    General, 3-28, 4-11, 6-6, 7-3, 7-18, 7-30, 8-15, 8-17, 9-16, 10-13, 10-14, 10-19, 10-20, 10-33, 10-41, 10-45
    Domains and Trusts, 10-19
    Extensions, 5-18
    Installation Wizard, 10-6, 10-19
    Load Balancing, 10-45
    Migrating, See ADMT
    Replication, 9-2
    Schema, 10-23
    Sites and Services, 10-19
    Users and Computers MMC, 7-3, 8-7, 8-9, 10-19, 10-20-, 10-24, 10-34
Active directory load balancing (ADLB), 10-45
Active Directory Migration Tool (ADMT), 5-21 to 5-24
AD. *See* Active Directory
Address Resolution Protocol, 8-32
administrators
    account, 6-15, 7-1, 7-37,7-39,8-2, 10-16, 10-22, 10-33
    group, 5-23, 7-19, 10-20, 10-41
    Terminal Services, 7-19
    name/description changes, 11-42 to 11-43
    mailboxes, 15-124
    password changes, 11-24 to 11-25
    vs. user mode, 11-49 to 11-54
ADMT. *See* Active Directory Migration Tool
after active directory (AAD), 5-19
alerts/triggers
    IIS, 8-3
    Monitoring, 8-3, 8-39 to 8-41, 10-21, 10-41

SharePoint, 4-4, 6-12, 7-25
System, 10-39
anti-virus, 6-14
anti-virus tools, 5-16, 5-18, 5-24
API. *See* application programming interface
Application filters, 6-20 to 6-21
Application programming interface, 3-3
applications
   client, 7-13, 8-5, 8-20 to 8-21
   events, 8-50
   Mobile, 8-26
   Office, 7-26
   server, 6-22
   SharePoint, 7-25
   SNMP, 7-20 to 7-21
   Volume Shadow Service, 8-36
   WinSock (Windows socket), 5-23, 6-20 to 6-22
ARP. *See* Address Resolution Protocol
ASR. *See* automated system recovery
attachments
   disable, 7-31
   e-mail, 7-23
   general use, 7-35
   removing/blocking, 7-10
   Shared, 7-26
Authentication, 8-17, 8-25, 8-45, 8-47, 10-22, 10-27-10-29, 12-18
automated system recovery (ASR), 6-15, 10-37 to 10-38
AV. See anti-virus

B
Backups, 3-22, 4-14 to 4-15, 6-15, 8-34, 9-8 to 9-9, 10-14, 10-36 to 10-38,
   10-42
BAD. *See* before active directory
bandwidth usage, 6-79, 12-20
before active directory, 5-19
blue screen of death, 10-2
booting, 5-9
broadband 3-8, 3-13, 4-6, 5-3 to 5-4, 7-7 to 7-8, 8-4, 11-16
browsers, s*ee* Internet Explorer (IE)
BSOD. *See* blue screen of death
business, 1-1 to 1-5, 2-7, 2-16, 3-1, 3-21, 4-1, 4-14, 6-1 to 6-2, 7-11, 8-38,
   10-43, 12-2

C

cabling, 3-6

CA. *See* certificate authority

CAL. *See* client access licenses (CALs)

cell phones/cellular, 5-27

CEICW. *See* Configure E-mail and Internet Connection Wizard

certificate authority, 7-10, 7-47

certificates, 6-2, 7-9 to 7-10, 8-48, 10-22

certification, 8-56, 9-10 to 9-11, 10-29, 10-37, 10-46, 11-1, 11-3, 11-15, 11-17, 12-2, 12-8

Certified Netware Engineer, 6-7

client access licenses (CALs), 2-9, 3-11, 5-24, 7-14, 9-6, 10-5, 10-8 to 10-9

client computer, 2-11, 3-13, 7-26, 8-20, 8-23 to 8-24, 10-32

CNE. *See* Certified Netware Engineer

CompanyWeb, 7-26 to 7-27

Computers, 7-39, 8-1, 8-5, 8-13, 8-21, 8-29 to 8-30, 8-46, 8-52, 10-21 to 10-22, 10-24, 10-30 to 10-31, 10-40 to 10-41

conferences, 11-6

Configure E-mail and Internet Connection Wizard (CEICW), 4-6 to 4-7, 4-20, 5-13, 6-19, 7-7 to 7-11, 7-18, 7-23 to 7-24, 7-29 to 7-30, 7-35 to 7-36, 8-7

Connect Computer page, 8-14 to 8-16, 8-24, 9-4

consulting, 12-6 to 12-7, 12-17

CPU performance, 4-26, 5-2 to 5-3, 8-41, 10-45

CRM (Customer Relationship Management), 2-6, 2-9, 2-35,10-17, 12-10

D

Data, 2-11, 2-15, 2-17, 2-36, 3-3 to 3-7, 4-4 to 4-5, 4-14, 4-16 to 4-18, 5-6, 5-10, 5-15 to 5-17, 5-19, 6-2, 6-9, 6-14, 7-22, 7-25, 8-14, 8-33 to 8-36, 8-38 to 8-39, 8-55, 9-8 to 9-10, 10-27, 10-39, 10-47, 12-10

Databases, 5-25, 8-34, 9-10

DCs. *See* domain controllers

DBMS (database management system), 3-3

deployment, 4-12, 5-1, 5-10 to 5-11, 8-19, 10-44, 12-12

DFS (Distributed File System), 4-24, 8-17, 9-8

DHCP. *See* Dynamic Host Configuration Protocol (DHCP)

DNS. *See* domain name system

Dialup, 8-28

digital subscriber line, 4-6

disaster recovery, 4-15, 5-6, 5-16, 8-32, 8-37,9-8

disk space, 4-9, 5-2 to 5-6, 7-39 to 7-40, 8-36,8-41, 10-2, 10-4, 10-6 to 10-7

domain controllers (DCs), 4-19, 5-33, 7-4, 9-1 to 9-3, 9-5 to 9-6, 9-11, 10-45

domain name system (DNS), 4-7, 5-10, 5-20 to 5-22, 5-25, 5-30, 7-8, 7-10, 7-17 to 7-19, 8-18, 8-31, 8-49, 9-6, 10-6, 10-19, 10-22, 10-26, 10-44 to 10-45

domain names, 6-4, 6-20 to 6-22, 6-35
domains, 7-4, 8-9, 8-12, 10-8 to 10-9, 10-12, 10-19, 10-22 to 10-23, 10-25
drivers, 5-16 to 5-17, 5-20, 7-37, 8-45 to 8-47, 10-6, 10-11, 10-31
DSL. *See* digital subscriber line
Dynamic Host Configuration Protocol (DHCP), 5-20, 5-29, 7-15, 9-6, 10-6,
   10-8, 10-22, 10-26, 10-28
dynamic IP, 4-7, 8-5, 9-4

E

ECMA. *See* European Computer Manufacturers Association
EFS. *See* encrypted file system
e-mail, 3-2, 3-4, 3-9, 3-11, 4-3, 4-5 to 4-7, 4-10 to 4-11, 4-15, 5-25, 6-6, 7-1
   to 7-2, 7-7, 7-10 to 7-13, 7-23, 7-29 to 7-33, 7-40, 8-4, 8-23, 8-28, 8-35,
   8-43, 10-43
emergency repair disk (ERD), 5-20, 10-38
encrypted file system, 8-17, 10-54
End-User License Agreement (EULA), 10-2
European Computer Manufacturers Association, 7-23
event logs, 8-3, 8-14, 8-41, 8-50
Exchange, 1-5, 2-9, 4-4, 4-10, 5-17, 5-21, 7-10, 7-21 to 7-23, 7-28 to 7-32,
   7-35, 8-27, 9-6, 9-10
Exmerge, 5-31

F

Fax, 3-2, 3-9 to 3-10, 4-3, 5-4, 5-10, 5-16, 7-11, 7-13, 7-37, 8-16, 8-20, 8-43,
   9-1
file protection, 8-34
File replication service (FRS), 9-8
file transfer protocol (FTP), 6-21 to 6-22, 7-9, 7-35 to 7-36
firewalls, 2-9, 3-8, 5-23, 6-17 to 6-18 to 6-22, 7-8, 7-16 to 7-20, 7-36
formatting disk, 3-29
FQDN. *See* fully qualified domain name
free disk space, 8-41
FTP. *See* file transfer protocol
full backup, 8-35, 9-9 to 9-10, 10-36 to 10-37
fully qualified domain name, 5-28, 8-26

G

GAL. *See* Global Address List
GC. *See* global catalog
General Packet Radio Service, 8-23
Generally Accepted Accounting Principles (GAAP), 2-12
Global Address List, 7-1

global catalog, 10-52
Google, 8-31, 10-44
GPMC. *See* Group Policy Management Console
GPO. *See* group policy objects (GPOs), group policies
GPRS. *See* General Packet Radio Service
graphical user interface (GUI), 5-8, 10-3, 10-20
group policies
Group Policy Management Console, 7-6, 8-9, 10-30
group policy objects (GPOs), 5-20, 6-15, 8-1, 8-9,to 8-13, 8-19, 8-22 to 8-23,
  8-29, 10-32, 10-44
groups, distribution, 5-24, 7-1 to 7-3, 8-4
groups, security, 5-24, 6-3 to 6-4, 6-8, 7-1 to 7-5, 8-6, 10-24
GUI. *See* graphical user interface

H

Hackers, 4-14, 7-33
HAL. *See* hardware abstraction layer
hands-on labs, 1-3 to 1-5, 4-15, 8-26, 8-32, 9-3, 10-15, 11-11, 12-9
hard drives, 3-7 to 3-8, 4-14, 4-16 to 4-17, 8-37
hardware, 2-2, 3-2, 3-5 to 3-12, 4-8 to 4-10, 4-15 to 4-18, 5-2 to 5-7, 8-31,
  10-4, 10-11, 10-25, 10-44, 10-46
hardware abstraction layer, 5-7
Health Insurance Portability and Accountability Act of 1996, 8-37
Hewlett Packard (HP), 1-4, 2-6, 2-31
high performance file system (HPFS), 5-6
HIPAA. *See* Health Insurance Portability and Accountability Act of 1996
Hypertext Transfer Protocol/Secure Hypertext Transfer Protocol (HTTP/
  HTTPS), 4-4, 6-17, 6-20 to 6-22, 7-9 to 7-10, 7-24, 8-47
Hypertext Transfer Protocol total time to live (HTTP TTL), 6-32

I

IAMCP (International Association of Microsoft Certified Partners), 2-5, 2-7
IAS. *See* Internet Authentication Service
IDE. *See* integrated development environment
IE. *See* Internet Explorer
IIS. *See* Internet Information Services
IM. *See* instant messaging
IMAP4. *See* Internet Message Access Protocol Version 4
Independent Software Vendors, xxvi, 7-21
installation. 1-2, 2-6, 2-8, 2-25, 3-7, 3-12, 4-12, 5-4 to 5-6, 5-10, 8-6, 8-53,
  10-2, 10-15
instant messaging, 2-9, 4-4, 7-28
integrated development environment, 3-8

Internet Authentication Service, 10-22
Internet Connection Wizard, see Configure E-mail and Internet Connection Wizard
Internet Explorer (IE), 5-23, 7-23 to 7-24, 8-46, 8-48, 10-30
Internet Information Services (IIS), 5-20 to 5-21, 7-34, 7-36, 8-46, 10-7, 10-22
Internet Message Access Protocol Version 4, 7-33
Internet Protocol, 4-6
Internet Security and Acceleration, 2-7, 3-8, 5-20
Internet Service Provider (ISP), 4-4, 4-7, 7-7 to 7-10, 7-29, 10-43
IP. *See* Internet Protocol
IPSec, 8-18, 10-28
ISA. *See* Internet Security and Acceleration
ISA Server 2000, 3-8, 3-18, 5-10, 5-12 to 5-13, 6-2, 6-17 to 6-25
ISP. *See* Internet Service Provider
ISV. *See* Independent Software Vendors
IT Light – Strategic, 12-12 to 12-14

J

Junk, data, folder. 5-16, 7-32, 8-34, 8-38
junk e-mail. *See* spam

K

keyword searches, 7-21

L

L2TP (Layer 2 Tunneling Protocol), 7-11, 8-18, 8-25, 10-28, to 10-29
LAN. *See* Local Area Network
Laptops, 3-11, 8-52
LAT (Local Address Table), 6-18, 6-21
LDAP. *See* Lightweight Directory Access Protocol
licensing. *See* client access licenses (CALs)
licensing, 7-14 to 7-15, 8-5, 10-3, 10-9, 12-9, 12-12, 12-16
Lightweight Directory Access Protocol, 10-33
Ligman, Eric, 2-29
Line of Business (LOB) applications, 3-7, 3-15, 4-9, 5-19, 5-25, 6-8, 7-19, 10-12
LPD (Linux printing database), 7-38
Local Area Network, 4-5, 9-1
log files, 4-15 to 4-16, 5-8, 8-41, 8-46, 8-51, 9-10, 10-4
logon/logoff, 4-3, 5-22, 5-26, 6-3, 7-31, 8-11, 8-47, 9-6, 10-31, 11-4

M

MAC address, 8-32, 8-49
mailboxes, private/public, 5-21, 5-25, 7-10, 7-29 to 7-31

marketing, 12-2 to 12-3, 12-8, 12-13
MBS. *See* Microsoft Business Solutions
MCSE. *See* Microsoft Certified System Engineer
MCP. *See* Microsoft Certified Professional
MCT. *See* Microsoft Certified Trainer
memory, 3-7, 3-11, 4-16, 8-41, 10-2, 10-39
Microsoft Business Solutions, 2-12
Microsoft Certified System Engineer (MCSE), 1-7, 2-15, 2-21, 2-23, 8-11, 8-14,
   8-51, 10-1, 10-40
Microsoft Certified Professional, 1-4, 2-13, 6-7
Microsoft Certified Trainer, 1-10
Microsoft Management Console, 10-31
Microsoft Office Curriculum (MOC), 1-10, 1-11, 4-2
Microsoft Operations Manager (MOM), 2-10, 10-40 to 10-41
Microsoft Partner Program, 2-6
Microsoft Product Support Services, 1-2, 6-6, 7-19
Microsoft TS2 event, 1-3
Microsoft Worldwide Partner Conference (WPC), 2-2, 2-31
MMC. *See* Microsoft Management Console
MOC. *See* Microsoft Office Curriculum
monitoring, 4-13, 5-14, 5-28, 6-14, 8-13, 8-39 to 8-41, 10-40, 10-46
MPPE (Microsoft Point-to-Point encryption), 10-27
MSDE (Microsoft SQL Server Desktop Engine), 5-11, 7-25
MSPP. *See* Microsoft Partner Program

N
NAT (Network Address Translation Service), 3-8, 4-7, 5-5, 6-18 to 6-20, 7-8,
   10-26 to 10-27
network adapter cards, NICs, 3-10 to 3-11, 5-5, 5-9, 5-16, 6-19, 7-8, 7-17, 8-17,
   10-29, 10-45
Network Monitor, 8-32, 8-49, 10-40
Networks, 3-8, 3-10, 4-16, 6-1 to 6-2, 6-18, 7-18, 7-20 to 7-21, 7-31, 10-10,
   10-18, 10-45, 12-7
NIC (network interface card), 3-8, 5-5, 8-7
NTFS (NT file system), 3-14, 5-6, 6-2 to 6-5, 6-10 to 6-14, 7-5, 10-3, 10-32,
   10-38, 10-43
NTLM, security, 8-17

O
OAB (online address book), 8-28
OEM (original equipment manufacturer), 1-4, 11-1
Office 2003, 1-12, 2-8, 2-10, 2-12, 7-26, 11-11 to 11-13, 12-9
OMA (Outlook Mobile Access), 7-7, 7-9, 7-31 to 7-32

Open Value and Software Assurance licensing, 12-16
OPK (OEM Preinstallation Kit), 1-4, 1-12, 2-8, 2-9, 11-1
organizational units (OUs), MyBusiness, 7-3, 8-9 to 8-13, 10-22, 10-24, 10-33 to 10-34
Outlook 2003, 2-9, 3-9, 3-12, 5-27, 7-32 to 7-33, 8-16, 8-20, 8-26 to 8-27
Outlook Mobile Access (see OMA)
Outlook Web Access (OWA), 7-9 to 7-10, 7-23 to 7-28, 7-30 to 7-32, 8-46 to 8-48
OWA. *See* Outlook Web Access (OWA)

P

packet filtering, 6-17 to 6-19, 8-32
PDAs (personal digital assistants), 7-31
peer-to-peer network, 2-23, 3-3, 3-13, 7-10, 8-14, 10-14, 12-7
PEP (Partner Engagement Program), 2-26
POP3 (Post Office Protocol 3), 10-6
PPPoE (Point-to-Point Protocol over Ethernet), 4-7
PPTP (Point-to-Point Tunneling Protocol), 10-27
print servers, 7-37, 10-15
PSS (product support services), 1-1, 6-6
public folders, 5-19, 5-21, 7-40 to 7-41

Q

quotas, disk 5-6, 5-22, 5-31, 6-5, 7-12 to 7-13, 7-39 to 7-40, 8-13, 9-5, 10-15
quotas, mailbox, 5-24

R

RAID 0, 1, 5 configuration (redundant array of independent disks), 3-8, 4-17 to 4-18, 5-6 to 5-7, 8-37, 10-3 to 10-4
RAM (Random Access Memory), 3-7
RAS (Remote Access Service), 10-22, 10-28 to 10-29
RDP (Remote Desktop Protocol), 8-52 to 8-53, 10-42
Registry, 4-14, 8-20, 8-34, 10-4
Remote Desktop Connection (RDC), 8-52
Remote Desktop Protocol (RDP), 8-13, 8-52, 10-42, 12-12
Remote Desktop Users (RDU), 8-54
Remote Protocol Call (RPC) filter, 12-56 to 12-57
Remote Web Workplace (RWW), 4-3, 4-7 to 4-8, 7-9 to 7-11, 7-24, 8-23
RF (radio frequency), 3-10
ROI (return on investment), 1-12, 2-17
Routers, 3-5 to 3-7, 7-8, 7-20, 10-22, 10-26
RRAS (Routing and Remote Access Service), 3-8, 4-23, 5-20 to 5-21, 6-18, to 6-19, 7-8, 7-11, 10-22 to 10-28
RWW. *See* Remote Web Workplace

S

SATA (Serial Advanced Technology Attachment), 3-8, 4-19
SBSmigration.com, 9-11
SBS-MPV (Small Business Server Most Valuable Professional), 2-20
Scripting, 8-45, 8-49
SCSI (Small Computer System Interface), 3-8, 5-6 to 5-7, 10-3 to 10-4
Secure Socket Layer (SSL), 7-9, 7-31, 8-48
SecureNAT clients, 6-18 to 6-22, 8-47
Server Management console, 4-11 to 4-13, 4-15, 5-13, 5-15, 6-5, 6-7 to 6-8, 7-2, 7-19, 7-27, 7-34, 7-37 to 7-38, 7-41, 8-1 to 8-8, 8-14, 8-22 to 8-24, 8-26, 8-39 to 8-40, 9-3
Server Status Reports, 8-3, 8-41
Shared Fax Service, 3-12, 7-13, 8-16, 8-19
SharePoint Services Intranet site, *See* Windows SharePoint Services (WSS)
SIDs (security identifiers), 5-21, 10-24 to 10-25
Simple Network Management Protocol (SNMP), 7-20 to 7-21, 10-41, Appendix B
SKU (stock-keeping unit), 2-8, 5-7, 9-3
Smartphone, 5-3, 5-4
S/MIME (Secure Multipurpose Internet Mail Extensions), 7-30
SMTP (Simple Mail Transfer Protocol), 5-20 to 5-21, 7-2, 7-9 to 7-10, 7-30, 7-33, 8-44, 9-6
Software Assurance, 7-28, 12-16
Software Update Service (SUS), 6-15 to 6-16, 8-10, 8-29 to 8-30
SP2 (Service Pack 2), 10-11
Spam, 4-13, 7-30, 8-44
SQL Server 2000, 2-11, 4-8, 5-10 to 5-12, 7-25, 10-9
SSL (Secure Socket Layer), 7-9, 7-31, 8-48

T

tape devices/backups, 4-14, 8-4, 8-34 to 8-39, 8-46, 10-35 to 10-38, 10-42
TCO. *See* total cost of ownership
TCP/IP, 3-10, 6-18, 6-21, 7-18, 7-37 to 7-38, 8-32, 8-52 to 8-53, 10-21
Technet, 7-21, 9-7
TelNet, 7-9
Terminal Services (TS), 8-53 to 8-54, 9-4 to 9-6, 10-7
Terminal Services Connection Configuration (TSCC), 8-54
time synchronization, 10-8
total cost of ownership, 3-5, 5-1

U

UDP (user datagram protocol), 6-18
UpnP (Universal Plug and Play), 4-7, 7-17

Uninterruptible power supply (UPS), 5-7
Universal Naming Code (UNC), 8-20
USB, 4-14, 7-37, 8-6, 8-8, 8-45 to 8-46
user templates, 6-4 to 6-8, 7-13 to 7-14, 7-23, 8-6

V

Value Added Reseller (VAR), 2-13
Virtual PC (VPC), 4-8, 10-15, 11-15
Virtual Private Network (VPN), 3-9, 7-9, 7-11, 7-13, 8-23, 8-25 to 8-26, 8-43,
    9-6, 10-27 to 10-29, 10-42
Virtual Storage Services (VSS) of Shadow Copy, 4-9, 8-4, 8-36
virus protection 4-13, 5-23
VoIP (Voice over Internet Protocol), 6-2
Volume Shadow Copy Restore, 4-9, 7-39, 8-12, 8-33 to 8-34 to 8-37, 9-8, 10-35
Volume Shadow Service (VSS), 4-9, 8-35, 9-8
VPN. *See* Virtual Private Network

W

WAN (wide area network), 9-5
WAP (Wireless Application Protocol) keys, 7-31
WINS (Windows Internet Naming Service), 7-18, 8-32, 9-6, 10-7, 10-26
Windows Media Services (WMS), 10-6
Windows Scripting Host (WSH), 8-45
WSS (Windows Sharepoint Services), 2-7, 2-10, 2-12, 4-4 to 4-15, 6-12, 7-9,
    7-12 to 7-13, 7-24 to 7-28, 10-6
Windows Update Service (WUS), 8-30

X

XML, 8-41

Y

Z

REGISTER THIS BOOK!

By registering this book with SMB Nation, you'll receive discounts on future SMB Nation books, conferences, and workshops. You will automatically be registered for our free SBS e-mail newsletter.

SPECIAL OFFER

When you register this book with SMB Nation, you will receive a free PDF e-book version of MICROSOFT SMALL BUSINESS SPECIALIST PRIMER & 70-282 EXAM PREPARATION GUIDE! Registration also grants you access to MORE test questions and a BONUS CHAPTER!

Complete the following information and fax to 425-488-3646 or scan and e-mail to sbs@nethealthmon.com.

Name*_____

Address*_____

City*_____ State*_____

Country*_____ Postal Code*_____

E-mail address*_____

Second e-mail address:_____

(as a backup address)

Telephone:_____

* Required information

How did you hear about MICROSOFT SMALL BUSINESS SPECIALIST PRIMER & 70-282 EXAM PREPARATION GUIDE!?

___ Referral/Word of mouth   ___ Advertisement

___ Newsgroup   ___ Microsoft web site

___ Other web site   ___ Search engine query

How did you purchase MICROSOFT SMALL BUSINESS SPECIALIST PRIMER & 70-282 EXAM PREPARATION GUIDE!?

___ Online directly from SMB Nation

___ Online from book seller (e.g. Amazon)

___ Off the shelf at a national retailer (e.g. Barnes and Noble)

___ Off the shelf at a local book reseller (e.g. San Diego Technical Books)

___ **Follow-up.** Please contact me about SMB Nation conferences, workshops, books, writing for SMB Nation Press, completing a follow-up survey, etc.

SUBSCRIBE TO FREE SBS NEWSLETTER!

Join over 10,000 readers who want to stay in touch bi-weekly via the SBS newsletter, *SMB Technology Watch*. This newsletter presents both technical and business topics surrounding SBS and other Microsoft SMB products.

Now in its third year, *SMB Technology Watch*, shown in the figure below, has built a reputation for delivering the most current news on SBS. This includes breaking news announcements such as product alerts!

For your free subscription to *SMB Technology Watch,* visit the SMB Nation site at www.smbnation.com and sign-up!

Attend SMB Nation Annual Conference and Workshops!

Plan on attending the annual SMB Nation Annual Conference that features SBS and other SMB technology solutions. In September 2005, SMB Nation will be held in Seattle and Redmond, Washington. You'll be able to interact directly with members of the SBS development and marketing teams and see the Microsoft campus.

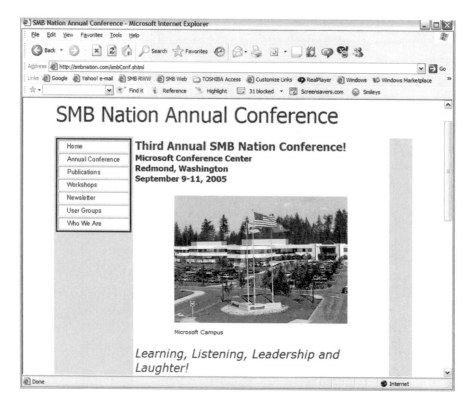

Visit the SMB Nation web site to sign up for the annual conference at www.smbnation.com

-AND-

Don't forget we have one-day SMB Nation Summits that travel worldwide! Information and sign-up at www.smbnation.com